W9-AFN-266

GLOBAL STUDIES

LATIN AMERICA

TWELFTH EDITION

Dr. Paul B. Goodwin Jr.
University of Connecticut, Storrs

OTHER BOOKS IN THE GLOBAL STUDIES SERIES
- Africa
- China
- Europe
- India and South Asia
- Islam and the Muslim World
- Japan and the Pacific Rim
- Russia, the Eurasian Republics, and
   Central/Eastern Europe
- The Middle East
- The World at a Glance

McGraw-Hill/Contemporary Learning Series
2460 Kerper Boulevard, Dubuque, Iowa 52001
Visit us on the Internet—http://www.mhcls.com

Staff

Larry Loeppke	*Managing Editor*
Susan Brusch	*Senior Developmental Editor*
Beth Kundert	*Production Manager*
Jane Mohr	*Project Manager*
Nancy Meissner	*Editorial Assistant*
Lori Church	*Permissions Coordinator*
Maggie Lytle	*Cover*
Tara McDermott	*Design Specialist*
Kari Voss	*Typesetting Supervisor*
Jean Smith	*Typesetter*
Sandy Wille	*Typesetter*
Karen Spring	*Typesetter*
Julie Keck	*Senior Marketing Manager*
Mary Klein	*Marketing Communications Specialist*
Alice Link	*Marketing Coordinator*
Tracie Kammerude	*Senior Marketing Assistant*

Sources for Statistical Reports

U.S. State Department, *Background Notes* (2000–2001).
The World Factbook (2001).
World Statistics in Brief (2001).
World Almanac (2001).
The Statesman's Yearbook (2001).
Demographic Yearbook (2001).
Statistical Yearbook (2001).
World Bank, World Development Report (2000–2001).

Copyright

Cataloging in Publication Data
Main entry under title: Global Studies: Latin America. 12th ed.
        1. Latin America—History. 2. Central America—History. 3. South America—History.
I. Title: Latin America. II. Goodwin, Paul, Jr., *comp*.
ISBN-13 978–0–07–340406–6   ISBN 0–07–340406–3   954   94–71536   ISSN 1061-2831

Twelfth Edition
Printed in the United States of America   1234567890QPDQPD09876   Printed on Recycled Paper

LATIN AMERICA

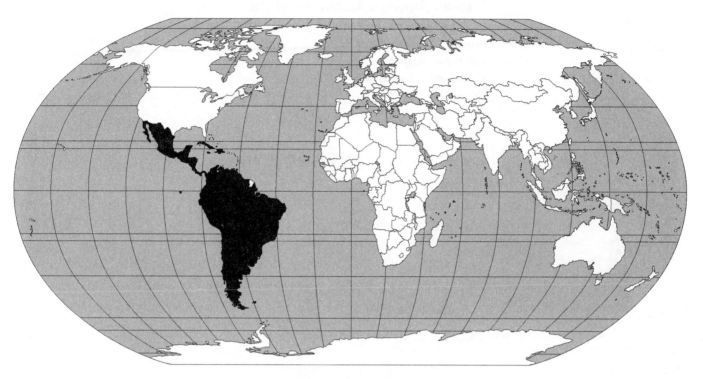

AUTHOR/EDITOR

Dr. Paul B. Goodwin Jr.

The author/editor for *Global Studies: Latin America* is a professor emeritus of Latin American history at the University of Connecticut, Storrs. Dr. Goodwin has written, reviewed, and lectured extensively at universities in the United States and many other countries. His particular areas of interest are modern Argentina and Anglo–Latin American relations. Dr. Goodwin has lectured frequently for the Smithsonian Institution, and he has authored or edited three books and numerous articles.

SERIES CONSULTANT

H. Thomas Collins
PROJECT LINKS
George Washington University

Contents

Regional Articles

Mexico Articles

Central America Articles

South America Articles

Caribbean Articles

Using Global Studies: Latin America

THE GLOBAL STUDIES SERIES

The Global Studies series was created to help readers acquire a basic knowledge and understanding of the regions and countries in the world. Each volume provides a foundation of information—geographic, cultural, economic, political, historical, artistic, and religious—that will allow readers to better assess the current and future problems within these countries and regions and to comprehend how events there might affect their own well-being. In short, these volumes present the background information necessary to respond to the realities of our global age.

Each of the volumes in the Global Studies series is crafted under the careful direction of an author/editor—an expert in the area under study. The author/editors teach and conduct research and have traveled extensively through the regions about which they are writing.

In *Global Studies: Latin America*, the author/editor has written several regional essays and country reports for each of the countries included.

MAJOR FEATURES OF THE GLOBAL STUDIES SERIES

The Global Studies volumes are organized to provide concise information on the regions and countries within those areas under study. The major sections and features of the books are described here.

Regional Essays

For *Global Studies: Latin America*, the author/editor has written several essays focusing on the religious, cultural, socio-political, and economic differences and similarities of the countries and peoples in the various subregions of the Latin America. Regional maps accompany the essays.

Country Reports

Concise reports are written for each of the countries within the region under study. These reports are the heart of each Global Studies volume. *Global Studies: Latin America, Twelfth Edition,* contains 24 country reports, including 2 Mexico reports, 6 reports for Central America, 9 for South America, and 2 for the Caribbean. The reports cover each *independent country* in Latin America.

The country reports are composed of five standard elements. Each report contains a detailed map visually positioning the country among its neighboring states; a summary of statistical information; a current essay providing important historical, geographical, political, cultural, and economic information; a historical timeline, offering a convenient visual survey of a few key historical events; and four "graphic indicators," with summary statements about the country in terms of development, freedom, health/welfare, and achievements.

A Note on the Statistical Reports

The statistical information provided for each country has been drawn from a wide range of sources. (The most frequently referenced are listed on page ii.) Every effort has been made to provide the most current and accurate information available.

However, sometimes the information cited by these sources differs to some extent; and, all too often, the most current information available for some countries is somewhat dated. Aside from these occasional difficulties, the statistical summary of each country is generally quite complete and up to date. Care should be taken, however, in using these statistics (or, for that matter, any published statistics) in making hard comparisons among countries. We have also provided comparable statistics for the United States and Canada, which can be found on pages x and xi.

World Press Articles

Within each Global Studies volume is reprinted a number of articles carefully selected by our editorial staff and the author/editor from a broad range of international periodicals and newspapers. The articles have been chosen for currency, interest, and their differing perspectives on the subject countries. There are 24 articles in *Global Studies: Latin America, Twelfth Edition.*

WWW Sites

An extensive annotated list of selected World Wide Web sites can be found on the facing page (ix) in this edition of *Global Studies: Latin America.* In addition, the URL addresses for country-specific Web sites are provided on the statistics page of most countries. All of the Web site addresses were correct and operational at press time. Instructors and students alike are urged to refer to those sites often to enhance their understanding of the region and to keep up with current events.

Glossary, Bibliography, Index

At the back of each Global Studies volume, readers will find a glossary of terms and abbreviations, which provides a quick reference to the specialized vocabulary of the area under study and to the standard abbreviations used throughout the volume.

Following the glossary is a bibliography that lists general works, national histories, and current-events publications and periodicals that provide regular coverage on Latin America.

The index at the end of the volume is an accurate reference to the contents of the volume. Readers seeking specific information and citations should consult this standard index.

Currency and Usefulness

Global Studies: Latin America, like the other Global Studies volumes, is intended to provide the most current and useful information available necessary to understand the events that are shaping the cultures of the region today.

This volume is revised on a regular basis. The statistics are updated, regional essays and country reports revised, and world press articles replaced. In order to accomplish this task, we turn to our author/editor, our advisory boards, and—hopefully—to you, the users of this volume. Your comments are more than welcome. If you have an idea that you think will make the next edition more useful, an article or bit of information that will make it more current, or a general comment on its organization, content, or features that you would like to share with us, please send it in for serious consideration.

Selected World Wide Web Sites for Global Studies: Latin America

All of these Web sites are hot-linked through the *Global Studies* home page:
http://www.mhcls.com/globalstudies (just click on a book).

Some Web sites are continually changing their structure and content, so the information listed may not always be available.

GENERAL SITES

CNN Online Page
http://www.cnn. com
U.S. 24-hour video news channel. News is updated every few hours.

C-SPAN Online
http://www.c-span.org
See especially C-SPAN International on the Web for International Programming Highlights and archived C-SPAN programs.

GlobalEdge
http://globaledge.msu.edu/ibrd/ibrd.asp
Connect to several international business links from this site. Included are links to a glossary of international trade terms, exporting data, international trade, current laws, and data on GATT, NAFTA, and MERCOSUR.

International Information Systems (University of Texas)
http://inic.utexas.edu
Gateway has pointers to international sites, including all Latin American countries.

Library of Congress Country Studies
http://lcweb2.loc.gov/frd/cs/cshome.html#toc
An invaluable resource for facts and analysis of 100 countries' political, economic, social, and national-security systems and installations.

Political Science Resources
http://www.psr.keele.ac.uk
Dynamic gateway to sources available via European addresses. Listed by country name, this site includes official government pages, official documents, speeches, election information, and political events.

ReliefWeb
http://www.reliefweb.int
UN's Department of Humanitarian Affairs clearinghouse for international humanitarian emergencies. It has daily updates, including Reuters and VOA, and PANA.

Social Science Information Gateway (SOSIG)
http://soig.esrc.bris.ac.uk/
Project of the Economic and Social Research Council (ESRC). It catalogs 22 subjects and lists developing countries' URL addresses.

United Nations System
http://www.sosig.ac.ulc/
The official Web site for the United Nations system of organizations. Everything is listed alphabetically, and data on UNICC and Food and Agriculture Organization are available.

UN Development Programme (UNDP)
http://www.undp.org
Publications and current information on world poverty, Mission Statement, UN Development Fund for Women, and much more. Be sure to see the Poverty Clock.

UN Environmental Programme (UNEP)
http://www.unep.org
Official site of UNEP with information on UN environmental programs, products, services, events, and a search engine.

U.S. Agency for International Development (USAID)
http://www.info.usaid.gov
Graphically presented U.S. trade statistics with Latin America and the Caribbean.

U.S. Central Intelligence Agency Home Page
http://www.odci.gov/ cia/publications/factbook/index.htm
This site includes publications of the CIA, such as the World Factbook, Factbook on Intelligence, Handbook of International Economic Statistics, CIA Maps and Publications, and much more.

U.S. Department of State Home Page
http://www.state.gov/ www/ind.html
Organized alphabetically (i.e., Country Reports, Human Rights, International Organizations, and more).

World Bank Group
http://www.worldbank.org
News (press releases, summary of new projects, speeches), publications, topics in development, and countries and regions. Links to other financial organizations are available.

World Health Organization (WHO)
http://www.who.ch
Maintained by WHO's headquarters in Geneva, Switzerland, the site uses Excite search engine to conduct keyword searches.

World Trade Organization
http://www.wto.org
Topics include foundation of world trade systems, data on textiles, intellectual property rights, legal frameworks, trade and environmental policies, and recent agreements.

MEXICO

The Mexican Government
http://world.presidencia.gob.mx
This site offers a brief overview of the organization of the Mexican Republic, including the Executive, Legislative, and Judicial Branches of the federal government.

Documents on Mexican Politics
http://www.cs.unb.ca/~alopez-o/polind.html
An archive of a large number of articles on Mexican democracy, freedom of the press, political parties, NAFTA, the economy, Chiapas, and so forth can be found on this Web site.

CENTRAL AMERICA

Central America News/Planeta
http://www.planeta.com/ecotravel/period/pubcent.html
Access to data that includes individual country reports, politics, economic news, travel, media coverage, and links to other sites are available here.

Latin World
http://www.latinworld.com
Connecting links to data on the economy and finance, businesses, culture, government, and other areas of interest are available on this site.

SOUTH AMERICA

South America Daily
http://www.southamericadaily.com
Everything you want to know about South America is available from this site—from arts and culture, to government data, to environment issues, to individual countries.

CARIBBEAN

Caribbean Studies
http://www.hist.unt.edu/09w-blk4.htm
A complete site for information about the Caribbean. Topics include general information, Caribbean religions, English Caribbean Islands, Dutch Caribbean Islands, French Caribbean Islands, Hispanic Caribbean Islands, and the U.S. Virgin Islands.

Library of Congress Report on the Islands of the Commonwealth Caribbean
http://lcweb2.loc.gov/frd/cs/extoc.html
An extended study of the Caribbean is possible from this site.

We highly recommend that you review our Web site for expanded information and our other product lines. We are continually updating and adding links to our Web site in order to offer you the most usable and useful information that will support and expand the value of your book. You can reach us at: *http://www.mhcls.com.*

The United States (United States of America)

GEOGRAPHY

Area in Square Miles (Kilometers): 3,717,792 (9,629,091) (about 1/2 the size of Russia)

Capital (Population): Washington, D.C. (3,997,000)

Environmental Concerns: air and water pollution; limited freshwater resources, desertification; loss of habitat; waste disposal; acid rain

Geographical Features: vast central plain, mountains in the west, hills and low mountains in the east; rugged mountains and broad river valleys in Alaska; volcanic topography in Hawaii

Climate: mostly temperate, but ranging from tropical to arctic

PEOPLE

Population

Total: 293,000,000

Annual Growth Rate: 0.89%

Rural/Urban Population Ratio: 24/76

Major Languages: predominantly English; a sizable Spanish-speaking minority; many others

Ethnic Makeup: 77% white; 13% black; 4% Asian; 6% Amerindian and others

Religions: 56% Protestant; 28% Roman Catholic; 2% Jewish; 4% others; 10% none or unaffiliated

Health

Life Expectancy at Birth: 74 years (male); 80 years (female)

Infant Mortality: 6.69/1,000 live births

Physicians Available: 1/365 people

HIV/AIDS Rate in Adults: 0.61%

Education

Adult Literacy Rate: 97% (official)

Compulsory (Ages): 7–16; free

COMMUNICATION

Telephones: 194,000,000 main lines

Daily Newspaper Circulation: 238/1,000 people

Televisions: 776/1,000 people

Internet Users: 165,750,000 (2002)

TRANSPORTATION

Highways in Miles (Kilometers): 3,906,960 (6,261,154)

Railroads in Miles (Kilometers): 149,161 (240,000)

Usable Airfields: 14,695

Motor Vehicles in Use: 206,000,000

GOVERNMENT

Type: federal republic

Independence Date: July 4, 1776

Head of State/Government: President George W. Bush is both head of state and head of government

Political Parties: Democratic Party; Republican Party; others of relatively minor political significance

Suffrage: universal at 18

MILITARY

Military Expenditures (% of GDP): 3.2%

Current Disputes: various boundary and territorial disputes; "war on terrorism"

ECONOMY

Per Capita Income/GDP: $37,800/$10.98 trillion

GDP Growth Rate: 4%

Inflation Rate: 2.2%

Unemployment Rate: 6.2%

Population Below Poverty Line: 13%

Natural Resources: many minerals and metals; petroleum; natural gas; timber; arable land

Agriculture: food grains; feed crops; fruits and vegetables; oil-bearing crops; livestock; dairy products

Industry: diversified in both capital and consumer-goods industries

Exports: $723 billion (primary partners Canada, Mexico, Japan)

Imports: $1.148 trillion (primary partners Canada, Mexico, Japan)

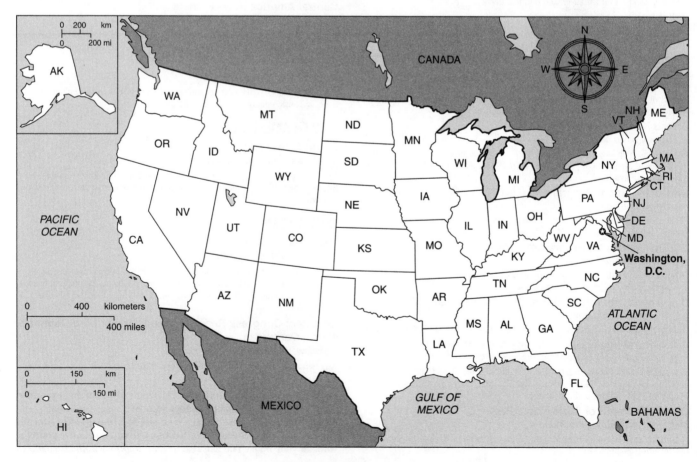

Canada

GEOGRAPHY
Area in Square Miles (Kilometers):
3,850,790 (9,976,140) (slightly larger than
the United States)
Capital (Population): Ottawa (1,094,000)
Environmental Concerns: air and water
pollution; acid rain; industrial damage to
agriculture and forest productivity
Geographical Features: permafrost in the
north; mountains in the west; central plains;
lowlands in the southeast
Climate: varies from temperate to arctic

PEOPLE
Population
Total: 31,903,000
Annual Growth Rate: 0.96%
Rural/Urban Population Ratio: 23/77
Major Languages: both English and French
are official
Ethnic Makeup: 28% British Isles origin;
23% French origin; 15% other European;
6% others; 2% indigenous; 26% mixed
Religions: 46% Roman Catholic; 36%
Protestant; 18% others

Health
Life Expectancy at Birth: 76 years (male); 83
years (female)
Infant Mortality: 4.95/1,000 live births
Physicians Available: 1/534 people

HIV/AIDS Rate in Adults: 0.3%
Education
Adult Literacy Rate: 97%
Compulsory (Ages): primary school

COMMUNICATION
Telephones: 20,803,000 main lines
Daily Newspaper Circulation: 215/1,000
people
Televisions: 647/1,000 people
Internet Users: 16,840,000 (2002)

TRANSPORTATION
Highways in Miles (Kilometers): 559,240
(902,000)
Railroads in Miles (Kilometers): 22,320
(36,000)
Usable Airfields: 1,419
Motor Vehicles in Use: 16,800,000

GOVERNMENT
Type: confederation with parliamentary
democracy
Independence Date: July 1, 1867
Head of State/Government: Queen Elizabeth
II; Prime Minister Stephen Harper
Political Parties: Progressive Conservative
Party; Liberal Party; New Democratic
Party; Bloc Québécois; Canadian Alliance
Suffrage: universal at 18

MILITARY
Military Expenditures (% of GDP): 1.1%
Current Disputes: maritime boundary
disputes with the United States

ECONOMY
Currency ($U.S. equivalent): 1.46 Canadian
dollars = $1
Per Capita Income/GDP: $27,700/$875
billion
GDP Growth Rate: 2%
Inflation Rate: 3%
Unemployment Rate: 7%
Labor Force by Occupation: 74% services;
15% manufacturing; 6% agriculture and
others
Natural Resources: petroleum; natural gas;
fish; minerals; cement; forestry products;
wildlife; hydropower
Agriculture: grains; livestock; dairy
products; potatoes; hogs; poultry and eggs;
tobacco; fruits and vegetables
Industry: oil production and refining;
natural-gas development; fish products;
wood and paper products; chemicals;
transportation equipment
Exports: $273.8 billion (primary partners
United States, Japan, United Kingdom)
Imports: $238.3 billion (primary partners
United States, European Union, Japan)

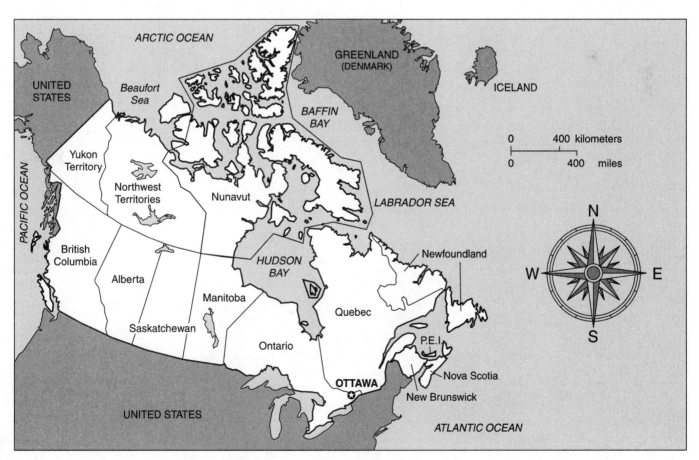

This map is provided to give you a graphic picture of where the countries of the world are located, the relationship they have with their region and neighbors, and their positions relative to major powers and power blocs. We have focused on certain areas to illustrate these crowded regions more clearly.

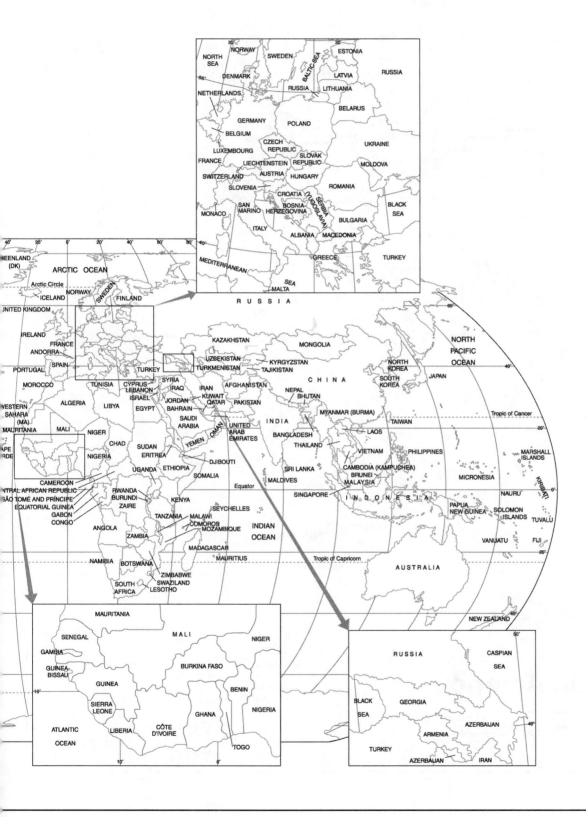

Latin America

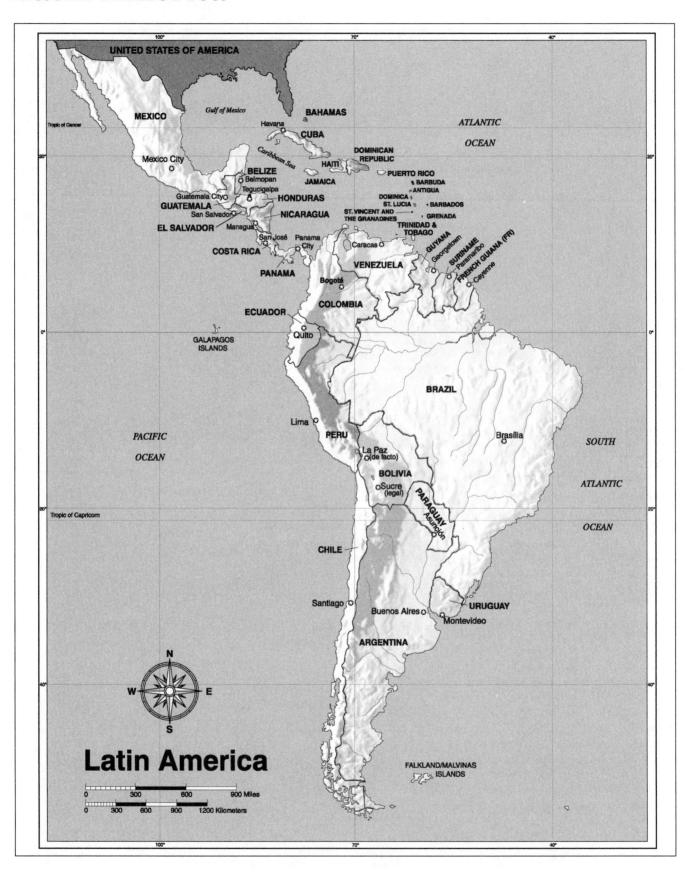

Latin America

Latin America: Myth and Reality

Much of the world still tends to view Latin Americans in terms of stereotypes. Latin American leaders are in many cases still perceived as dictators or demagogues, either from the left or the right sides of the political spectrum with scant attention paid to their actual goals and policies. The popular image of the mustachioed bandit sporting a large sombrero and draped with cartridge belts has been replaced by the figure of the modern-day guerrilla or drug lord, but the same essential image, of lawlessness and violence, persists. Another common stereotype is that of the lazy Latin American who constantly puts things off until *mañana* ("tomorrow"). The implied message here is that Latin Americans lack industry and do not know how to make the best use of their time. A third widespread image is that of the Latin lover and the cult of *machismo* (manliness).

Many of those outside the culture find it difficult to conceive of Latin America as a mixture of peoples and cultures, each one distinct from the others. Indeed, it was not so long ago that then–U.S. president Ronald Reagan, after a tour of the region, remarked with some surprise that all of the countries were "different." Stereotypes spring from ignorance and bias; images are not necessarily a reflection of reality. In the words of Spanish philosopher José Ortega y Gasset: "In politics and history, if one takes accepted statements at face value, one will be sadly misled."

THE LATIN AMERICAN REALITY

The reality of Latin America's multiplicity of cultures is, in a word, complexity. Europeans, Africans, Asians, and the indigenous peoples of Latin America have all contributed substantially to these cultures. If one sets aside non-Hispanic influences for a moment, is it possible to argue, as does historian Claudio Veliz, that "the Iberian [Spanish and Portuguese] inheritance is an essential part of our lives and customs; Brazil and Spanish America [i.e., Spanish-speaking] have derived their personality from Iberia"?

Many scholars would disagree. For example, political scientist Lawrence S. Graham argues that "what is clear is that generalizations about Latin American cultural unity are no longer tenable." And that "one of the effects of nationalism has been to … lead growing numbers of individuals within the region to identify with their own nation-state before they think in terms of a more amorphous land mass called Latin America."

Granted, Argentines speak of their Argentinity and Mexicans of their *Mejicanidad*. It is true that there are profound differences that separate the nations of the region. But there exists a cultural bedrock that ties Latin America to Spain and Portugal, and beyond—to the Roman Empire and the great cultures of the Mediterranean world. African influence, too, is substantial in many parts of the region. Latin America's Indians, of course, trace their roots to indigenous sources. In countries such as Bolivia, however, where indigenous peoples are in the majority, in recent years there has emerged a strong movement that exalts indigenous cultures over those derived from the West.

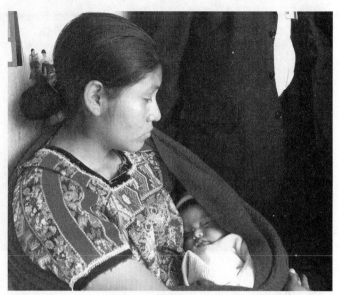

(World Bank/Foto Anckerman/WB042806GTBWhealth2)

In Latin America, the family is an important element in the cultural context. A woman is holding her baby at the Community Center of Basic Health in Chimaltenango, Guatemala.

To understand the nature of Latin American culture, one must remember that there exist many exceptions to the generalizations; the cultural mold is not rigid. Much of what has happened in Latin America, including the evolution of its cultures, is the result of a fortunate—and sometimes an unfortunate—combination of various factors.

THE FAMILY

Let us first consider the Latin American family. The family unit has survived even Latin America's uneven economic development and the pressures of modernization. Family ties are strong and dominant. These bonds are not confined to the nuclear family of father, mother, and children. The same close ties are found in the extended family (a network of second cousins, godparents, and close friends of blood relatives). In times of difficulty, the family can be counted on to help. It is a fortress against the misery of the outside world; it is the repository of dignity, honor, and respect.

AN URBAN CIVILIZATION

In a region where the interaction of networks of families is the rule and where frequent human contact is sought out, it is not surprising to find that Latin Americans are, above all, an urban people. There are more cities of over half a million people in Latin America than in the United States.

Latin America's high percentage of urban dwellers is unusual, for urbanization is usually associated with industrializa-

(Royalty-Free/CORBIS/DILIND085)
The role of the indigenous woman in Latin America has been defined by centuries of tradition. This woman is carrying a bundle of firewood, just as her ancestors did.

tion. In Latin America, urban culture was not created by industrial growth; it actually predated it. As soon as the opportunity presented itself, the Spanish conquerors of the New World, in Veliz's words, "founded cities in which to take refuge from the barbaric, harsh, uncivilized, and rural world outside.... For those men civilization was strictly and uniquely a function of well-ordered city life."

The city, from the Spanish conquest until the present, has dominated the social and cultural horizon of Latin America. Opportunity is found in the city, not in the countryside. This cultural fact of life, in addition to economic motives, accounts for the continuing flow of population from rural to urban areas in Latin America.

A WORLD OF APPEARANCES

Because in their urban environment Latin Americans are in close contact with many people, appearances are important to them. There is a constant quest for prestige, dignity, status, and honor. People are forever trying to impress one another with their public worth. Hence, it is not unusual to see a blue-collar worker traveling to work dressed in a suit, briefcase in hand. It is not uncommon to see jungles of television antennas over shantytowns, although many are not connected to anything.

It is a society that, in the opinion of writer Octavio Paz, hides behind masks. Latin Americans convey an impression of importance, no matter how menial their position. Glen Dealy, a political scientist, writes: "And those of the lower class who must wait on tables, wash cars, and do gardening for a living can help to gain back a measure of self-respect by having their shoes shined by someone else, buying a drink for a friend..., or concealing their occupation by wearing a tie to and from work."

MACHISMO

Closely related to appearances is *machismo*. The term is usually understood solely, and mistakenly, in terms of virility—the image of the Latin lover, for example. But machismo also connotes generosity, dignity, and honor. In many respects, macho behavior is indulged in because of social convention; it is expected of men. Machismo is also a cultural trait that cuts through class lines, for the macho is admired regardless of his social position.

THE ROLE OF WOMEN

If the complex nature of machismo is misunderstood by those outside the culture, so too is the role of women. The commonly held stereotype is that Latin American women are submissive and that the culture is dominated by males. Again, appearances mask a far more complex reality, for Latin American cultures actually allow for strong female roles. Political scientist Evelyn Stevens, for example, has found that *marianismo*—the female counterpart of machismo—permeates all strata of Latin American society. Marianismo is the cult of feminine spiritual superiority that "teaches that women are semi-divine, morally superior to and spiritually stronger than men."

When Mexico's war for independence broke out in 1810, a religious symbol—the Virgin of Guadalupe—was identified with the rebels and became a rallying point for the first stirrings of Mexican nationalism. It was not uncommon in Argentine textbooks to portray Eva Perón (1919–1952), President Juan Perón's wife, in the image of the Virgin Mary, complete with a blue veil and halo. In less religious terms, one of Latin America's most popular novels, *Doña Barbara*, by Rómulo Gallegos, is the story of a female *caudillo* ("man on horseback") on the plains of Venezuela. One need not look to fiction, for in 2006 Chile elected a woman as president. Importantly,

(United Nations photo/Jerry Frank/UN144060)

Agriculture is the backbone of much of Latin America's cultures and economies. These workers are harvesting sugarcane on a plantation in the state of Pernambuco, Brazil.

she won on her own merits: equally important, she was careful to cultivate an image of a caring mother.

The Latin American woman dominates the family because of a deep-seated respect for motherhood. Personal identity is less of a problem for her because she retains her family name upon marriage and passes it on to her children. Women who work outside the home are also supposed to retain respect for their motherhood, which is sacred. In any conflict between a woman's job and the needs of her family, the employer, by custom, must grant her a leave to tend to the family's needs. Recent historical scholarship has also revealed that Latin American women have long enjoyed rights denied to women in other, more "advanced" parts of the world. For example, Latin American women were allowed to own property and to sign for mortgages in their own names even in colonial days. In the 1920s, they won the right to vote in local elections in Yucatán, Mexico, and in San Juan, Argentina.

Here again, though, appearances can be deceiving. Many Latin American constitutions guarantee equality of treatment, but reality is burdensome for women in many parts of the region. They do not have the same kinds of access to jobs that men enjoy; they seldom receive equal pay for equal work; and family life, at times, can be brutalizing.

WORK AND LEISURE

Work, leisure, and concepts of time in Latin America correspond to an entirely different cultural mindset than exists in Northern Europe and North America. The essential difference was demonstrated in a North American television commercial

for a wine, in which two starry-eyed people were portrayed giving the Spanish toast *Salud, amor, y pesetas* ("Health, love, and money"). For a North American audience, the message was appropriate. But the full Spanish toast includes the tag line *y el tiempo para gozarlos* ("and the time to enjoy them").

In Latin America, leisure is viewed as a perfectly rational goal. It has nothing to do with being lazy or indolent. Indeed, in *Ariel*, by writer José Enrique Rodó, leisure is described within the context of the culture: "To think, to dream, to admire—these are the ministrants that haunt my cell. The ancients ranked them under the word *otium*, well-employed leisure, which they deemed the highest use of being truly rational, liberty of thought emancipated of all ignoble chains. Such leisure meant that use of time which they opposed to mere economic activity as the expression of a higher life. Their concept of dignity was linked closely to this lofty conception of leisure." Work, by contrast, is often perceived as a necessary evil.

CONCEPTS OF TIME

Latin American attitudes toward time also reveal the inner workings of the culture. Exasperated North American business-people have for years complained about the *mañana, mañana* attitude of Latin Americans. People often are late for appointments; sometimes little *appears* to get done.

For the North American who believes that time is money, such behavior appears senseless. However, Glen Dealy, in his perceptive book *The Public Man*, argues that such behavior is perfectly rational. A Latin American man who spends hours over lunch or over coffee in a café is not wasting time. For here, with his friends

5

and relatives, he is with the source of his power. Indeed, networks of friends and families are the glue of Latin American society. "Without spending time in this fashion he would, in fact, soon have fewer friends. Additionally, he knows that to leave a café precipitously for an 'appointment' would signify to all that he must not keep someone else waiting—which further indicates his lack of importance. If he had power and position the other person would wait upon his arrival. It is the powerless who wait." Therefore, friends and power relationships are more important than rushing to keep an appointment. The North American who wants the business deal will wait. In a sense, then, the North American is the client and the Latin American is the *patrón* (the "patron," or wielder of power).

Perceptions of time in Latin America also have a broader meaning. North American students who have been exposed to Latin American literature are almost always confused by the absence of a "logical," chronological development of the story. Time, for Latin Americans, tends to be circular rather than linear. That is, the past and the present are perceived as equally relevant—both are points on a circle. The past is as important as the present.

MYTH AND REALITY MERGE

The past that is exposed in works of Latin American literature as well as scholarly writings reflects wholly different attitudes toward what people from other cultures identify as reality. For example, in Nobel Prize–winning writer Gabriél García Márquez's classic novel *One Hundred Years of Solitude*—a fictional history of the town of Macondo and its leading family—fantasy and tall tales abound. But García Márquez drew his inspiration from stories he heard at his grandmother's knee about Aracataca, Colombia, the real town in which he grew up. The point here is that the fanciful story of the town's origins constitutes that town's memory of its past. The stories give the town a common heritage and memory.

From a North American or Northern European perspective, the historical memory is faulty. From the Latin American perspective, however, it is the perception of the past that is important, regardless of its factual accuracy. Myth and reality, appearances and substance, merge.

POLITICAL CULTURE

The generalizations drawn here about Latin American society apply also to its political culture, which is essentially authoritarian and oriented toward power and power relationships. Ideology—be it liberalism, conservatism, or communism—is little more than window dressing. It is the means by which contenders for power can be separated. As Claudio Veliz has noted, regardless of the aims of revolutionary leaders, the great upheavals in Latin America in the twentieth century, without exception, ended up by strengthening the political center, which is essentially authoritarian. This was true of the Mexican Revolution (1910), the Bolivian Revolution (1952), the Cuban Revolution (1958), and the Nicaraguan Revolution (1979).

Ideology has never been a decisive factor in the historical and social reality of Latin America. But charisma and the ability to lead are crucial ingredients. José Velasco Ibarra, five times the president of Ecuador in the twentieth century, once boasted: "Give me a balcony and I will be president!" He saw his personality, not his ideology, as the key to power.

In the realm of national and international relations, Latin America often appears to those outside the culture to be in a constant state of turmoil and chaos. It seems that every day there are reports that a prominent politician has fallen from power, border clashes have intensified, or guerrillas have taken over another section of a country. But the conclusion that chaos reigns in Latin America is most often based on the visible political and social violence, not on the general nature of a country. Political violence is often local in nature, and the social fabric of the country is bound together by the enduring social stability of the family. Again, there is the dualism of what *appears to be* and what *is*.

Much of this upheaval can be attributed to the division in Latin America between the people of Mediterranean background and the indigenous Indian populations. There may be several hundred minority groups within a single country. The problems that may arise from such intense internal differences, however, are not always necessarily detrimental, because they contribute to the texture and color of Latin American culture.

SEEING BEHIND THE MASK

In order to grasp the essence of Latin America, one must ignore the stereotypes, appreciate appearances for what they are, and attempt to see behind the mask. Latin America must be appreciated as a culture in its own right, as an essentially Mediterranean variant of Western civilization.

A Latin American world view tends to be dualistic. The family constitutes the basic unit; here one finds generosity, warmth, honor, and love. Beyond the walls of the home, in the world of business and politics, Latin Americans don their masks and enter "combat." It is a world of power relationships, of macho bravado, and of appearances. This dualism is deepseated; scholars such as Richard Morse and Glen Dealy have traced its roots to the Middle Ages. For Latin Americans, one's activities are compartmentalized into those fit for the City of God, which corresponds to religion, the home, and one's intimate circle of friends; and those appropriate for the City of Man, which is secular and often ruthless and corrupt. North Americans, who tend to measure both their public and private lives by the same yardstick, often interpret Latin American dualism as hypocrisy. Nothing could be further from the truth.

For the Latin American, life exists on several planes, has purpose, and is perfectly rational. Indeed, one is tempted to suggest that many Latin American institutions—particularly the supportive network of families and friends—are more in tune with a world that can alienate and isolate than are our own. As you will see in the following reports, the social structure and cultural diversity of Latin America add greatly to its character and, paradoxically, to its stability.

Mexico (United Mexican States)

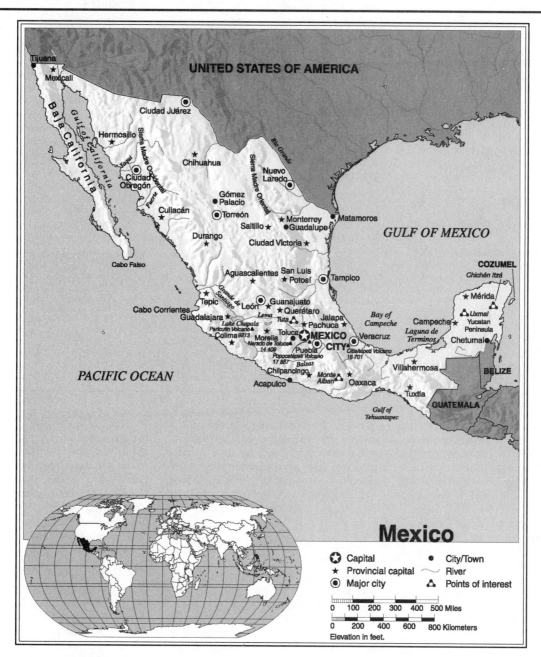

Mexico Statistics

GEOGRAPHY

Area in Square Miles (Kilometers):
764,000 (1,978,000) (about 3 times the size of Texas)

Capital (Population): Mexico City (8,500,000)

Environmental Concerns: Scarce freshwater resources; water pollution; deforestation; soil erosion; serious air pollution

Geographical Features: high, rugged mountains; low coastal plains; high plateaus; desert

Climate: varies from tropical to desert

PEOPLE

Population

Total: 104,959,594
Annual Growth Rate: 1.18%
Rural/Urban Population Ratio: 26/74

Major Languages: Spanish; various Maya, Nahuatl, and other regional indigenous languages

Ethnic Makeup: 60% Mestizo; 30% Amerindian; 9% white; 1% others

Religions: 89% Roman Catholic; 6% Protestant; 5% others

Health

Life Expectancy at Birth: 72 years (male); 77 years (female)

7

Infant Mortality Rate (Ratio): 21.69/1,000
Physicians Available (Ratio): 1/613

Education

Adult Literacy Rate: 92.2%
Compulsory (Ages): 6–12; free

COMMUNICATION

Telephones: 15,958,700 main lines
Daily Newspaper Circulation: 115 per 1,000 people
Televisions: 192 per 1,000
Internet Users: 10.033 million (2002)

TRANSPORTATION

Highways in Miles (Kilometers): 204,761 (329,532)
Railroads in Miles (Kilometers): 12,122 (19,510)
Usable Airfields: 1,827
Motor Vehicles in Use: 12,230,000

GOVERNMENT

Type: federal republic
Independence Date: September 16, 1810 (from Spain)
Head of State/Government: President Vicente Fox is both head of state and head of government
Political Parties: Institutional Revolutionary Party; National Action Party; Party of the Democratic Revolution; Mexican Green Ecologist Party; Workers Party
Suffrage: universal and compulsory at 18

MILITARY

Military Expenditures (% of GDP): 0.9%
Current Disputes: none

ECONOMY

Currency ($U.S. Equivalent): 10.79 pesos = $1
Per Capita Income/GDP: $9,000/$942.2 billion
GDP Growth Rate: 1.2%
Inflation Rate: 4%
Unemployment Rate: 3.3% urban; plus considerable underemployment
Labor Force: 41.5 million
Natural Resources: petroleum; silver; copper; gold; lead; zinc; natural gas; timber
Agriculture: corn; wheat; soybeans; rice; beans; cotton; coffee; fruit; tomatoes; livestock products; wood products
Industry: food and beverages; tobacco; chemicals; iron and steel; petroleum; mining; textiles; clothing; motor vehicles; consumer durables; tourism
Exports: $164.8 billion (primary partners United States, Canada)
Imports: $168.9 billion (primary partners United States, Japan, China)

SUGGESTED WEBSITE

http://www.cia.gov/cia/
publications/factbook/geos/
mx.html#geo

Mexico Country Report

There is a story that Hernán Cortéz, the conqueror of the Aztec Empire in the sixteenth century, when asked to describe the landscape of New Spain (Mexico), took a piece of paper in his hands and crumpled it. The analogy is apt. Mexico is a tortured land of mountains and valleys, of deserts in the north and rain forests in the south. Geography has helped to create an intense regionalism in Mexico, and the existence of hundreds of *patrias chicas* ("little countries") has hindered national integration.

Much of Mexico's territory is vulnerable to earthquakes and volcanic activity. In 1943, for example, a cornfield in one of Mexico's richest agricultural zones sprouted a volcano instead of maize. In 1982, a severe volcanic eruption in the south took several hundred lives, destroyed thousands of head of livestock, and buried crops under tons of ash. Thousands of people died when a series of earthquakes struck Mexico City in 1985.

Mexico is a nation of climatic extremes. Much-needed rains often fall so hard that most of the water runs off before it can be absorbed by the soil. When rains fail to materialize, crops die in the fields. The harsh face of the land, the unavailability of water, and erosion limit the agricultural potential of Mexico. Only 10 to 15 percent of Mexico's land can be planted with crops; but because of unpredictable weather or natural disasters, good harvests can be expected from only 6 to 8 percent of the land in any given year. Hurricanes have also taken a toll on Mexico's Atlantic and Pacific coasts. In 2005 severe storms struck Cancun where they not only wreaked havoc with the lucrative tourism industry but also caused significant losses in farming areas in the south.

MEXICO CITY

Mexico's central region has the best cropland. It was here that the Aztecs built their capital city, the foundations of which lie beneath the current Mexican capital, Mexico City. Given their agricultural potential as well as its focus as the commercial and administrative center of the nation, Mexico City and the surrounding region have always supported a large population. For decades, Mexico City has acted as a magnet for rural poor who have given up attempts to eke out a living from the soil. In the 1940s and 1950s, the city experienced a great population surge. In that era, however, it had the capacity to absorb the tens of thousands of migrants, and so a myth of plentiful money and employment was created. Even today, that myth exercises a strong influence in the countryside; it partially accounts for the tremendous growth of the city and its greater metropolitan area, now home to approximately 18 million people.

The size and location of Mexico City have spawned awesome problems. Because it lies in a valley surrounded by mountains, air pollution is trapped. Mexico City has the worst smog in the Western Hemisphere. Traffic congestion is among the worst in the world. And essential services—including the provision of drinkable water, electricity, and sewers—have failed to keep pace with the city's growth in population.

Social and Cultural Changes

Dramatic social and cultural changes have accompanied Mexico's population growth. These are particularly evident in Mexico City, which daily becomes less Mexican and more cosmopolitan and international.

As Mexico City has become more worldly, English words have become more common in everyday vocabulary. "Okay," "coffee break," and "happy hour" are some examples of English idioms that have slipped into popular usage. In urban centers, quick lunches and coffee breaks have replaced the traditional large meal that was once served at noon. For most people, the afternoon siesta ("nap") is a fondly remembered custom of bygone days.

Mass communication has had an incalculable impact on culture. Television commercials primarily use models who are ethnically European in appearance—preferably white, blue-eyed, and blonde. As if in defiance of the overwhelmingly Mestizo (mixed Indian and white) character of the population, Mexican newspapers and magazines carry advertisements for products guaranteed to lighten one's skin. Success has become associated with light skin.

Another symbol of success is ownership of a television. Antennas cover rooftops even in the poorest urban slums. Acute observers might note, however, that many of the antennas are not connected to anything; the residents of many hovels merely want to convey the impression that they can afford one.

Television, however, has helped to educate the illiterate. Some Mexican soap operas, for instance, incorporate educational materials. On a given day, a show's characters may attend an adult-education class that stresses basic reading and writing skills. Both the television characters and the home-viewing audience sit in on the class. Literacy is portrayed as being essential to one's success and well-being. Mexican *telenovelas*, or "soaps," have a special focus on teenagers and problems common to adolescents. Solutions are advanced within a traditional cultural context and reaffirm the central role of the family.

Cultural Survival: Compadrazgo

Despite these obvious signs of change, distinct Mexican traditions and customs have not only survived Mexico's transformation

but have also flourished because of it. The chaos of city life, the hundreds of thousands of migrants uprooted from rural settings, and the sense of isolation and alienation common to city dwellers the world over are in part eased by the Hispanic institution of *compadrazgo* ("cogodparenthood" or "sponsorship").

DEVELOPMENT

Mexico's economy ended 2005 with a lackluster 3 percent growth and has fallen far short of the 1 million new jobs needed to keep pace with population growth. Chinese goods have flooded Mexican markets, which has resulted in lost jobs in the textile, electronics, and toy industries. Mexico's trade deficit with China in 2005 was in excess of $14 billion.

Compadrazgo is found at all levels of Mexican society and in both rural and urban areas. It is a device for building economic and social alliances that are more enduring than simple friendship. Furthermore, it has a religious dimension as well as a secular, or everyday, application. In addition to basic religious occasions (such as baptism, confirmation, first communion, and marriage), Mexicans seek sponsors for minor religious occasions, such as the blessing of a business, and for

events as common as a graduation or a boy's first haircut.

Anthropologist Robert V. Kemper observes that the institution of compadrazgo reaches across class lines and knits the various strands of Mexican society into a whole cloth. Compadrazgo performs many functions, including providing assistance from the more powerful to the less powerful and, reciprocally, providing homage from the less powerful to the more powerful. The most common choices for *compadres* are neighbors, relatives, fellow migrants, coworkers, and employers. A remarkably flexible institution, compadrazgo is perfectly compatible with the tensions and anxieties of urban life.

Yet even compadrazgo—a form of patron/client relationship—has its limitations. As Mexico City has sprawled ever wider across the landscape, multitudes of new neighborhoods have been created. Many are the result of well-planned land seizures, orchestrated by groups of people attracted by the promise of the city. Technically, such land seizures are illegal; and a primary goal of the *colonos* (inhabitants of these low-income communities) is legitimization and consequent community participation.

Beginning in the 1970s, colonos forcefully pursued their demands for legitimization through protest movements and demonstrations, some of which revealed a

(AP photo/Jose Luis Magana/CatlSubF)

A man from the state of Puebla asks for money outside a jewelry store in Mexico City, hoping to raise enough funds to supply the peasants of his community with the water and electricity that the government has been unable to provide.

surprising degree of radicalism. In response, the Mexican government adopted a two-track policy: It selectively repressed the best-organized and most radical groups of colonos, and it tried to co-opt the remainder through negotiation. In the early 1980s, the government created "Citizen Representation" bodies, official channels within Mexico City through which colonos could participate, within the system, in the articulation of their demands.

From the perspective of the colonos, the establishment of the citizen organizations afforded them an additional means to advance their demands for garbage collection, street paving, provision of potable water, sewage removal, and, most critically, the regularization of land tenure—that is, legitimization. In the government's view, representation for the colonos served to win supporters for the Mexican political structure, particularly the authority of the official ruling party, at a time of outspoken challenge from other political sectors.

Citizens are encouraged to work within the system; potential dissidents are transformed through the process of co-optation into collaborators. In today's Mexico City, then, patronage and clientage have two faces: the traditional one of compadrazgo, the other a form of state paternalism that promotes community participation.

THE BORDER

In the past few decades, driven by poverty, unemployment, and underemployment, many Mexicans have chosen not Mexico City but the United States as the place to improve their lives. Mexican workers in the United States are not a new phenomenon. During World War II, the presidents of both nations agreed to allow Mexican workers, called *braceros*, to enter the United States as agricultural workers. They were strictly regulated. In contrast, the new wave of migrants is largely unregulated. Each year, hundreds of thousands of undocumented Mexicans illegally cross the border in search of work. It has been estimated that at any given time, between 4 million and 6 million Mexicans pursue an existence as illegal aliens in the United States.

Thousands of Mexicans are able to support families with the fruits of their labors, but, as undocumented workers, they are not protected by the law. Many are callously exploited by those who smuggle them across the border as well as by employers in the United States. For the Mexican government, however, such mass emigration has been a blessing in disguise. It has served as a kind of sociopolitical safety valve, and it has resulted in an inflow of dollars sent home by the workers.

In recent years, U.S. companies and the governments of Mexican states along the border have profited from the creation of assembly plants known as *maquiladoras*. Low wages and a docile labor force are attractive to employers, while the Mexican government reaps the benefits of employment and tax dollars. Despite the appearance of prosperity along the border, it must be emphasized that chronic unemployment in other parts of Mexico ensures the misery of millions of people. The North American Free Trade Agreement (NAFTA) hoped to alter these harsh realities, but after 10 years real wages are lower, the distribution of income has become more unequal, and Mexicans still cross the U.S. border in large numbers.

THE INDIAN "PROBLEM"

During the 1900s, urbanization and racial mixing changed the demographic face of Mexico. A government official once commented: "A country predominately Mestizo, where Indian and white are now minorities, Mexico preserves the festivity and ceremonialism of the Indian civilizations and the religiosity and legalism of the Spanish Empire." The quotation is revealing, for it clearly identifies the Indian as a marginal member of society, as an object of curiosity.

FREEDOM

In February 2006 Subcomandante Marcos, leader of the Zapatista rebel group, emerged from the state of Chiapas and began a six-month tour of Mexico to promote a new, nonviolent political movement. The government, which considers Marcos a rebel and an outlaw, has not moved to arrest him. In the event of his incarceration, Marcos directed his followers not to resist but to "Run away and spread the word … and bring me tobacco."

In Mexico, as is the case with indigenous peoples in most of Latin America, Indians in many quarters are viewed as obstacles to national integration and economic progress. There exist in Mexico more than 200 distinct Indian tribes or ethnic groups, who speak more than 50 languages or dialects. In the view of "progressive" Mexicans, the "sociocultural fragmentation" caused by the diversity of languages fosters political misunderstanding, insecurity, and regional incomprehension. Indians suffer from widespread discrimination. Language is not the only barrier to their economic progress. They have long endured the unequal practices of a ruling white and Mestizo elite. Indians may discover, for example, that they cannot expand a small industry, such as a

furniture-making enterprise, because few financial institutions will lend a large amount of money to an Indian.

NATIONAL IDENTITY

Mexico's Mestizo face has had a profound impact on the attempts of intellectuals to understand the meaning of the term "Mexican." The question of national identity has always been an important theme in Mexican history; it became a particularly burning issue in the aftermath of the Revolution of 1910. Octavio Paz believes that most Mexicans have denied their origins: They do not want to be either Indian or Spaniard, but they also refuse to see themselves as a mixture of both. One result of this essential denial of one's ethnic roots is a collective inferiority complex. The Mexican, Paz writes, is insecure. To hide that insecurity, which stems from his sense of "inferiority," the Mexican wears a "mask." Machismo (the cult of manliness) is one example of such a mask. In Paz's estimation, aggressive behavior at a sporting event, while driving a car, or in relationships with women reflects a deep-seated identity crisis.

Perhaps an analogy can be drawn from Mexican domestic architecture. Traditional Mexican homes are surrounded by high, solid walls, often topped with shards of glass and devoid of windows looking out onto the street. From the outside, these abodes appear cold and inhospitable. Once inside (once behind the mask), however, the Mexican home is warm and comfortable. Here, appearances are set aside and individuals can relax and be themselves. By contrast, many homes in the United States have vast expanses of glass that allow every passerby to see within. That whole style of open architecture, at least for homes, is jolting for many Mexicans (as well as other Latin Americans).

THE FAILURE OF THE 1910 REVOLUTION

In addition to the elusive search for Mexican identity, one of Mexican intellectuals' favorite themes is the Revolution of 1910 and what they perceive as its shortcomings. That momentous struggle (1910–1917) cost more than 1 million lives, but it offered Mexico the promise of a new society, free from the abuses of past centuries. It began with a search for truth and honesty in government; it ended with an assertion of the dignity and equality of all men and women.

The goals of the 1910 Revolution were set forth in the Constitution of 1917, a remarkable document—not only in its own era, but also today. *Article 123*, for example, which concerns labor, includes the following provisions: an eight-hour workday, a general minimum wage, and a six-week leave with pay for pregnant women before the approximate birth date plus a six-week leave with pay following the birth. During the nursing period, the mother must be given extra rest periods each day for nursing the baby. Equal wages must be paid for equal work, regardless of sex or nationality. Workers are entitled to a participation in the profits of an enterprise (i.e., profit sharing). Overtime work must carry double pay. Employers are responsible for and must pay appropriate compensation for injuries received by workers in the performance of their duties or for occupational diseases. In 1917, such provisions were viewed as astounding and revolutionary.

Unfulfilled Promises

Unfortunately, many of the goals of 1917 have yet to be achieved. A number of writers, frustrated by the slow pace of change, concluded long ago that the Mexican Revolution was dead. Leading thinkers and writers, such as Carlos Fuentes, have bitterly criticized the failure of the Revolution to shape a more equitable society. Corruption, abuse of power, and self-serving opportunism characterize Mexico today.

One of the failed goals of the Revolution, in the eyes of critics, was an agrarian-reform program that fell short of achieving a wholesale change of land ownership or even of raising the standard of living in rural areas. Over the years, however, small-scale agriculture has sown the seeds of its own destruction. Plots of land that are barely adequate for subsistence farming have been further divided by peasant farmers anxious to satisfy the inheritance rights of their sons. More recently, government price controls on grain and corn have driven many marginal producers out of the market and off their lands.

Land Reform: One Story

Juan Rulfo, a major figure in the history of postrevolutionary literature, captured the frustration of peasants who have "benefited" from agrarian reform. "But sir," the peasant complained to the government official overseeing the land reform, "the earth is all washed away and hard. We don't think the plow will cut into the earth … that's like a rock quarry. You'd have to make with a pick-axe to plant the seed, and even then you can't be sure that anything will come up…." The official, cold and indifferent, responded: "You can state that in writing. And now you can go. You should be attacking the large-estate owners and not the government that is giving you the land."

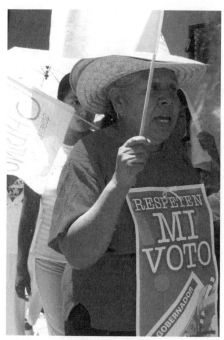

(Courtesy of Heather Haddon/haddon01)

Mexican women won the right to vote in 1955. This woman demonstrates her political consciousness in response to an especially disputed gubernatorial election in the state of Oaxaca in August 2004.

More frequently, landowners have attacked peasants. During the past several years in Mexico, insistent peasant demands for a new allocation of lands have been the occasion of a number of human-rights abuses—some of a very serious character. Some impatient peasants who have occupied lands in defiance of the law have been killed or have "disappeared." In one notorious case in 1982, 26 peasants were murdered in a dispute over land in the state of Puebla. The peasants, who claimed legal title to the land, were killed by mounted gunmen, reportedly hired by local ranchers. Political parties reacted to the massacre in characteristic fashion—all attempted to manipulate the event to their own advantage rather than to address the problem of land reform. Yet years later, paramilitary bands and local police controlled by political bosses or landowners still routinely threatened and/or killed peasant activists. Indeed, access to the land was a major factor in the Maya uprising in the southern state of Chiapas that began in 1994 and, in 2006, remains unresolved.

The Promise of the Revolution

While critics of the 1910 Revolution are correct in identifying its failures, the Constitution of 1917 represents more than dashed hopes. The radical nature of the document allows governments (should they desire) to pursue aggressive egalitarian policies and

still be within the law. For example, when addressing citizens, Mexican public officials often invoke the Constitution—issues tend to become less controversial if they are placed within the broad context of 1917. When President Adolfo López Mateos declared in 1960 that his government would be "extremely leftist," he quickly added that his position would be "within the Constitution." But some authorities argue that constitutional strictures can inhibit needed change. For example, the notoriously inefficient state petroleum monopoly (PEMEX) has been critically short of investment capital for years. To allow private companies to invest in the oil industry would require a constitutional change that many Mexicans equate to a form of *vendepatria* (selling out the country). Indeed, in 2003–2004 Congress routinely rejected discussions of even limited private participation in a national industry.

Women's Rights

Although the Constitution made reference to the equality of women in Mexican society, it was not until World War II that the women's-rights movement gathered strength. Women won the right to vote in Mexico in 1955; by the 1970s, they had challenged laws and social customs that were prejudicial to women. Some women have served on presidential cabinets, and one became governor of the state of Colima. The most important victory for women occurred in 1974, however, when the Mexican Congress passed legislation that, in effect, asked men to grant women full equality in society—including jobs, salaries, and legal standing.

But attitudes are difficult to change with legislation, and much social behavior in Mexico still is sexist. The editor of the Mexican newspaper *Noroeste* has asserted that the most important challenge confronting president Vicente Fox is to "break the paternalistic culture." But commentator Lourdes Galaz has noted that the absence of professional women in positions of responsibility on Fox's government teams is an indication that "he lacks any commitment to the female vote."

Many Mexican men feel that there are male and female roles in society, regardless of law. Government, public corporations, private businesses, the Roman Catholic Church, and the armed forces represent important areas of male activity. The home, private religious rituals, and secondary service roles represent areas of female activity. One is clearly dominant, the other subordinate.

The Role of the Church

Under the Constitution of 1917, no religious organization is allowed to administer or teach in Mexico's primary, secondary, or normal (higher education) schools; nor may clergy participate in the education of workers or peasants. Yet between 1940 and 1979, private schools expanded to the point where they enrolled 1.5 million of the country's 17 million pupils. Significantly, more than half of the private-school population attended Roman Catholic schools. Because they exist despite the fact that they are prohibited by law, the Catholic schools demonstrate the kinds of accommodation and flexibility that are possible in Mexico. It is in the best interests of the ruling party to satisfy as many interest groups as is possible.

From the perspective of politicians, the Roman Catholic Church has increasingly tilted the balance in the direction of social justice in recent years. Some Mexican bishops have been particularly outspoken on the issue; but when liberal or radical elements in the Church embrace social change, they may cross into the jurisdiction of the state. Under the Constitution, the state is responsible for improving the welfare of its people. Some committed clergy, however, believe that religion must play an active role in the transformation of society; it must not only have compassion for the poor but must also act to relieve poverty and eliminate injustice.

In 1991, Mexican bishops openly expressed their concern about the torture and mistreatment of prisoners, political persecution, corruption, discrimination against indigenous peoples, mistreatment of Central American refugees, and electoral fraud. In previous years, the government would have reacted sharply against such charges emanating from the Church. But, in this case, there had been a significant rapprochement between the Catholic Church and the state in Mexico. The new relationship culminated with the exchange of diplomatic representatives and Pope John Paul II's successful and popular visit to Mexico in 1990. Despite better relations at the highest level, in 1999 the bishop of Chiapas vigorously criticized the government for backing away from a 1996 accord between the state and leaders of a guerrilla insurgency and returning to a policy of violent repression.

MEXICO'S STABILITY

The stability of the Mexican state, as has been suggested, depends on the ability of the ruling elite to maintain a state of relative equilibrium among the multiplicity of interests and demands in the nation. The whole political process is characterized by bargaining among elites with various views on politics, social injustice, economic policy, and the conduct of foreign relations.

It was the Institutional Revolutionary Party (PRI), which held the presidency from 1929 until 2000, that set policy and decided what was possible or desirable. All change was generated from above, from the president and his advisers. Although the Constitution provides for a federal system, power was effectively centralized. In the words of one authority, Mexico, with its one-party rule, was not a democracy but, rather, "qualified authoritarianism." In the PRI era, Peruvian author Mario Vargas Llosa referred to Mexico as a "perfect dictatorship." Indeed, the main role of the PRI in the political system was political domination, not power sharing. Paternalistic and all-powerful, the state controlled the bureaucracies that directed the labor unions, peasant organizations, student groups, and virtually every other dimension of organized society. Even though the PRI lost the presidency in 2000, it remains the most powerful political party and retains a strong influence in Mexico's power centers.

HEALTH/WELFARE

Violence against women in Mexico first became an issue of public policy when legislation was introduced in 1990 to amend the penal code with respect to sexual crimes. Among the provisions were specialized medical and social assistance for rape victims and penalties for sexual harassment.

Historically, politicians have tended to be more interested in building their careers than in responding to the demands of their constituents. According to political scientist Peter Smith, Mexican politicians are forever bargaining with one another, seeking favors from their superiors, and communicating in a language of "exaggerated deference." They have learned how to maximize power and success within the existing political structure. By following the "rules of the game," they move ahead. The net result is a consensus at the upper echelons of power.

In the past few decades, that consensus has been undermined. One of the great successes of the Revolution of 1910 was the rise to middle-class status of millions of people. But recent economic crises alienated that upwardly mobile sector from the PRI. People registered their dissatisfaction at the polls; in 1988, in fact, the official party finished second in Mexico City and other urban centers. In 1989, the PRI's unbroken winning streak of 60 years, facilitated by widespread electoral corruption, was broken in the state of Baja California del Norte, where the right-wing National Action Party (PAN) won the governorship.

A decade of worrisome political losses prompted the PRI to consider long overdue reforms. That concern did not prevent the PRI from flagrant electoral fraud in 1988 that handed the presidency to Carlos Salinas Gortari. When it seemed apparent that the PRI would lose, the vote count was interrupted because of "computer failures." In the words of the recent autobiography of former president Miguel de la Madrid, who presided over the fraud, he was told by the PRI president: "You must proclaim the triumph of the PRI. It is a tradition that we cannot break without alarming the citizens." That "tradition" was about to end. Clearly, the PRI had lost touch with critical constituencies who were interested in fundamental change rather than party slogans and were fed up with the rampant corruption of PRI functionaries. Opposition parties continued to win elections.

In the summer of 1997, the left-of-center Party of the Democratic Revolution (PRD) scored stunning victories in legislative, gubernatorial, and municipal elections. For the first time, the PRI lost its stranglehold on the Chamber of Deputies, the lower house of Congress. Significantly, Cuauhtemoc Cardenas of the PRD was swept into power as mayor of Mexico City in the first direct vote for that position since 1928. In gubernatorial contests, the PAN won two elections and controlled an impressive seven of Mexico's 31 governorships.

Within the PRI, a new generation of leaders now perceived the need for political and economic change. President Ernesto Zedillo, worried about his party's prospects in the general elections of 2000, over the objections of old-line conservatives pushed a series of reforms in the PRI. For the first time, the party used state primaries and a national convention to choose the PRI's presidential candidate. This democratization of the party had its reflection in Zedillo's stated commitment to transform Mexican politics by giving the opposition a fair playing field. Voting was now more resistant to tampering and, as a consequence, the three major parties had to campaign for the support of the voters.

In July 2000, Vicente Fox headed a coalition of parties that adopted the name Alliance for Change and promised Mexico's electorate a "Revolution of Hope." It was a formula for success, as the PRI was swept from power. Although Fox was labeled a conservative, his platform indicated that he was above all a pragmatic politician who realized that his appeal and policies had to resonate with a wide range of sectors. Mexican voters saw in Fox someone who identified with human rights, social activism, indigenous rights, women, and the poor. He promised to be a "citizen president."

Pundits described his election as a shift from an "imperial presidency" to an "entrepreneurial presidency." Indeed, Fox's economic policies, if implemented, would promote an annual growth rate of 7 percent, lower inflation, balance the budget, raise tax revenues, and improve the standard of living for Mexico's poor (who number 40 million). The private sector would drive the economy; and strategic sectors of the economy, notably electricity generation and petrochemicals, would be opened to private capital. Labor reforms would be initiated that would link salaries to productivity.

President Fox also promised a renewed dialogue with rebels in the southern state of Chiapas. There, beginning in 1994, Maya insurgents had rebelled against a government that habitually supported landowners against indigenous peoples, essentially marginalizing the latter. Led by Subcomandante Marcos, a shrewd and articulate activist who quickly became a hero not only in Chiapas but also in much of the rest of Mexico, the rebels symbolized widespread dissatisfaction with the promises of the PRI. A series of negotiations with the government from time to time interrupted the climate of violence and culminated in 1996 with the Agreements of San Andres. The government assured the Maya of their independence over issues of local governance. But lack of implementation of the agreements, in combination with attacks by the military on the Maya, doomed the accord from the outset.

The inability of President Fox to implement fully his programs, Mexico's far-from-satisfactory economic performance, and a general trend in Latin America that has put populist regimes in power, have set the stage for an interesting and contentious general election in July 2006. The election, which was likely the cleanest in Mexican history, was also the closest, with PAN candidate Felipe Calderón apparently winning by half a percent of the votes. Calderón, who did well in the north and among middle and upper-class voters, favors a free-market approach to the economy and wants to allow the participation of private investment in the state-controlled energy markets. Runner-up Andrés Manuel Lopez Obrador of the PRD has challenged the results of the election and has called for a recount, which could delay the process until September 6. A populist, he favors the involvement of the state in public works projects to stimulate construction and ease unemployment. He also advocates broad-ranging social programs to address the plight of millions of impoverished Mexicans. The PRI finished a distant third. Regardless of the final outcome, it is clear that

the election revealed a polarized nation, divided geographically between the north and the south, and between the rich and the poor. The ultimate winner does not have a mandate and must work with the other party to address Mexico's many problems.

ORGANIZED LABOR

Organized labor provides an excellent example of the ways in which power is wielded in Mexico and how social change occurs. Mexican trade unions have the right to organize, negotiate, and strike. Most unions historically have not been independent of the government. The major portion of the labor movement is still affiliated with the PRI through an umbrella organization known as the Confederation of Mexican Workers (CTM). The Confederation, with a membership of 3.5 million, is one of the PRI's most ardent supporters. Union bosses truck in large crowds for campaign rallies, help PRI candidates at election time, and secure from union members approval of government policies. Union bosses have been well rewarded by the system they have helped to support. Most have become moderately wealthy and acquired status and prestige. Fully one third of Mexico's senators and congressional representatives, as well as an occasional governor, come from the ranks of union leadership.

ACHIEVEMENTS

Mexican writers and artists have won world acclaim. The works of novelists such as Carlos Fuentes, Mariano Azuela, and Juan Rulfo have been translated into many languages. The graphic-art styles of Posada and the mural art of Diego Rivera, José Clemente Orozco, and David Siqueiros are distinctively Mexican.

Such a relationship must be reciprocal if it is to function properly. The CTM has used an impressive array of left-wing slogans for years to win gains for its members. It has projected an aura of radicalism when, in fact, it is not. The image is important to union members, however, for it gives them the feeling of independence from the government, and it gives a role to the true radicals in the movement. In the 1980s, cracks began to appear in the foundation of union support for the government. The economic crisis of that decade resulted in sharp cutbacks in government spending. Benefits and wage increases fell far behind the pace of inflation; layoffs and unemployment led many union members to question the value of their special relationship with the PRI. Indeed, during the 1988 elections, the Mexican newspaper *El Norte* reported that

Joaquín Hernández Galicia, the powerful leader of the Oil Workers' Union, was so upset with trends within the PRI that he directed his membership to vote for opposition candidates. Not surprisingly, then, President Salinas responded by naming a new leader to the Oil Workers' Union.

Independent unions outside the Confederation of Mexican Workers capitalized on the crisis and increased their memberships. For the first time, these independent unions possessed sufficient power to challenge PRI policies. To negate the challenge from the independents, the CTM invited them to join the larger organization. Incorporation of the dissidents into the system is seen as the only way in which the system's credibility can be maintained. It illustrates the state's power to neutralize opposing forces by absorbing them into its system. The demands of labor today are strong, which will present a significant challenge to the winner of the 2006 presidential election. If labor is to win benefits, it will have to collaborate, but the government must also be prepared for a reciprocal relationship.

ECONOMIC CRISIS

As has been suggested, a primary threat to the consensus politics of the PRI came from the economic crisis that began to build in Mexico and other Latin American countries (notably Brazil, Venezuela, and Argentina) in the early 1980s. In the 1970s, Mexico undertook economic policies designed to foster rapid and sustained industrial growth. Credit was readily available from international lending agencies and banks at low rates of interest. Initially, the development plan seemed to work, and Mexico achieved impressive economic growth rates, in the range of 8 percent per year. The government, confident in its ability to pay back its debts from revenues generated by the vast deposits of petroleum beneath Mexico, recklessly expanded its economic infrastructure.

A glut on the petroleum market in late 1981 and 1982 led to falling prices for Mexican oil. Suddenly, there was not enough money available to pay the interest on loans that were coming due, and the government had to borrow more money—at very high interest rates—to cover the unexpected shortfall. By the end of 1982, between 35 and 45 percent of Mexico's export earnings were devoured in interest payments on a debt of $80 billion. Before additional loans could be secured, foreign banks and lending organizations, such as the International Monetary Fund, demanded that the Mexican government drastically reduce state spending. This demand translated into layoffs, inadequate

13

funding for social-welfare programs, and a general austerity that devastated the poor and undermined the high standard of living of the middle class.

Although political reform was important to then-president Salinas, he clearly recognized that economic reform was of more compelling concern. Under Salinas, the foreign debt was renegotiated and substantially reduced.

It was hoped that the North American Free Trade Agreement (NAFTA) among Mexico, the United States, and Canada would shore up the Mexican economy and generate jobs. After a decade there is a wide range of disagreement over NAFTA's success. The Carnegie Endowment of International Peace concluded in November 2003 that the agreement failed to generate significant job growth and actually hurt hundreds of thousands of subsistence farmers who could not compete with "highly efficient and heavily subsidized American farmers." A World Bank report argued that NAFTA had "brought significant economic and social benefits to the Mexican economy," and that Mexico would have been worse off without the pact. Part of the problem lies with the globalization of the economy. Mexico has lost thousands of jobs to China as well as El Salvador, where labor is 20 percent cheaper and less strictly regulated. Five hundred of Mexico's 3,700 *maquiladoras* have closed their doors since 2001. Opposition politicians, nationalists, and those concerned with the more negative aspects of capitalism have generally fought all free-trade agreements, which they see as detrimental to Mexico's sovereignty and independence of action. Perhaps the most interesting development is not economic, but political. Analysts have noted that NAFTA has contributed to a trend toward more representative government in Mexico and that globalization of the economy undercut the state-centered regime of the PRI. Despite advances in some areas, there are still far too many Mexicans whose standard of living is below the poverty level. Of the 40 million poor, 18 million are characterized as living in "extreme poverty." Income distribution is skewed, with the richest 20 percent of the population in control of 58 percent of the nation's wealth, while the poorest 20 percent control only 4 percent.

Many of those unemployed workers, now estimated at 150,000 per year, will continue to make their way to the U.S. border, which remains accessible despite the passage of immigration-reform legislation and more rigorous patrolling of the border. Others will be absorbed by the so-called informal sector, or underground economy.

When walking in the streets of Mexico City, one quickly becomes aware that there exists an economy that is not recognized, licensed, regulated, or "protected" by the government. Yet in the 1980s, this informal sector of the economy produced 25 to 35 percent of Mexico's gross domestic product and served as a shield for millions of Mexicans who might otherwise have been reduced to destitution. According to George Grayson, "Extended families, which often have several members working and others hawking lottery tickets or shining shoes, establish a safety net for upward of one third of the workforce in a country where social security coverage is limited and unemployment compensation is nonexistent."

FOREIGN POLICY

The problems created by Mexico's economic policy have been balanced by a visibly successful foreign policy. Historically, Mexican foreign policy, which is noted for following an independent course of action, has been used by the government for domestic purposes. In the 1980s, President Miguel de la Madrid identified revolutionary nationalism as the historical synthesis, or melding, of the Mexican people. History, he argued, taught Mexicans to be nationalist in order to resist external aggression, and history made Mexico revolutionary in order to enable it to transform unequal social and economic structures. These beliefs, when tied to the formulation of foreign policy, have fashioned policies with a definite leftist bias. The country has often been sympathetic to social change and has identified, at least in principle, with revolutionary causes all over the globe. The Mexican government opposed the economic and political isolation of Cuba that was so heartily endorsed by the United States. It supported the Marxist regime of Salvador Allende in Chile at a time when the United States was attempting to destabilize his government. Mexico was one of the first nations to break relations with President Anastasio Somoza of Nicaragua and to recognize the legitimacy of the struggle of the Sandinista guerrillas. In 1981, Mexico joined with France in recognizing the opposition front and guerrilla coalition in El Salvador. In the 1990s Mexico, together with several other Latin American countries, urged a negotiated solution to the armed conflict in Central America. In the event of a populist victory in 2006 it is likely that Mexico would move closer to other populist regimes in the hemisphere, including Brazil, Argentina, Chile, Bolivia, Uruguay, and perhaps, Venezuela—very much to the displeasure of the United States. On the other

Timeline: PAST

1519
Hernán Cortés lands at Vera Cruz

1521
Destruction of the Aztec Empire

1810
Mexico proclaims its independence from Spain

1846–1848
War with the United States; Mexico loses four-fifths of its territory

1862–1867
The French take over the Mexican throne and install Emperor Maximillian

1876–1910
Era of dictator Porfirio Díaz: modernization

1910–1917
The Mexican Revolution

1934–1940
Land distribution under President Cárdenas

1938
Nationalization of foreign petroleum companies

1955
Women win the right to vote

1968
The Olympic Games are held in Mexico City; riots and violence

1980s
Severe economic crisis; the peso is devalued; inflation soars; the foreign-debt crisis escalates; Maya insurgency in the state of Chiapas

1990s
NAFTA is passed; the PRI loses ground in legislative, gubernatorial, and municipal elections

PRESENT

2000s
The PRI is ousted from power
Vicente Fox is elected president
Presidential elections scheduled for 2006

hand, the PAN has warned that a populist victory would undermine Mexican democracy and cites the example of the Chavez regime in Venezuela.

Mexico's leftist foreign policy balances conservative domestic policies. A foreign policy identified with change and social justice has the effect of softening the impact of leftist demands in Mexico for land reform or political change. Mexicans, if displeased with government domestic policies, were soothed by a vigorous foreign policy that placed Mexico in a leadership role, often in opposition to the United States. With a PAN victory in 2006, Mexico's foreign policy would continue to be centrist, especially with regard to economic-policy formulations and negotiation of free-trade agreements. A populist win would move Mexico away from the open market desires of Washington.

HARD TIMES

Mexico's future is fraught with uncertainty. In December 1994, the economy collapsed after the government could no longer sustain an overvalued peso. In just a few months, the peso fell in value by half, while the stock market, in terms of the peso, suffered a 38 percent drop. The crash was particularly acute because the Salinas government had not invested foreign aid in factories and job creation, but had instead put most of the money into Mexico's volatile stock market. It then proceeded to spend Mexico's reserves to prop up the peso when the decline gathered momentum. Salinas's successor, President Ernesto Zedillo, had to cut public spending, sell some state-owned industries, and place strict limits on wage and price increases.

To further confound the economic crisis, the Maya insurgency in Chiapas succeeded in generating much antigovernment support in the rest of Mexico. President Zedillo claimed that the rebels, who call themselves the Zapatista Army of National Liberation (EZLN, named for Emiliano Zapata, one of the peasant leaders of the Mexican Revolution), were "neither popular, nor indigenous, nor from Chiapas." Nobel Laureate Octavio Paz condemned the uprising as an "interruption of Mexico's ongoing political and economic liberalization." The interests of the EZLN leadership, he said, were those of intellectuals rather than those of the peasantry. In other words, what happened in Chiapas was an old story of peasant Indians being used by urban intellectuals—in this instance, to challenge the PRI. Indeed, the real identity of "Subcomandante Marcos"

was revealed as Rafael Sebastian Guillen Vicente, a former professor from a rich provincial family who had worked with Tzotzil and Tzeltal Maya Indians since 1984.

George Collier, however, argues that the rebellion is a response to changing governmental policies, agricultural modernization, and cultural and economic isolation. While the peasants of central Chiapas profited from PRI policies, those in the eastern part of the state were ignored. Thus, the rebellion, in essence, was a demand to be included in the largesse of the state. The demands of the EZLN were instructive: democratic reform by the state, limited autonomy for indigenous communities, an antidiscrimination law, teachers, clinics, doctors, electricity, better housing, childcare centers, and a radio station for indigenous peoples. Only vague statements were made about subdivision of large ranches.

During the presidential campaign of 2000, Fox promised to address the complaints raised by the EZLN. Legislation introduced in Congress in the spring of 2001 was designed to safeguard and promote the rights of indigenous peoples. To call attention to the debate, the Zapatistas, with government protection, embarked on a two-week-long march to Mexico City. Significantly, the marchers carried not only the flag of the EZLN but also that of Mexico. But Congress felt that the legislation could damage the nation's unity and harm the interests of local landlords in the south. When a watered-down version of the legislation was passed, Subcomandante Marcos vowed to continue the rebellion. President Fox urged that the talks continue and publicly complained about the congressional action. This was an astute move, because the EZLN could lose an important ally if it adopted an intransigent position.

On the other hand, the Zapatistas were in danger of fading into the background if

they lost the ability to attract the attention of the media. Indeed, the government has essentially ignored them in recent years and much Zapatista support in Mexico has shifted to the populism of the PRD. It is no surprise that Subcomandante Marcos emerged from the jungle and embarked on a nationwide tour in 2006, not only to prevent his movement from becoming irrelevant in the minds of Mexicans, but also to attack the PRD presidential candidate as a "traitor" who would betray Mexico's indigenous peoples.

In summary, the insurgency can be seen to have several roots and to serve many purposes. It is far more complex than a "simple" uprising of an oppressed people.

THE FUTURE

Journalist Igor Fuser, writing in the Brazilian newsweekly *Veja*, observed: "For pessimists, the implosion of the PRI is the final ingredient needed to set off an apocalyptic bomb composed of economic recession, guerrilla war, and the desperation of millions of Mexicans facing poverty. For optimists, the unrest is a necessary evil needed to unmask the most carefully camouflaged dictatorship on the planet."

The elections of 2000 tore away that mask, but persistent problems remain. Corruption, endemic drug-related violence, poverty, unemployment and underemployment, high debt, and inflation are daunting. President Fox admitted in his state of the nation address in September 2003 that he had failed to implement the "historic transformations our times demand." Congress has blocked many of his initiatives, the conflict with the Zapatista of Chiapas continued to simmer, jobs are being lost to the globalization of the economy, and there is a very good chance that an opposition party could win back the presidency in 2006. Change is critical but the policies of transformation render it problematic.

Central America

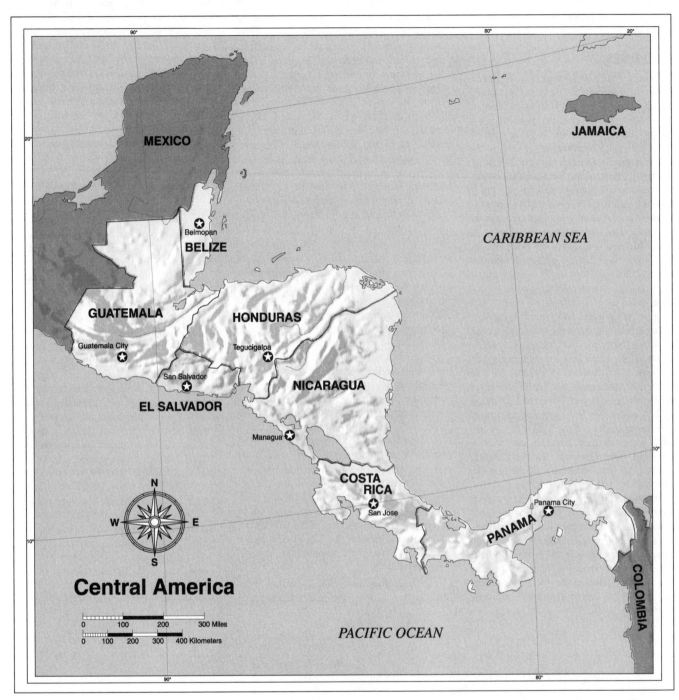

Central America

Much of Central America shares important historical milestones. In 1821, the states of Guatemala, Honduras, El Salvador, Costa Rica, and Nicaragua declared themselves independent of Spain. In 1822, they joined the Empire of Mexico; in 1823, they formed the United Provinces of Central America. This union lasted until 1838, when each member state severed its relations with the federation and went its own way. Since 1838, there have been more than 25 attempts to restore the union—but to no avail.

Central America Lands in Turmoil

LIFE IN THE MOUTH OF THE VOLCANO

Sons of the Shaking Earth, a well-known study of Middle America by anthropologist Eric Wolf, captures in its title the critical interplay between people and the land in Central America. It asserts that the land is violent and that the inhabitants of the region live in an environment that is often shaken by natural disaster.

The dominant geographical feature of Central America is the impressive and forbidding range of volcanic mountains that runs from Mexico to Panama. These mountains have always been obstacles to communication, to the cultivation of the land, and to the national integration of the countries in which they lie. The volcanoes rest atop major fault lines; some are dormant, others are active, and new ones have appeared periodically. Over the centuries, eruptions and earthquakes have destroyed thousands of villages. Some have recovered, but others remain buried beneath lava and ash. Nearly every Central American city has been destroyed at one time or another; and some, such as Managua, Nicaragua, have suffered repeated devastation.

An ancient Indian philosophy speaks of five great periods of time, each doomed to end in disaster. The fifth period, which is the time in which we now live, is said to terminate with a world-destroying earthquake. "Thus," writes Wolf, "the people of Middle [Central] America live in the mouth of the volcano. Middle America … is one of the proving grounds of humanity."

Earthquakes and eruptions are not the only natural disasters that plague the region. Rains fall heavily between May and October each year, and devastating floods are common. On the Caribbean coast, hurricanes often strike in the late summer and early autumn, threatening coastal cities and leveling crops.

The constant threat of natural disaster has had a deep impact on Central Americans' views of life and development. Death and tragedy have conditioned their attitudes toward the present and the future.

GEOGRAPHY

The region is not only violent but also diverse. In political terms, Central America consists of seven independent nations: Belize, Costa Rica, El Salvador, Guatemala, Honduras, Nicaragua, and Panama. With the exception of Costa Rica and Panama, where national borders coincide with geographical and human frontiers, political boundaries are artificial and were marked out in defiance of both the lay of the land and the cultural groupings of the region's peoples.

Geographically, Central America can be divided into four broad zones: Petén–Belize; the Caribbean coasts of Guatemala, Honduras, and Nicaragua; the Pacific volcanic region; and Costa Rica–Panama.

The northern Guatemalan territory of Petén and all of Belize are an extension of Mexico's Yucatán Peninsula. The region is heavily forested with stands of mahogany, cedar, and pine, whose products are a major source of revenue for Belize.

The Caribbean lowlands, steamy and disease-ridden, are sparsely settled. The inhabitants of the Caribbean coast in Nicaragua include Miskito Indians and the descendants of English-speaking blacks who first settled the area in the seventeenth century. The Hispanic population there was small until recently. Coastal Honduras, however, presents a different picture. Because of heavy investments by foreign companies in the region's banana industry, it is a pocket of relative prosperity in the midst of a very poor country whose economy is based on agricultural production and textiles.

The Pacific volcanic highlands are the cultural heartland of Central America. Here, in highland valleys noted for their spring like climate, live more than 80 percent of the population of Central America; here are the largest cities. In cultural terms, the highlands are home to the whites, mixed bloods, Hispanicized Indians known as Ladinos, and pure-blooded Indians who are descended from the Maya. These highland groups form a striking ethnic contrast to the Indians (such as the Miskito), mulattos, and blacks of the coastlands. The entire country of El Salvador falls within this geographical zone. Unlike its neighbors, there is a uniformity to the land and people of El Salvador.

The fourth region, divided between the nations of Costa Rica and Panama, constitutes a single geographical unit. Mountains form the spine of the isthmus. In Costa Rica, the Central Mesa has attracted 70 percent of the nation's population, because of its agreeable climate.

CLIMATE AND CULTURE

The geographic and biological diversity of Central America—with its cool highlands and steaming lowlands, its incredible variety of microclimates and environments, its seemingly infinite types of flora and fauna, and its mineral wealth—has been a major factor in setting the course of the cultural history of Central America. Before the Spanish conquest, the environmental diversity favored the cultural cohesion of peoples. The products of one environmental niche could easily be exchanged for the products of another. In a sense, valley people and those living higher up in the mountains depended on one another. Here was one of the bases for the establishment of the advanced culture of the Maya.

The cultural history of Central America has focused on the densely populated highlands and Pacific plains—those areas most favorable for human occupation. Spaniards settled in the same regions, and centers of national life are located there today. But if geography has been a factor in bringing peoples together on a local level, it has also contributed to the formation of regional differences, loyalties, interests, and jealousies. Neither Maya rulers nor Spanish bureaucrats could triumph over the natural obstacles presented by the region's harsh geography. The mountains and rain forests have mocked numerous attempts to create a single Central American state.

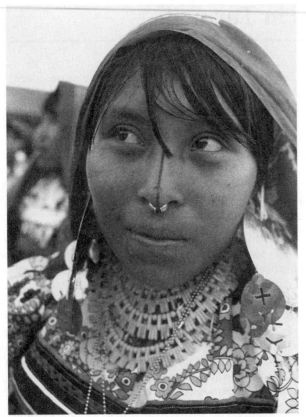

(United Nations photo/Jerry Frank/UN130329)

Central American Indians are firmly tied to their traditional beliefs and have strongly resisted the influence of European culture, as evidenced by this Cuna woman of Panama's Tubala Island.

CULTURES IN CONFLICT

Although physical geography has interacted with culture, the contact between Indians and Spaniards since the sixteenth century has profoundly shaped the cultural face of today's Central America. According to historian Ralph Woodward, the religious traditions of the indigenous peoples, with Christianity imperfectly superimposed over them, "together with the violence of the Conquest and the centuries of slavery or serfdom which followed, left clear impressions on the personality and mentality of the Central American Indian."

To outsiders, the Indians often appear docile and obedient to authority, but beneath this mask may lie intense emotions, including distrust and bitterness. The Indians' vision is usually local and oriented toward the village and family; they do not identify themselves as Guatemalan or Nicaraguan. When challenged, Indians have fought to defend their rights, and a long succession of rebellions from colonial days until the present attests to their sense of what is just and what is not. The Indians, firmly tied to their traditional beliefs and values, have tried to resist modernization, despite government programs and policies designed to counter what urbanized whites perceive as backwardness and superstition.

Population growth, rather than government programs and policies, has had a great impact on the region's Indian peoples and has already resulted in the recasting of cultural traditions. Peasant villages in much of Central America have traditionally organized their ritual life around the principle of *mayordomía,* or sponsor-

ship. Waldemar Smith, an anthropologist who has explored the relationship between the *fiesta* (ceremony) system and economic change, has shown the impact of changing circumstances on traditional systems. In any Central American community in any given year, certain families are appointed *mayordomos,* or stewards, of the village saints; they are responsible for organizing and paying for the celebrations in their names. This responsibility ordinarily lasts for a year. One of the outstanding features of the fiesta system is the phenomenal costs that the designated family must bear. An individual might have to expend the equivalent of a year's earnings or more to act as a sponsor in a community fiesta. Psychological and social burdens must also be borne by the mayordomos, for they represent their community before its saints. Mayordomos, who in essence are priests for a year, are commonly expected to refrain from sexual activity for long periods as well as to devote much time to ritual forms.

The office, while highly prestigious, can also be dangerous. Maya Indians, for example, believe that the saints use the weather as a weapon to punish transgressions, and extreme weather is often traced to ritual error or sins on the part of the mayordomo, who might on such occasions actually be jailed.

Since the late 1960s, the socioeconomic structure of much of the area heavily populated by Indians has changed, forcing changes in traditional cultural forms, including the fiesta system. Expansion of markets and educational opportunity, the absorption of much of the workforce in seasonal plantation labor, more efficient transportation systems, and population growth have precipitated change. Traditional festivals in honor of a community's saints have significantly diminished in importance in a number of towns. Costs have been reduced or several families have been made responsible for fiesta sponsorship. This reflects not only modernization but also crisis. Some communities have become too poor to support themselves—and the expensive fiestas have, naturally, suffered.

This increasing poverty is driven in part by population growth, which has exerted tremendous pressure on people's access to land. Families that cannot be sustained on traditional lands must now seek seasonal wage labor on sugarcane, coffee, or cotton plantations. Others emigrate. The net result is a culture under siege. Thus, while the fiestas may not vanish, they are surely in the process of change.

The Ladino World

The word *Ladino* can be traced back to the Roman occupation of Spain. It referred to someone who had been "Latinized" and was therefore wise in the ways of the world. The word has several meanings in Central America. In Guatemala, it refers to a person of mixed blood, or *Mestizo.* In most of the rest of Central America, however, it refers to an Indian who has adopted white culture.

The Ladinos are caught between two cultures, both of which initially rejected them. The Ladinos attempted to compensate for their lack of cultural roots and cultural identity by aggressively carving out a place in Central American society. Often acutely status-conscious, Ladinos typically contrast sharply with the Indians they physically resemble. Ladinos congregate in the larger towns and cities, speak Spanish, and seek a livelihood as shopkeepers or landowners. They compose the local elite in Guatemala, Nicaragua, Honduras, and El Salvador (the

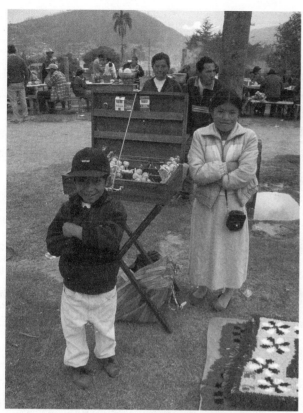

(Courtesy of Omar Sahyoun/Sahyoun01)

An estimated 40 million children throughout Latin America between three and 18 are living and working on the streets. Children, as pictured above, sell trinkets to supplement the family income where parents earn well below a living wage.

latter country was almost entirely Ladinoized by the end of the nineteenth century), and they usually control regional politics. They are often the most aggressive members of the community, driven by the desire for self-advancement. Their vision is frequently much broader than that of the Indian; they have a perspective that includes the capital city and the nation. The vast majority of the population speak Spanish; few villages retain the use of their original, native tongues.

The Elite

For the elite, who are culturally "white," the city dominates their social and cultural horizons. For them, the world of the Indian is unimportant—save for the difficult questions of social integration and modernization. Businesspeople and bureaucrats, absentee landlords, and the professional class of doctors, lawyers, and engineers constitute an urban elite who are cosmopolitan and sophisticated. Wealth, status, and "good blood" are the keys to elite membership.

The Disadvantaged

The cities have also attracted disadvantaged people who have migrated from poverty-stricken rural regions in search of economic opportunity. Many are self-employed as peddlers, small-scale traders, or independent craftspeople. Others seek low-paying, unskilled positions in industry, construction work, and transporta-

tion. Most live on the edge of poverty and are the first to suffer in times of economic recession. But there exist Hispanic institutions in this harsh world that help people of all classes to adjust. In each of the capital cities of Central America, lower-sector people seek help and sustenance from the more advantaged elements in society. They form economic and social alliances that are mutually beneficial. For example, a tradesman might approach a well-to-do merchant and seek advice or a small loan. In return, he can offer guaranteed service, a steady supply of crafts for the wholesaler, and a price that is right. It is a world built on mutual exchanges.

These networks, when they function, bind societies together and ease the alienation and isolation of the less advantaged inhabitants. Of course, networks that cut through class lines can effectively limit class action in pursuit of reforms; and, in many instances, the networks do not exist or are exploitive.

POPULATION MOVEMENT

For many years, Central Americans have been peoples in motion. Migrants who have moved from rural areas into the cities have often been driven from lands they once owned, either because of the expansion of landed estates at the expense of the smaller landholdings, population pressure, or division of the land into plots so small that subsistence farming is no longer possible. Others have moved to the cities in search of a better life.

Population pressure on the land is most intense in El Salvador. No other Latin American state utilizes the whole of its territory to the extent that El Salvador does. Most of the land is still privately owned and is devoted to cattle farming or to raising cotton and coffee for the export market. There is not enough land to provide crops for a population that has grown at one of the most rapid rates in the Western Hemisphere. There are no unpopulated lands left to occupy. Agrarian reform, even if successful, will still leave hundreds of thousands of peasants without land.

Many Salvadorans have moved to the capital city of San Salvador in search of employment. Others have crossed into neighboring countries. In the 1960s, thousands moved to Honduras, where they settled on the land or were attracted to commerce and industry. By the end of that decade, more than 75 percent of all foreigners living in Honduras had crossed the border from El Salvador. Hondurans, increasingly concerned by the growing presence of Salvadorans, acted to stem the flow and passed restrictive and discriminatory legislation against the immigrants. The tension, an ill-defined border, and festering animosity ultimately brought about a brief war between Honduras and El Salvador in 1969.

Honduras, with a low population density (about 139 persons per square mile, as compared to El Salvador's 721), has attracted population not only from neighboring countries but also from the Caribbean. Black migrants from the "West Indian" Caribbean islands known as the Antilles have been particularly attracted to Honduras's north coast, where they have been able to find employment on banana plantations or in the light industry that has increasingly been established in the area. The presence of these Caribbean peoples in moderate numbers has more sharply focused regional differences in Honduras. The coast, in many respects, is Caribbean in its peoples' identity and outlook; while peoples of the highlands

(World Bank photo/Jaime Martin-Escobal/ WBescobal)

The migration of poor rural people to Central American urban centers has caused large numbers of squatters to take up residence in slums. The crowded conditions in urban El Salvador, as shown in this photograph, are typical results of this phenomenon.

of the interior identify with the capital city of Tegucigalpa, which is Hispanic in culture.

THE REFUGEE PROBLEM

Recent turmoil in Central America created yet another group of people on the move—refugees from the fighting in their own countries or from the persecution by extremists of the political left and right. For example, thousands of Salvadorans crowded into Honduras's western province. In the south, Miskito Indians, fleeing from Nicaragua's Sandinista government, crossed the Río Coco in large numbers. Additional thousands of armed Nicaraguan counterrevolutionaries camped along the border. Only in 1990–1991 did significant numbers of Salvadorans move back to their homeland. With the declared truce between Sandinistas and Contras and the election victory of Violeta Chamorro, Nicaraguan refugees were gradually repatriated. Guatemalan Indians sought refuge in southern Mexico, and Central Americans of all nationalities resettled in Costa Rica and Belize.

El Salvadorans, who began to emigrate to the United States in the 1960s, did so in much greater numbers with the onset of the El Salvadoran Civil War, which killed approximately 70,000 people and displaced about 25 percent of the nation's population. The Urban Institute, a Washington, D.C.–based research group, estimated in 1986 that there were then about ¾ million El Salvadorans—of a total population of just over 5 million—living in the United States. Those emigrants became a major source of dollars for El Salvador; it is estimated that they now send home about $500 million a year.

While that money has undoubtedly helped to keep the nation's economy above water, it has also generated, paradoxically, a good deal of anti–U.S. sentiment in El Salvador. Lindsey Gruson, a reporter for *The New York Times*, studied the impact of expatriate dollars in Intipuca, a town 100 miles southwest of the capital, and concluded that they had a profound impact on Intipuqueño culture. The influx of money was an incentive not to work, and townspeople said that the "free" dollars "perverted cherished values" and were "breaking up many families."

THE ROOTS OF VIOLENCE

Central America still feels the effects of civil war and violence. Armies, guerrillas, and terrorists of the political left and right have exacted a high toll on human lives and property. The civil wars and guerrilla movements that spread violence to the region sprang from each of the societies in question.

A critical societal factor was (and remains) the emergence of a middle class in Central America. In some respects, people of the middle class resemble the Mestizos or Ladinos, in that their wealth and position have placed them above the masses. But, like the Mestizos and Ladinos, they have been denied access to the upper reaches of power, which is the special preserve of the elite. Since World War II, it has been members of the middle class who have called for reform and a more equitable distribution of the national wealth. They have also attempted to forge alliances of opportunity with workers and peasants.

Nationalistic, assertive, restless, ambitious, and, to an extent, ruthless, people of the middle class (professionals, intellectuals, junior officers in the armed forces, office workers, businesspeople, teachers, students, and skilled workers) demand a greater voice in the political world. They want governments that are responsive to their interests and needs; and, when governments have proven unresponsive or hostile, elements of the middle class have chosen confrontation.

In the civil war that removed the Somoza family from power in Nicaragua in 1979, for example, the middle class played a critical leadership role. Guerrilla leaders in El Salvador were middle class in terms of their social origins, and there was significant middle-class participation in the unrest in Guatemala.

Indeed, Central America's middle class is among the most revolutionary groups in the region. Although middle-class people are well represented in antigovernment forces, they also resist changes that would tend to elevate those below them on the social scale. They are also significantly represented among right-wing groups, whose reputation for conservative views is accompanied by systematic terror.

Other societal factors also figure prominently in the violence in Central America. The rapid growth of population since the 1960s has severely strained each nation's resources. Many rural areas have become overpopulated, poor agricultural practices have caused extensive soil erosion, the amount of land available to subsistence farmers is inadequate, and poverty and misery are pervasive. These problems have combined to compel rural peoples to migrate to the cities or to whatever frontier lands are still available. In Guatemala, government policy drove Indians from ancestral villages in the highlands to "resettlement" villages in the low-lying, forested Petén to the north. Indians displaced in this manner often—not surprisingly—joined guerrilla movements. They were not attracted to insurgency by the allure of socialist or communist ideology; they simply responded to violence and the loss of their lands with violence against the governments that pursued such policies.

The conflict in this region does not always pit landless, impoverished peasants against an unyielding elite. Some members of the elite see the need for change. Most peasants have not taken up arms, and the vast majority wish to be left in peace. Others who desire change may be found in the ranks of the military or within the hierarchy of the Roman Catholic Church. Reformers are drawn from all sectors of society. It is thus more appropriate to view the conflict in Central America as a civil war rather than a class struggle, as civil wars cut through the entire fabric of a nation.

Much of today's criminal violence in urban areas of Central America, and particularly in El Salvador and Honduras, is a direct consequence of the years of civil war. Young children of refugees, who relocated to large United States cities as adolescents, often imitated the gang culture to which they were exposed. When they returned to Central America and encountered a society that they did not recognize, they could not find jobs and the gang culture was replicated. Indeed, violent crime, most of which was attributed to youth gangs, was a central issue in presidential elections in Honduras in 2005.

ECONOMIC PROBLEMS

Central American economies, always fragile, have in recent years been plagued by a combination of vexing problems. Foreign debt, inflation, currency devaluations, recession, and, in some instances, outside interference have had deleterious effects on the standard of living in all the countries. Civil war, insurgency, corruption and mismanagement, and population growth have added fuel to the crisis—not only in the region's economies but also in their societies. Nature, too, has played an important contributory role in the region's economic and social malaise. Hurricane Mitch, which struck Central American in 1998, killed thousands, destroyed crops and property, and disrupted the infrastructure of roads and bridges in Honduras, Nicaragua, Guatemala, and El Salvador.

Civil war in El Salvador brought unprecedented death and destruction and was largely responsible for economic deterioration and a decline of well over one-third of per capita income from 1980 to 1992. Today, fully two-thirds of the working-age population are either unemployed or underemployed. The

struggle of the Sandinista government of Nicaragua against U.S.–sponsored rebels routinely consumed 60 percent of government spending; even with peace, much of the budget was earmarked for economic recovery. In Guatemala, a savage civil war lasted more than a generation; took more than 140,000 lives; strained the economy; depressed wages; and left unaddressed pressing social problems in education, housing, and welfare. Although the violence has subsided, the lingering fears conditioned by that violence have not. U.S. efforts to force the ouster of Panamanian strongman Manuel Antonio Noriega through the application of economic sanctions probably harmed middle-class businesspeople in Panama more than Noriega.

Against this backdrop of economic malaise there have been some creative attempts to solve, or at least to confront, pressing problems. In 1987, the Costa Rican government proposed a series of debt-for-nature swaps to international conservation groups, such as the Nature Conservancy. The first of the transactions took place in 1988, when several organizations purchased more than $3 million of Costa Rica's foreign debt at 17 percent of face value. The plan called for the government to exchange with the organizations part of Costa Rica's external debt for government bonds; the conservation groups would then invest the earnings of the bonds in the management and protection of Costa Rican national parks. According to the National Wildlife Federation, while debt-for-nature swaps are not a cure-all for the Latin American debt crisis, at least the swaps can go some distance toward protecting natural resources and encouraging ecologically sound, long-term economic development.

INTERNAL AND EXTERNAL DIMENSIONS OF CONFLICT

The continuing violence in much of Central America suggests that internal dynamics are perhaps more important than the overweening roles formerly ascribed to Havana, Moscow, and Washington. The removal of foreign "actors" from the stage lays bare the real reasons for violence in the region: injustice, power, greed, revenge, and racial and ethnic discrimination. Havana, Moscow, and Washington, among others, merely used Central American violence in pursuit of larger policy goals. And Central American governments and guerrilla groups were equally adept at using foreign powers to advance their own interests, be they revolutionary or reactionary.

Panama offers an interesting scenario in this regard. It, like the rest of Central America, is a poor nation comprised of subsistence farmers, rural laborers, urban workers, and unemployed and underemployed people dwelling in the shantytowns ringing the larger cities. For years, the pressures for reform in Panama were skillfully rechanneled by the ruling elite toward the issue of the Panama Canal. Frustration and anger were deflected from the government, and an outdated social structure was attributed to the presence of a foreign power—the United States—in what Panamanians regarded as their territory.

Central America, in summary, is a region of diverse geography and is home to peoples of many cultures. It is a region of strong local loyalties; its problems are profound and perplexing. The violence of the land is matched by the violence of its peoples as they fight for something as noble as justice or human rights, or as ignoble as political power or self-promotion.

Belize

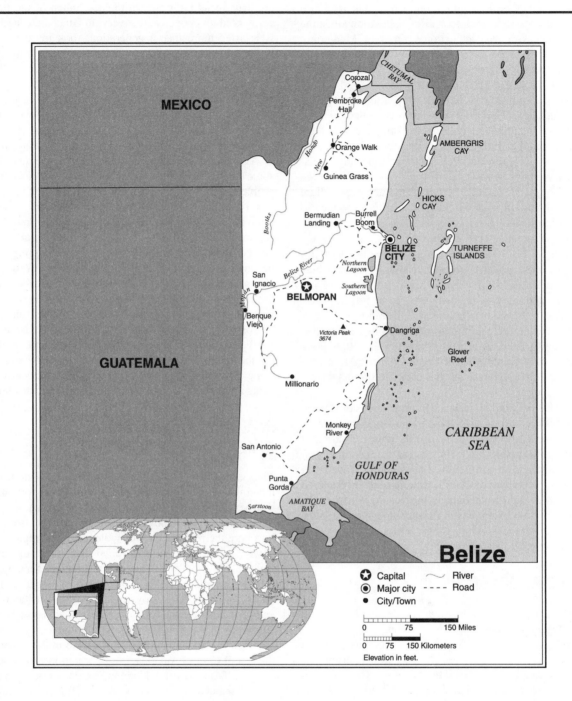

Belize Statistics

GEOGRAPHY

Area in Square Miles (Kilometers): 8,866 (22,963) (about the size of Massachusetts)

Capital (Population): Belmopan (6,800)

Environmental Concerns: deforestation; water pollution

Geographical Features: flat, swampy coastal plain; low mountains in south

Climate: tropical; very hot and humid

PEOPLE

Population

Total: 272,945

Annual Growth Rate: 2.39%

Rural/Urban Population Ratio: 54/46

Ethnic Makeup: 48.7% Mestizo; 24.9% Creole; 10.6% Maya; 6.1% Garifuna; 9.7% others

Major Languages: English; Spanish; Maya; Garifuna

Religions: 49.6% Roman Catholic; 27% Protestant; 14% others; 9.4% unaffiliated

Health

Life Expectancy at Birth: 70 years (male); 74 years (female)
Infant Mortality Rate (Ratio): 26.37/1,000
Physicians Available (Ratio): 1/1,546

Education

Adult Literacy Rate: 70.3%
Compulsory (Ages): 5–14

COMMUNICATION

Telephones: 31,300 main lines
Televisions: 109 per 1,000 people
Internet Users: 30,000

TRANSPORTATION

Highways in Miles (Kilometers): 1,723 (2,872)
Railroads in Miles (Kilometers): none
Usable Airfields: 44
Motor Vehicles in Use: 5,600

GOVERNMENT

Type: parliamentary democracy
Independence Date: September 21, 1981 (from the United Kingdom)
Head of State/Government: Governor General Sir Colville Young (represents Queen Elizabeth II); Prime Minister Said Musa
Political Parties: People's United Party; United Democratic Party; National Alliance for Belizean Rights
Suffrage: universal at 18

MILITARY

Military Expenditures (% of GDP): 2%
Current Disputes: border dispute with Guatemala

ECONOMY

Currency ($U.S. Equivalent): 2.00 Belize dollars = $1
Per Capita Income/GDP: $4,900/$1.28 billion
GDP Growth Rate: 3.7%
Inflation Rate: 1.9%
Unemployment Rate: 9.1%
Labor Force: 90,000
Natural Resources: arable land; timber; fish; hydropower
Agriculture: bananas; cocoa; citrus fruits; sugarcane; lumber; fish; cultured shrimp
Industry: garment production; food processing; tourism; construction
Exports: $207.8 million (primary partners Mexico, United States, European Union)
Imports: $500.6 million (primary partners United States, Mexico, United Kingdom)

SUGGESTED WEBSITE

http://www.cia.gov/cia/
publications/factbook/geos/
bh.html#Geo

Belize Country Report

THE "HISPANICIZATION" OF A COUNTRY

Belize was settled in the late 1630s by English woodcutters who also indulged in occasional piracy at the expense of the Spanish crown. The loggers were interested primarily in dye-woods, which, in the days before chemical dyes, were essential to British textile industries. The country's name is derived from Peter Wallace, a notorious buccaneer who, from his base there, haunted the coast in search of Spanish shipping. The natives shortened and mispronounced Wallace's name until he became known as "Belize."

As a British colony (called British Honduras), Belize enjoyed relative prosperity as an important entrepôt, or storage depot for merchandise, until the completion of the Panama Railway in 1855. With the opening of a rail route to the Pacific, commerce shifted south, away from Caribbean ports. Belize entered an economic tailspin (from which it has never entirely recovered). Colonial governments attempted to diversify the colony's agricultural base and to attract foreign immigration to develop the land. But, except for some Mexican settlers and a few former Confederate soldiers who came to the colony after the U.S. Civil War, the immigration policy failed. Economically depressed, its population exposed to the ravages of yellow fever, malaria, and dengue (a tropical fever), Be-

lize was once described by British novelist Aldous Huxley in the following terms: "If the world had ends, Belize would be one of them."

Living conditions improved markedly by the 1950s, and the colony began to move toward independence from Great Britain. Although self-governing by 1964, Belize did not become fully independent until 1981, because of Guatemalan threats to invade what it even today considers a lost province, stolen by Britain. British policy calls for a termination of its military presence, even though Guatemalan intentions toward Belize are ambivalent.

DEVELOPMENT
Belize has combined its tourism and environmental-protection offices into one ministry, which holds great promise for ecotourism. Large tracts of land have been set aside to protect jaguars and other endangered species. But there is also pressure on the land from rapid population growth.

For most of its history Belize has been culturally British with Caribbean overtones. English common law is practiced in the courts, and politics are patterned on the English parliamentary system. A large percent of the people are Protestants. The Belizeans are primarily working-class poor

and middle-class shopkeepers and merchants. There is no great difference between the well-to-do and the poor in Belize, and few people fall below the absolute poverty line.

Thirty percent of the population are Creole (black and English mixture), 6 percent Garifuna (black and Indian mixture). The Garifuna originally inhabited the Caribbean island of St. Vincent. In the eighteenth century, they joined with native Indians in an uprising against the English authorities. As punishment, virtually all the Garifuna were deported to Belize.

Despite a pervasive myth of racial democracy in Belize, discrimination exists. Belize is not a harmonious, multiethnic island in a sea of violence. For example, sociologist Bruce Ergood notes that in Belize it "is not uncommon to hear a light Creole bad-mouth 'blacks,' even though both are considered Creole. This reflects a vestige of English colonial attitude summed up in the saying, 'Best to be white, less good to be mulatto, worst to be black....'"

FREEDOM
Legislation was passed in October 2000 that calls on trade unions and employers to negotiate over unionization of the workplace if that is the desire of the majority of workers.

A shift in population occurred in the 1980s because of the turmoil in neighboring Central American states. For years, well-educated, English-speaking Creoles had been leaving Belize in search of better economic opportunities in other countries; but this was more than made up for by the inflow of perhaps as many as 40,000 Latin American refugees fleeing the fighting in the region. Spanish is now the primary language of a significant percentage of the population, and some Belizeans are concerned about the "Hispanicization" of the country.

HEALTH/WELFARE

In a speech to the Christian Workers Union, Prime Minister Said Musa noted: "Higher wages will not mean much if families cannot obtain quality and affordable health care services. What good are higher wages if there are not enough classrooms in which to place the children? What good are higher wages if we are forced to live in fear of the criminal elements in society? A workers' movement must ... concern itself not only with wages but also with the overall quality of life of its members."

Women in Belize suffer discrimination that is deeply rooted in the cultural, social, and economic structures of the society, even though the government promotes their participation in the nation's politics and development process. Great emphasis is placed on education and health care. Tropical diseases, once the primary cause of death in Belize, were brought under control by a government program of insect spraying. Better health and nutritional awareness are emphasized in campaigns to encourage breastfeeding and the selection and preparation of meals using local produce.

ACHIEVEMENTS

Recent digging by archaeologists has uncovered several Maya sites that have convinced scholars that the indigenous civilization in the region was more extensive and refined than experts had previously believed.

With the new millennium, Belize has increasingly turned its attention to the impact of globalization. Concern was expressed by the government about job security and the need for education and training in the skills necessary to compete in a global marketplace. National Trade Union Congress president Dorene Quiros noted that "global institutions are not meeting the basic needs of people," and promises by international organizations to do better have produced only modest results. Worrying, too, is the rising incidence of violent urban crime and growing involvement in the South American drug trade.

In 2006 petroleum was discovered in the western part of the country close to the border with Guatemala. With expec-

tations that the oil field could yield about 50,000 barrels of oil per day, exports could provide a modest boost to the economy. But the discovery could lead to friction with Guatemala. Although Guatemala recognized the independence of Belize in 1992, the oil was found in a disputed border area.

Timeline: PAST

1638
Belize is settled by English Logwood cutters

1884
Belize is declared an independent Crown colony

1972
Guatemala threatens to invade

1981
Independence from Great Britain

1990s
Belize becomes an ecotourism destination
Said Musa is elected prime minister

PRESENT

2000s
Guatemala continues territorial claims to Belize

Negotiations with Guatemala over border issues continue

Costa Rica (Republic of Costa Rica)

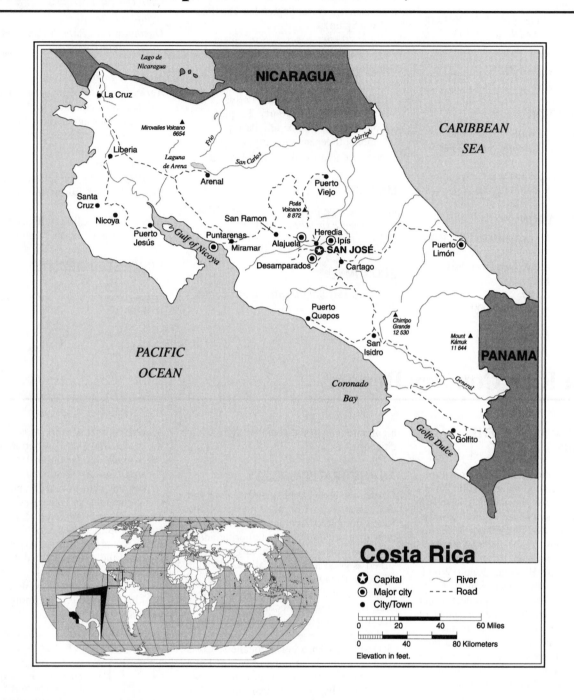

Costa Rica Statistics

GEOGRAPHY

Area in Square Miles (Kilometers):
19,700 (51,022) (about the size of West Virginia)

Capital (Population): San José (325,000)

Environmental Concerns: deforestation; soil erosion

Geographical Features: coastal plains separated by rugged mountains

PEOPLE

Population

Total: 3,956,507

Annual Growth Rate: 1.52%

Rural/Urban Population Ratio: 50/50

Major Language: Spanish

Ethnic Makeup: 96% white (including a few Mestizos); 2% black; 1% Indian; 1% Chinese

Religions: 76.3% Roman Catholic; 13.7% Evangelical; 5% others

Health

Life Expectancy at Birth: 74 years (male);
79 years (female)
Infant Mortality Rate (Ratio): 10.26/1,000
Physicians Available (Ratio): 1/763

Education

Adult Literacy Rate: 95%
Compulsory (Ages): 6–15; free

COMMUNICATION

Telephones: 1.132 million main lines
Daily Newspaper Circulation: 102 per
1,000 people
Televisions: 102 per 1,000 people
Internet Users: 800,000 (2000)

TRANSPORTATION

Highways in Miles (Kilometers): 21,363
(37,273)
Railroads in Miles (Kilometers): 593
(950)
Usable Airfields: 155
Motor Vehicles in Use: 119,000

GOVERNMENT

Type: democratic republic
Independence Date: September 15, 1821
(from Spain)
Head of State/Government: President
Oscar Arias is both head of state and
head of government
Political Parties: Social Christian Unity
Party; National Liberation Party;
National Integration Party; People
United Party; Democratic Party;
National Independent Party; others
Suffrage: universal and compulsory at 18

MILITARY

*Military Expenditures (% of Central Gov-
ernment Expenditures):* 0.4%
Current Hostilities: none

ECONOMY

Currency ($U.S. Equivalent): 365 colons
= $1

Per Capita Income/GDP: $7,100/$26
billion
GDP Growth Rate: 7%
Inflation Rate: 10.8%
Unemployment Rate: 5.7%; 7.5%
underemployment
Labor Force: 1,377,000
Natural Resources: hydropower
Agriculture: coffee; bananas; sugar; corn;
rice; beans; potatoes; beef; timber
Industry: microprocessors; food
processing; textiles and clothing;
construction materials; fertilizer; plastic
products; tourism
Exports: $6.4 billion (primary partners
United States, European Union, Central
America)
Imports: $7.5 billion (primary partners
United States, Japan, Mexico)

SUGGESTED WEBSITE

http://www.cia.gov/cia/
publications/factbook/geos/
cs.html

Costa Rica Country Report

COSTA RICA: A DIFFERENT TRADITION?

Costa Rica has often been singled out as politically and socially unique in Latin America. It is true that the nation's historical
development has not been as directly influenced by Spain as its neighbors' have, but
this must not obscure the essential Hispanic
character of the Costa Rican people and
their institutions. Historian Ralph Woodward observes that historically, Costa
Rica's "uniqueness was the product of her
relative remoteness from the remainder of
Central America, her slight economic importance to Spain, and her lack of a non-
white subservient class and corresponding
lack of a class of large landholders to exploit its labors." Indeed, in 1900, Costa
Rica had a higher percentage of farmers
with small- and medium-range operations
than any other Latin American country.

The nature of Costa Rica's economy allowed a wider participation in politics and
fostered the development of political institutions dedicated to the equality of all people, which existed only in theory in other
Latin American countries. Costa Rican
politicians, since the late nineteenth century, have endorsed programs that have
been largely middle class in content. The
government has consistently demonstrated

a commitment to the social welfare of its
citizens.

AN INTEGRATED SOCIETY

Despite the recent atmosphere of crisis and
disintegration in Central America, Costa
Rica's durable democracy has avoided the
twin evils of oppressive authoritarianism
and class warfare. But what might be construed as good luck is actually a reflection
of Costa Rica's history. In social, racial,
linguistic, and educational terms, Costa
Rica is an integrated country without the
fractures and cleavages that typify the rest
of the region.

Despite its apparent uniqueness, Costa
Rica is culturally an integral part of Latin
America and embodies what is most positive about Hispanic political culture. The
government has long played the role of benevolent patron to the majority of its citizens. Opposition and antagonism have
historically been defused by a process of
accommodation, mutual cooperation, and
participation. In the early 1940s, for example, modernizers who wanted to create a
dynamic capitalist economy took care to
pacify the emerging labor movement with
appropriate social legislation and benefits.
Moreover, to assure that development did
not sacrifice social welfare, the state assumed a traditional role with respect to the

economy—that is, it took an active role in
the production and distribution of income.
After much discussion, in 1993, the Costa
Rican Congress authorized the privatization of the state-owned cement and fertilizer companies. In both cases, according to
Latin American Regional Reports, "a 30%
stake [would] be reserved for employees,
20% [would] be offered to private investors, and the remainder [would] be shared
out between trade unions ... and cooperatives." Tight controls were retained on
banking, insurance, oil refining, and public
utilities.

DEVELOPMENT

In recent years the country has
moved away from its traditional
dependence on exports of
coffee, bananas, and beef.
Tourism is now Costa Rica's main source of
revenue. In the late 1990s a large computer
chip plants promised further diversification of
the economy and high-tech jobs. But
fluctuating world demand for microchips has
been the cause of some concern.

Women, who were granted the right to
vote in the 1940s, have participated freely
in Costa Rica's elections. Women have
served as a vice president, minister of foreign commerce, and president of the Legis-

(Courtesy of Don Evelio Tarrazu Farm/tarrazucafe01924)

Modern growing and distribution techniques are making more and better coffee available, both for export and for the domestic market. Here two workers are pouring coffee cherries down the measuring machine on a plantation in Costa Rica.

lative Assembly. Although in broader terms the role of women is primarily domestic, they are legally unrestricted. Equal work, in general, is rewarded by equal pay for men and women. But women also hold, as a rule, lower-paying jobs.

POLITICS OF CONSENSUS

Costa Rica's political stability is assured by the politics of consensus. Deals and compacts are the order of the day among various competing elites. Political competition is open, and participation by labor and peasants is expanding. Election campaigns provide a forum to air differing viewpoints, to educate the voting public, and to keep politicians in touch with the population at large.

Costa Rica frequently has had strong, charismatic leaders who have been committed to social democracy and have rejected a brand of politics grounded in class differences. The country's democracy has always reflected the paternalism and personalities of its presidents.

This tradition was again endorsed when José María Figueres Olsen won the presidential election on February 6, 1994. Figueres was the son of the founder of the modern Costa Rican democracy, and he promised to return to a reduced version of the welfare state. But, by 1996, in the face of a sluggish economy, the populist champion adopted policies that were markedly pro-business. As a result, opinion polls rapidly turned against him. In the 1998 presidential election, an unprecedented 13 political parties ran candidates, which indicated to the three leading parties that citizens no longer believed in them and that political reforms were in order.

A low voter turnout of 65 percent in presidential elections in 2006 signaled further dissatisfaction with the nation's traditional parties. In 2004 evidence of high-level corruption resulted in the jailing of two former presidents on charges of graft. Although former president (1986–1990) and Nobel Prize–winner Oscar Arias was expected to win easily, the vote was evenly split. Only after a manual recount and a series of legal challenges did Otton Solís concede defeat.

Other oft-given reasons for Costa Rica's stability are the high levels of tolerance exhibited by its people and the absence of a military establishment. Costa Rica has had no military establishment since a brief civil war in 1948. Government officials have long boasted that they rule over a country that has more teachers than soldiers. There is also a strong public tradition that favors demilitarization. Costa Rica's auxiliary

forces, however, could form the nucleus of an army in a time of emergency.

The Costa Rican press is among the most unrestricted in Latin America, and differing opinions are openly expressed. Human-rights abuses are virtually nonexistent in the country, but there is a general suspicion of Communists in this overwhelmingly middle-class, white society. And some citizens are concerned about the antidemocratic ideas expressed by ultra-conservatives.

The aftermath of Central America's civil wars is still being felt. Although thousands of refugees returned to Nicaragua with the advent of peace, many thousands more remained in Costa Rica. Economic malaise in Nicaragua combined with the devastation of Hurricane Mitch in 1998 sent thousands of economic migrants across the border into Costa Rica. "Ticos" are worried by the additional strain placed on government resources in a country where more than 80 percent of the population are covered by social-security programs, and approximately 60 percent are provided with pensions and medical benefits.

FREEDOM

Despite Costa Rica's generally enviable human-rights record, there is some de facto discrimination against blacks, Indians, and women (domestic violence against women is a serious problem). The press is free. A stringent libel law, however, makes the media cautious in reporting of personalities.

HEALTH/WELFARE

Costa Ricans enjoy the highest standard of living in Central America. But Costa Rica's indigenous peoples, in part because of their remote location, have inadequate schools, health care, and access to potable water. Fully 20 percent of the population live in poverty.

The economy has been under stress since 1994, and President Figueres was forced to reconsider many of his statist policies. While the export sector remained healthy, domestic industry languished and the internal debt ballooned. The Costa Rican–American Chamber of Commerce observed that "Costa Rica, with its tiny $8.6 billion GDP and 3.5 million people, can not afford a government that consistently overspends its budget by 5 percent or more and then sells short-term bonds, mostly to state institutions, to finance the deficit." In 1997, there was a vigorous debate over the possible privatization of many state entities in an effort to reduce the debt quickly. But opponents of privatization noted that state institutions were important contributors to the high standard of living in the country.

Acknowledging that the world had entered a new phase of development, President Miguel Angel Rodríguez introduced a new economic program in January 2001. Called *Impulso* ("Impulse"), the plan, as reported in *The Tico Times*, noted that for Costa Rica to compete in the new global economy, "knowledge, technology, quality of human resources and the development of telecommunication and transportation infrastructures are fundamental determinants of national prosperity." The old model of economic development, which, according to the president, was characterized by "a diversification of exports, liberalized markets and high levels of foreign investment," must be replaced with a fresh approach "rooted in advanced technological development, a highly qualified labor force, and exports of greater value." President Abel Pacheco, elected in April 2002, embraced a similar approach to economic development. But he was unable to fulfill his promises in part because of falling commodity prices and continued trade and fiscal deficits and in part because of political opposition to tax reforms, privatization of some sectors of the economy, and his free trade philosophy. President Arias is also committed to free-trade, but his narrow victory in 2006 signal the need for compromise and flexibility in his economic policy.

THE ENVIRONMENT

At a time when tropical rain forests globally are under assault by developers, cattle barons, and land-hungry peasants, Costa Rica has taken concrete action to protect its environment. Minister of Natural Resources Álvaro Umana was one of those responsible for engineering an imaginative debt-for-nature swap. In his words: "We would like to see debt relief support conservation … a policy that everybody agrees is good." Since 1986, the Costa Rican government has authorized the conversion of $75 million in commercial debt into bonds. Interest generated by those bonds has supported a variety of projects, such as the enlargement and protection of La Amistad, a 1.7 million-acre reserve of tropical rain forest.

ACHIEVEMENTS

In a region torn by civil war and political chaos, Costa Rica's years of free and democratic elections stand as a remarkable achievement in political stability and civil rights. President Óscar Arias was awarded the Nobel Peace Prize in 1987; he remains a respected world leader.

About 13 percent of Costa Rica's land is protected currently in a number of national parks. It is hoped that very soon about 25 percent of the country will be designated as national parkland in order to protect tropical rain forests as well as the even more endangered tropical dry forests.

Much of the assault on the forests typically has been dictated by economic necessity and/or greed. In one all-too-common scenario, a small- or middle-size cacao grower discovers that his crop has been decimated by a blight. Confronted by disaster, he will usually farm the forest surrounding his property for timber and then torch the remainder. Ultimately, he will likely sell his land to a cattle rancher, who will transform what had once been rain forest or dry forest into pasture.

Timeline: PAST

1522
Spain establishes its first settlements in Costa Rica

1821
Independence from Spain

1823
Costa Rica is part of the United Provinces of Central America

1838
Costa Rica Becomes independent as a separate state

1948
Civil war; reforms; abolition of the army

1980s
Costa Rica takes steps to protect its tropical rain forests and dry forests

1990s
Ecotourism to Costa Rica increases

PRESENT

2000s
Two former presidents jailed on corruption charges

Oscar Arias elected president in 2006

In an effort to break this devastating pattern, at least one Costa Rican environmental organization has devised a workable plan to save the forests. Farmers are introduced to a variety of cash crops so that they will not be totally dependent on a single crop. Also, in the case of cacao, for example, the farmer will be provided with a disease- or blight-resistant strain to lessen further the chances of crop losses and subsequent conversion of land to cattle pasture.

Scientists in Costa Rica are concerned that tropical forests are being destroyed before their usefulness to humankind can be fully appreciated. Such forests contain a treasure-trove of medicinal herbs. In Costa Rica, for example, there is at least one plant common to the rain forests that might be beneficial in the struggle against AIDS.

El Salvador (Republic of El Salvador)

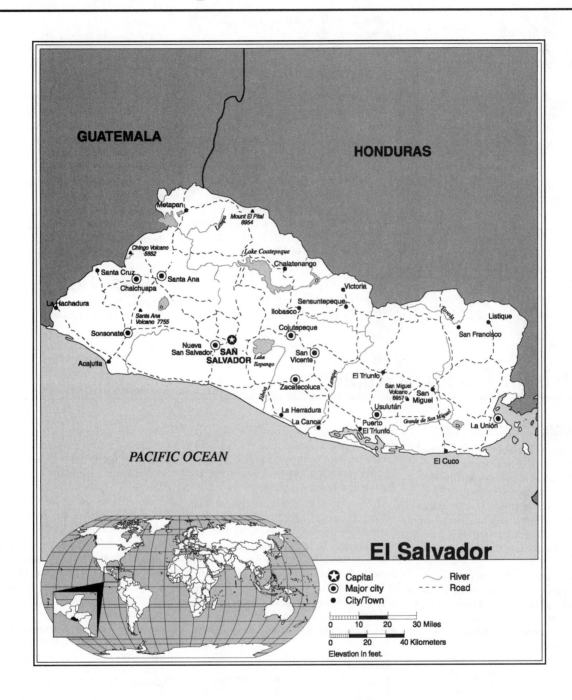

El Salvador Statistics

GEOGRAPHY

Area in Square Miles (Kilometers): 8,292 (21,476) (about the size of Massachusetts)

Capital (Population): San Salvador (1,214,000)

Environmental Concerns: deforestation; soil erosion; water pollution; soil contamination

Geographical Features: a hot coastal plain in south rises to a cooler plateau and valley region; mountainous in north, including many volcanoes

Climate: tropical; distinct wet and dry seasons

PEOPLE

Population

Total: 6,587,541

Annual Growth Rate: 1.78%

Rural/Urban Population Ratio: 55/45

Ethnic Makeup: 94% Mestizo;
Amerindian 1% white; 9%

Major Language: Spanish

Religions: 75% Roman Catholic; 25%
Protestant groups

Health

Life Expectancy at Birth: 67 years (male);
74 years (female)

Infant Mortality Rate (Ratio): 25.93/1,000

Physicians Available (Ratio): 1/1,219

Education

Adult Literacy Rate: 80.2%

Compulsory (Ages): 7–16; free

COMMUNICATION

Telephones: 483,000 main lines

Daily Newspaper Circulation: 53 per
1,000 people

Televisions: 91 per 1,000

Internet Users: 4 (2000)

TRANSPORTATION

Highways in Miles (Kilometers): 6,196
(9,977)

Railroads in Miles (Kilometers): 374 (602)

Usable Airfields: 85

Motor Vehicles in Use: 80,000

GOVERNMENT

Type: republic

Independence Date: September 15, 1821
(from Spain)

Head of State/Government: President
Francisco Flores is both head of state and
head of government

Political Parties: Farabundo Martí
National Liberation Front; National
Republican Alliance; National
Conciliation Party; Christian Democratic
Party; Democratic Convergence; others

Suffrage: universal at 18

MILITARY

Military Expenditures (% of GDP): 1.1%

Current Disputes: border disputes

ECONOMY

Currency ($U.S. Equivalent): U.S. Dollar

Per Capita Income/GDP: $4,800/$30.99
billion

GDP Growth Rate: 1.4%

Inflation Rate: 2.1%

Unemployment Rate: 6.5%

Labor Force: 2,350,000

Natural Resources: hydropower;
geothermal power; petroleum; arable land

Agriculture: coffee; sugarcane; corn; rice;
beans; oilseed; cotton; sorghum; beef;
dairy products; shrimp

Industry: food processing; beverages;
petroleum; chemicals; fertilizer; textiles;
furniture; light metals

Exports: $3.2 billion (primary partners
United States, Guatemala, Germany)

Imports: $5.5 billion (primary partners
United States, Guatemala, Mexico)

SUGGESTED WEBSITE

http://cia.gov/cia/publications/
factbook/index.html

El Salvador Country Report

EL SALVADOR: A TROUBLED LAND

El Salvador, a small country, was engaged until 1992 in a civil war that cut through class lines, divided the military and the Roman Catholic Church, and severely damaged the social and economic fabric of the nation. It was the latest in a long series of violent sociopolitical eruptions that have plagued the country since its independence in 1821.

In the last quarter of the nineteenth century, large plantation owners—spurred by the sharp increase in the world demand for coffee and other products of tropical agriculture—expanded their lands and estates. Most of the new land was purchased or taken from Indians and Mestizos (those of mixed white and Indian blood), who, on five occasions between 1872 and 1898, took up arms in futile attempts to preserve their land. The once-independent Indians and Mestizos were reduced to becoming tenant farmers, sharecroppers, day laborers, or peons on the large estates. Indians, when deprived of their lands, also lost much of their cultural and ethnic distinctiveness. Today, El Salvador is an overwhelmingly Mestizo society.

The uprooted peasantry was controlled in a variety of ways. Some landowners played the role of *patrón* and assured workers the basic necessities of life in return for their la-

bor. Laws against "vagabonds" (those who, when stopped by rural police, did not have a certain amount of money in their pockets) assured plantation owners a workforce and discouraged peasant mobility.

To enforce order further, a series of security organizations—the National Guard, the National Police, and the Treasury Police—were created by the central government. Many of these security personnel actually lived on the plantations and estates and followed the orders of the owner. Although protection of the economic system was their primary function, over time elements of these organizations became private armies.

DEVELOPMENT

Since 1991, the government has been able to attract substantial investment in a new industry of low-wage, duty-free assembly plants patterned after the maquiladora industries along Mexico's border with the United States. Advantageous tax laws and a free-market climate favorable to business are central to the government's development policy.

This phenomenon lay at the heart of much of the "unofficial" violence in El Salvador in recent years. In Salvadoran society, personal loyalties to relatives or local

strongmen competed with and often superseded loyalty to government officials. Because of this, the government was unable to control some elements within its security forces.

In an analysis of the Salvadoran Civil War, it is tempting to place the rich, rightwing landowners and their military allies on one side; and the poor, the peasantry, and the guerrillas on the other. Such a division is artificial, however, and fails to reflect the complexities of the conflict. Granted, the military and landowners had enjoyed a mutually beneficial partnership since 1945. But there were liberal and conservative factions within the armed forces, and, since the 1940s, there had been some movement toward needed social and economic reforms. It was a military regime in 1949 that put into effect the country's first social-security legislation. In 1950, a Constitution was established that provided for public-health programs, women's suffrage, and extended social-security coverage. The reformist impulse continued in the 1960s, when it became legal to organize opposition political parties.

A TIME FOR CHANGE

Food production increased in the 1970s by 44 percent, a growth that was second in Latin America only to Brazil's. Although much of the food grown was exported to world markets, some of the revenue generated was used for social programs in El Salvador. Life expectancy increased, the death rate fell, illiteracy declined, and the percentage of government expenditures on public health, housing, and education was among the highest in Latin America.

The programs and reforms, in classic Hispanic form, were generated by the upper classes. The elite believed that state-sponsored changes could be controlled in such a way that traditional balances in society would remain intact and elite domination of the government would be assured.

The origin of El Salvador's civil war may be traced to 1972, when the Christian Democratic candidate for president, José Napoleón Duarte, is believed to have won the popular vote but was deprived of his victory when the army declared the results false and handed the victory to its own candidate. Impatient and frustrated, middle-class politicians and student leaders from the opposition began to consider more forceful ways to oust the ruling class.

By 1979, guerrilla groups had become well established in rural El Salvador, and some younger army officers grew concerned that a successful left-wing popular revolt was a distinct possibility. Rather than wait for revolution from below, which might result in the destruction of the military as an institution, the officers chose to seize power in a coup and manipulate change from above. Once in power, this *junta*, or ruling body, moved quickly to transform the structure of Salvadoran society. A land-reform program, originally developed by civilian reformers and Roman

Catholic clergy, was adopted by the military. It would give the campesinos ("peasants") not only land but also status, dignity, and respect.

FREEDOM

The end of the civil war brought an overall improvement in human rights in El Salvador. News from across the political spectrum, often critical of the government, is reported in El Salvador, although foreign journalists seem to be the target of an unusually high level of muggings, robberies, and burglaries. Violence against women is widespread. Judges often dismiss rape cases on the pretext that the victim provoked the crime.

In its first year, 1980, the land-reform program had a tremendous impact on the landowning elite—37 percent of the lands producing cotton and 34 percent of the coffee-growing lands were confiscated by the government and redistributed. The junta also nationalized the banks and assumed control of the sale of coffee and sugar. Within months, however, several peasant members of the new cooperatives and the government agricultural advisers sent to help them were gunned down. The violence spread. Some of the killings were attributed to government security men in the pay of dispossessed landowners, but most of the killings may have been committed by the army.

In the opinion of a land-reform program official, the army was corrupt and had returned to the cooperatives that it had helped to establish in order to demand

money for protection and bribes. When the peasants refused, elements within the army initiated a reign of terror against them.

In 1989, further deterioration of the land-reform program was brought about by Supreme Court decisions and by policies adopted by the newly elected right-wing government of President Alfredo Cristiani. Former landowners who had property taken for redistribution to peasants successfully argued that seizures under the land reform were illegal. Subsequently, five successive land-reform cases were decided by the Supreme Court in favor of former property owners.

Cristiani, whose right-wing National Republican Alliance Party (ARENA) fought hard against land reform, would not directly attack the land-reform program—only because such a move would further alienate rural peasants and drive them into the arms of left-wing guerrillas. Instead, Cristiani favored the reconstitution of collective farms as private plots. Such a move, according to the government, would improve productivity and put an end to what authorities perceived as a form of U.S.–imposed "socialism." Critics of the government's policy charged that the privatization plan would ultimately result in the demise of land reform altogether.

Yet another problem was that many of the collectives established under the reform were (and remain) badly in debt. A 1986 study by the U.S. Agency for International Development reported that 95 percent of the cooperatives could not pay interest on the debt they were forced to acquire to compensate the landlords. *New York Times* reporter Lindsey Gruson noted

(Y. Nagata/PAS United Nations photo/ UN121035)

Civil strife disrupted much of El Salvador's agrarian production, and a lack of fishery planning necessitated importing from other parts of the world. With a new and efficient program to take advantage of fish in domestic waters, El Salvador has been able to develop an effective food industry from the sea.

that the world surplus of agricultural products as well as mismanagement by peasants who suddenly found themselves in the unfamiliar role of owners were a large part of the reason for the failures. But the government did not help. Technical assistance was not provided, and the tremendous debt gave the cooperatives a poor credit rating, which made it difficult for them to secure needed fertilizer and pesticides.

Declining yields and, for many families, lives of increasing desperation have been the result. Some peasants must leave the land and sell their plots to the highest bidder. This will ultimately bring about a reconcentration of land in the hands of former landlords.

HEALTH/WELFARE

Many Salvadorans suffer from parasites and malnutrition. El Salvador has one of the highest infant mortality rates in the Western Hemisphere, largely because of polluted water. Potable water is readily available to only 10 percent of the population.

Other prime farmland lay untended because of the civil war. Violence drove many peasants from the land to the slums of the larger cities. And free-fire zones established by the military (in an effort to destroy the guerrillas' popular base) and guerrilla attacks against cooperatives (in an effort to sabotage the economy and further destabilize the country) had a common victim: the peasantry.

Some cooperatives and individual families failed to bring the land to flower because of the poor quality of the soil they inherited. Reporter Gruson told the story of one family, which was, unfortunately, all too common:

José ... received 1.7 acres on a rock-pocked slope an hour's walk from his small shack. José ... used to sell some of his beans and rice to raise a little cash. But year after year his yields have declined. Since he cannot afford fertilizers or insecticides, the corn that survives the torrential rainy season produces pest-infested ears the size of a baby's foot. Now, he has trouble feeding his wife and seven children.

"The land is no good," he said. "I've been working it for 12 years and my life has gotten worse every year. I don't have anywhere to go, but I'll have to leave soon."

After the coup, several governments came and went. The original reformers retired, went into exile, or went over to the guerrillas. The civil war continued into 1992, when a United Nations–mediated cease-fire took effect.

HUMAN-RIGHTS ISSUES

Twelve years of war had cost 70,000 lives and given El Salvador the reputation of a bloody and abusive country. Tens of thousands of El Salvadorans were uprooted by the violence and many made their way to the United States. Despite the declared truce, the extreme right and left continued to utilize assassination to eliminate or terrorize both each other and the voices of moderation who dared to speak out.

Through 1992, human-rights abuses still occurred on a wide scale in El Salvador. Public order was constantly disrupted by military operations, guerrilla raids, factional hatreds, acts of revenge, personal grudges, pervasive fear, and a sense of uncertainty about the future. State-of-siege decrees suspended all constitutional rights to freedom of speech and press. However, self-censorship, both in the media and by individuals, out of fear of violent reprisals, was the leading constraint on free expression in El Salvador.

Eventually, as *Boston Globe* correspondent Pamela Constable reported, "a combination of war-weariness and growing pragmatism among leaders of all persuasions suggests that once-bitter adversaries have begun to develop a modus vivendi."

Release of the report in 1993 by the UN's "Truth Commission," a special body entrusted with the investigation of human-rights violations in El Salvador, prompted the right wing–dominated Congress to approve an amnesty for those named. But progress has been made in other areas. The National Police have been separated from the Defense Ministry; and the National Guard, Civil Defense forces, and the notorious Treasury Police have been abolished. A new National Civilian Police, comprised of 20 percent of National Police, 20 percent former Farabundo Martí National Liberation Front (FMLN) guerrillas, and 60 percent with no involvement on either side in the civil war, was instituted in 1994.

President Cristiani reduced the strength of the army from 63,000 to 31,500 by February 1993, earlier than provided for by the agreement; and the class of officers known as the *tondona*, who had long dominated the military and were likely responsible for human-rights abuses, were forcibly retired by the president on June 30, 1993. Land, judicial, and electoral reforms followed. Despite perhaps inevitable setbacks because of the legacy of violence and bitterness, editor Juan Comas wrote that "most analysts are inclined to believe that El Sal-

vador's hour of madness has passed and the country is now on the road to hope."

In El Salvador, as elsewhere in Latin America, the Roman Catholic Church was divided. The majority of Church officials backed government policy and supported the United States' contention that the violence in El Salvador was due to Cuban-backed subversion. Other clergy strongly disagreed and argued convincingly that the violence was deeply rooted in historical social injustice.

ACHIEVEMENTS

Despite the violence of war, political power has been transferred via elections at both the municipal and national levels. Elections have helped to establish the legitimacy of civilian leaders in a region usually dominated by military regimes.

Another endemic problem that confronts postwar El Salvador is widespread corruption. It is a human-rights issue because corruption and its attendant misuse of scarce resources contribute to persistent or increased poverty and undermine the credibility and stability of government at all levels. According to the nonprofit watchdog group *Probidad*, "El Salvador has a long history of corruption.... Before the first of many devastating earthquakes on January 13, 2001, El Salvador was the third poorest country in Latin America.... Influence peddling between construction companies and their friends and families in government and other corrupt practices resulted in many unnecessary deaths, infrastructure damage, and irregularities in humanitarian assistance distribution."

ECONOMIC ISSUES

In 1998, President Armando Calderón Sol surprised both supporters and opponents when he launched a bold program of reforms. The first three years of his administration had been characterized by indecision. Political scientist Tommie Sue Montgomery noted that his "reputation for espousing as policy the last viewpoint he has heard has produced in civil society both heartburn and black humor." But a combination of factors created new opportunities for Calderón. The former guerrillas of the FMLN were divided and failed to take advantage of ARENA's apparent weak leadership; a UN–sponsored program of reconstruction and reconciliation was short of funds and, by 1995, had lost momentum; and presidential elections were looming in 1999. A dozen years of war had left the economic infrastructure in disarray. The economy had, at best, remained static, and while the war raged, there had been no attempt to modernize. During his final year in office, Calderón developed reform policies of modernization, privatization, and free-market competition. Interestingly, his reforms generated opposition from former guerrillas, who are now represented in the Legislature by the FMLN, as well as from some members of the traditional conservative economic elite.

Perhaps one result of Calderón's reforms was the decisive victory of ARENA at the polls in 1999, and again in 2004. The FMLN, on the other hand, won municipal and legislative elections in 2003, which gave them the largest voting bloc in congress.

OUT-MIGRATION

El Salvador's civil war set into motion some profound changes in the nation. As noted, thousands of people fled to other countries, and especially to the United States. Once established, other family members tended to follow. Indeed, one of every nine people born in El Salvador will migrate to the United States. Salvadoran sociologist Raymundo Calderón, as reported in the *Los Angeles Times*, stated: "Most of the Salvadorans who have migrated ... are not well educated. But when they get to the U.S., they have access to better housing and better pay. Their view of the world changes, and they communicate this to their families in El Salvador." So many have departed that there is a labor shortage in the agricultural sector that has had to be filled by workers from Honduras and Nicaragua. In November 2005 the nation's minister of agriculture announced

that 15,000 foreign workers would be needed to cut sugarcane and harvest the cotton and coffee crops.

The labor shortage is directly related to a more serious issue. *Los Angeles Times* correspondent Hector Tobar notes concerns that Salvadorans are losing their "industrious self-image, a vision celebrated by poets such as Roque Dalton, whose 'Love Poem' recounted the exploits of Salvadoran laborers up and down the Americas." Remittances from the United States to El Salvador prompted one harvest supervisor for a large sugar refinery to say that money from families in the United States has made Salvadorans "comfortable, and they don't want to work cutting cane." This lament was echoed by the minister of the interior in his comments to a local newspaper: "Today people are telling us that their family remittances are sufficient [to live on]. It's not possible that we are abandoning our own fields and we have to bring in labor from abroad." What the minister finds impossible is that El Salvadoran rural workers, because of a labor surplus, had traditionally sought work in neighboring Honduras. Now the flow of labor is in the other direction. War, natural disasters, and out-migration have changed the very culture of the nation.

Finally, an unwelcome consequence of out-migration is that many youths, exposed to and emulating the gang cultures in several United States cities, have become a serious criminal problem for not only United States authorities, but also for those in El Salvador as gangs have made their appearance in urban areas. A BBC report notes: "Poverty, civil war, natural

Timeline: PAST

1524
Present-day El Salvador is occupied by Spanish settlers from Mexico

1821
Independence from Spain is declared

1822
El Salvador is part of the United Provinces of Central America

1838
El Salvador becomes independent as a separate state

1969
A brief war between El Salvador and Honduras

1970
Guerrilla warfare in El Salvador

1979
Army officers seize power in a coup; civil war

1990s
A cease-fire takes effect on February 1, 1992, officially ending the civil war

PRESENT

2000s
Earthquakes devastate towns and cities, with a heavy loss of life and extensive infrastructure damage

Anthony Saca wins 2004 presidential election

disaster, and consequent dislocations have left their mark on ... society, which is among the most violent and crime ridden in the Americas."

Guatemala (Republic of Guatemala)

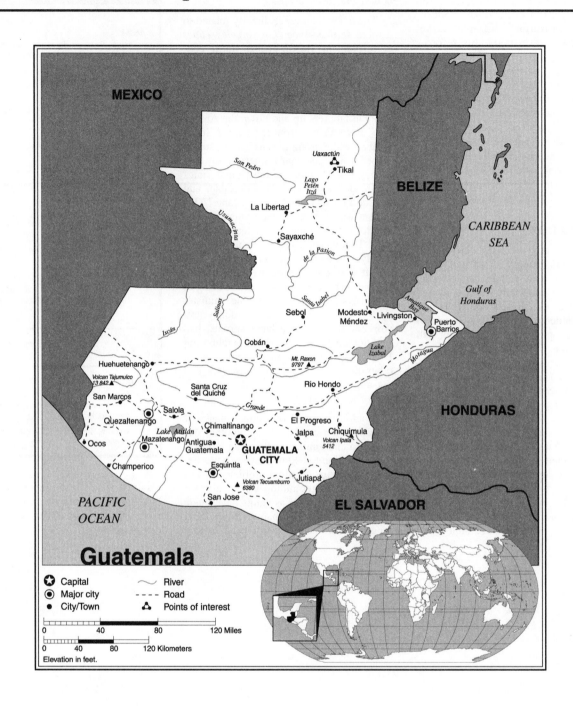

MEXICO

Uaxactún
Tikal

Lago Petén Itzá

BELIZE

San Pedro

La Libertad

CARIBBEAN SEA

Sayaxché

Usumacinta

de la Pasion

Santa Isabel

Gulf of Honduras

Amatique Bay

Sebol

Modesto Méndez
Livingston

Puerto Barrios

Salinas

Ixcán

Cobán

Lake Izabal

Motagua

Huehuetenango

Mt. Raxon 9797

Volcan Tajumulco 13,842

San Marcos

Santa Cruz del Quiché

Rio Hondo

Grande

Salola

El Progreso

HONDURAS

Quezaltenango

Chimaltinango

Jalpa

Chiquimula

Lake Atitlán

Volcan Ipala 5412

Mazatenango

Antigua Guatemala

GUATEMALA CITY

Ocos

Esquintla

Jutiapa

Champerico

Volcan Tecuamburro 6380

PACIFIC OCEAN

San Jose

EL SALVADOR

Guatemala

- ⊛ Capital
- ⊙ Major city
- ● City/Town
- ∾ River
- --- Road
- △ Points of interest

0   40   80   120 Miles
0   40   80   120 Kilometers
Elevation in feet.

Guatemala Statistics

GEOGRAPHY

Area in Square Miles (Kilometers): 42,000 (108,780) (about the size of Tennessee)

Capital (Population): Guatemala City (2,205,000)

Environmental Concerns: deforestation; soil erosion; water pollution
Geographical Features: mostly mountains, with narrow coastal plains and a rolling limestone plateau (Peten)
Climate: temperate in highlands; tropical on coasts

PEOPLE

Population

Total: 14,280,596
Annual Growth Rate: 2.63%
Rural/Urban Population Ratio: 61/39
    Ethnic Makeup: 56% Ladino (Mestizo

and Westernized Indian); 44%
Amerindian
Major Languages: Spanish; Maya
languages
Religions: predominantly Roman
Catholic; Protestant and Maya

Health

Life Expectancy at Birth: 64 years (male);
66 years (female); 44 years (Indian
population)
Infant Mortality Rate (Ratio): 36.91/1,000
Physicians Available (Ratio): 1/2,356

Education

Adult Literacy Rate: 70.6%
Compulsory (Ages): 7–14; free

COMMUNICATION

Telephones: 846,000 main lines
Daily Newspaper Circulation: 29 per
1,000 people
Televisions: 45 per 1,000
Internet Users: 400,000

TRANSPORTATION

Highways in Miles (Kilometers): 8,135
(13,100)

Railroads in Miles (Kilometers): 552 (884)
Usable Airfields: 477
Motor Vehicles in Use: 199,000

GOVERNMENT

Type: Constitutional democratic republic
Independence Date: September 15, 1821
(from Spain)
Head of State/Government: President
Oscar Jose Rafael Berger (January 2004)
is both head of state and head of
government
Political Parties: National Centrist Union;
Christian Democratic Party; National
Advancement Party; National Liberation
Movement; Social Democratic Party;
Revolutionary Party; Guatemalan
Republican Front; Democratic Union;
New Guatemalan Democratic Front
Suffrage: universal at 18

MILITARY

Military Expenditures (% of GDP): 0.8%
Current Disputes: border dispute with
Belize

ECONOMY

Currency ($U.S. Equivalent): 7.94
quetzals = $1
Per Capita Income/GDP: $4,100/$56.53
billion
GDP Growth Rate: 2.2%
Inflation Rate: 5.6%
Unemployment Rate: 7.5%
Labor Force: 4.2 million
Natural Resources: petroleum; nickel; rare
woods; fish; chicle; hydropower
Agriculture: sugarcane; corn; bananas;
coffee; beans; cardamom; livestock
Industry: sugar; textiles and clothing;
furniture; chemicals; petroleum; metals;
rubber; tourism
Exports: $2.7 billion (primary partners
United States, El Salvador, Honduras)
Imports: $5.7 billion (primary partners
United States, Mexico, South Korea, El
Salvador)

SUGGESTED WEBSITE

http://www.cia.gov/cia/
publications/factbook/index.html

Guatemala Country Report

GUATEMALA: PEOPLES IN CONFLICT

Ethnic relations between the descendants
of Maya Indians, who comprise 44 percent
of Guatemala's population, and whites and
Ladinos (Hispanicized Indians) have always been unfriendly and have contributed
significantly to the nation's turbulent history. During the colonial period and since
independence, Spaniards, Creoles (in Guatemala, whites born in the New World—as
opposed to in Nicaragua, where Creoles
are defined as native-born blacks), and Ladinos have repeatedly sought to dominate
the Guatemalan Indian population, largely
contained in the highlands, by controlling
the Indians' land and their labor.

The process of domination was accelerated between 1870 and 1920, as Guatemala's entry into world markets hungry for
tropical produce such as coffee resulted in
the purchase or extensive seizures of land
from Indians. Denied sufficient lands of
their own, Indians were forced onto the expanding plantations as debt peons. Others
were forced to labor as seasonal workers
on coastal plantations; many died there because of the sharp climatic differences.

THE INDIAN AND INTEGRATION

Assaulted by the Ladino world, highland
Indians withdrew into their own culture
and built social barriers between themselves and the changing world outside their
villages. Those barriers have persisted until the present.

DEVELOPMENT

Although the Peace Accords of
1996 called for distributing land
to peasant farmers, more land, in
fact, has been concentrated in
fewer hands. International institutions such as
the World Bank favor export models that
endorse "economies of scale," which result in
larger agricultural yields. One result is the
increasing out-migration of rural families to
urban areas or even to the United States.

For the Guatemalan governments that
have thought in terms of economic progress
and national unity, the Indians have always
presented a problem. A 2003 presidential
candidate stated: "Indigenous groups do not
speak of a 'political system'; they speak of
community consensus, and their conception of community is very local.... How do

you have a functioning nation state, one
where indigenous groups participate actively in protecting their political interests,
and yet still respect the cultural practices of
other indigenous groups for whom participation in Western political institutions is
deemed undesirable?"

According to anthropologist Leslie
Dow, Jr., Guatemalan governments too
easily explain the Indian's lack of material
prosperity in terms of the "deficiencies" of
Indian culture. Indian "backwardness" is
better explained by elite policies calculated
to keep Indians subordinate. Social, political, and economic deprivations have consistently and consciously been utilized by
governments anxious to maintain the Indian in an inferior status.

Between 1945 and 1954, however, there
was a period of remarkable social reform in
Guatemala. Before the reforms were cut
short by the resistance of landowners, factions within the military, and a U.S. Central
Intelligence Agency–sponsored invasion,
Guatemalan governments made a concerted effort to integrate the Indian into national life. Some Indians who lived in close
proximity to large urban centers such as the

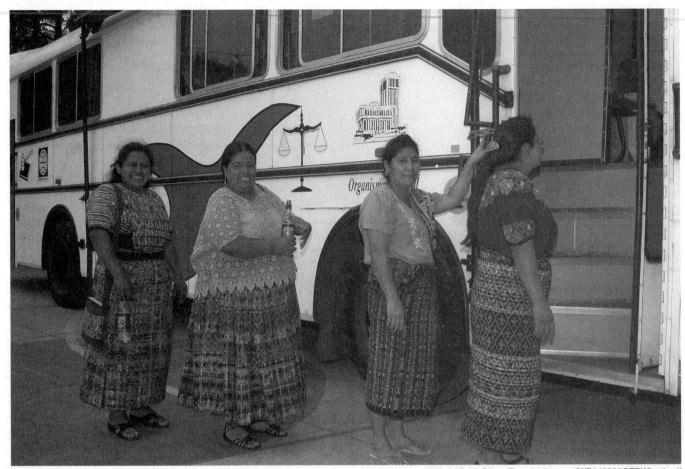

(World Bank Photo/Foto Anckerman/WB042806GTPWjustice1)

In recent years, Indians in Guatemala have pursued their rights by exercising their voting power. Here members of the Defense Fund for Indigenous Women are entering a mobile court in Jocotenango, Guatemala. The Fund provides psychological and social support to victims of violence and abuse.

capital, Guatemala City, learned that their vote had the power to effect changes to their benefit. They also realized that they were unequal not because of their illiteracy, "backwardness," poverty, or inability to converse in Spanish, but because of governments that refused to reform their political, social, and economic structures.

In theory, indigenous peoples in Guatemala enjoy equal legal rights under the Constitution. In fact, however, they remain largely outside the national culture, do not speak Spanish, and are not integrated into the national economy. Indian males are far more likely to be impressed into the army or guerrilla units. Indigenous peoples in Guatemala have suffered most of the combat-related casualties and repeated abuses of their basic human rights. There remains a pervasive discrimination against Indians in white society. Indians have on occasion challenged state policies that they have considered inequitable and repressive. But if they become too insistent on change, threaten violence

or societal upheaval, or support and/or join guerrilla groups, government repression is usually swift and merciless.

GUERRILLA WARFARE

A civil war, which was to last for 36 years, developed in 1960. Guatemala was plagued by violence, attributed both to left-wing insurgencies in rural areas and to armed forces' counterinsurgency operations. Led by youthful middle-class rebels, guerrillas gained strength because of several factors: the radical beliefs of some Roman Catholic priests in rural areas; the ability of the guerrillas to mobilize Indians for the first time; and the "demonstration effect" of events elsewhere in Central America. Some of the success is explained by the guerrilla leaders' ability to converse in Indian languages. Radical clergy increased the recruitment of Indians into the guerrilla forces by suggesting that revolution was an acceptable path to social justice. The excesses of the armed forces in their search for subversives drove other In-

dians into the arms of the guerrillas. In some parts of the highlands, the loss of ancestral lands to speculators or army officers was sufficient to inspire the Indians to join the radical cause.

According to the *Latin American Regional Report* for Mexico and Central America, government massacres of guerrillas and their actual or suspected supporters were frequent and "characterized by clinical savagery." At times, the killing was selective, with community leaders and their families singled out. In other instances, entire villages were destroyed and all the inhabitants slaughtered. "Everything depends on the army's perception of the local level of support for the guerrillas," according to the report.

To counterbalance the violence, once guerrillas were cleared from an area, the government implemented an "Aid Program to Areas in Conflict." Credit was offered to small farmers to boost food production in order to meet local demand, and displaced and jobless people were enrolled in food-for-work units to build roads or other public projects.

FREEDOM

Former president Ramiro de León Carpio warned those who would violate human rights, saying that the law would punish those guilty of abuses, "whether or not they are civilians or members of the armed forces." The moment has come, he continued, "to change things and improve the image of the army and of Guatemala."

By the mid-1980s, most of the guerrillas' military organizations had been destroyed. This was the result not only of successful counterinsurgency tactics by the Guatemalan military but also of serious errors of judgment by guerrilla leaders. Impatient and anxious for change, the guerrillas had overestimated the willingness of the Guatemalan people to rebel. They also had underestimated the power of the military establishment. Surviving guerrilla units maintained an essentially defensive posture for the remainder of the decade. In 1989, however, the guerrillas regrouped. The subsequent intensification of human-rights abuses and the climate of violence were indicative of the military's response.

There was some hope for improvement in 1993, in the wake of the ouster of President Jorge Serrano, whose attempt to emulate the "self-coup" of Peru's Alberto Fujimori failed. Guatemala's next president, Ramiro de León Carpio, was a human-rights activist who was sharply critical of security forces in their war against the guerrillas of the Guatemalan National Revolutionary Unity (URNG). Peace talks between the government and guerrillas had been pursued with the Roman Catholic Church as intermediary for several years, with sparks of promise but no real change. In July 1993, de León announced a new set of proposals to bring to an end the decades of bloodshed that had resulted in 140,000 deaths. Those proposals were the basis for the realization of a peace agreement worked out under the auspices of the United Nations in December 1996.

But the underlying causes of the violence still must be addressed. Colin Woodard, writing in *The Chronicle of Higher Education*, reported that the peace accords promised to "reshape Guatemala as a democratic, multicultural society." But an estimated 70 percent of the Maya Indians still live in poverty, and more than 80 percent are illiterate. Estuardo Zapeta, Guatemala's first Maya newspaper columnist, writes: "This is a multicultural, multilingual society…. As long as we leave the Maya illiterate, we're condemning them to being peasants. And if that happens, their

need to acquire farmland will lead us to another civil war." This, however, is only one facet of a multifaceted set of issues. The very complexity of Guatemalan society, according to political scientist Rachel McCleary, "make[s] it extremely difficult to attain a consensus at the national level on the nature of the problems confronting society." But the new ability of leaders from many sectors of society to work together to shape a meaningful peace is a hopeful sign.

Although the fighting has ended, fear persists. Journalist Woodard wrote in July 1997: "In many neighborhoods [in Guatemala City] private property is protected by razor wire and patrolled by guards with pump-action shotguns." One professor at the University of San Carlos observed, "It is good that the war is over, but I am pessimistic about the peace…. There is intellectual freedom now, but we are very unsure of the permanence of that freedom. It makes us very cautious."

URBAN VIOLENCE

Although most of the violence occurred in rural areas, urban Guatemala did not escape the horrors of the civil war. The following characterization of Guatemalan politics, written by an English traveler in 1839, is still relevant today: "There is but one side to the politics in Guatemala. Both parties have a beautiful way of producing unanimity of opinion, by driving out of the country all who do not agree with them."

HEALTH/WELFARE

While constitutional bars on child labor in the industrial sector are not difficult to enforce, in the informal and agricultural sectors such labor is common. It is estimated that 5,000 Guatemalan children live on the streets and survive as best they can. They are often targeted for elimination by police and death squads.

During the civil war, right-wing killers murdered dozens of leaders of the moderate political left to prevent them from organizing viable political parties that might challenge the ruling elite. These killers also assassinated labor leaders if their unions were considered leftist or antigovernment. Leaders among university students and professors "disappeared" because the national university had a reputation as a center of leftist subversion. Media people were gunned down if they were critical of the government or the right wing. Left-wing extremists also assassinated political leaders associated with "repressive" policies, civil servants (whose only "crime" was government employment), military personnel and

police, foreign diplomats, peasant informers, and businesspeople and industrialists associated with the government.

Common crime rose to epidemic proportions in Guatemala City (as well as in the capitals of other Central American republics). Many of the weapons that once armed the Nicaraguan militias and El Salvador's civil-defense patrols found their way onto the black market, where, according to the Managua newspaper *Pensamiento Propio*, they were purchased by the Guatemalan Army, the guerrillas of the URNG, and criminals.

Timeline: PAST

1523
Guatemala is conquered by Spanish forces from Mexico

1821
Independence

1822–1838
Guatemala is part of the United Provinces of Central America

1838
Guatemala becomes independent as a separate state

1944
Revolution; many reforms

1954
A CIA–sponsored coup deposes the reformist government

1976
An earthquake leaves 22,000 dead

1977
Human-rights abuses lead to the termination of U.S. aid

1990s
Talks between the government and guerrillas end 36 years of violence

PRESENT

2000s
Economic problems multiply

Oscar Berger elected president in November 2003

2005–2006
Rural and urban violence kills thousands

The fear of official or unofficial violence has always inhibited freedom of the press in Guatemala. Early in the 1980s, the Conference on Hemispheric Affairs noted that restrictions on the print media and the indiscriminate brutality of the death squads "turned Guatemala into a virtual no-man's land for journalists." Lingering fears and memories of past violence tend to limit the exercise of press freedoms guaranteed by the Constitution. The U.S. State Depart-

ment's Country Reports notes that "the media continues to exercise a degree of self-censorship on certain topics.... The lack of aggressive investigative reporting dealing with the military and human rights violations apparently is due to self-censorship."

HEALTH CARE AND NUTRITION

In rural Guatemala, half the people have a diet that is well below the minimum daily caloric intake established by the Food and Agricultural Organization. Growth in the staple food crops (corn, rice, beans, wheat) has failed to keep pace with population growth. Marginal malnutrition is endemic.

Health services vary, depending on location, but are uniformly poor in rural Guatemala. The government has begun pilot programs in three departments to provide basic primary health care on a wide scale. But some of these well-intentioned policies have failed because of a lack of sensitivity to cultural differences. Anthropologist Linda Greenberg has observed that the Ministry of Health, as part of its campaign to bring basic health-care services to the hinterlands, introduced midwives who were ignorant of Indian traditions. For Guatemalan Indians, pregnancy is considered an illness that demands specific care, calling for certain foods, herbs, body positions, and interpersonal relations between

expectant mother and Indian midwife. In Maya culture, traditional medicine has spiritual, psychological, physical, social, and symbolic dimensions. Ministry of Health workers too often dismiss traditional practices as superstitious and unscientific. Their insensitivity and ignorance create ineffectual health-care programs.

THE FUTURE

In February 1999, a UN–sponsored Commission for Historical Clarification, in a harsh nine-volume report, blamed the Guatemalan government for acts of genocide against the Maya during the long civil war. The purpose of the report was not to set the stage for criminal prosecutions but to examine the root causes of the civil war and explain how the conflict developed over time. It was hoped that the report signaled the first steps toward national reconciliation and the addressing of human-rights issues, long ignored by those in power.

But the high command of the military and its civilian allies, accused of planning and executing a broad range of atrocities against the Maya, may perceive the report as a threat to their position and their future. In fact, the government has done little to implement the recommendations called for in the 1996 peace accords that ended the civil war. Former President

Efraín Rios Montt, who engineered the assault against the Maya during the civil war, lost his congressional seat—and his immunity to prosecution—in 2004. Although he now faces charges of genocide for his scorched earth policy, Guatemala's current president, Oscar Berger, a wealthy farmer backed by the nation's traditional power brokers, has remained noncommittal on Ríos Montt's fate.

Not surprisingly, the poor and disadvantaged are increasingly frustrated. Illiteracy, infant mortality and malnutrition are among the highest in Central America while life expectancy is among the lowest. Two-thirds of Guatemala's children live in poverty. Violence remains endemic. In 2005 Guatemala's death toll as a direct result of violence in the countryside and urban crime, much of it gang-related, reached 3,000.

Honduras (Republic of Honduras)

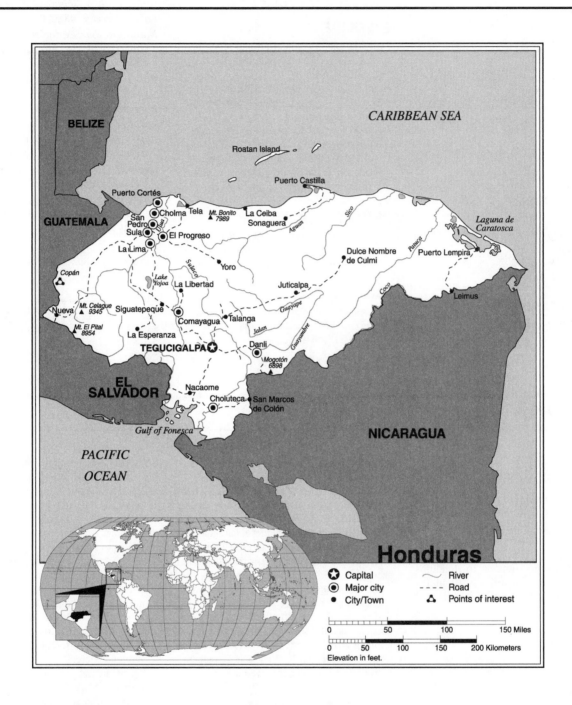

Honduras Statistics

GEOGRAPHY

Area in Square Miles (Kilometers): 43,267 (112,090) (slightly larger than Tennessee)

Capital (Population): Tegucigalpa (995,000)

Environmental Concerns: urbanization; deforestation; land degradation and soil erosion; mining pollution

Geographical Features: mostly mountainous in the interior; narrow coastal plains

Climate: subtropical, but varies with elevation (temperate highlands)

PEOPLE*

Population

Total: 6,823,568

Annual Growth Rate: 2.2%

Rural/Urban Population Ratio: 56/44

Ethnic Makeup: 90% Mestizo (European and Indian mix); 7% Indian; 2% African; 1% European, Arab, and Asian
Major Language: Spanish
Religions: 97% Roman Catholic; a small Protestant minority

Health

Life Expectancy at Birth: 65 years (male); 67 years (female)
Infant Mortality Rate (Ratio): 29.64/1,000
Physicians Available (Ratio): 1/1,586

Education

Adult Literacy Rate: 76.2%
Compulsory (Ages): 7–13; free

COMMUNICATION

Telephones: 322,500 main lines
Daily Newspaper Circulation: 45 per 1,000 people
Televisions: 29 per 1,000
Internet Users: 168,600

TRANSPORTATION

Highways in Miles (Kilometers): 9,563 (15,400)

Railroads in Miles (Kilometers): 369 (595)
Usable Airfields: 119
Motor Vehicles in Use: 185,000

GOVERNMENT

Type: democratic constitutional republic
Independence Date: September 15, 1821 (from Spain)
Head of State/Government: President Manuel Zelaya is both head of state and head of government
Political Parties: Liberal Party; National Party of Honduras; National Innovation and Unity Party–Social Democratic Party; Christian Democratic Party; others
Suffrage: universal and compulsory at 18

MILITARY

Military Expenditures (% of GDP): 1.5%
Current Disputes: boundary disputes with El Salvador and Nicaragua

ECONOMY

Currency ($U.S. Equivalent): 17.35 lempiras = $1 Per Capita Income/GDP: $2,600/$17.46 billion

GDP Growth Rate: 2.5%
Inflation Rate: 7.7%
Unemployment Rate: 27.5%
Labor Force: 2,300,000
Natural Resources: timber; gold; silver; copper; lead; zinc; iron ore; antimony; coal; fish; hydropower
Agriculture: bananas; coffee; citrus fruits; beef; timber; shrimp
Industry: sugar; coffee; textiles and clothing; wood products
Exports: $1.4 billion (primary partners United States, Japan, Germany)
Imports: $3.1 billion (primary partners United States, Guatemala, Netherland Antilles)

SUGGESTED WEBSITE

http://www.cia.gov/cia/
publications/factbook/geos/
ho.html

---

*Note: Estimates for Honduras explicitly take into account the effects of excess mortality due to AIDS.

Honduras Country Report

HONDURAS:
THE CONTAGION OF VIOLENCE

In political terms, Honduras resembles much of the rest of Central America. Frequent changes of government, numerous constitutions, authoritarian leaders, widespread corruption, and an inability to solve basic problems are common to Honduras and to the region. A historian of Honduras once wrote that his country's history could be "written in a tear."

DEVELOPMENT

The Central American Free Trade Zone, of which Honduras is a member, will reduce tariffs by 5 percent to 20 percent on more than 5,000 products traded within the region. In the coming years, more products will be included and tariffs will be progressively lowered.

In terms of social policy, however, Honduras stands somewhat apart from its neighbors. It was slower to modernize, there were no great extremes of wealth between landowners and the rest of the population, and society appeared more paternalistic and less exploitive than was the case in other Central

American states. "Ironically," notes journalist Loren Jenkins, "the land's precarious existence as a poor and unstable backwater has proven almost as much a blessing as a curse." Honduras lacks the sharp social divisions that helped to plunge Nicaragua, El Salvador, and Guatemala into rebellion and civil war. And Honduran governments have seemed somewhat more responsive to demands for change. Still, Honduras is a poor country. Its people have serious problems—widespread illiteracy, malnutrition, and inadequate health care and housing. The government itself reported an unemployment rate of 30 percent in 2005 and that 70 percent of the nation's population lived in poverty.

A WILLINGNESS TO CHANGE

In 1962 and 1975, agrarian-reform laws were passed and put into effect with relative success. The Honduran government, with the aid of peasant organizations and organized labor, was able to resettle 30,000 families on their own land. Today, two-thirds of the people who use the land either own it or have the legal right to its use. Labor legislation and social-security laws were enacted in the early 1960s. Even the Honduran military, usually corrupt, has at

times brought about reform. An alliance of the military and organized labor in the early 1970s produced a series of reforms in response to pressure from the less advantaged sectors of the population; in 1974, the military government developed a five-year plan to integrate the rural poor into the national economy and to increase social services in the area. The state has often shown a paternalistic face rather than a brutal, repressive one. The capacity for reform led one candidate in the 1981 presidential campaign to comment: "We Hondurans are different. There is no room for violence here."

There are now many signs of change. Agrarian reform slowed after 1976, prompting a peasant-association leader to remark: "In order to maintain social peace in the countryside, the peasants' needs will have to be satisfied to avoid revolt." In 1984, the Honduran government initiated a land-titling program and issued about 1,000 titles per month to landless peasants. The government's agrarian-reform program, which is under the control of the National Agrarian Institute, has always been characterized by the carrot and the stick. While some *campesinos* ("peasants") have been granted titles to land, others have been jailed or killed. Former military and security personnel apparently murdered several indigenous minority rights leaders in 2004.

Honduran campesinos, according to *Central America Report*, "have had a long and combative history of struggling for land rights." In 1987, hundreds of peasants were jailed as "terrorists" as a result of land invasions. Occupation of privately owned lands has become increasingly common in Honduras and reflects both population pressure on and land hunger of the peasantry. Land seizures by squatters are sometimes recognized by the National Agrarian Institute. In other cases, the government has promoted the relocation of people to sparsely populated regions of the country. Unfortunately, the chosen relocation sites are in tropical rain forests, which are already endangered throughout the region. The government wishes to transform the forests into rubber and citrus plantations or into farms to raise rice, corn, and other crops.

Peasants who fail to gain access to land usually migrate to urban centers in search of a better life. What they find in cities such as the capital, Tegucigalpa, are inadequate social services, a miserable standard of living, and a municipal government without the resources to help. In 1989, Tegucigalpa was deeply in debt, mortgaged to the limit, months behind in wage payments to city workers, and plagued by garbage piling up in the streets. In 2004 the capital city was plagued by a crime wave conducted by youth gangs, drug trafficking, police implication in high-profile crimes, and the murder of street children by death squads.

FREEDOM

Former president Reina reduced the power of the military. Constitutional reforms in 1994–1995 replaced obligatory military service and the press-gang recruitment system with voluntary service. As a result, the size of the army declined.

The nation's economy as a whole fared badly in the late 1980s. But by 1992, following painful adjustments occasioned by the reforms of the government of President Rafael Callejas, the economy again showed signs of growth. Real gross domestic product reached 3.5 percent, and inflation was held in check. Still, unemployment remained a persistent problem; some agencies calculated that two thirds of the workforce lacked steady employment. A union leader warned: "Unemployment leads to desperation and becomes a time bomb that could explode at any moment."

In addition to internal problems, pressure has been put on Honduras by the Inter-

national Monetary Fund. According to the *Caribbean & Central America Report*, the first phase of a reform program agreed to with the IMF succeeded in stabilizing the economy through devaluation of the lempira (the Honduran currency), public spending cuts, and increased taxes. But economic growth declined, and international agencies urged a reduction in the number of state employees as well as an accelerated campaign to privatize state-owned enterprises. The government admitted that there was much room for reform, but one official complained: "As far as they [the IMF] are concerned, the Honduran state should make gigantic strides, but our position is that this country cannot turn into General Motors overnight."

Opposition to the demands of international agencies was quick to materialize. One newspaper warned that cuts in social programs would result in violence. Trade-union and Catholic Church leaders condemned the social costs of the stabilization program despite the gains recorded in the credit-worthiness of Honduras.

HUMAN AND CIVIL RIGHTS

In theory, despite the continuing violence in the region, basic freedoms in Honduras are still intact. The press is privately owned and free of government censorship. There is, however, a quietly expressed concern about offending the government, and self-censorship is considered prudent. Moreover, it is an accepted practice in Honduras for government ministries and other agencies to have journalists on their payrolls.

Honduran labor unions are free to organize and have a tradition of providing their rank-and-file certain benefits. Unions are allowed to bargain, but labor laws guard against "excessive" activity. A complex procedure of negotiation and arbitration must be followed before a legal strike can be called. If a government proves unyielding, labor will likely pass into the ranks of the opposition.

In 1992, Honduras's three major workers' confederations convinced the private sector to raise the minimum wage by 13.7 percent, the third consecutive year of increases. Nevertheless, the minimum wage, which varies by occupation and location, is not adequate to provide a decent standard of living, especially in view of inflation. One labor leader pointed out that the minimum wage will "not even buy tortillas." To compound workers' problems, the labor minister admitted that about 30 percent of the enterprises under the supervision of his office paid wages *below* the minimum. To survive, families must pool the resources of all their working members. Predictably,

health and safety laws are usually ignored. As is the case in the rural sector, the government has listened to the complaints of workers—but union leaders have also on occasion been jailed.

The government is also confronted with the problem of an increasing flow of rural poor into the cities. Employment opportunities in rural areas have declined as landowners have converted cropland into pasture for beef cattle. Because livestock raising requires less labor than growing crops, the surplus rural workers seek to better their opportunities in the cities. But the new migrants have discovered that Honduras's commercial and industrial sectors are deep in recession and cannot provide adequate jobs.

HEALTH/WELFARE

Honduras remains one of the region's poorest countries. Serious shortcomings are evident in education and health care, and economic growth is essentially erased by population growth. Approximately half of the population live in poverty.

Fortunately, many of the 300,000 refugees from Nicaragua and El Salvador have returned home. With the election of President Violeta Chamorro in Nicaragua, most of the 20,000 rebel Contras laid down their arms and went home, thus eliminating—from the perspective of the Honduran government—a source of much violence in its border regions.

To the credit of the Honduran government, which is under strong pressure from conservative politicians and businesspeople as well as elements within the armed forces for tough policies against dissent, allegations vis-à-vis human-rights abuses are taken seriously. (In one celebrated case, the Inter-American Court of Human Rights, established in 1979, found the government culpable in at least one person's "disappearance" and ordered the payment of an indemnification to the man's family. While not accepting any premise of guilt, the government agreed to pay. More important, according to the COHA *Washington Report*, the decision sharply criticized "prolonged isolation" and "incommunicado detention" of prisoners and equated such abuses with "cruel and inhuman punishment.") Former president Carlos Roberto Reina was a strong advocate of human rights as part of his "moral revolution." In 1995, he took three steps in this direction: a special prosecutor was created to investigate human-rights violations, human-rights inquiries were taken out of the hands of the military and given to a new civilian Department of Criminal Investigation, and promises were made to follow up on cases of disappearances during previous administrations. While Honduras may no longer be characterized as "the peaceable kingdom," the government has not lost touch with its people and still acts out a traditional role of patron.

From the mid-1980s to the mid-1990s, the most serious threat to civilian government came from the military. The United States' Central American policy boosted the prestige, status, and power of the Honduran military, which grew confident in its ability to forge the nation's destiny. With the end of the Contra–Sandinista armed struggle in Nicaragua, there was a dramatic decline in military assistance from the United States. This allowed President Reina to assert civilian control over the military establishment.

ACHIEVEMENTS

The small size of Honduras, in terms of territory and population, has produced a distinctive literary style that is a combination of folklore and legend.

The sharp drop in U.S. economic assistance to Honduras—it fell from $229 million in 1985 to about $50 million in 1997—has revealed deep problems with the character of that aid. *Wall Street Journal* reporter Carla Anne Robbins writes that "Honduras's experience suggests that massive, politically motivated cash transfers ... can buy social peace, at least temporarily, but can't guarantee lasting economic growth or social development." Rather, such unconditional aid "may have slowed development by making it possible for the government to put off economic reform." On the other hand, some of the aid that found its way to programs that were not politically motivated has also been lost. One program provided access to potable water and was credited

with cutting the infant mortality rate by half. Other programs funded vaccinations and primary-education projects. In the words of newspaperman and development expert Juan Ramón Martínez: "Just when you [the United States] started getting it right, you walked away."

President Reina's "moral revolution" also moved to confront the problem of endemic official corruption. In June 1995, Reina alluded to the enormity of the task when he said that if the government went after all of the guilty, "there would not be enough room for them in the prisons." In 1998, just as the Honduran economy was beginning to recover from economic setbacks occasioned by turmoil in the influential Asian financial markets, Hurricane Mitch wreaked havoc on the nation's infrastructure. Roads, bridges, schools, clinics, and homes were destroyed, and thousands of lives were lost. Freshwater wells had to be reconstructed. Banana plantations were severely damaged. Recovery from this natural disaster will be prolonged and costly.

Although the press in Honduras is legally "free," *Honduras This Week* notes that many journalists have close ties to the business community and allow these contacts "rather than impartial journalism" to determine the substance of their articles. Moreover, there is a disturbing tendency for the media to praise the government in power as a "means of gaining favor with that administration."

President Ricardo Maduro made a determined effort to crack down on a rampant crime wave. Undoubtedly his focus was sharpened by the loss of his son to criminal violence in 1998. Presidential elections in 2005 were dominated by the growing incidence of violent crime, much of it attributed to youth gangs. Both candidates stressed law and order issues. The candidate of the ruling National Party urged a hard line policy against gangs. He endorsed the government's "Mano Duro"

Timeline: PAST

1524
Honduras is settled by Spaniards from Guatemala

1821
Independence from Spain

1822–1838
Honduras is part of the United Provinces of Central America

1838
Honduras becomes independent as a separate country

1969
Brief border war with El Salvador

1980s
Tensions with Nicaragua grow

1990s
Hurricane Mitch causes enormous death and destruction

PRESENT

2000s
AIDS is an increasing problem

Manuel Zelaya elected president in 2005

Increasing gang-related violence

(Tough Hand) Law, by which membership in a gang was made a felony, and sought reinstatement of the death penalty, which had been abolished in 1937. The victor in the elections, the Liberal Party's Manuel Zelaya, is opposed the death penalty as well as the tough anti-gang legislation. Crime, he argues, in part springs from basic social problems. Poverty and unemployment drive youth into gangs, he asserted. The close results of the election indicate that Hondurans are badly divided over issues of crime and poverty.

Nicaragua (Republic of Nicaragua)

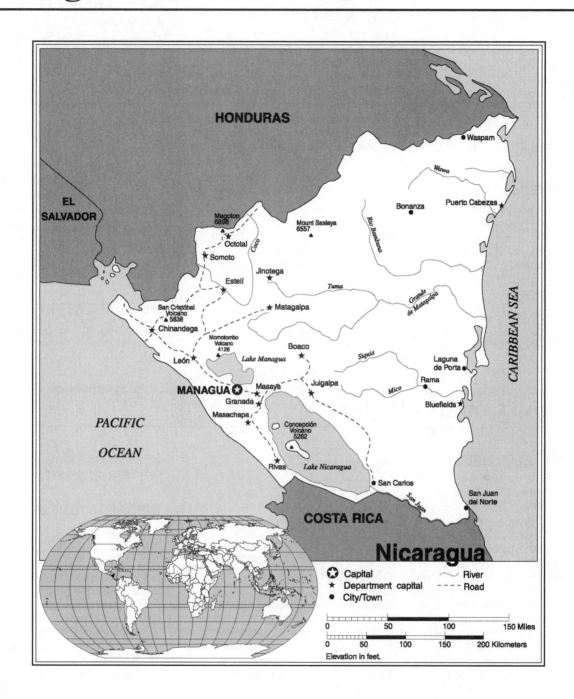

Nicaragua Statistics

GEOGRAPHY

Area in Square Miles (Kilometers): 49,985 (129,494) (about the size of New York)

Capital (Population): Managua (1,124,000)

Environmental Concerns: deforestation; soil erosion; water pollution

Geographical Features: extensive Atlantic coastal plains rising to central interior mountains; narrow Pacific coastal plain interrupted by volcanoes

Climate: tropical, but varies with elevation (temperate highlands)

PEOPLE

Population

Total: 5,359,759

Annual Growth Rate: 1.97%

Rural/Urban Population Ratio: 37/63

Ethnic Makeup: 69% Mestizo; 17% white;
  9% black; 5% Amerindian
Major Language: Spanish
Religions: 95% Roman Catholic; 5%
  Protestant

Health

Life Expectancy at Birth: 67 years (male);
  72 years (female)
Infant Mortality Rate (Ratio): 34.7/1,000
Physicians Available (Ratio): 1/1,566

Education

Adult Literacy Rate: 67.5%
Compulsory (Ages): 7–13; free

COMMUNICATION

Telephones: 171,600 main lines
Daily Newspaper Circulation: 31 per
  1,000 people
Televisions: 48 per 1,000
Internet Users: 90,000

TRANSPORTATION

Highways in Miles (Kilometers): 9,829
  (16,382)
Railroads in Miles (Kilometers): none

Usable Airfields: 182
Motor Vehicles in Use: 145,000

GOVERNMENT

Type: republic
Independence Date: September 15, 1821
  (from Spain)
Head of State/Government: President
  Enrique Bolaños Geyer is both head of
  state and head of government
Political Parties: Independent Liberal
  Party; Liberal Alliance; Neoliberal Party;
  Conservative Party; National Action
  Party; Sandinista National Liberation
  Front; many others
Suffrage: universal at 16

MILITARY

Military Expenditures (% of GDP): 1.2%
Current Disputes: territorial or boundary
  disputes with Colombia, Honduras, and
  El Salvador

ECONOMY

Currency ($U.S. Equivalent): 14.06
  córdobas oros = $1

Per Capita Income/GDP: $2,200/$11.49
  billion
GDP Growth Rate: 1.4%
Inflation Rate: 5.3%
Unemployment Rate: 22% (official rate);
  substantial underemployment
Labor Force: 1,700,000
Natural Resources: gold; silver; copper;
  tungsten; lead; zinc; timber; fish
Agriculture: coffee; bananas; sugarcane;
  cotton; rice; corn; tobacco; soya; beans;
  livestock
Industry: food processing; chemicals;
  machinery; metals products; textiles and
  clothing; petroleum; beverages;
  footwear; wood
Exports: $632 million (primary partners
  United States, Germany, El Salvador)
Imports: $1.6 billion (primary partners
  United States, Costa Rica, Guatemala)

SUGGESTED WEBSITE

http://www.cia.gov/cia/
  publications/factbook/index.html

Nicaragua Country Report

NICARAGUA: A NATION IN RECOVERY

Nicaraguan society, culture, and history have been molded to a great extent by the country's geography. A land of volcanoes and earthquakes, the frequency of natural disasters in Nicaragua has profoundly influenced its peoples' perceptions of life, death, and fate. What historian Ralph Woodward has written about Central America is particularly apt for Nicaraguans: Fatalism may be said to be a "part of their national mentality, tempering their attitudes toward the future. Death and tragedy always seem close in Central America. The primitive states of communication, transportation, and production, and the insecurity of human life, have been the major determinants in the region's history…."

Nicaragua is a divided land, with distinct geographic, cultural, racial, ethnic, and religious zones. The west-coast region, which contains about 90 percent of the total population, is overwhelmingly white or Mestizo (mixed blood), Catholic, and Hispanic. The east coast is a sharp contrast, with its scattered population and multiplicity of Indian, Creole (in Nicaragua, native-born blacks), and Hispanic ethnic groups.

The east coast's geography, economy, and isolation from Managua, the nation's

DEVELOPMENT

The possibility of the construction of a "dry canal" across Nicaragua has raised the hopes of thousands for a better future. A group of Asian investors is investigating the construction of a 234-mile-long rail link between the oceans to carry container cargo.

capital city, have created a distinct identity among its people. Many east-coast citizens think of themselves as *costeños* ("coast dwellers") rather than Nicaraguans. Religion reinforces this common identity. About 70 percent of the east-coast population, regardless of ethnic group, are members of the Protestant Moravian Church. After a century and a half of missionary work, the Moravian Church has become "native," with locally recruited clergy. Among the Miskito Indians, Moravian pastors commonly replace tribal elders as community leaders. The Creoles speak English and originally arrived either as shipwrecked or escaped slaves or as slave labor introduced by the British to work in the lumber camps and plantations in the seventeenth century. Many Creoles and Miskitos feel a greater sense of allegiance to the

British than to Nicaraguans from the west coast, who are regarded as foreigners.

SANDINISTA POLICIES

Before the successful 1979 Revolution that drove the dictator Anastasio Somoza from power, Nicaraguan governments generally ignored the east coast. Revolutionary Sandinistas—who took their name from a guerrilla, Augusto César Sandino, who fought against occupying U.S. forces in the late 1920s and early 1930s—adopted a new policy toward the neglected region. The Sandinistas were concerned with the east coast's history of rebelliousness and separatism, and they were attracted by the economic potential of the region (palm oil and rubber). Accordingly, they hastily devised a bold campaign to unify the region with the rest of the nation. Roads, communications, health clinics, economic development, and a literacy campaign for local inhabitants were planned. The Sandinistas, in defiance of local customs, also tried to organize the local population into mass formations—that is, organizations for youth, peasants, women, wage earners, and the like. It was believed in Managua that such groups would unite the people behind

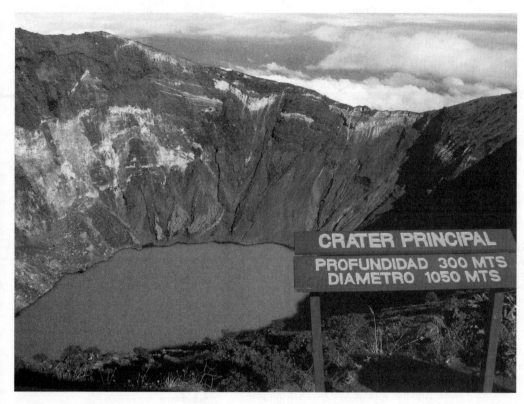

CRATER PRINCIPAL
PROFUNDIDAD 300 MTS
DIAMETRO 1050 MTS

(Courtesy of Chris and Erin Ratay/ Ratay02)

Known to the Spaniards as the "Gates of Hell," the craters of Volcán Masaya National Park are the most easily accessible active volcanoes in Nicaragua. Santiago crater is still active and is often seen steaming and smoking.

the government and the Revolution and facilitate the economic, political, and social unification of the region.

In general, the attempt failed, and regional tensions within Nicaragua persist to this day. Historically, costeños were unimpressed with the exploits of the guerrilla Sandino, who raided U.S. companies along the east coast in the 1930s. When the companies left or cut back on operations, workers who lost their jobs blamed Sandino rather than the worldwide economic crisis of the 1930s. Consequently, there was a reluctance to accept Sandino as the national hero of the new Nicaragua. Race and class differences increased due to an influx of Sandinistas from the west. Many of the new arrivals exhibited old attitudes and looked down on the east-coast peoples as "uncivilized" or "second class."

The Miskito Question

In 1982, the government forced 10,000 Indians from their ancestral homes along the Río Coco because of concern with border security. As a result, many Indians joined the Contras, U.S.–supported guerrillas who fought against the Sandinista regime.

In an attempt to win back the Miskito and associated Indian groups, the government decided on a plan of regional autonomy. The significance of the Sandinista policy was that the government finally appreciated how crucial regional differences are in Nicaragua. Cultural and ethnic differences must be respected if Managua ex-

pects to rule its peoples effectively. The lesson learned by the Sandinistas was taken to heart by the subsequent Chamorro government, which was the first in history to appoint a Nicaraguan of Indian background to a ministerial-level position. A limited self-government granted to the east-coast region by the Sandinistas in 1987 has been maintained; local leaders were elected to office in 1990.

A Mixed Record

The record of the Sandinista government was mixed. When the rebels seized power in 1979, they were confronted by an economy in shambles. Nineteen years of civil war had taken an estimated 50,000 lives and destroyed half a billion dollars' worth of factories, businesses, medical facilities, and dwellings. Living standards had tumbled to 1962 levels, and unemployment had reached an estimated 25 percent.

Despite such economic difficulties, the government made great strides in the areas of health and nutrition. A central goal of official policy was to provide equal access to health services. The plan had more success in urban areas than in rural ones. The government emphasized preventive, rather than curative, medicine. Preventive medicine included the provision of clean water, sanitation, immunization, nutrition, and maternal and child care. People were also taught basic preventive medical techniques. National campaigns to wipe out malaria, measles, and polio had reasonable

success. But because of restricted budgets, the health system was overloaded, and there was a shortage of medical supplies. In the area of nutrition, basic foodstuffs such as grains, oil, eggs, and milk were paid for in part by the government in an effort to improve the general nutritional level of Nicaraguans.

By 1987, the Sandinista government was experiencing severe economic problems that badly affected all social programs. In 1989, the economy, for all intents and purposes, collapsed. Hyperinflation ran well over 100 percent a month; and in June 1989, following a series of mini-devaluations, the nation's currency was devalued by an incredible 100 percent. Commerce was virtually paralyzed.

The revolutionary Sandinista government, in an attempt to explain the economic debacle, with some justice argued that the Nicaragua that it had inherited in 1979 had been savaged and looted by former dictator Somoza. The long-term costs of economic reconstruction; the restructuring of the economy to redistribute wealth; the trade embargo erected by the United States and North American diplomatic pressure, designed to discourage lending or aid from international institutions such as the International Monetary Fund; and the high cost of fighting a war against the U.S.–supported Contra rebels formed the backdrop to the crisis. Opposition leaders added to this list various Sandinista economic policies that discouraged private business.

The impact of the economic crisis on average Nicaraguans was devastating. Overnight, prices of basic consumer goods such as meat, rice, beans, milk, sugar, and cooking oil were increased 40 to 80 percent. Gasoline prices doubled. School-teachers engaged in work stoppages in an effort to increase their monthly wages of about $15, equal to the pay of a domestic servant. (To put the teachers' plight into perspective, note that the cost of a liter of milk absorbed fully 36 percent of a day's pay.)

FREEDOM

Diverse points of view have been freely and openly discussed in the media. Radio, the most important medium for news distribution in Nicaragua, has conveyed a broad range of opinion.

As a hedge against inflation, other Nicaraguans purchased U.S. dollars on the black market. *Regionews*, published in Managua, noted that conversion of córdobas into dollars was "seen as a better proposition than depositing them in savings accounts."

Economic travail inevitably produces dissatisfaction; opinion polls taken in July 1989 signaled political trouble for the Sandinistas. The surveys reflected an electorate with mixed feelings. While nearly 30 percent favored the Sandinistas, 57 percent indicated that they would not vote for President Daniel Ortega.

The results of the election of 1990 were not surprising, for the Sandinistas had lost control of the economy. They failed to survive a strong challenge from the opposition, led by the popular Violeta Chamorro.

Sandinista land reform, for the most part, consisted of the government's confiscation of the huge estates of the ousted Somoza family. These lands amounted to more than 2 million acres, including about 40 percent of the nation's best farmland. Some peasants were given land, but the government preferred to create cooperatives. This policy prompted the criticism that the state had simply become an old-style landowner. The Sandinistas replied that "the state is not the same state as before; it is a state of producers; we organized production and placed it at the disposal of the people." In 1990, there were several reports of violence between Sandinista security forces and peasants and former Contras who petitioned for private ownership of state land.

The Role of the Church

The Revolution created a sharp division within the Roman Catholic Church in Nicaragua. Radical priests, who believed that Christianity and Marxism share similar goals and that the Church should play a leading role in social change and revolution, were at odds with traditional priests fearful of "godless communism." Since 1979, many radical Catholics had become involved in social and political projects; several held high posts in the Sandinista government.

One priest of the theology of liberation was interviewed by *Regionews*. The interviewer stated that an "atheist could say, 'These Catholics found a just revolution opposed by the Church hierarchy. They can't renounce their religion and are searching for a more convenient theology. But it's their sense of natural justice that motivates them.'" The priest replied: "I think that's evident and that Jesus was also an 'atheist,' an atheist of the religion as practiced in his time. He didn't believe in the God of the priests in the temples who were allied with Caesar. Jesus told of a new life. And the 'atheist' that exists in our people doesn't believe in the God that the hierarchy often offers us. He believes in life, in man, in development. God manifests Himself there. A person who believes in life and justice in favor of the poor is not an atheist." The movement, he noted, would continue "with or without approval from the hierarchy."

The Drift to the Left

As has historically been the case in revolutions, after a brief period of unity and excitement, the victors begin to disagree over policies and power. For a while in Nicaragua, there was a perceptible drift to the left, and the Revolution lost its image of moderation. While radicalization was a dynamic inherent in the Revolution, it was also pushed in a leftward direction by a hostile U.S. foreign policy that attempted to bring down the Sandinista regime through its support of the Contras. In 1987, however, following the peace initiatives of Latin American governments, the Sandinista government made significant efforts to project a more moderate image. *La Prensa*, the main opposition newspaper, which the Sandinistas had shut down in 1986, was again allowed to publish. Radio Católica, another source of opposition to the government, was given permission to broadcast after its closure the year before. And anti-government demonstrations were permitted in the streets of Managua.

Significantly, President Ortega proposed reforms in the country's election laws in April 1989, to take effect before the national elections in 1990. The new Nicaraguan legislation was based on Costa Rican and Venezuelan models, and in some instances was even more forward-looking.

An important result of the laws was the enhancement of political pluralism, which allowed for the National Opposition Union (UNO) victory in 1990. Rules for organizing political parties, once stringent, were loosened; opposition parties were granted access to the media; foreign funding of political parties was allowed; the system of proportional representation permitted minority parties to maintain a presence; and the opposition was allowed to monitor the elections closely.

HEALTH/WELFARE

Nicaragua's deep debt and the austerity demands of the IMF have had a strongly negative effect on citizens' health. As people have been driven from the health service by sharp cuts in government spending, the incidence of malnutrition in children has risen. Reported deaths from diarrhea and respiratory problems are also on the increase.

The Sandinistas realized that to survive, they had to make compromises. In need of breathing space, the government embraced the Central American Peace Plan designed by Costa Rican president Óscar Arias and designed moderate policies to isolate the United States.

On the battlefield, the cease-fire unilaterally declared by the Sandinistas was eventually embraced by the Contras as well, and both sides moved toward a political solution of their differences. Armed conflict formally ended on June 27, 1990, although sporadic violence continued in rural areas.

A PEACEFUL TRANSITION

It was the critical state of the Nicaraguan economy that in large measure brought the Sandinistas down in the elections of 1990. Even though the government of Violeta Chamorro made great progress in the demilitarization of the country and national reconciliation, the economy remained a time bomb.

ACHIEVEMENTS

The Nicaraguan poet Rubén Darío was the most influential representative of the Modernist Movement, which swept Latin America in the late nineteenth century. Darío was strongly critical of injustice and oppression.

The continuing economic crisis and disagreements over policy directions destroyed the original base of Chamorro's political support. Battles between the legislative and executive branches of government virtually paralyzed the country. At the end of 1992, President Chamorro closed the Assembly building and called for new elections. But by July 1995, an accord had been reached between the two contending branches of government. Congress passed a "framework law" that created the language necessary to implement changes in the Sandinista Constitution of 1987. The Legislative Assembly, together with the executive branch, are pledged to the passage of laws on matters such as property rights, agrarian reform, consumer protection, and taxation. The July agreement also provided for the election of the five-member Consejo Supremo Electoral (Supreme Electoral Council), which oversaw the presidential elections in November 1996.

The election marked something of a watershed in Nicaraguan political history. Outgoing president Chamorro told reporters at the inauguration of Arnoldo Alemán Lâcayo: "For the first time in more than 100 years ... one civilian, democratically elected president will hand over power to another." But the election did not mask the fact that Nicaragua was still deeply polarized and that the Sandinistas only grudgingly accepted their defeat.

President Alemán sought a dialogue with the Sandinistas, and both sides agreed to participate in discussions to study poverty, property disputes occasioned by the Sandinista policy of confiscation, and the need to attract foreign investment.

The Alemán administration confronted a host of difficult problems. In the Western Hemisphere, only Haiti is poorer. Perhaps 80 percent of the population are unemployed or underemployed, and an equal percentage live below the poverty line. Just as the economy began to show some signs of recovery from years of war, Hurricane Mitch devastated the country in 1998 and profoundly set back development efforts, as all available resources had to be husbanded to reconstruct much of Nicaragua's infrastructure.

Economic malaise compounded by allegations of corruption and illegal enrichment undermined the credibility of the Alemán government. Dissatisfaction among voters was registered at the polls, resulting in Sandinista victories in Managua and nine of 17 provincial capitals in municipal elections in November 2000. A contributing factor was the emergence of the Conservative Party, which split the anti-Sandinista vote. Interestingly, the Sandinista victor in Managua, Herty Lewites, has styled himself as a "revolutionary businessman and defender of social justice"—that is, a popular pragmatist.

Organized labor has shown a similar pragmatic dimension in Nicaragua. Labor leaders have quietly supported both globalization and the policies of the World Trade Organization because of the jobs that would be created. Another effect of globalization, not only in Nicaragua but also throughout the region, has been the further erosion of the *siesta* (nap) tradition. In the words of a Nicaraguan-government official, the emerging world economy demands that "we stay open all day."

The administration of President Enrique Bolaño Geyer, elected in 2002, has seen some improvement. There was some economic growth in 2003, private investment has increased, and exports have risen. For the foreseeable future, however, Nicaragua will remain poor.

President Bolaños has become politically isolated, however. His campaign against government corruption, which ensnared former President Alemán, led to his abandonment by his own conservative Constitutionalist Liberal Party. Remarkably, the conservatives have allied with Daniel Ortega's Sandinista Party with the object, in the words of the *New York Times,*

"to regain power without holding an election that neither man could win." The state electoral commission, under Ortega's direction, "lowered the threshold for averting a runoff election to 35 percent of the vote from 45 percent." Presidential elections are scheduled for November 2006, when the Nicaraguan people will try to make choices in the midst of political fratricide.

Timeline: PAST

1522
Nicaragua is explored by Gil González

1821
Independence from Spain

1823
Nicaragua joins the United Provinces of Central America

1838
Nicaragua becomes independent as a separate state

1855
William Walker and filibusters (U.S. insurgents) invade Nicaragua

1928–1934
Augusto César Sandino leads guerrillas against occupying U.S. forces

1934–1979
Domination of Nicaragua by the Somoza family

1979
Sandinista guerrillas oust the Somoza family

1990s
A cease-fire allows an opening for political dialogue; Hurricane Mitch devastates the country

PRESENT

2000s
Sandinistas win municipal elections in November 2000

Enrique Bolaño Geyer elected president in 2002

Presidential elections scheduled for 2006

Panama (Republic of Panama)

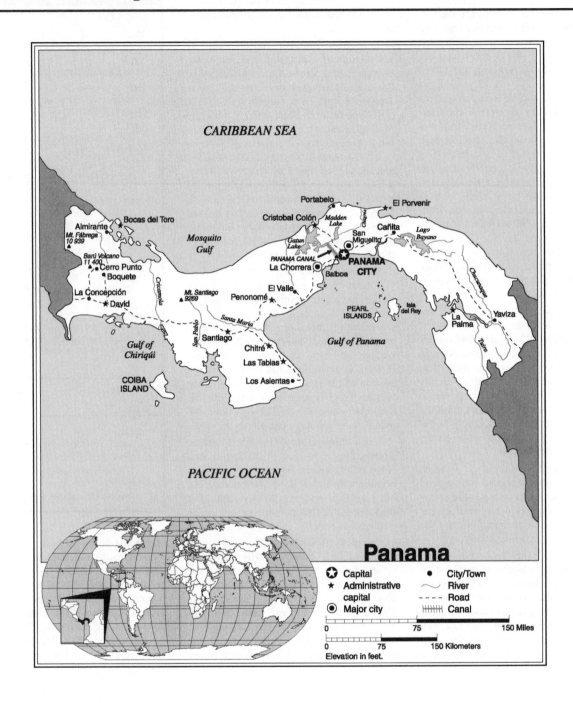

CARIBBEAN SEA

Portabelo
El Porvenir
Cristobal Colón
Madden Lake
Bocas del Toro
Almirante
Mt. Fábrega 10 939
Mosquito Gulf
San Miguelito
Cañita
Lago Bayano
Gatun Lake
PANAMA CANAL
Barú Volcano 11 400
Cerro Punto
Boquete
La Chorrera
PANAMA CITY
Balboa
La Concepción
Cricamola
Mt. Santiago 9269
El Valle
Chucunaque
David
San Pablo
Penonomé
PEARL ISLANDS
Isla del Rey
La Palma
Yaviza
Santa María
Gulf of Chiriquí
Santiago
Chitré
Gulf of Panama
Tuira
Las Tablas
Los Asientas
COIBA ISLAND

PACIFIC OCEAN

Panama

- ⍟ Capital
- ★ Administrative capital
- ◉ Major city
- ● City/Town
- ∼ River
- - - - Road
- ┼┼┼┼ Canal

0   75   150 Miles
0   75   150 Kilometers
Elevation in feet.

Panama Statistics

GEOGRAPHY

Area in Square Miles (Kilometers): 30,185 (78,200) (about the size of South Carolina)

Capital (Population): Panama City (465,000)

Environmental Concerns: water pollution; deforestation; land degradation; soil erosion

Geographical Features: interior mostly steep, rugged mountains and dissected upland plains; coastal areas largely plains and rolling hills

Climate: tropical marine

PEOPLE

Population

Total: 3,000,463
Annual Growth Rate: 1.34%

48

Rural/Urban Population Ratio: 44/56

Major Languages: Spanish; English

Ethnic Makeup: 70% Mestizo; 14% West Indian; 10% white; 6% Indian and others

Religions: 85% Roman Catholic; 15% Protestant and others

Health

Life Expectancy at Birth: 69 years (male); 74 years (female)

Infant Mortality Rate (Ratio): 20.8/1,000

Physicians Available (Ratio): 1/856

Education

Adult Literacy Rate: 92.6%

Compulsory (Ages): for 6 years between 6–15; free

COMMUNICATION

Telephones: 366,000 main lines

Daily Newspaper Circulation: 62 per 1,000 people

Televisions: 13 per 1,000

Internet Users 120,000

TRANSPORTATION

Highways in Miles (Kilometers): 6,893 (11,100)

Railroads in Miles (Kilometers): 208 (355)

Usable Airfields: 105

Motor Vehicles in Use: 227,000

GOVERNMENT

Type: constitutional democracy

Independence Date: November 3, 1903 (from Colombia)

Head of State/Government: President Mireya Elisa Moscoso Rodriguez is both head of state and head of government

Political Parties: Nationalist Republican Liberal Movement; Solidarity Party; Authentic Liberal Party; Arnulfista Party; Christian Democratic Party; Papa Egoro Movement; Democratic Revolutionary Party; Independent Democratic Union; National Liberal Party; Labor Party; others

Suffrage: universal and compulsory at 18

MILITARY

Military Expenditures (% of GDP): 1.2%

Current Disputes: none

ECONOMY

Currency ($U.S. Equivalent): 1.00 balboa = $1

Per Capita Income/GDP: $6,300/$18.62 billion

GDP Growth Rate: 3.24%

Inflation Rate: 1.3%

Unemployment Rate: 14.5%

Labor Force: 1,044,000

Natural Resources: copper; mahogany forests; shrimp; hydropower

Agriculture: bananas; rice; corn; coffee; sugarcane; vegetables; livestock; fishing

Industry: construction; petroleum; brewing; sugar; canal traffic/tourism

Exports: $5.2 billion (primary partners United States, Sweden, Costa Rica)

Imports: $6.6 billion (primary partners United States, Central America and Caribbean)

SUGGESTED WEBSITE

http://www.cia.gov/cia/ publications/factbook/index.html

Panama Country Report

PANAMA: A NATION AND A CANAL

The Panama Canal, opened to shipping in 1914, has had a sharp impact on Panamanian political life, foreign policy, economy, and society. Panama is a country of minorities and includes blacks, Mestizos (mixed Indian and white), Indians, and Chinese. Many of the blacks and Chinese are the children or grandchildren of the thousands of workers who were brought to Panama to build the canal. Unable to return home, they remained behind, an impoverished people, ignored for decades by a succession of Panamanian governments.

DEVELOPMENT

Because many new ships can no longer transit the Panama Canal it has become imperative to add new, larger locks, and to widen the existing channel. This will require billions of dollars in new investment.

The government has usually been dominated by whites, although all of the country's minorities are politically active. In areas where Indians comprise a majority of the population, they play significant roles in provincial political life. Some, such as the San Blas

islanders—famous for the art form known as Mola, which consists of different colored fabrics that are cut away to make designs—live in self-governing districts. Although Indians are not restricted to tribal areas, most remain by choice, reflecting a long tradition of resistance to assimilation and defense of their cultural integrity.

Panama's economy has both profited and suffered from the presence of the canal. Because governments traditionally placed too much reliance on the direct and indirect revenues generated by the canal tolls, they tended to ignore other types of national development. Much of Panama's economic success in the 1980s, however, was the result of a strong service sector associated with the presence of a large number of banks, the Panama Canal, and the Colón Free Zone. Agriculture and industry, on the other hand, usually experienced slow growth rates.

Because of U.S. control of the canal and the Canal Zone, this path between the seas continuously stoked the fires of Panamanian nationalism. The high standard of living and the privileges enjoyed by U.S. citizens residing in the Canal Zone contrasted sharply with the poverty of Panamanians. President Omar Torrijos became

a national hero in 1977 when he signed the Panama Canal Treaties with U.S. president Jimmy Carter. The treaties provided for full Panamanian control over the canal and its revenues by 1999.

FREEDOM

In 2005 the Torrijos government repealed restrictive media laws that punished journalists and radio and television personalities for alleged "insults" against state officials. Panama's media is now free to present news and commentary.

Panamanian officials spoke optimistically of their plans for the bases they would soon inherit, citing universities, modern container ports, luxury resorts, and retirement communities. But there was much concern over the loss of an estimated $500 million that tens of thousands of American troops, civilians, and their dependents had long pumped into the Panamanian economy. Moreover, while all agreed that the canal itself would be well run, because Panamanians had been phased into its operation, there was pessimism about the lack of planning for ancillary facilities.

(Courtesy Dr. Paul Goodwin/panama2)

The Panama Canal has been of continuing importance to the country since it opened in 1914. Full control of the canal was turned over to Panama in 1999, marking the end of U.S. involvement and representing a source of Panamanian nationalism.

In 1995, more than 300 poor, landless people a day were moving into the Zone and were clearing forest for crops. The rain forest in the Canal Basin supplies not only the water essential to the canal but also the drinking water for about 40 percent of Panama's population. Loss of the rain forest could prove catastrophic. One official noted: "If we lose the Canal Basin we do not lose only our water supply, it will also be the end of the Canal itself."

A RETURN TO CIVILIAN GOVERNMENT

President Torrijos, who died in a suspicious plane crash in 1981, left behind a legacy that included much more than the treaties. He elevated the National Guard to a position of supreme power in the state and ruled through a National Assembly of community representatives.

The 1984 elections appeared to bring to fruition the process of political liberalization initiated in 1978. But even though civilian rule was officially restored, the armed forces remained the real power behind the throne. Indeed, spectacular revelations in 1987 strongly suggested that Defense Forces chief general Manuel Antonio Noriega had rigged the 1984 elections. He was also accused of drug trafficking, gun running, and money laundering.

In February 1988, Noriega was indicted by two U.S. grand juries and charged with using his position to turn Panama into a center for the money-laundering activities of the Medellín, Colombia, drug cartel and providing protection for cartel members living temporarily in Panama.

Attempts by Panamanian president Eric Arturo Delvalle to oust the military strongman failed, and Delvalle himself was forced into hiding. Concerted efforts by the United States to remove Noriega from power—including an economic boycott, plans to kidnap the general and have the CIA engineer a coup, and saber-rattling by the dispatch of thousands of U.S. troops to the Canal Zone—proved fruitless.

The fraud and violence that accompanied an election called by Noriega in 1989 to legitimize his government and the failure of a coup attempt in October ultimately resulted in the invasion of Panama by U.S. troops in December. Noriega was arrested, brought to the United States for trial, and eventually was convicted on drug-trafficking charges.

HEALTH/WELFARE

 The Care Group, which is affiliated with Harvard Medical School, Beth Israel Hospital, and Panama's excellent Hospital Nacionál, reached agreement to create the region's first teaching hospital in the area of emergency care. Physicians from all of Latin America would be welcomed to the facility.

The U.S. economic sanctions succeeded in harming the wrong people. Noriega and his cronies were shielded from the economic crisis by their profits from money laundering. But many other Panamanians were devastated by the U.S. policy.

Nearly a decade after the invasion by U.S. troops to restore democracy and halt drug trafficking, the situation in Panama remains problematic. The country is characterized by extremes of wealth and poverty, and corruption is pervasive. The economy is still closely tied to drug-money laundering, which has reached levels higher than during the Noriega years.

Elections in 1994 reflected the depth of popular dissatisfaction. Three quarters of the voters supported political movements that had risen in opposition to the policies and politics imposed on Panama by the U.S. invasion. The new president, Ernesto Pérez Balladares, a 48-year-old economist and businessman and a former supporter of Noriega, promised "to close the Noriega chapter" in Panama's history. During his term, he pushed ahead with privatization, the development of the Panama Canal Zone, a restructuring of the foreign debt, and initiatives designed to enhance tourism.

Unfortunately, Pérez seemed to have inherited some of the personalist tendencies of his predecessors. In 1998, he pushed for a constitutional change that would have allowed him to run for reelection in 1999. When put to a referendum in August 1998, Panamanians resoundingly defeated the ambitions of the president.

The 1999 elections, without the participation of Pérez, produced a close campaign between Martín Torrijos, the son of Omar, and Mireya Moscoso, the widow of the president who had been ousted by Omar Torrijos. Moscoso emerged as a winner, with 44 percent of the vote, and became Panama's first woman president.

Moscoso opposed many of Pérez's free-market policies and was especially critical of any further plans to privatize state-owned industries. Moscoso identified her administration with the inauguration of a "new era" for Panama's poor. Her social policies stood in direct contrast to the more economically pragmatic approach of her predecessors. Continued domination of the Legislature by the opposition render social reform difficult, but the president felt that she had to intercede on behalf of the poor, who constitute one-third of the population. Diversification of the economy remains a need, as Panama is still overly dependent on canal revenues and traditional agricultural exports. As supplement to the income produced by the canal, the Panama Canal Railway has been refurbished so that it will be able to transport container cargo in less time than it takes for a ship to transit the canal.

SOCIAL POLICIES

As is the case in most Latin American nations, Panama's Constitution authorizes the state to direct, regulate, replace, or create economic activities designed to increase the nation's wealth and to distribute the benefits of the economy to the greatest number of people. The harsh reality is that the income of one-third of Panama's population frequently fails to provide for families' basic needs.

Women, who won the right to vote in the 1940s, are accorded equal political rights under the law and hold a number of important government positions, including the presidency. But as in all of Latin Amer-ica, women do not enjoy the same opportunities for advancement as men. There are also profound domestic constraints to their freedom. Panamanian law, for example, does not recognize community property; divorced or deserted women have no protection and can be left destitute, if that is the will of their former spouses. Many female heads-of-household from poor areas are obliged to work for the government, often as street cleaners, in order to receive support funds from the authorities.

ACHIEVEMENTS

The Panama Canal, which passed wholly to Panamanian control in 1999, is one of the greatest engineering achievements of the twentieth century. A maze of locks and gates, it cuts through 50 miles of the most difficult terrain on Earth.

With respect to human rights, Panama's record is mixed. The press and electronic media, while theoretically free, have experienced some harassment. In 1983, the Supreme Court ruled that journalists need not be licensed by the government. Nevertheless, both reporters and editors still exercise a calculated self-censorship, and press conduct in general is regulated by an official "Morality and Ethics Commission," whose powers are broad and vague. In 2001, some journalists complained that the Moscoso government used criminal antidefamation laws to intimidate the press in general, and its critics in particular.

In May 2004 Martín Torrijos was elected president with about 47 percent of the vote. Although he is the flag bearer of a political party built by military strongmen, including his father and Noriega, he has promised change. Cloaking himself in the garb of a populist, Torrijos has presented an image in both the cities and the countryside as the defender of the poor. He has in-

Timeline: PAST

1518
Panama City is established

1821–1903
Panama is a department of Colombia

1903
Independence from Colombia

1977
The signing of the Panama Canal Treaties

1980s
The death of President Omar Torrijos creates a political vacuum; American troops invade Panama; Manuel Noriega surrenders to face drug charges in the United States

1990s
Mireya Moscoso is elected as Panama's first woman president; the last U.S. troops leave Panama; the Panama Canal passes to wholly local control

PRESENT

2000s
Climatic changes have been accelerated by deforestation

Martín Torrijos elected president in 2004

herited a government widely accused of corruption and a national pension system close to collapse because of overspending. His economic policies will likely embrace a significant reconstruction of the Panama Canal to allow the passage of larger ships. The need for huge amounts of private investment will tend to temper his populism. Panama's problems are daunting, and one Panamanian university professor told the *New York Times*: "There is no way [Torrijos] is going to be able to live up to people's expectations. He is going to have a short honeymoon."

South America

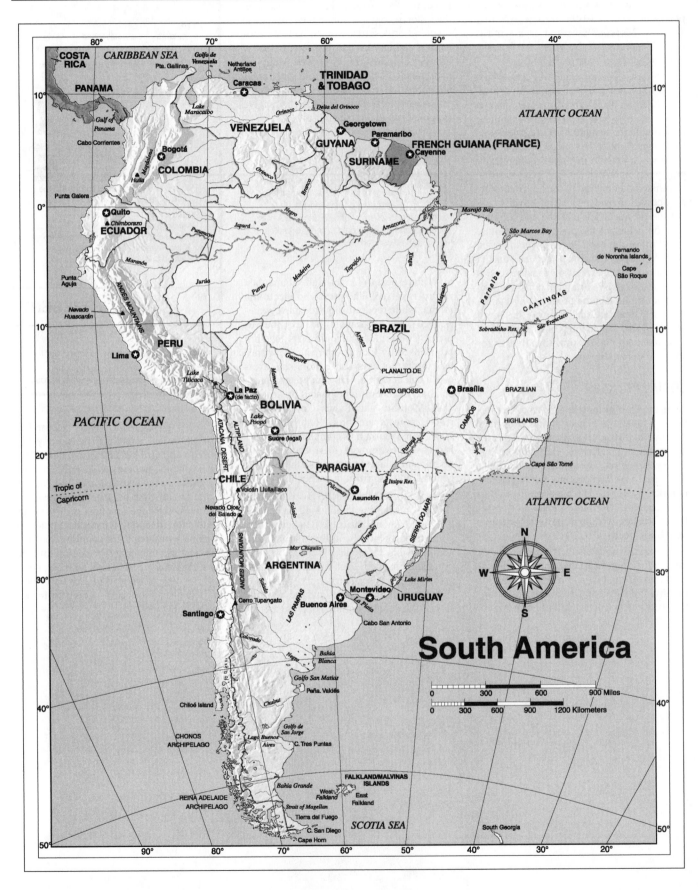

CARIBBEAN SEA

COSTA RICA
PANAMA
Pta. Gallinas
Golfo de Venezuela
Netherland Antilles
TRINIDAD & TOBAGO
Caracas
ATLANTIC OCEAN
Gulf of Panama
Lake Maracaibo
Orinoco
Delta del Orinoco
Cabo Corrientes
VENEZUELA
Georgetown
Bogotá
GUYANA
Paramaribo
FRENCH GUIANA (FRANCE)
COLOMBIA
Orinoco
SURINAME
Cayenne
Huila
Branco
Punta Galera
Quito
Chimborazo
ECUADOR
Negro
Amazona
Marajó Bay
São Marcos Bay
Japurá
Fernando de Noronha Islands
Marañón
Putumayo
Cape São Roque
Punta Aguja
Jurúa
Purus
Madeira
Tapajós
Xingu
Parnaíba
Nevado Huascarán
ANDES MOUNTAINS
CAATINGAS
BRAZIL
PERU
Guaporé
Sobradinho Res.
São Francisco
Lima
Mamoré
PLANALTO DE
Lake Titicaca
La Paz (de facto)
MATO GROSSO
Brasília
BRAZILIAN
BOLIVIA
Lake Poopó
Arinos
CAMPOS
HIGHLANDS
ALTIPLANO
Sucre (legal)
Paraná
ATACAMA DESERT
PACIFIC OCEAN
PARAGUAY
Cape São Tomé
CHILE
Pilcomayo
Itaipu Res.
Volcán Llullaillaco
Asunción
SIERRA DO MAR
ATLANTIC OCEAN
Nevado Ojos del Salado
Salado
Uruguay
N
ANDES MOUNTAINS
Mar Chiquito
W   E
ARGENTINA
Lake Mirim
Montevideo
S
Cerro Tupangato
Salado
LAS PAMPAS
Buenos Aires
La Plata
URUGUAY
Santiago
Colorado
Cabo San Antonio
Negro
Bahía Blanca
South America
Golfo San Matías
Peña. Valdés
Chubut
Chiloé Island
Golfo de San Jorge
0   300   600   900 Miles
CHONOS ARCHIPELAGO
Lago Buenos Aires
C. Tres Puntas
0   300   600   900   1200 Kilometers
FALKLAND/MALVINAS ISLANDS
REINA ADELAIDE ARCHIPELAGO
Bahía Grande
West Falkland
East Falkland
Strait of Magellan
Tierra del Fuego
C. San Diego
SCOTIA SEA
South Georgia
Cape Horn

South America An Imperfect Prism

Any overview of South America must first address the incredible geographic and climatic diversity of the region. Equatorial rain forests are found in Brazil, Ecuador, Colombia, Venezuela, and other countries; and the coastal deserts in Peru and northern Chile are among the driest and most forbidding in the world (naturalist Charles Darwin described the area as "a complete and utter desert"). More hospitable are the undulating pampas and plains of Argentina, Uruguay, central Venezuela, eastern Colombia, and southeastern Brazil. The spine of the continent is formed by the Andes Mountains, majestic and snowcapped. Because of its topography and the many degrees of latitude in which it lies, South America has extremes of temperature, ranging from desert heat to the steaming humidity of the tropics to the cold gales of Tierra del Fuego, which lies close to the Antarctic Circle. To add further to the perils of generalization, wide-ranging differences often occur within a country. Geography has played a critical role in the evolution of each of the nations of South America; it has been one of several major influences in their histories and their cultures.

NATURE'S CHALLENGE

Nature has presented the inhabitants of South America with an unrelenting challenge. On the west coast, most of the major cities are located in geologically active zones. All too frequently, earthquakes, tidal waves, volcanic activity, and landslides have taken a staggering toll of human life. And throughout the region, floods and droughts make agriculture a risky business. Periodically, for example, the appearance of a warm current off the coasts of Peru and Ecuador, a phenomenon known as *El Niño*, produces significant atmospheric events worldwide. For Peru and Ecuador, *El Niño* brings devastating floods with heavy loss of life and extensive damage to the area's infrastructure. Further economic damage results from the profound disruption of the fishing industry.

REGIONALISM

South America's diverse topography has also helped to foster a deep-seated regionalism that has spawned innumerable civil wars and made national integration an extremely difficult task. In Colombia, for instance, the Andes fan out into three distinct ranges, separated by deep valleys. Each of the nation's three major cities—Bogotá, Medellín, and Cali—dominates a valley and is effectively isolated from the others by the mountains. The broad plains to the east have remained largely undeveloped because of the difficulty of access from the centers of population. Troubling to Colombian governments is the fact that, in terms of topography, the eastern plains are tied to Venezuela and not to the Colombian cities to the west.

(Photo Lisa Clyde/Sar4)

The northern Andes Mountains meet the Caribbean Sea in Venezuela.

(Courtesy of Chris & Erin Ratay/Ratay01)

The cultures of the countries of the southern Cone—Argentina, Uruguay, Paraguay, and Chile—have been profoundly influenced by the geography of their vast, fertile plains. These latter-day gauchos are packing their bags for a trekking journey.

Similarly, mountains divide Ecuador, Peru, Bolivia, and Venezuela. In all of these nations, there is a permanent tension between the capital cities and the hinterlands. As is the case in those republics that have large Indian populations, the tension often is as much cultural as it is a matter of geography. But in the entire region, physical geography interacts with culture, society, politics, and economics. Regionalism has been a persistent theme in the history of Ecuador, where there has been an often bitter rivalry between the capital city of Quito, located high in the central mountains, and the port city of Guayaquil. Commonly, port cities, with their window on the world outside, tend to be more cosmopolitan, liberal, and dynamic than cities that are more isolated. Such is the case with freewheeling Guayaquil, which stands in marked contrast to conservative, traditional, deeply Catholic Quito.

Venezuela boasts six distinct geographical regions, which include mountains and valleys, plains and deserts, rivers and jungles, and a coastline. Historian John Lombardi observes that each of these regions has had an important role in identifying and defining the character of Venezuela's past and present: "Over the centuries the geographical focus has shifted from one region to another in response to internal arrangements and external demands."

THE SOUTHERN CONE

The cultures of the countries of the so-called Southern Cone— Argentina, Uruguay, Paraguay, and Chile—have also been shaped by the geographical environment. Argentina, Uruguay, and Brazil's southern state of Rio Grande do Sul developed subcultures that reflected life on the vast, fertile plains, where cattle grazed by the millions. The *gaucho* ("cowboy") became symbolic of the "civilization of leather." Fierce, independent, a law unto himself, the gaucho was mythologized by the end of the nineteenth century. At a time when millions of European immigrants were flooding into the region, the gaucho emerged as a nationalist symbol of Argentina and Uruguay, standing firm in the face of whatever natives viewed as "foreign."

Landlocked Paraguay, surrounded by powerful neighbors, has for most of its history been an introspective nation, little known to the outside world. Because of its geography, most of Paraguay's population is concentrated near the capital city of Asunción. A third of the nation is tropical and swampy—not suitable for settlement. To the west, the desolate Chaco region, with its lack of adequate sources of drinkable water, is virtually uninhabitable.

Chile, with a coastline 2,600 miles long, is a country of topographic and climatic extremes. If superimposed on a map of North America, Chile would stretch from Mexico's Baja California to the Yukon in Alaska. It is on Chile's border with Argentina that the Andes soar to their greatest heights. Several peaks, including Aconcagua, reach to nearly 23,000 feet in elevation. That mountain barrier has historically isolated Chile from eastern South America and from Europe. The central valley of Chile is the political, industrial, social, and cultural heart of the nation. With the capital city of Santiago and the large port of Valparaíso, the valley holds about 70 percent of Chile's population. The valley's Mediterranean climate and fertile soil have long acted as a magnet for Chileans from other, less hospitable, parts of the country.

BRAZIL

Historian Rollie Poppino has noted that the "major miracle of Brazil is its existence as a single nation." What he implies is that Brazil embraces regions that are so distinct that they could well be separate countries. "There are actually many Brazils within the broad expanse of the national territory, and the implication of uniformity conveyed by their common flag and language is often deceptive." In Brazil, there exists a tremendous range of geographical, racial, cultural, and economic contrasts. But part of the Brazilian "miracle" lies in the ability of its people to accept the diversity as normal. Many Brazilians were unaware of the great differences within their country for years, until the improvement of internal transportation and communications as well as the impact of the mass media informed them not only of their common heritage but also of their profound regional differences.

DIVERSE PEOPLES

In many respects, the peoples of South America are as diverse as its geography. While the populations of Argentina and Uruguay are essentially European, with virtually no Indian intermixture, Chilean society is descended from Spanish conquerors and the Indians they dominated. The Indian presence is strongest in the Andean republics of Bolivia, Peru, and Ecuador— the heart of the ancient Inca civilization. Bolivia is the most Indian, with well over half its population classified as such. Mestizos (mixed white and Indian) constitute about a quarter of the population, and whites make up only about one-tenth.

Three ethnic groups are found among the populations of Colombia and Venezuela: Spanish and Indian predominate, and there are small black minorities. About 60 percent of the populations of both countries are of Mestizo or pardo (mixed blood) origin. One of Brazil's distinctive features is the rich racial mixture of its population. Peoples of Indian, European, African, and

Japanese heritage live in an atmosphere largely free of racial enmity, if not degrees of prejudice.

Taken as a whole, the predominant culture is Iberian (that is, Spanish or Portuguese), although many mountain areas are overwhelmingly Indian in terms of ethnic makeup. With the conquest and colonization of South America in the sixteenth century, Spain and Portugal attempted to fasten their cultures, languages, and institutions on the land and its peoples. Spanish cities in South America—laid out in the familiar grid pattern consisting of a large central plaza bordered by a Catholic church, government buildings, and the dwellings of the ruling elite—represented the conscious intention of the conquerors to impose their will, not only on the defeated Indian civilizations but also on nature itself.

By way of contrast, the Brazilian cities that were laid out by early Portuguese settlers tended to be less formally structured, suggesting that their planners and builders were more flexible and adaptable to the new world around them. Roman Catholicism, however, was imposed on all citizens by the central authority. Government, conforming to Hispanic political culture, was authoritarian in the colonial period and continues to be so today. The conquerors created a stratified society of essentially two sectors: a ruling white elite and a ruled majority. But Spain and Portugal also introduced institutions that knit society together. Paternalistic patron–client relationships that bound the weak to the strong were common; they continue to be so today.

INDIAN CULTURE

Among the isolated Indian groups of Ecuador, Peru, and Bolivia, Spanish cultural forms were strongly and, for the most part, successfully resisted. Suspicious and occasionally hostile, the Indians refused integration into the white world outside their highland villages. By avoiding integration, in the words of historian Frederick Pike, "they maintain the freedom to live almost exclusively in the domain of their own language, social habits, dress and eating styles, beliefs, prejudices, and myths."

Only the Catholic religion was able to make some inroads, and that was (and still is) imperfect. The Catholicism practiced by Quechua- and Aymara-speaking Indians is a blend of Catholic teachings and ancient folk religion. For example, in an isolated region in Peru where eight journalists were massacred by Indians, a writer who investigated the incident reported in *The New York Times* that while Catholicism was "deeply rooted" among the Indians, "it has not displaced old beliefs like the worship of the *Apus*, or god mountains." When threatened, the Indians are "zealous defenders of their customs and mores." The societies' two cultures have had a profound impact on the literature of Ecuador, Peru, and Bolivia. The plight of the Indian, social injustice, and economic exploitation are favorite themes of these nations' authors.

Other Indian groups more vulnerable to the steady encroachment of "progress" did not survive. In the late nineteenth century, pampas Indians were virtually destroyed by Argentine cavalry armed with repeating rifles. Across the Andes, in Chile, the Araucanian Indians met a similar fate in the 1880s. Unfortunately, relations between the "civilized" world and the "primitive" peoples clinging to existence in the rain forests of Brazil, Peru, Bolivia, and Venezuela have generally improved little.

(PhotoLink/Getty Images/DIL5104)

South America's Indian cultures and modern development have never really mixed. The native cultures persist in many areas, as exemplified at a market in Ecuador.

But beginning in the early 1990s events in Bolivia, Brazil, Ecuador, and Venezuela signaled a marked shift toward greater Indian rights. Bolivians elected an Aymara Indian leader and activist as president in 2006. Indigenous peoples throughout the Amazon Basin, however, are still under almost daily assault from settlers hungry for land, road builders, developers, miners, loggers, and speculators—most of whom care little about the cultures they are annihilating.

AFRICAN AMERICAN CULTURE

In those South American countries where slavery was widespread, the presence of a large black population has contributed yet another dimension to Hispanic culture (or, in the case of Guyana and Suriname, English and Dutch culture). Slaves, brutally uprooted from their cultures in Africa, developed new cultural forms that were often a combination of Christian and other beliefs. To insulate themselves against the rigors of forced labor and to forge some kind of common identity, slaves embraced folk religions that were heavily oriented toward magic. Magic helped blacks to face an uncertain destiny, and folk religions built bridges between peoples facing a similar, horrible fate. Folk religions not only survived the emancipation of slaves but have remained a common point of focus for millions of Brazilian blacks.

This phenomenon had become so widespread that in the 1970s, the Roman Catholic Church made a concerted effort to win Afro-Brazilians to a religion that was more Christian and less pagan. This effort was partly negated by the development of close relations between Brazil and Africa, which occurred at the same time as the Church's campaign. Brazilian blacks became more acutely aware of their African origins and began a movement of "re-Africanization." So pervasive had the folk religions become that one authority stated that Umbada (one of the folk religions) was now the religion of Brazil. The festival of *Carnaval* ("Carnival") in Rio de Janeiro, Brazil, is perhaps the best-known example of the blending of Christianity with spiritism. Even the samba, a dance form that is central to the Carnaval celebration, had its origins in black folk religions.

IMMIGRATION AND CULTURE

Italians, Eastern and Northern Europeans, Chinese, and Japanese have also contributed to the cultural, social, and economic development of several South American nations. The great outpouring of Europe's peoples that brought millions of immigrants to the shores of the United States also brought millions to South America. From the mid-1800s to the outbreak of World War I in 1914, great numbers of Italians and Spaniards, and much smaller numbers of Germans, Russians, Welsh, Scots, Irish, and English boarded ships that would carry them to South America.

Many were successful in the "New World." Indeed, immigrants were largely responsible for the social restructuring of Argentina, Uruguay, and southern Brazil, as they created a large and dynamic middle class where none had existed before.

Italians

Many of the new arrivals came from urban areas, were literate, and possessed a broad range of skills. Argentina received the greatest proportion of immigrants. So great was the influx that an Argentine political scientist labeled the years 1890–1914 the "alluvial era" (flood). His analogy was apt, for by 1914, half the population of the capital city of Buenos Aires were foreign-born. Indeed, 30 percent of the total Argentine population were of foreign extraction. Hundreds of thousands of immigrants also flocked into Uruguay.

In both countries, they were able to move quickly into middle-class occupations in business and commerce. Others found work on the docks or on the railroads that carried the produce of the countryside to the ports for export to foreign markets. Some settled in the interior of Argentina, where they usually became sharecroppers or tenant farmers, although a sizable number were able to purchase land in the northern province of Santa Fe or became truck farmers in the immediate vicinity of Buenos Aires. Argentina's wine industry underwent a rapid transformation and expansion with the arrival of Italians in the western provinces of Mendoza and San Juan. In the major cities of Argentina, Uruguay, Chile, Peru, and Brazil, Italians built

hospitals and established newspapers; they formed mutual aid societies and helped to found the first labor unions. Their presence is still strong today, and Italian words have entered into everyday discourse in Argentina and Uruguay.

Other Groups

Other immigrant groups also made their contributions to the formation of South America's societies and cultures. Germans colonized much of southern Chile and were instrumental in creating the nation's dairy industry. In the wilds of Patagonia, Welsh settlers established sheep ranches and planted apple, pear, and cherry trees in the Río Negro Valley.

In Buenos Aires, despite the 1982 conflict over the Falkland Islands, there remains a distinct British imprint. Harrod's is the largest department store in the city, and one can board a train on a railroad built with English capital and journey to suburbs with names such as Hurlingham, Temperley, and Thames. In both Brazil and Argentina, soccer was introduced by the English, and two Argentine teams still bear the names "Newell's Old Boys" and "River Plate." Collectively, the immigrants who flooded into South America in the late nineteenth and early twentieth centuries introduced a host of new ideas, methods, and skills. They were especially important in stimulating and shaping the modernization of Argentina, Uruguay, Chile, and southern Brazil.

In other countries that were bypassed earlier in the century, immigration has become a new phenomenon. Venezuela—torn by political warfare, its best lands long appropriated by the elite, and its economy developing only slowly—was far less attractive than the lands of opportunity to its north (the United States) and south (Argentina, Uruguay, and Brazil). In the early 1950s, however, Venezuela embarked on a broadscale development program that included an attempt to attract European immigrants. Thousands of Spaniards, Portuguese, and Italians responded to the economic opportunity. Most of the immigrants settled in the capital city of Caracas, where some eventually became important in the construction business, retail trade, and the transportation industry.

INTERNAL MIGRATION

Paralleling the movement of peoples from across the oceans to parts of South America has been the movement of populations from rural areas to urban centers. In every nation, cities have been gaining in population for years. What prompts people to leave their homes and strike out for the unknown? In the cases of Bolivia and Peru, the very real prospect of famine has driven people out of the highlands and into the larger cities. Frequently, families will plan the move carefully. Vacant lands around the larger cities will be scouted in advance, and suddenly, in the middle of the night, the new "settlers" will move in and erect a shantytown. With time, the seizure of the land is usually recognized by city officials and the new neighborhood is provided with urban services. Where the land seizure is resisted, however, violence and loss of life are common.

Factors other than famine also force people to leave their ancestral homes. Population pressure and division of the land into parcels too small to sustain families compel people to migrate.

(United Nations photo/M. Grant/UN155045)

Colombia, as is the case with many other Latin American nations, has experienced rapid urbanization. Large numbers of migrants from rural areas have spread into slums on the outskirts of cities, as exemplified by this picture of a section of Colombia's capital, Bogotá. Most of the migrants are poorly paid, and the struggle to meet basic needs precludes political activism.

Others move to the cities in search of economic opportunities or chances for social advancement that do not exist in rural regions. Tens of thousands of Colombians illegally crossed into Venezuela in the 1970s and 1980s in search of employment. As is the case with Mexicans who enter the United States, Colombians experienced discrimination and remained on the margins of urban society, mired in low-paying, unskilled jobs. Those who succeeded in finding work in industry were a source of anger and frustration to Venezuelan labor-union members, who resented Colombians who accepted low rates of pay. Other migrants sought employment in the agricultural sector on coffee plantations or the hundreds of cattle ranches that dot the *llanos*, or plains. In summary, a combination of push-and-pull factors are involved in a person's decision to begin a new life.

Since World War II, indigenous migration in South America has rapidly increased urban populations and has forced cities to reorganize. Rural people have been exposed to a broad range of push–pull pressures to move to the cities. Land hunger, extreme poverty, and rural violence might be included among the push factors; while hope for a better job, upward social mobility, and a more satisfying life help to explain the attraction of a city. The phenomenon can be infinitely complex.

In Lima, Peru, there has been a twofold movement of people. While the unskilled and illiterate, the desperately poor and unemployed, the newly arrived migrant, and the delinquent have moved to or remained in inner-city slums, former slum dwellers have in turn moved to the city's perimeter. Although less centrally located, they have settled in more spacious and socially desirable shantytowns. In this way, some 16,000 families created a squatter settlement practically overnight in the south of Lima. Author Hernando DeSoto, in his groundbreaking and controversial book *The Other Path*, captures the essence of the shantytowns: "Modest homes cramped together on city perimeters, a myriad of workshops in their midst, armies of vendors hawking their wares on the street, and countless minibus lines crisscrossing them—all seem to have sprung from nowhere, pushing the city's boundaries ever outward."

Significantly, DeSoto notes, collective effort has increasingly been replaced by individual effort, upward mobility exists even for the inner-city slum dwellers, and urban culture and patterns of consumption have been transformed. Opera, theater, and *zarzuela* (comic opera) have gradually been replaced by movies, soccer, folk festivals, and television. Beer, rice, and table salt are now within the reach of much of the population; consumption of more expensive items, however, such as wine and meat, has declined.

On the outskirts of Buenos Aires there exists a *villa miseria* (slum) built on the bottom and sides of an old clay pit. Appropriately, the *barrio*, or neighborhood, is called La Cava (literally "The Digging"). The people of La Cava are very poor; most have moved there from rural Argentina or from Paraguay. Shacks seem to be thrown together from whatever is available—scraps of wood, packing crates, sheets of tin, and cardboard. There is no source of potable water, garbage litters the narrow alleyways, and there are no sewers. Because of the concave character of the barrio, the heat is unbearable in the summer. Rats and flies are legion. At times, the smells are repulsive. The visitor to La Cava experiences an assault on the senses; this is Latin America at its worst.

But there is another side to the slums of Buenos Aires, Lima, Santiago, and Rio de Janeiro. A closer look at La Cava, for example, reveals a community in transition. Some of the housing is more substantial, with adobe replacing the scraps of wood and tin; other homes double as places of business and sell general merchandise, food, and bottled drinks. One advertises itself as a food store, bar, and butcher shop. Another sells watches and repairs radios. Several promote their merchandise or services in a weekly newspaper that circulates in La Cava and two other *barrios de emergencia* ("emergency"—that is, temporary—neighborhoods). The newspaper addresses items of concern to the inhabitants. There are articles on hygiene and infant diarrhea; letters and editorials plead with people not to throw their garbage in the streets; births and deaths are recorded. The newspaper is a chronicle of progress as well as frustration: people are working together to create a viable neighborhood; drainage ditches are constructed with donated time and equipment; collections and raffles are held to provide materials to build sewers and, in some cases, to provide minimal street lighting; and men and women who have contributed their labor are singled out for special praise.

The newspaper also reproduces municipal decrees that affect the lives of the residents. The land on which the barrio sits was illegally occupied, the stores that service the neighborhood were opened without the necessary authorization, and the housing was built without regard to municipal codes, so city ordinances such as the following aimed at the barrios de emergencia are usually restrictive: "The sale, renting or transfer of *casillas* [homes] within the boundaries of the barrio de emergencia is prohibited; casillas can not be inhabited by single men, women or children; the opening of businesses within the barrio is strictly prohibited, unless authorized by the Municipality; dances and festivals may not be held without the express authorization of the Municipality." But there are also signs of accommodation: "The Municipality is studying the problem of refuse removal." For migrants, authority and the legal system typically are not helpful; instead, they are hindrances.

Hernando DeSoto found this situation to be true also of Peru, where "the greatest hostility the migrants encountered was from the legal system." Until the end of World War II, the system had either absorbed or ignored the migrants "because the small groups who came were hardly likely to upset the status quo." But when the rural-to-urban flow became a flood, the system could no longer remain disinterested. Housing and education were barred to them, businesses would not hire them. The migrants discovered over time that they would have to fight for every right and every service from an unwilling establishment. Thus, to survive, they became part of the informal sector, otherwise known as the underground or parallel economy.

On occasion, however, municipal laws can work to the advantage of newly arrived migrants. In the sprawling new communities that sprang up between Lima and its port city of Callao, there are thousands of what appear to be unfinished homes. In almost every instance, a second floor was begun but, curiously, construction ceased. The reason for the incomplete projects relates to taxes—they are not assessed until a building is finished.

These circumstances are true not only of the squatter settlements on the fringes of South America's great cities but also of the inner-city slums. Slum dwellers have been able to improve their market opportunities and have been able to acquire better housing and some urban services, because they have organized on their own, outside formal political channels. In the words of sociologist Susan Eckstein, "They refused to allow dominant class and state interests to determine and restrict their fate. Defiance and resistance won them concessions which quiescence would not."

DeSoto found this to be the case with Lima: Migrants, "if they were to live, trade, manufacture, or even consume … had to do so illegally. Such illegality was not antisocial in intent, like trafficking in drugs, theft, or abduction, but was designed to achieve such essentially legal objectives as building a house, providing a service, or developing a business."

This is also the story of Buenos Aires's La Cava. To open a shop in the barrio with municipal approval, an aspiring businessperson must be a paragon of patience. Various levels of bureaucracy, with their plethora of paperwork and fees, insensitive municipal officials, inefficiency, and interminable waiting, drive people outside the system where the laws do not seem to conform to social need.

Disturbing, however, is the destruction of the social fabric of some of these "illegal" communities in the environs of Rio de Janeiro. In the *favelas* of this Brazilian city a drug and gang culture has taken root. The accompanying violence has torn families apart and resulted in the deaths of many people who stood in the way drug lords who have appropriated the *favelas* as a base of operations.

AN ECCLESIASTICAL REVOLUTION

During the past few decades, there have been important changes in the religious habits of many South Americans. Virtually everywhere, Roman Catholicism, long identified with the traditional order, has been challenged by newer movements such as Evangelical Protestantism and the Charismatics. Within the Catholic Church, the theology of liberation once gained ground. The creation of Christian communities in the barrios, people who bond together to discuss their beliefs and act as agents of change, has become a common phenomenon throughout the region. Base communities from the Catholic perspective instill Christian values in the lives of ordinary people. But it is an active form of religion that pushes for change and social justice. Hundreds of these communities exist in Peru, thousands in Brazil.

NATIONAL MYTHOLOGIES

In the midst of geographical and cultural diversity, the nations of South America have created national mythologies designed to unite people behind their rulers. Part of that mythology is rooted in the wars of independence that tore through much of the region between 1810 and 1830. Liberation from European colonialism imparted to South Americans a sense of their own national histories, replete with military heroes such as José de San Martín, Simón Bolívar, Bernardo O'Higgins, and Antonio

José de Sucre, as well as a host of revolutionary myths. This coming to nationhood paralleled what the United States experienced when it won its independence from Britain. South Americans, at least those with a stake in the new society, began to think of themselves as Venezuelans, Chileans, Peruvians, or Brazilians. The architects of Chilean national mythology proclaimed the emergence of a new and superior being who was the result of the symbolic and physical union of Spaniards and the tough, heroic Araucanian Indians. The legacy of Simón Bolívar lives on in particular in Venezuela, his homeland; even today, the nation's foreign policymakers speak in Bolivarian terms about Venezuela's rightful role as a leader in Latin American affairs. In some instances, the mythology generated by the wars for independence became a shield against foreign ideas and customs and was used to force immigrants to become "Argentines" or "Chileans." It was an attempt to bring national unity out of diversity.

Argentines have never solved the question of their identity. Many consider themselves European and hold much of the rest of Latin America in contempt. Following Argentina's loss in the Falklands War with Britain, one scholar suggested that perhaps Argentines should no longer consider themselves as "a forlorn corner of Europe" but should wake up to the reality that they are Latin Americans. Much of Argentine literature reflects this uncertain identity and may help to explain author Jorge Luis Borges's affinity for English gardens and Icelandic sagas. It was also an Argentine military government that invoked Western Catholic civilization in its fight against a "foreign" and "godless" communism in the 1970s.

National mythologies also tend artificially to homogenize a country's history and often ignore large segments of the population and their cultures that differ from the "official" version. Recent events in Bolivia have laid bare long-existing cleavages.

The non-Indian elite is clearly concerned by the election of an Aymara as president and his vision of the nation's history and future. The "white" inhabitants of Santa Cruz in eastern Bolivia have loudly proclaimed their cultural, ethnic, and social differences with the indigenous population of the highlands and have talked of secession.

THE ARTIST AND SOCIETY

There is a strongly cultured and humane side of South America. Jeane Franco, an authority on Latin American cultural movements, observes that to "declare oneself an artist in Latin America has frequently involved conflict with society." The art and literature of South America in particular and Latin America in general represent a distinct tradition within the panorama of Western civilization.

The art of South America has as its focus social questions and ideals. It expresses love for one's fellow human beings and "has kept alive the vision of a more just and humane form of society." It rises above purely personal relationships and addresses humanity.

Much change is also evident at the level of popular culture. Andean folk music, for example, is being replaced by the more urban and upbeat chicha music in Peru; and in Argentina, the traditional tango has lost much of its early appeal. Radio and television programs are more and more in the form of soap operas, adventure programs, or popular entertainment, once considered vulgar by cosmopolitan city dwellers. South America is rather like a prism. It can be treated as a single object or region. Yet when exposed to a shaft of sunlight of understanding, it throws off a brilliant spectrum of colors that exposes the diversity of its lands and peoples.

Argentina (Argentine Republic)

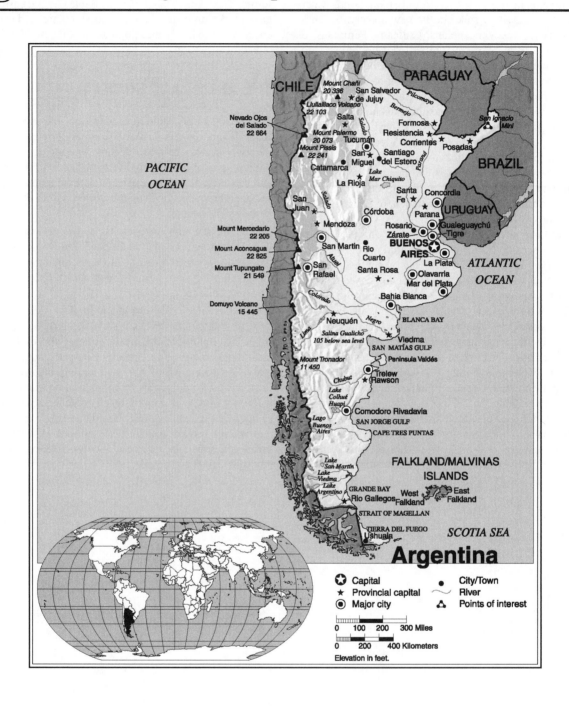

Mount Chañi 20 336
San Salvador de Jujuy
Llullaillaco Volcano 22 103
Nevado Ojos del Salado 22 664
Mount Palermo 20 073
Mount Pissis 22 241
Salta
Tucumán
San Miguel
Catamarca
Lake Mar Chiquito
La Rioja
PACIFIC OCEAN
San Juan
Córdoba
Santa Fe
Concordia
Paraná
URUGUAY
Mount Mercedario 22 205
Mendoza
Rosario
Gualeguaychú
Zárate
Tigre
BUENOS AIRES
Mount Aconcagua 22 825
San Martin
Río Cuarto
Mount Tupungato 21 549
San Rafael
Santa Rosa
La Plata
ATLANTIC OCEAN
Olavarría
Mar del Plata
Domuyo Volcano 15 445
Bahía Blanca
Neuquén
Negro
BLANCA BAY
Salina Gualicho 105 below sea level
Viedma
SAN MATÍAS GULF
Mount Tronador 11 450
Peninsula Valdés
Chubut
Trelew
Rawson
Lake Colhué Huapí
Comodoro Rivadavia
Lago Buenos Aires
SAN JORGE GULF
CAPE TRES PUNTAS
Lake San Martín
Lake Viedma
Lake Argentino
GRANDE BAY
Río Gallegos
FALKLAND/MALVINAS ISLANDS
West Falkland
East Falkland
STRAIT OF MAGELLAN
TIERRA DEL FUEGO
Ushuaia
SCOTIA SEA

CHILE
PARAGUAY
Pilcomayo
Bermejo
Formosa
Resistencia
Corrientes
Posadas
San Ignacio Mini
BRAZIL
Santiago del Estero
Paraná
Saladó

Argentina

⊛ Capital
★ Provincial capital
◉ Major city
• City/Town
∿ River
△ Points of interest

0 100 200 300 Miles
0 200 400 Kilometers
Elevation in feet.

Argentina Statistics

GEOGRAPHY

Area in Square Miles (Kilometers): 1,100,000 (2,771,300) (about 4 times the size of Texas)

Capital (Population): Buenos Aires (11,802,000)

Environmental Concerns: soil erosion and degradation; air and water pollution; desertification.

Geographical Features: rich plains of the Pampas in the north; the flat to rolling plateau of Patagonia in the south; the rugged Andes along western border

Climate: varied; mostly temperate; subantarctic in southwest

PEOPLE

Population

Total: 39,144,753

Annual Growth Rate: 1.02%

Rural/Urban Population Ratio: 12/88

Major Languages: Spanish; Italian Ethnic Makeup: 97% white; 3% Mestizo, Indian, and others

Religions: 90% Roman Catholic (fewer than 20% practicing); 2% Protestant; 2% Jewish; 6% others

Health

Life Expectancy at Birth: 72 years (male); 76 years (female)

Infant Mortality Rate (Ratio): 15.66/1,000

Physicians Available (Ratio): 1/376

Education

Adult Literacy Rate: 97.1%

Compulsory (Ages): 6–14; free

COMMUNICATION

Telephones: 8,009,400 main lines

Daily Newspaper Circulation: 138 per 1,000 people

Televisions: 347 per 1,000 people

Internet Users: 41 million

TRANSPORTATION

Highways in Miles (Kilometers): 135,549 (218,276)

Railroads in Miles (Kilometers): 23,542 (37,910)

Usable Airfields: 1,359

Motor Vehicles in Use: 6,100,000

GOVERNMENT

Type: republic

Independence Date: July 9, 1816 (from Spain)

Head of State/Government: President Néstor Kirchner is both head of state and head of government

Political Parties: Radical Civic Union; Justicialist Party (Peronist); Union of the Democratic Center; others

Suffrage: universal at 18

MILITARY

Military Expenditures (% of GDP): 1.3%

Current Disputes: indefinite boundary with Chile; claims UK-administered South Georgia and South Sandwich Islands, and Falkland Islands (Islas Malvinas); territorial claim in Antarctica

ECONOMY

Currency ($U.S. Equivalent): 2.9 pesos = $1

Per Capita Income/GDP: $11,200/$432 billion

GDP Growth Rate: 8%

Inflation Rate: 3.7%

Unemployment Rate: 16.3%; substantial underemployment

Labor Force: 15,000

Natural Resources: fertile plains; lead; zinc; tin; copper; iron ore; manganese; petroleum; uranium

Agriculture: wheat; corn; sorghum; fruits; soybeans; tobacco; tea; livestock

Industry: food processing; motor vehicles; consumer durables; textiles; chemicals and petrochemicals; printing; metallurgy; steel

Exports: $29.5 billion (primary partners Brazil, European Union, United States)

Imports: $13.2 billion (primary partners European Union, United States, Brazil)

SUGGESTED WEBSITE

http://www.cia.gov/cia/
publications/factbook/index.html

Argentina Country Report

ARGENTINA: THE DIVIDED LAND

Writers as far back as the mid-1800s have perceived two Argentinas. Domingo F. Sarmiento, the president of Argentina in the 1860s, entitled his classic work about the country *Civilization and Barbarism*. More contemporary writers speak of Argentina as a divided land or as a city and a nation. All address the relationship of the capital city, Buenos Aires, to the rest of the country. Buenos Aires is cultured, cosmopolitan, modern, and dynamic. The rural interior is in striking contrast in terms of living standards, the pace of life, and, perhaps, expectations as well. For many years, Buenos Aires and other urban centers have drawn population away from the countryside: Today, Argentina is 88 percent urban.

There are other contrasts. The land is extremely rich and produces a large share of the world's grains and beef. Few Argentines are malnourished, and the annual per capita consumption of beef is comparable to that of the United States. Yet this land of promise, which seemed in the 1890s to have a limitless future, has slowly decayed. Its greatness is now more mythical than real. Since the Great Depression of the 1930s, the Argentine economy has, save for brief spurts, never been able to return to the sustained growth of the late nineteenth and early twentieth centuries.

In the 1990s, the Argentine economy enjoyed a brief period of stability and growth. Inefficient and costly state enterprises were privatized, with the exception of the petroleum industry, traditionally a strategic sector reserved to the state. A peso tied to the dollar brought inflation under control, and the pace of business activity, employment, and foreign investment quickened.

The nation's economy is vulnerable to events in other parts of the world, however. The collapse of the Mexican peso in the early 1990s and the economic crises in Russia and, especially, Asia in the late 1990s had profound negative effects in Argentina. The global slowdown in the new millennium further complicated the economic situation.

By the first quarter of 2002, the economy was in crisis. A foreign debt of $142 billion (which works out to $3,000 for every man, woman, and child in the country), declining export revenues, high unemployment, and the inability of the government to win International Monetary Fund support for additional loans forced a devaluation of the currency.

Argentine economic history has been typified by unrealized potential and unfulfilled promises. Much depends on the confidence of the Argentine people in the leadership and policies of their elected representatives. Five changes of government between December 2001 and March 2002 suggest a wholesale *lack* of confidence.

DEVELOPMENT

Argentina convinced the IMF to help its economic recovery without following the strict full fiscal discipline measures usually required. Economic recovery was well underway in 2004.

AUTHORITARIAN GOVERNMENT

In political terms, Argentina has revealed a curious inability to bring about the kind of stable democratic institutions that seemed assured in the 1920s. Since 1930, the military has seized power at least half a dozen times. It must be noted, however, that it has been civilians who have encouraged the generals to play an active role in politics.

Historian Robert Potash writes: "The notion that Argentine political parties or other important civilian groups have consistently opposed military takeovers bears little relation to reality."

Argentina has enjoyed civilian rule since 1983, but the military is still a presence. Indeed, one right-wing faction, the *carapintadas* ("painted faces"), responsible for mutinies against President Raúl Alfonsín in 1987 and 1988, have organized a nationwide party and have attracted enough votes to rank as an important political force. An authoritarian tradition is very much alive in Argentina, as is the bitter legacy of the so-called Dirty War.

THE DIRTY WAR

What made the latest era of military rule different is the climate of political violence that gripped Argentina starting in the late 1960s. The most recent period of violence began with the murder of former president Pedro Aramburu by left-wing guerrillas (Montoneros) who claimed to be fighting on behalf of the popular but exiled leader Juan Perón (president from 1946 to 1955 and from 1973 to 1974). The military responded to what it saw as an armed challenge from the left with tough antisubversion laws and official violence against suspects. Guerrillas increased their activities and intensified their campaign to win popular support.

Worried by the possibility of a major popular uprising and divided over policy, the military called for national elections in 1973, hoping that a civilian government would calm passions. The generals could then concentrate their efforts on destroying the armed left. The violence continued, however, and even the brief restoration of Juan Perón to power failed to bring peace.

FREEDOM

 Some 40 retired military officers accused of human-rights violations during the Dirty War have been stripped of their immunity from extradition to Spain where they face criminal charges. This is seen as a major advance in international law.

In March 1976, with the nation on the verge of economic collapse and guerrilla warfare spreading, the military seized power once again and declared a state of internal war, popularly called the Dirty War. Between 1976 and 1982, between 10,000 and 30,000 Argentine citizens "disappeared." Torture, the denial of basic human rights, harsh press censorship, officially directed death squads, and widespread fear came to characterize Argentina.

The labor movement—the largest, most effective, and most politically active on the continent—was, in effect, crippled by the military. Identified as a source of leftist subversion, the union movement was destroyed as an independent entity. Collective-bargaining agreements were dismantled, pension plans were cut back, and social-security and public-health programs were eliminated. The military's intent was to destroy a labor movement capable of operating on a national level.

The press was one of the immediate victims of the 1976 coup. A law was decreed warning that anyone spreading information derived from organizations "dedicated to subversive activities or terrorism" would be subject to an indefinite sentence. To speak out against the military was punishable by a 10-year jail term. The state also directed its terrorism tactics against the media, and approximately 100 journalists disappeared. Hundreds more received death threats, were tortured and jailed, or fled into exile. Numerous newspapers and magazines were shut down, and one, *La Opinión*, passed to government control.

The ruling junta justified these excesses by portraying the conflict as the opening battle of "World War III," in which Argentina was valiantly defending Western Christian values and cultures against hordes of Communist, "godless" subversives. It was a "holy war," with all of the unavoidable horrors of such strife.

By 1981, leftist guerrilla groups had been annihilated. Argentines slowly began to recover from the shock of internal war

(United Nations photo/P. Teuscher/UN133443)

Well known for its abundant grains and beef, Argentina also has a large fishing industry. These fishing boats are in the bay of the Plata River in Buenos Aires.

and talked of a return to civilian government. The military had completed its task; the nation needed to rebuild. Organized labor attempted to re-create its structure and threw the first tentative challenges at the regime's handling of the economy. The press carefully criticized both the economic policies of the government and the official silence over the fate of *los desaparecidos* ("the disappeared ones"). Human-rights groups pressured the generals with redoubled efforts.

OPPOSITION TO THE MILITARY

Against this backdrop of growing popular dissatisfaction with the regime's record, together with the approaching 150th anniversary of Great Britain's occupation of Las Islas Malvinas (the Falkland Islands), President Leopoldo Galtieri decided in 1982 to regain Argentine sovereignty and attack the Falklands. A successful assault, the military reasoned, would capture the popular imagination with its appeal to Argentine nationalism. The military's tarnished image would regain its luster. Forgiven would be the excesses of the Dirty War. But the attack ultimately failed.

In the wake of the fiasco, which cost thousands of Argentine and British lives, the military lost its grip on labor, the press, and the general population. Military and national humiliation, the continuing economic crisis made even worse by war costs, and the swelling chorus of discontent lessened the military's control over the flow of information and ideas. Previously forbidden subjects—such as the responsibility for the disappearances during the Dirty War—were raised in the newspapers.

The labor movement made a rapid and striking recovery and is now in the forefront of renewed political activity. Even though the movement is bitterly divided into moderate and militant wings, it is a force that cannot be ignored by political parties on the rebound.

HEALTH/WELFARE

In recent years, inflation has had an adverse impact on the amount of state spending on social services. Moreover, the official minimum wage falls significantly lower than the amount considered necessary to support a family.

The Falklands War may well prove to be a watershed in recent Argentine history. A respected Argentine observer, Torcuato DiTella, argues that the Falklands crisis was a "godsend," for it allowed Argentines to break with "foreign" economic models that had failed in Argentina. Disappointed

with the United States and Europe over their support of Great Britain, he concludes: "We belong in Latin America and it is better to be a part of this strife-torn continent than a forlorn province of Europe."

Popularly elected in 1983, President Raúl Alfonsín's economic policies initially struck in bold new directions. He forced the International Monetary Fund to renegotiate Argentina's huge multi-billion-dollar debt in a context more favorable to Argentina, and he was determined to bring order out of chaos.

One of his most difficult problems centered on the trials for human-rights abuses against the nation's former military rulers. According to *Latin American Regional Reports*, Alfonsín chose to "distinguish degrees of responsibility" in taking court action against those who conducted the Dirty War. Impressively, Alfonsín put on trial the highest authorities, to be followed by action against those identified as responsible for major excesses.

Almost immediately, however, extreme right-wing nationalist officers in the armed forces opposed the trials and engineered a series of mutinies that undermined the stability of the administration. In 1987, during the Easter holiday, a rebellion of dissident soldiers made its point, and the Argentine Congress passed legislation that limited the prosecution of officers who killed civilians during the Dirty War to those only at the highest levels. Mini-mutinies in 1988 resulted in further concessions to the mutineers by the Alfonsín government, including reorganization of the army high command and higher wages.

Political scientist Gary Wynia aptly observed: "The army's leadership is divided between right-wing officers willing to challenge civilian authorities with force and more romantic officers who derive gratification from doing so. Many of the latter refuse to accept the contention that they are 'equal' to civilians, claiming that they have a special role that prevents their subordination to civilian authorities." To this day, the Argentine military has come to terms neither with itself nor with democratic government.

Carlos Menem was supported by the military in the presidential election of May 1989, with perhaps 80 percent of the officer corps casting their votes for the Peronist Party. Menem adopted a policy of rapprochement with the military, which included the 1990 pardon of former junta members convicted of human-rights abuses. Historian Peter Calvert argues that Menem chose the path of amnesty because elements in the armed forces "would not be content until they got it." Rebellious middle-rank officers were well

disposed toward Peronists, and Menem's pardon was "a positive gain in terms of the acceptance of the Peronists among the military themselves." In essence, then, Menem's military policy was consistent with other policies in terms of its pragmatic core. And the military seems to have been contained; military spending has been halved, the army has been reduced from 100,000 to 20,000 soldiers, military enterprises have been divested, and mandatory service has been abandoned in favor of a professional force.

Significant progress has been made with regard to "disappeared" people. In 1992, President Menem agreed to create a commission to deal with the problem of children of the disappeared who were adopted by other families. Many have had their true identities established as a result of the patient work of "The Grandmothers of the Plaza de Mayo" and by the technique of cross-generational genetic analysis. (In 1998, former junta chief Admiral Emilio Massera was arrested on charges of kidnapping—that is, the distribution to families of babies born to victims of the regime.) In 1995, the names of an additional 1,000 people were added to the official list of the missing. Also, a retired military officer revealed his part in pushing drugged prisoners out of planes over the South Atlantic Ocean.

ECONOMIC TRAVAIL

The Argentine economy under President Alfonsín was virtually out of control. Inflation soared. The sorry state of the economy and spreading dissatisfaction among the electorate forced the president to hand over power to Carlos Menem six months early.

ACHIEVEMENTS

Argentine citizens have won four Nobel Prizes—two for peace and one each for chemistry and medicine. The nation's authors— Jorge Luis Borges, Julio Cortazar, Manuel Puig, and Ricardo Guiraldes, to name only a few—are world-famous.

Menem's new government worked a bit of an economic miracle, despite an administration nagged by corruption and early policy indecision, which witnessed the appointment of 21 ministers to nine cabinet positions during his first 18 months in office. In Menem's favor, he was not an ideologue but, rather, an adept politician whose acceptance by the average voter was equaled by his ability to do business with almost anyone. He quickly identified the source of much of Argentina's chronic inflation: the state-owned enterprises. From the time of Perón, these industries were regarded as wellsprings of employment and cronyism rather than as instruments for the production of goods or the delivery of services such as electric power and telephone service. "Ironically," says Luigi Manzetti, writing in *North-South FOCUS*, "it took a Peronist like Menem to dismantle Perón's legacy." While Menem's presidential campaign stressed "traditional Peronist themes like social justice and government investments" to revive the depressed economy, once he was in power, "having inherited a bankrupt state and under pressure from foreign banks and domestic business circles to enact a stiff adjustment program, Menem reversed his stand." He embraced the market-oriented policies of his political adversaries, "only in a much harsher fashion." State-owned enterprises were sold off in rapid-fire order. Argentina thus underwent a rapid transformation, from one of the world's most closed economies to one of the most open.

Economic growth began again in 1991, but the social costs were high. Thousands of public-sector workers lost their jobs; a third of Argentina's population lived below the poverty line, and the gap between the rich and poor tended to increase. But both inflation and the debt were eventually contained, foreign investment increased, and confidence began to return to Argentina.

In November 1993, former president Alfonsín supported a constitutional reform that allowed Menem to serve another term. Menem accepted some checks on executive power, including reshuffling the Supreme Court, placing members of the political opposition in charge of certain state offices, creating a post similar to that of prime minister, awarding a third senator to each province, and shortening the presidential term from six to four years. With these reforms in place, Menem easily won another term in 1995.

Convinced that his mandate should not end with the conclusion of his second term, Menem lobbied hard in 1998 for yet another constitutional reform to allow him to run again. This was not supported by the Supreme Court.

The Radical Party won the elections in 1999. Almost immediately President Fernando de la Rua confronted an economy mired in a deepening recession. Rising unemployment, a foreign debt that stood at 50 percent of gross domestic product, and fears of a debt default prompted the government to announce tax increases and spending cuts to meet IMF debt targets. At the end of 2001, the economic crisis triggered rioting

in the streets and brought down the de la Rua administration and three others that followed in rapid succession.

By the end of 2002 the economy was in such shambles that some provinces began to issue their own currencies, farmers resorted to barter—exchanging soy beans for agricultural equipment—and many Argentines seriously considered emigration. Crime rates rose and people lost faith in governments that seemed incapable of positive policies and all-to-susceptible to corruption.

This dismal picture began to change with the election of Néstor Kirchner in May 2003. During his first year in office he called on Congress to begin impeachment proceedings against the widely hated Supreme Court. The justices were accused of producing verdicts that reflected payoffs and political favors. Kirchner also laid siege to Argentina's security forces: he ordered more than 50 admirals and generals into early retirement and dismissed 80 percent of the high command of the notoriously corrupt Federal Police.

Finally, after years of severe malaise, the economy began to turn around in 2003. Kirchner noted that the IMF had abandoned Argentina in 2001 as its economy spiraled downward. Consequently the Argentine president, in the words of *New York Times* reporter Tony Smith, "felt justified in resolutely refusing to make a series of concessions that negotiators for the monetary fund wanted in exchange for refinancing $21.6 billion in debt that Argentina owes to multilateral institutions…" In March 2005, President Kirchner announced a debt settlement that paid the nation's creditors as little as 30 cents on the dollar. Argentina, in effect, worked out a deal in accord with Argentine economic realities.

FOREIGN POLICY

The Argentine government's foreign policy has usually been determined by realistic appraisals of the nation's best interests. From 1946, the country moved between the two poles of pro-West and nonaligned. President Menem firmly supported the foreign-policy initiatives of the United States and the UN. Argentine participation in the Persian Gulf War and the presence of Argentine troops under United Nations command in Croatia, Somalia, and other trouble spots paid dividends: Washington agreed to supply Argentina with military supplies for the first time since the Falklands War in 1982. President Kirchner has assumed an independent posture. The U.S. invasion of Iraq was cast as a violation of

international law and Argentina has moved closer to Latin American regimes not in the good graces of Washington, that is, Brazil, Venezuela, and Cuba.

President Kirchner, having stood up to the demands of the IMF, has now moved steadily away from Washington's free trade agenda. He has also moved closer to Hugo Chávez of Venezuela and signed a series of economic agreements. By identifying with populist leaders in South America Kirchner has established Argentina's independence from the United States; it may also be seen as an attempt to become a more popular leader himself at home.

ARGENTINA'S FUTURE

Renewed confidence in government and economic recovery auger well for Argentina. Experts predict a 4 percent annual growth from 2004 to 2006 while inflation should decline from double digits to about 7 percent.

Timeline: PAST

1536
Pedro de Mendoza establishes the first settlement at Buenos Aires

1816
Independence of Spain

1865–1870
War with Paraguay

1912
Electoral reform: Compulsory male suffrage

1946–1955 and **1973–1974**
Juan Perón is in power

1976–1982
The Dirty War

1980s
War with Great Britain over the Falkland Islands; military mutinies and economic chaos

1990s
Economic crises in Mexico, Russia, and Asia slow the economy

PRESENT

2000s
Argentina Struggles to climb out of recession

Néstor Kirchner elected president in May 2003

2005–2006
Argentina moves to the left

Bolivia (Republic of Bolivia)

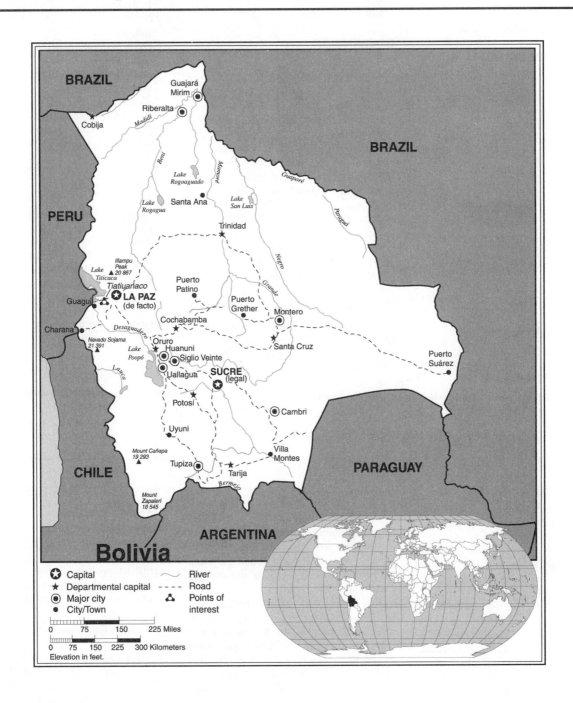

Map legend:
- ☆ Capital
- ★ Departmental capital
- ◉ Major city
- ● City/Town
- ～ River
- - - - Road
- ⌂ Points of interest

0   75   150   225 Miles
0   75   150   225   300 Kilometers
Elevation in feet.

Bolivia Statistics

GEOGRAPHY

Area in Square Miles (Kilometers): 424,162 (1,098,160) (about 3 times the size of Montana)

Capital (Population): La Paz (de facto) (740,000); Sucre (legal)

Environmental Concerns: deforestation; soil erosion; desertification; loss of biodiversity; water pollution

Geographical Features: rugged Andes Mountains with a highland plateau (Altiplano), hills, lowland plains of the Amazon Basin

Climate: varies with altitude; from humid and tropical to semiarid and cold

PEOPLE

Population

Total: 8,724,156

Annual Growth Rate: 1.56%
Rural/Urban Population Ratio: 39/61
Major Languages: Spanish; Quechua; Aymara
Ethnic Makeup: 30% Quechua; 25% Aymara; 30% Mestizo; 15% white
Religions: 95% Roman Catholic; Protestant

Health

Life Expectancy at Birth: 65 years (male); 67 years (female)
Infant Mortality Rate (Ratio): 60.4/1,000
Physicians Available (Ratio): 1/3,663

Education

Adult Literacy Rate: 87.2%
Compulsory (Ages): 6–14; free

COMMUNICATION

Telephones: 563,900 main lines
Daily Newspaper Circulation: 69 per 1,000 people
Televisions: 202 per 1,000
Internet Users: 270,000

TRANSPORTATION

Highways in Miles (Kilometers): 32,426 (52,216)
Railroads in Miles (Kilometers): 2,292 (3,691)
Usable Airfields: 1,109
Motor Vehicles in Use: 432,000

GOVERNMENT

Type: republic
Independence Date: August 6, 1825 (from Spain)
Head of State/Government: President Evo Morales is both head of state and head of government
Political Parties: Movement Toward Socialism; Free Bolivia Movement; Revolutionary Front of the Left; Nationalist Revolutionary Movement; Christian Democratic Party; Nationalist Democratic Action; popular Patriotic Movement; Unity and Progress Movement; many others
Suffrage: universal and compulsory at 18 if married, at 21 if single

MILITARY

Military Expenditures (% of GDP): 1.6%
Current Disputes: dispute with Chile over water rights; seeks sovereign corridor to the South Pacific Ocean

ECONOMY

Currency ($U.S. Equivalent): 7.66 bolivianos = $1
Per Capita Income/GDP: $2,400/$20.88 billion
GDP Growth Rate: 2.1%
Inflation Rate: 2.1%
Unemployment Rate: 7.6%; substantial underemployment
Labor Force: 2,500,000
Natural Resources: tin; natural gas; petroleum; zinc; tungsten; antimony; silver; iron; lead; gold; timber; hydropower
Agriculture: soybeans; coffee; coca; cotton; corn; sugarcane; rice; potatoes; timber
Industry: mining; smelting, petroleum; food and beverages; tobacco; handicrafts; clothing
Exports: $1.5 billion (primary partners United Kingdom, United States, Peru)
Imports: $1.6 billion (primary partners United States, Japan, Brazil)

SUGGESTED WEBSITE

http://www.cia.gov/cia/
publications/factbook/geos/
bl.html

Bolivia Country Report

BOLIVIA: AN INDIAN NATION

Until recently, the images of Bolivia captured by the world's press were uniformly negative. Human-rights abuses were rampant, a corrupt and brutal military government was deeply involved in cocaine trafficking, and the nation was approaching bankruptcy.

Other images might include Bolivia's complex society. So intermixed has this multiethnic culture become that one's race is defined by one's social status. So-called whites, who look very much like the Indians with whom their ancestors intermarried, form the upper classes only because of their economic, social, and cultural positions—that is, the degree to which they have embraced European culture.

DEVELOPMENT

Bolivia's economic development stalled as a result of indigenous demands with regard to basic rights.

Another enduring image fixed in the literature is Bolivia's political instability.

The actual number of governments over the past 200 years is about 80, however, and not the 200 commonly noted. Indeed, elected governments have been in power for the past two decades. What outsiders perceive as typical Latin American political behavior clouds what is unusual and positive about Bolivia.

One nineteenth-century leader, Manuel Belzu, played an extremely complex role that combined the forces of populism, nationalism, and revolution. Belzu encouraged the organization of the first trade unions, abolished slavery, promoted land reform, and praised Bolivia's Indian past.

In 1952, a middle-class–led and popularly supported revolution swept the country. The ensuing social, economic, and political reforms, while not erasing an essentially dual society of "whites" and Indians, did significantly ease the level of exploitation. Most of the export industries, including those involved with natural resources, were nationalized. Bolivia's evolution—at times progressive, at times regressive—continues to reflect the impulse for change.

THE SOCIETY: POSITIVE AND NEGATIVE ASPECTS

Bolivia, despite the rapid and startling changes that have occurred in the recent past, remains an extremely poor society. In terms of poverty, life expectancy, death rates, and per capita income, the country ranks among the worst in the Western Hemisphere.

Rights for women have made slow progress, even in urban areas. In 1975, a woman was appointed to the Bolivian Supreme Court; and in 1979, the Bolivian Congress elected Lidia Gueiler Tejada, leader of the lower house, as president. Long a supporter of women's rights, Tejada had drafted and pushed through Congress a bill that created a government ministry to provide social benefits for women and children. That remarkably advanced legislation has not guaranteed that women enjoy a social status equal to that of men, however. Furthermore, many women are likely unaware of their rights under the law.

Bolivia's press is reasonably free, although many journalists are reportedly paid by politicians, drug traffickers, and

(Courtesy of Jorge Tutor/tutor_bol1)

Bolivia has a complex society, tremendously affected by the continued interplay of multiethnic cultures. The influence of indigenous peoples on Bolivia remains strong.

officials to increase their exposure or suppress negative stories. A few journalists who experienced repression under previous governments still practice self-censorship.

URBANIZATION

Santa Cruz has been transformed in the last 50 years from an isolated backwater into a modern city with links to the other parts of the country and to the rest of South America. From a population of 42,000 in 1950, the number of inhabitants quickly rose to half a million in the mid-1980s and is now growing at the rate of about 8 percent a year. Bolivia's second largest city, its population now exceeds that of the de facto capital, La Paz.

Most of the city's population growth has been the result of rural-to-urban migration, a phenomenon closely studied by geographer Gil Green. On paper, Santa Cruz is a planned city, but, since the 1950s, there has been a running battle between city planners and new settlers wanting land. "Due to the very high demand for cheap land and the large amount of flat, empty, nonvaluable land surrounding it, the city has tended to expand by a process of land invasion and

squatting. Such invasions are generally overtly or covertly organized by political parties seeking electoral support of the low-income population." In the wake of a successful "invasion," the land is divided into plots that are allocated to the squatters, who then build houses from whatever materials are at hand. Then begins the lengthy process of settlement consolidation and regularization of land tenure. Once again the new land is subdivided and sold cheaply to the low-income population.

FREEDOM

 A corrupt judicial system, overcrowded prisons, and violence and discrimination against women and indigenous peoples are perennial problems in Bolivia, despite protective legislation.

Perhaps the pace of urbanization as a result of internal migration is most pronounced in El Alto, which hardly existed on maps 30 years ago. It is now a "city" of 700,000 and overlooks La Paz. The rapid growth actually reflects a profound crisis in Bolivia. Tens of thousands of Aymara and Quechua-speaking miners and peasant

farmers have been driven to El Alto by their inability to make a living in rural areas. Over the past five years it has become, in the works of a local newspaper editor, "the capital of social protest in Bolivia." In fact, a rebellion centered in El Alto succeeded in driving President Gonzalo Sánchez from power in 2003 and threatened to do the same to his successor, Carlos Mesa.

The character of what has been termed the "Ideology of Fury" is complex and springs from a broad range of contexts. Perhaps most important, Bolivia's indigenous majority has suffered centuries of neglect and abuse. President Mesa noted as much when he explained the uprising as an "eruption of deeply held positions, over many centuries, that have been accumulating." There appear to have been two more immediate catalysts: U.S. insistence on the eradication of coca and the government's proposal to export natural gas to the United States through the construction of a pipeline to Chile.

With respect to coca cultivation, Bolivian politicians for years have promised to put an end to the trade and substitute other crops such as pineapples, coffee, black pepper, oregano, and passion fruit. Unfortunately most of the government's efforts were put on eradication and not alternative development. The United States, according to economist Jeffrey Sachs, "has constantly made demands on an impoverished country without any sense of reality or an economic framework and strategy to help them in development." The net result was the impoverishment of thousands of peasant farmers, who have since migrated to El Alto and become the taproot of the "Ideology of Fury." Indigenous uprisings first backed program of coca eradication. What is not appreciated by Washington and Bolivian politicians who are fearful of losing U.S. aid money, is that coca is central to indigenous culture. Certainly much is exported in the form of coca paste or cocaine. In the 1990s it was calculated that illegal exports contributed the equivalent of 13 to 15 percent of Bolivia's gross domestic product and that coca by-products accounted for as much as 40 percent of total exports, both legal and illicit. Today, about 400,000 Bolivians are estimated to live off coca and cocaine production. U.S. wishes run afoul of the multifaceted heritage of coca, the sacred plant of the Incas. There is virtually no activity in domestic, social, or religious life in which coca does not play a role; thus, attempts to limit its cultivation have had profound repercussions among the peasantry.

HEALTH/WELFARE

Provisions against child labor in Bolivia are frequently ignored; many children may be found shining shoes, selling lottery tickets, and as street vendors.

Indigenous resistance to coca eradication now centers on Evo Morales, the head of the coca growers' federation, who emerged victorious in the presidential elections of 2005. Morales's new party, the Movement Toward Socialism, will push for modification of the laws against coca cultivation, regardless of the wishes of the United States. "There has to be a change, to a policy that is truly Bolivian, not one that is imposed by foreigners with the pretext that eradication will put an end to narcotics trafficking," said a member of Congress

and an ally of Morales. The president-elect himself coined the phrase: "Yes to coca, no to cocaine."

ACHIEVEMENTS

The Bolivian author Armando Chirveches, in his political novel *La Candidatura de Rojas* (1909), produced one of the best examples of this genre in all of Latin America. The book captures the politics of the late nineteenth century extraordinarily well.

The second catalyst involved the proposed gas pipeline. While there are good historical reasons for Bolivian antipathy towards Chile (Chile deprived Bolivia its access to the Pacific as a result of territorial adjustments following the War of the Pacific in 1879–1880), resistance to the pipeline also has a social dimension. As reported in *The New York Times*, a Chilean pollster noted: "Part of the democratic process is assuring that people are going to get a piece of the cake, and that has been lacking in Bolivia. Bolivians are suspicious of whoever is making the deal because they think the "elite always puts money in its own pockets, and we are left on the streets with nothing to eat." Regionalism also plays a role in the controversy. Gas-producing regions, those with large deposits of lithium, and even farmers in Santa Cruz who have experienced a boom in soybean exports, now demand a significant voice in the distribution of the wealth they produce as well as a degree of autonomy from La Paz.

The success of the indigenous majority in Bolivia in toppling one government and then winning the presidency has both emboldened their leaders, who relish their new found power, and awakened a sense of racial pride among the Aymara and Quechua. As one unemployed carpenter told reporter Larry Rohter: "They may still say that we are only Indians, but now we can see what is happening and what the Aymara nation can do when it is united."

President Morales will now have to put his rhetoric into action if he is to mollify

the demands of an awakened and angry indigenous population. It will be impossible for Bolivia to develop its extensive natural resources in the face of an indigenous and regional resistance that does not take into account their needs. If the government can link development to the creation of jobs, if it finally begins to deliver on years of unfulfilled promises with regard to health care and education, and if it can pursue a coca policy that respects the culture of the majority of the population and stems from Bolivian reality and not Washington's wishes, then perhaps a modus vivendi can be reached. If not, the future will bring further economic malaise and political upheaval.

Brazil (Federative Republic of Brazil)

Brazil Statistics

GEOGRAPHY

Area in Square Miles (Kilometers):
3,285,670 (8,512,100) (slightly smaller than the United States)
Capital (Population): Brasília (1,738,000)

Environmental Concerns: deforestation; water and air pollution; land degradation

Geographical Features: mostly flat to rolling lowlands in the north; some

plains, hills, mountains, and a narrow coastal belt

Climate: mostly tropical or semitropical; temperate zone in the south

PEOPLE*

Population

Total: 184,101,109

Annual Growth Rate: 1.11%

Rural/Urban Population Ratio: 21/79

Ethnic Makeup: 55% white; 38% mixed; 6% black; 1% others

Major Languages: Portuguese; Spanish; English; French

Religions: 70% nominal Roman Catholic; 30% others

Health

Life Expectancy at Birth: 67 years (male); 75 years (female)

Infant Mortality Rate (Ratio): 30.66/1,000

Physicians Available (Ratio): 1/681

Education

Adult Literacy Rate: 86.4%

Compulsory (Ages): 7–14; free

COMMUNICATION

Telephones: 38.81 million main lines

Daily Newspaper Circulation: 47 per 1,000 people

Televisions: 193 per 1,000 people

Internet Users: 14.3 million

TRANSPORTATION

Highways in Miles (Kilometers): 1,229,580 (1,980,000)

Railroads in Miles (Kilometers): 16,702 (26,895)

Usable Airfields: 3,277

Motor Vehicles in Use: 18,030,000

GOVERNMENT

Type: federal republic

Independence Date: September 7, 1822 (from Portugal)

Head of State/Government: President Luiz Inacio "Lula" Da Silva is both head of state and head of government

Political Parties: Brazilian Democratic Movement Party; Liberal Front Party; Workers' Party; Brazilian Workers' Party; Democratic Labor Party; Popular Socialist Party; Liberal Party; others

Suffrage: voluntary at 16; compulsory between 19 and 70; voluntary over 70

MILITARY

Military Expenditures (% of GDP): 2.1%

Current Disputes: boundary disputes with Uruguay

ECONOMY

Currency ($U.S. Equivalent): 3.08 reals = $1

Per Capita Income/GDP: $7,600/$1.38 trillion

GDP Growth Rate: 0.1%

Inflation Rate: 9.3%

Unemployment Rate: 12.2%

Labor Force: 74,000,000

Natural Resources: bauxite; gold; iron ore; manganese; nickel; phosphates; platinum; tin; uranium; petroleum; hydropower; timber

Agriculture: coffee; rice; corn; sugarcane; soybeans; cotton; manioc; oranges

Industry: textiles; shoes; chemicals; cement; lumber; iron ore; tin; steel; aircraft; motor vehicles and parts; other machinery and equipment

Exports: $73.3 billion (primary partners United States, Argentina, Germany)

Imports: $48.7 billion (primary partners United States, Argentina, Germany)

SUGGESTED WEBSITE

http://www.cia.gov/cia/
publications/factbook/geos/
br.html

*Note: Estimates explicitly take into account the effects of excess mortality due to AIDS.

Brazil Country Report

BRAZIL: A TROUBLED GIANT

In 1977, Brazilian president Ernesto Geisel stated that progress was based on "an integrated process of political, social, and economic development." Democracy, he argued, was the first necessity in the political arena. But democracy could only be achieved "if we also further social development…, if we raise the standard of living of Brazilians." The standard of living, he continued, "can only be raised through economic development."

It was clear from his remarks that the three broad objectives of democratization, social progress, and economic development were interconnected. He could not conceive of democracy in a poor country or in a country where there were "gaps, defects, and inadequacies in the social realm."

CONCEPTS OF PROGRESS

Geisel's comments offer a framework within which to consider not only the cur-

rent situation in Brazil but also historical trends that reach back to the late nineteenth century—and, in some instances, to Portugal. Historically, most Brazilians have believed that progress would take place within the context of a strong, authoritarian state. In the nineteenth century, for example, a reform-minded elite adapted European theories of modernization that called for government-sponsored changes. The masses would receive benefits from the state; in this way, the elite reasoned, pressure for change from the poorer sectors of society would be eliminated. There would be progress with order. *Ordem e Progresso* ("Order and Progress") is the motto that graces the Brazilian flag; the motto is as appropriate today as it was in 1889, when the flag first flew over the new republic.

The tension among modernization, social equity, and order and liberty was first obvious in the early 1920s, when politically isolated middle-class groups united with junior military officers (*tenentes*) to chal-

lenge an entrenched ruling class of coffee-plantation owners. By the mid-1920s, the tenentes, bent on far-reaching reforms, conceived a new role for themselves. With a faith that bordered at times on the mystical and a philosophy that embraced change in the vaguest of terms, they felt that only the military could shake Brazil from its lethargy and force it to modernize. Their program demanded the ouster of conservative, tradition-minded politicians; an economic transformation of the nation; and, eventually, a return to strong, centralized constitutional rule. The tenentes also proposed labor reforms that included official recognition of trade unions, a minimum wage and maximum workweek, restraints on child labor, land reform, nationalization of natural resources, and a radical expansion of educational facilities. Although the tenentes were frustrated in their attempts to mold policy, many of their reforms were taken up by Getulio Vargas, who seized power in 1930 and imposed a strong, authoritarian state on Brazil.

Certain areas of Brazil attract enormous numbers of visitors from all over the world. This beach in Rio de Janeiro has one of the most famous skylines in South America.

THE 1964 REVOLUTION

In some respects, the goals of the tenentes were echoed in 1964, when a broad coalition of civilians—frustrated by an economy that seemed to be disintegrating, concerned with the "leftist" slant of the government of João Goulart, and worried about a social revolution that might well challenge the status and prestige of the wealthy and the middle classes—called on the military to impose order on the country.

The military leaders did not see their intervention as just another coup but, rather, as a revolution. They foresaw change but believed that it would be dictated from above. Government was highly centralized, the traditional parties were virtually frozen out of the political process, and the military and police ruthlessly purged Brazil of elements considered "leftist" or "subversive." (The terms were used interchangeably.) Order and authority triumphed over liberty and freedom. The press was muzzled, and human-rights abuses were rampant.

Brazil's economic recovery eventually began to receive attention. The military gave economic growth and national security priority over social programs and political

liberalization. Until the effects of the oil crisis generated by the Organization of Petroleum Exporting Countries (OPEC) in 1973 began to be felt, the recovery of the Brazilian economy was dubbed a "miracle," with growth rates averaging 10 percent a year.

The benefits of that growth went primarily to the upper and middle classes, who enjoyed the development of industries based largely on consumer goods. Moreover, Brazil's industrialization was flawed. It was heavily dependent on foreign investment, foreign technology, and foreign markets. It required large investments in machinery and equipment but needed little labor, and it damaged the environment through pollution of the rivers and air around industrial centers. Agriculture was neglected to the point that even basic foodstuffs had to be imported.

THE IMPACT OF RURAL-TO-URBAN MIGRATION

The stress on industrialization tremendously increased rural-to-urban migration and complicated the government's ability to keep up with the expanded need for public health and social services. In 1970,

nearly 56 percent of the population were concentrated in urban areas; by the late 1990s, 79 percent of the population were so classified. These figures also illustrate the inadequacies of an agrarian program based essentially on a "moving frontier." Peasants evicted from their plots have run out of new lands to exploit, unless they move to the inhospitable Amazon region. As a result, many have been attracted by the cities.

The pressure of the poor on the cities, severe shortages of staple foods, and growing tension in rural areas over access to the land forced the government to act. In 1985, the civilian government of José Sarney announced an agrarian-reform plan to distribute millions of acres of unused private land to peasants. Implementation of the reform was not easy, and confrontations between peasants and landowners occurred.

MILITARY RULE IS CHALLENGED

Nineteen seventy-four was a crucial year for the military government of Brazil. The virtual elimination of the urban-guerrilla threat challenged the argument that demo-

71

(United Nations Photo/UN152113)

By the late 1980s, agrarian reforms that were designed to establish peasants in plots of workable land had caused the depletion of Brazilian jungle and, as space and opportunities diminished, there was a large movement of these people to the cities. The profound urban crowding in Brazil is illustrated by this photo of a section of Rio de Janeiro.

cratic institutions could not be restored because of national security concerns.

Pressure grew from other quarters as well. Many middle- and upper-class Brazilians were frightened by the huge state-controlled sector in the economy that had been carved out by the generals. The military's determination to promote the rapid development of the nation's resources, to control all industries deemed vital to the nation's security, and to compete with multinational corporations concerned Brazil-

ian businesspeople, who saw their role in the economy decreasing.

Challenges to the military regime also came from the Roman Catholic Church, which attacked the government for its brutal violations of human rights and constantly called for economic and social justice. One Brazilian bishop publicly called the government "sinful" and in "opposition to the plans of God" and noted that it was the Church's moral and religious obligation to fight it. After 1974, as Brazil's

economic difficulties mounted, the chorus of complaints grew insistent.

THE RETURN OF DEMOCRACY

The relaxation of political repression was heralded by two laws passed in 1979. The Amnesty Bill allowed for the return of hundreds of political exiles; the Party Reform Bill in essence reconstructed Brazilian politics. Under the provisions of the Party Reform Bill, new political parties could be established—provided they were repre-

sented in nine states and in 20 percent of the counties of those states. The new parties were granted the freedom to formulate political platforms, as long as they were not ideological and did not favor any single economic class. The Communist Party was outlawed, and the creation of a workers' party was expressly forbidden. (Communist parties were legalized again in 1985.)

DEVELOPMENT

Since 2000 trade with China has tripled. China is now Brazil's fourth largest market. The bulk of the trade consists of soya beans, iron ore, and steel.

The law against the establishment of a workers' party reflected the regime's concern that labor, increasingly anxious about the state of the economy, might withdraw its traditional support for the state. Organized labor had willingly cooperated with the state since the populist regime of Getulio Vargas (1937–1945). For Brazilian workers in the 1930s, the state was their "patron," the source of benefits. This dependence on the government, deeply rooted in Portuguese political culture, replaced the formation of a more independent labor movement and minimized industrial conflict. The state played the role of mediator between workers and management. President Vargas led the workers to believe that the state was the best protector of their interests. (Polls have indicated that Brazilian workers still cling to that belief.)

If workers expect benefits from the state, however, the state must then honor those expectations and allocate sufficient resources to assure labor's loyalty. A deep economic crisis, such as the one that occurred in the early 1960s and again in the early 1990s, endangers the state's control of labor. In 1964, organized labor supported the coup, because workers felt that the civilian regime had failed to perform its protective function. This phenomenon also reveals the extremely shallow soil in which Brazilian democracy has taken root.

Organized labor tends not to measure Brazilian governments in political terms, but within the context of the state's ability to address labor's needs. For the rank-and-file worker, it is a question not of democracy or military authoritarianism, but of bread and butter. President Sarney, in an effort to keep labor loyal to the government, sought the support of union leaders for a proposal to create a national pact with businesspeople, workers, and his government. But pervasive corruption, inefficient government, and a continuing economic crisis eventually eroded the legitimacy of

the elites and favored nontraditional parties in the 1989 election. The candidacy of Luís Inácio da Silva, popularly known as Lula and leader of the Workers' Party, "was stunning evidence of the Brazilian electorate's dissatisfaction with the conduct of the country's transition to democracy and with the political class in general." He lost the election by a very narrow margin. In 2002, he won the election and promised to "end hunger."

Workers continue to regard the state as the source of benefits, as do other Brazilians. Many social reformers, upset with the generals for their neglect of social welfare, believe that social reform should be dispensed from above by a strong and paternalistic state. Change is possible, even welcome—but it must be the result of compromise and conciliation, not confrontation or nonnegotiable demands.

THE NEW CONSTITUTION

The *abertura* (political liberalization) of Brazil climaxed in January 1985 with the election of President Sarney, a civilian, following 21 years of military rule. Importantly, the Brazilian military promised to respect the Constitution and promised a policy of nonintervention in the political process. In 1987, however, with the draft of a new constitution under discussion, the military strongly protested language that removed its responsibility for internal law and order and restricted the military's role to that of defense of the nation against external threats. According to *Latin American Regional Reports: Brazil*, the military characterized the draft constitution as "confused, inappropriate, at best a parody of a constitution, just as Frankenstein was a gross and deformed imitation of a human being."

Military posturing aside, the new Constitution went into effect in October 1988. It reflects the input of a wide range of interests: The Constituent Assembly—which also served as Brazil's Congress—heard testimony and suggestions from Amazonian Indians, peasants, and urban poor as well as from rich landowners and the military. The 1988 Constitution is a document that captures the byzantine character of Brazilian politics and influence peddling and reveals compromises made by conservative and liberal vested interests.

The military's fears about its role in internal security were removed when the Constituent Assembly voted constitutional provisions to grant the right of the military independently to ensure law and order, a responsibility it historically has claimed. But Congress also arrogated to itself the responsibility for appropriating federal mon-

ies. This is important, because it gives Congress a powerful check on both the military and the executive office.

FREEDOM

Violence against street children, indigenous peoples, homosexuals, and common criminals at the hands of the police, landowners, vigilante groups, gangs, and hired thugs is commonplace. Homicide committed by police is the third-leading cause of death among children and adolescents. Investigation of such crimes is lax and prosecution of the perpetrators sporadic. Indians continue to clash with miners and landowners.

Nationalists won several key victories. The Constituent Assembly created the concept of "a Brazilian company of national capital" that can prevent foreigners from engaging in mining, oil-exploration risk contracts, and biotechnology. Brazilian-controlled companies were also given preference in the supply of goods and services to local, state, and national governments. Legislation reaffirmed and strengthened the principle of government intervention in the economy should national security or the collective interest be at issue.

Conservative congressional representatives were able to prevail in matters of land reform. They defeated a proposal that would have allowed the compulsory appropriation of property for land reform. Although a clause that addressed the "social function" of land was included in the Constitution, it was clear that powerful landowners and agricultural interests had triumphed over Brazil's landless peasantry.

In other areas, however, the Constitution is remarkably progressive on social and economic issues. The workweek was reduced to a maximum of 44 hours, profit sharing was established for all employees, time-and-a-half was promised for overtime work, and paid vacations were to include a bonus of 30 percent of one's monthly salary. Day-care facilities were to be established for all children under age six, maternity leave of four months and paternity leave of five days were envisaged, and workers were protected against "arbitrary dismissal." The Constitution also introduced a series of innovations that would increase significantly the ability of Brazilians to claim their guaranteed rights before the nation's courts and ensure the protection of human rights, particularly the rights of Indians and peasants involved in land disputes.

Despite the ratification of the 1988 Constitution, a functioning Congress, and an independent judiciary, the focus of power in Brazil is still the president. A legislative majority in the hands of the opposition in no way erodes the executive's ability to govern as he or she chooses. Any measure introduced by the president automatically becomes law after 40 days, even without congressional action. Foreign observers perceive "weaknesses" in the new parties, which in actuality are but further examples of well-established political practices. The parties are based on personalities rather than issues, platforms are vague, goals are so broad that they are almost illusions, and party organization conforms to traditional alliances and the "rules" of patronage. Democratic *forms* are in place in Brazil; the *substance* remains to be realized.

The election of President Fernando Collor de Mello, who assumed office in March 1990, proves the point. As political scientist Margaret Keck explains, Collor fit well into a "traditional conception of elite politics, characterized by fluid party identifications, the predominance of personal relations, a distrust of political institutions, and reliance on charismatic and populist appeals to *o povo*, the people." Unfortunately, such a system is open to abuse; revelations of widespread corruption that reached all the way to the presidency brought down Collor's government in 1992 and gave Brazilian democracy its most difficult challenge to date. Populist President Lula da Silva's government has also been increasingly dogged by charges of corruption. In September 2005 thousands of protesters, including workers, students, and businessmen took to the streets and accused the ruling Workers Party of bribing lawmakers and complicity in illicit campaign funding. Such scandals bring to light a range of strengths and weaknesses that presents insights into the Brazilian political system.

THE PRESS AND THE PRESIDENCY

Brazil's press was severely censored and harassed from the time of the military coup of 1964 until 1982. Not until passage of the Constitution of 1988 was the right of free speech and a free press guaranteed. It was the press, and in particular the news magazine *Veja*, that opened the door to President Collor's impeachment. In the words of *World Press Review*, "Despite government pressure to ease off, the magazine continued to uncover the president's malfeasance, tugging hard at the threads of Collor's unraveling administration. As others in the media followed suit, Congress was forced to begin an investigation and, in the end, indict Collor." The importance of the event to Brazil's press, according to *Veja* editor Mario Sergio Conti, is that "It

will emerge with fewer illusions about power and be more rigorous. Reporting has been elevated to a higher plane…."

While the failure of Brazil's first directly elected president in 29 years was tragic, it should not be interpreted as the demise of Brazilian democracy. Importantly, according to Brazilian journalist Carlos Eduardo Lins da Silva, writing in *Current History*, many "Brazilians and outside observers saw the workings of the impeachment process as a sign of the renewed strength of democratic values in Brazilian society. They were also seen as a healthy indicator of growing intolerance to corruption in public officials."

The military, despite persistent rumors of a possible coup, has to date allowed the constitutional process to dictate events. For the first time, most civilians do not see the generals as part of the solution to political shortcomings. But many Brazilians still assume that most politicians are "crooked."

THE RIGHTS OF WOMEN AND CHILDREN

Major changes in Brazilian households have occurred over the last decade as the number of women in the workforce has dramatically increased. In 1990, just over 35 percent of women were in the workforce, and the number was expected to grow. As a result, many women are limiting the size of their families. More than 20 percent use birth-control pills, and Brazil is second only to China in the percentage of women who have been sterilized. The traditional family of 5.0 or more children has shrunk to an average of 3.4. With two wage earners, the standard of living has risen slightly for some families. Many homes now have electricity and running water. Television sales increased by more than 1,000 percent in the last decade.

HEALTH/WELFARE

The quality of education in Brazil varies greatly from state to state, in part because there is no system of national priorities. The uneven character of education has been a major factor in the maintenance of a society that is profoundly unequal. The provision of basic health needs remains poor, and land reform is a perennial issue.

In relatively affluent, economically and politically dynamic urban areas, women are more evident in the professions, education, industry, the arts, media, and political life. In rural areas, however, especially in the northeast, traditional cultural attitudes, which call upon women to be submissive, are still well entrenched.

Women are routinely subjected to physical abuse in Brazil. Americas Watch, an international human-rights group, reports that more than 70 percent of assault, rape, and murder cases take place in the home and that many incidents are unreported. Even though Brazil's Supreme Court struck down the outmoded concept of a man's "defense of honor," local courts routinely acquit men who kill unfaithful wives. Brazil, for all intents and purposes, is still a patriarchy.

Children are also in many cases denied basic rights. According to official statistics, almost 18 percent of children between the ages of 10 and 14 are in the labor force, and they often work in unhealthy or dangerous environments. Violence against urban street children has reached frightening proportions. Between January and June 1992, 167 minors were killed in Rio de Janeiro; 306 were murdered in São Paulo over the first seven months of the year. In July 1993, the massacre in a single night of seven street children in Rio de Janeiro resulted, for a time, in cries for an investigation of the matter. In February 1997, however, five children were murdered on the streets of Rio.

THE STATUS OF BLACKS

Scholars continue to debate the actual status of blacks in Brazil. Not long ago, an elected black member of Brazil's federal Congress blasted Brazilians for their racism. However, argues historian Bradford Burns, Brazil probably has less racial tension and prejudice than other multiracial societies.

A more formidable barrier, Burns says, may well be class. "Class membership depends on a wide variety of factors and their combination: income, family history and/or connections, education, social behavior, tastes in housing, food and dress, as well as appearance, personality and talent." But, he notes, "The upper class traditionally has been and still remains mainly white, the lower class principally colored." Upward mobility exists and barriers can be breached. But if such advancement depends upon a symbolic "whitening out," does not racism still exist?

This point is underscored by the 1988 celebration of the centennial of the abolition of slavery in Brazil. In sharp contrast to the government and Church emphasis on racial harmony and equality were the public protests by militant black groups claiming that Brazil's much-heralded "racial democracy" was a myth. In 1990, blacks earned 40 percent less than whites in the same professions.

(United Nations photo/Shelley Rotner/UN152106)

The status of blacks in Brazil is considered better than most other multiracial societies. The class structure is determined by a number of factors: income, family history, education, social behavior, cultural tastes, and talent. Still, the upper class remains mainly white, and the lower class principally of color.

THE INDIAN QUESTION

Brazil's estimated 200,000 Indians have suffered greatly in recent decades from the gradual encroachment of migrants from the heavily populated coastal regions and from government efforts to open the Amazon region to economic development. Highways have penetrated Indian lands, diseases for which the Indians have little or no immunity have killed thousands, and additional thousands have experienced a profound culture shock. Government efforts to protect the Indians have been largely ineffectual.

The two poles in the debate over the Indians are captured in the following excerpts from *Latin American Regional Reports: Brazil.* A Brazilian Army officer observed that the "United States solved the problem

with its army. They killed a lot of Indians. Today everything is quiet there, and the country is respected throughout the world." And in the words of a Kaingang Indian woman: "Today my people see their lands invaded, their forests destroyed, their animals exterminated and their hearts lacerated by this brutal weapon that is civilization."

Sadly, the assault against Brazil's Indian peoples has accelerated, and disputes over land have become more violent. One case speaks for itself. In the aftermath of a shooting incident in which several Yanomamö Indians were killed by prospectors, the Brazilian federal government declared that all outsiders would be removed from Yanomamö lands, ostensibly to protect the Indians. Those expelled by

the government included anthropologists, missionaries, doctors, and nurses. A large number of prospectors remained behind. By the end of 1988, while medical personnel had not been allowed back in, the number of prospectors had swelled to 50,000 in an area peopled by 9,000 Yanomamö. The Indians have been devastated by diseases, particularly malaria, and by mercury poisoning as a result of prospecting activities upriver from Yanomamö settlements. In 1991, cholera began to spread among indigenous Amazon peoples, due to medical waste dumped into rivers in cholera-ridden Peru and Ecuador.

The new Constitution devotes an entire chapter to the rights of Indians. For the first time in the country's history, Indians have the authority to bring suits in court to defend their rights and interests. In all such cases, they will be assisted by a public prosecutor. Even though the government established a large protected zone for Brazil's Yanomamö Indians in 1991, reports of confrontations between Indians and prospectors have persisted. There are also Brazilian nationalists who insist that a 150-mile-wide strip along the border with Venezuela be excluded from the reserve as a matter of national security. The Yanomamö cultural area extends well into Venezuela; such a security zone would bisect Yanomamö lands.

THE BURNING OF BRAZIL

Closely related to the destruction of Brazil's Indians is the destruction of the tropical rain forests. The burning of the forests by peasants clearing land in the traditional slash-and-burn method, or by developers and landowners constructing dams or converting forest to pasture, has become a source of worldwide concern and controversy.

Ecologists are horrified by the mass extinction of species of plants, animals, and insects, most of which have not even been catalogued. The massive annual burning (equivalent in one recent year to the size of Kansas) also fuels the debate on the greenhouse effect and global warming. The problem of the burning of Brazil is indeed global, because we are all linked to the tropics by climate and the migratory patterns of birds and animals.

ACHIEVEMENTS

Brazil's cultural contributions to the world are many. Authors such as Joaquim Maria Machado de Assis, Jorge Amado, and Graciliano Ramos are evidence of Brazil's high rank in terms of important literary works. Brazilian music has won millions of devotees throughout the world, and Brazil's *Cinema Novo* (New Cinema) has won many awards.

World condemnation of the destruction of the Amazon basin has produced a strong xenophobic reaction in Brazil. Foreign Ministry Secretary-General Paulo Tarso Flecha de Lima informed a 24-nation conference on the protection of the environment that the "international community cannot try to strangle the development of Brazil in the name of false ecological theories." He further noted that foreign criticism of his government in this regard was "arrogant, presumptuous and aggressive." The Brazilian military, according to Latin American Regional Reports: Brazil, has adopted a high-profile posture on the issue. The military sees the Amazon as "a kind of

strategic reserve vital to national security interests." Any talk of transforming the rain forests into an international nature reserve is rejected out of hand.

Over the next decade, however, Brazilian and foreign investors will create a 2.5 million-acre "green belt" in an already devastated area of the Amazon rain forest. Fifty million seedlings have been planted in a combination of natural and commercial zones. It is hoped that responsible forestry will generate jobs to maintain and study the native forest and to log the commercial zones. Steady employment would help to stem the flow of migrants to cities and to untouched portions of the rain forest. On the other hand, to compound the problem, landless peasants in 16 of Brazil's states launched violent protests in May 2000 to pressure the government to provide land for 100,000 families, as well as to grant millions of dollars in credits for poor rural workers.

FOREIGN POLICY

If Brazil's Indian and environmental policies leave much to be desired, its foreign policy has won it respect throughout much of Latin America and the developing world. Cuba, Central America, Angola, and Mozambique seemed far less threatening during the Cold War to the Brazilian government than they did to Washington. Brazil is more concerned about its energy needs, capital requirements, and trade opportunities.

President Lula da Silva's foreign policy has been characterized by the United States as "leftward" leaning, especially since it has moved closer to other populist governments in the region, such as Venezuela (Hugo Chavez), or Bolivia (Evo Morales). Closer relations have also been established with Castro's Cuba. Lula continues to attack the United States' invasion of Iraq and is distrustful of Washington's free-trade agenda. It must be understood that Brazil's current foreign policy, both in terms of its economic and political contexts, has another dimension. Standing up to the United States plays well at home and in the region and may be used to balance domestic policies that fall short of the radical solutions many of his followers expected. Lula himself disdains political labels such as "leftist" and, as he told a *New York Times* reporter, the class struggle was about results for the people and he didn't care if it was called "Socialism or Christianity or simply ethics." Brazil's foreign policy likewise should not be labeled but seen as one of pragmatism.

ECONOMIC POLICY

In mid-1993, Finance Minister Fernando Henrique Cardoso announced a plan to restore life to an economy in shambles. The so-called Real Plan, which pegged the new Brazilian currency (the real) to the dollar, brought an end to hyperinflation and won Cardoso enough popularity to carry him to the presidency. Inflation, which had raged at a rate of 45 percent per month in July 1994, was only 2 percent per month in February 1995. His two-to-one victory in elections in October 1994 was the most one-sided win since 1945.

Timeline: PAST

1500
Pedro Alvares Cabral discovers and claims Brazil for Portugal

1822
Declaration of Brazil's independence

1888
The Golden Law abolishes slavery

1889
The republic is proclaimed

1944
The Brazilian Expeditionary Force participates in the Italian campaign

1964
The military seizes power

1980s–1990s
Economic, social, and ecological crises

1990s
President Fernando Collor de Mello is convicted; the Asian financial crisis plunges Brazil into deep recession

PRESENT

2000s
Brazil wins praise for its handling of its HIV/AIDS problem

Luis Inacio da Silva, "Lula," elected president in 2002; Brazil pursues independent foreign and economic policies

Presidential elections scheduled for 2006

President Cardoso transformed the economy through carefully conceived and brilliantly executed constitutional reforms. A renovated tax system, an overhauled social-security program, and extensive privatization of state-owned enterprises were supported by a new generation of legislators pledged to support broad-based reform.

But, as was the case in much of Latin America in 1995, Mexico's financial crisis spread quickly to affect Brazil's economy, in large measure because foreign investors were unable to distinguish between Mexico and other Latin American nations. A similar problem occurred in 1998 with the collapse of Asian financial markets. Again, foreign investors shied away from Brazil's economy, and President Cardoso was forced to back away from a promise not to devalue the real. With devaluation in 1999 and signs of recovery in Asian markets, Brazil's economic prospects brightened considerably. Exports rose, and Brazil was able to finance its foreign debt through bond issues. In 2000 and 2001, however, the economy slowed, and concerns were expressed about energy supplies and costs, and the default of Brazil's major trading partner, Argentina, on its foreign debt. Economic uncertainty emboldened Congress to initiate a probe against corruption in government. Life for average Brazilians remained difficult. Cardoso's loss of popularity opened the door to the political opposition who were able to capitalize on presidential elections in 2002, when Luis Inacio da Silva, or "Lula" as he is popularly known, won a resounding triumph at the polls.

Lula, who worried many foreign observers because of his "leftist" ideology has begun to tackle Brazil's myriad problems in a pragmatic fashion. Labor unions, who supported his presidency and expected all of the benefits of political patronage, have been somewhat disillusioned. Lula, in attempt to bring the nation's spending under control, significantly culled the public workforce. With regard to the economy, his policies have not been "leftist" but have more closely adhered to classical economic approaches. This has calmed the fears of foreign investors.

Cardoso's laudable economic reforms did not succeed in transforming the quality of Brazilian democracy.

The lament of Brazilian journalist Lins da Silva is still accurate: "Brazilian elites have once again shown how capable they are of solving political crises in a creative and peaceful manner but also how unwilling to promote change in inequitable social structures." The wealth of the nation still remains in the hands of a few, and the educational system has failed to absorb and train as many citizens as it should. Police continue routinely to abuse their power. Lula, who's own family roots lie in the favelas, is deeply sensitive to the needs of Brazil's poor and disadvantaged. He has made a point of visiting the slums, of listening to the complaints and needs of people, of behaving, in short, like the classic "patron."

On a positive note, Brazil's progress in the struggle against AIDS, a disease that contributed to the deaths of 9,600 people in Brazil in 1996, is among the best in the world. In simple terms, the government uses language in the Paris Convention of 1883 to produce low-cost generic drugs similar to costlier medications manufactured abroad. Everyone in Brazil infected with the HIV virus is provided with a "cocktail" of drugs, and with training in how to take them effectively. More than 100,000 Brazilians are on the drug regimen, at an annual cost of $163 million. In 2000, AIDS–related deaths declined to 1,200, and the rate of transmission was sharply reduced.

At a broader level, Brazil has prospered from its membership in Mercosur, a regional trade organization that consists of Argentina, Brazil, Paraguay, and Uruguay. The success of Mercosur has expanded relations with other countries, especially Chile, which became an "associate" member in 1997. Lula, like Cardoso before him, is opposed to Washington's efforts to forge a Free Trade Area of the Americas (FTAA), in part because Mercosur and Brazil consider Europe a more important market and do not send a high percentage of their exports to the United States. Brazil has kept the pressure on other South American governments to convince them to join with Mercosur, not only in a "South American Free Trade Agreement," but in closer ties with the European Union. This independent policy has provided Brazil with leverage in the era of globalization.

Chile (Republic of Chile)

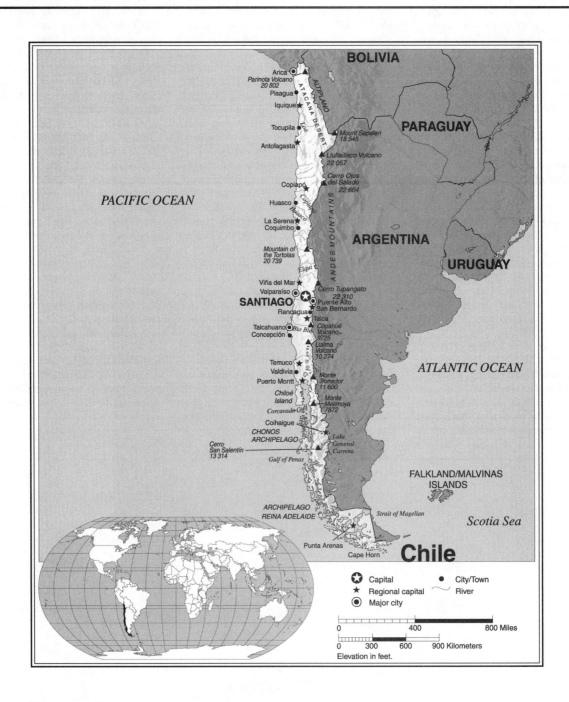

Chile Statistics

GEOGRAPHY

Area in Square Miles (Kilometers):
292,280 (756,945) (about twice the size of Montana)

Capital (Population): Santiago (4,642,000)

Environmental Concerns: air and water pollution; deforestation; loss of biodiversity; soil erosion; desertification

Geographical Features: low coastal mountains; a fertile central valley; rugged Andes Mountains in the east

Climate: temperate; desert in the north; Mediterranean in the center; cool and damp in the south

PEOPLE

Population

Total: 15,823,957

Annual Growth Rate: 1.01%

Rural/Urban Population Ratio: 16/84

Major Language: Spanish

Ethnic Makeup: 95% European and
Mestizo; 3% Indian; 2% others
Religions: 89% Roman Catholic; 11%
Protestant

Health

Life Expectancy at Birth: 72 years (male);
79 years (female)
Infant Mortality Rate (Ratio): 9.6/1,000
Physicians Available (Ratio): 1/875

Education

Adult Literacy Rate: 96.2%
Compulsory (Ages): for 8 years; free

COMMUNICATION

Telephones: 3.5 million main lines
Daily Newspaper Circulation: 101 per
1,000 people
Televisions: 280 per 1,000 people
Internet Users: 3.6 million

TRANSPORTATION

Highways in Miles (Kilometers): 49,556
(79,800)
Railroads in Miles (Kilometers): 4,212
(6,782)

Usable Airfields: 370
Motor Vehicles in Use: 1,375,000

GOVERNMENT

Type: republic
Independence Date: September 18, 1810
(from Spain)
Head of State/Government: President
Michelle Bechelet is both head of state
and head of government
Political Parties: Christian Democratic
Party; Party for Democracy; Socialist
Party; National Renewal; Independent
Democratic Union; others
Suffrage: universal and compulsory at 18

MILITARY

Military Expenditures (% of GDP): 4.1%
Current Disputes: boundary or territorial
disputes with Argentina, and Bolivia;
territorial claim in Antarctica

ECONOMY

Currency ($U.S. Equivalent): 691.43
pesos = $1

Per Capita Income/GDP: $9,900/$154.6
billion
GDP Growth Rate: 3.2%
Inflation Rate: 1.1%
Unemployment Rate: 8.5%
Labor Force: 5,800,000
Natural Resources: copper; timber; iron
ore; nitrates; precious metals;
molybdenum; fish; hydropower
Agriculture: wheat; corn; grapes; beans;
sugar beets; potatoes; fruit; beef; poultry;
wool; timber; fish
Industry: copper and other minerals;
foodstuffs; fish processing; iron and
steel; wood and wood products; transport
equipment; cement; textiles
Exports: $20.44 billion (primary partners,
European Union, United States, Japan)
Imports: $17 billion (primary partners
United States, European Union,
Argentina)

SUGGESTED WEBSITE

http://www.cia.gov/cia/
publications/factbook/
geos.ci.html

Chile Country Report

CHILE: A NATION ON THE REBOUND

In September 1973, the Chilean military, with the secret support of the U.S. Central Intelligence Agency (CIA), seized power from the constitutionally elected government of President Salvador Allende. Chile, with its long-standing traditions of free and honest elections, respect for human rights, and freedom of the press, was quickly transformed into a brutal dictatorship that arrested, tortured, and killed thousands of its own citizens. In the larger sweep of Chilean history, however, the coup seemed to be the most recent and severe manifestation of a lengthy conflict between social justice, on the one hand, and the requirements of order dictated by the nation's ruling elite, on the other. This was true in the colonial period, when there was conflict between the Roman Catholic Church and landowners over Indian rights. It was also apparent in later confrontations among Marxists, reformers, and conservatives.

FORM, NOT SUBSTANCE

Form, as opposed to substance, had characterized the rule of the Christian Democrats in the 1960s, when they created many separate rural unions, supposedly to address

the needs of *campesinos* ("peasants"). A divided union movement in effect became a form of government control that prevented the emergence of a single powerful rural organization.

DEVELOPMENT

 Chile, with an average gross domestic product growth of 6 percent over the last decade, has become a model for other Latin American nations. Bilateral trade agreements have continued with Mexico, Venezuela, and Bolivia. Trade agreements were also signed with the United States and the European Union.

In the early 1970s, President Allende—despite his talk of socialism and his genuine attempt to destroy the institutions and values of an old social order—used as his weapon of transformation, a centralized bureaucracy that would have been recognized by sixteenth-century viceroys and nineteenth-century presidents. Allende's attempts to institute far-reaching social change led to a strong reaction from powerful sectors of Chilean society who felt threatened.

THE 1973 COUP D'ETAT

When the military ousted Allende, it had the support of many Chileans, including the majority of the middle class, who had been hurt by the government's economic policies, troubled by continuous political turmoil, and infuriated by official mismanagement. The military, led by General Augusto Pinochet, began a new experiment with another form of centrist rule: military authoritarianism. The generals made it clear that they had not restored order merely to return it to the "discredited" constitutional practices of the past. They spoke of regeneration, of a new Chile, and of an end to the immorality, corruption, and incompetence of all civilian politics. The military announced in 1974 that, "guided by the inspiration of [Diego] Portales"—one of nineteenth-century Chile's greatest civilian leaders—"the government of Chile will energetically apply the principle of authority and drastically punish any outburst of disorder and anarchy."

The political, economic, and social reforms proposed by the military aimed at restructuring Chile to such an extent that there would no longer be a need for traditional political parties. Economic policy favored free and open competition as the main regulator

(Department of Defense photo by R. D. Ward/
DofDBachelet_1)

President Michelle Bechelet is both head
of state and head of government.

of economic and social life. The Chilean
state rid itself of hundreds of state-owned
corporations, struck down tariffs designed to
protect Chilean industry from foreign competition, and opened the economy to widespread foreign investment. The changes
struck deeply at the structure of the Chilean
economy and produced a temporary but
sharp recession, high unemployment, and
hundreds of bankruptcies. A steep decline in
the standard of living for most Chileans was
the result of the government's anti-inflation
policy.

FREEDOM

Chile's first woman president,
Michelle Bechelet, who was
elected in 2006, was arrested,
tortured, and exiled by the
Pinochet dictatorship. Her father died while in
prison. She said that she "was a victim of
hatred, and I have dedicated my life to
reversing that hatred."

Social-welfare programs were reduced
to a minimum. The private sector was encouraged to assume many functions and
services once provided by the state. Pensions were moved entirely to the private
sector as all state programs were phased
out. In this instance, the state calculated
that workers tied through pensions and
other benefits to the success of private en-

terprise would be less likely to be attracted
to "non-Chilean" ideologies such as Marxism, socialism, and even Christian democracy. State-sponsored health programs
were also cut to the bone, and many of the
poor now paid for services once provided
by the government.

THE DEFEAT OF A DICTATOR

To attain a measure of legitimacy, Chileans
expected the military government to produce economic achievement. By 1987, and
continuing into 1989, the regime's economic policies seemed successful; the economic growth rate for 1988 was an
impressive 7.4 percent. However, it
masked critical weaknesses in the Chilean
economy. For example, much of the
growth was overdependent on exports of
raw materials—notably, copper, pulp, timber, and fishmeal.

Modest economic success and an inflation rate of less than 20 percent convinced
General Pinochet that he could take his political scenario for Chile's future to the voters for their ratification. But in the October
5, 1988, plebiscite, Chile's voters upset the
general's plans and decisively denied him
an additional eight-year term. (He did,
however, continue in office until the next
presidential election determined his successor.) The military regime (albeit reluctantly) accepted defeat at the polls, which
signified the reemergence of a deep-rooted
civic culture and long democratic tradition.

Where had Pinochet miscalculated?
Public-opinion surveys on the eve of the
election showed a sharply divided electorate. Some political scientists even spoke of
the existence of "two Chiles." In the words
of government professor Arturo Valenzuela and *Boston Globe* correspondent Pamela Constable, one Chile "embraced those
who had benefited from the competitive
economic policies and welfare subsidies
instituted by the regime and who had been
persuaded that power was best entrusted to
the armed forces." The second Chile "consisted of those who had been victimized by
the regime, who did not identify with Pinochet's anti-Communist cause, and who
had quietly nurtured a belief in democracy." Polling data from the respected Center for Public Policy Studies showed that
72 percent of those who voted against the
regime were motivated by economic factors. These were people who had lost
skilled jobs or who had suffered a decrease
in real wages. While Pinochet's economic
reforms had helped some, it had also created a disgruntled mass of downwardly
mobile wage earners.

Valenzuela and Constable explain how
a dictator allowed himself to be voted out

of power. "To a large extent Pinochet had
been trapped by his own mythology. He
was convinced that he would be able to win
and was anxious to prove that his regime
was not a pariah but a legitimate government. He and other officials came to believe their own propaganda about the
dynamic new Chile they had created." The
closed character of the regime, with all
lines of authority flowing to the hands of
one man, made it "impossible for them to
accept the possibility that they could lose."
And when the impossible occurred and the
dictator lost an election played by his own
rules, neither civilians on the right nor the
military were willing to override the constitutional contract they had forged with
the Chilean people.

HEALTH/WELFARE

Since 1981, all new members of
Chile's labor force have been
required to contribute 10 percent
of their monthly gross earnings to
private-pension-fund accounts, which they
own. Unfortunately, in 2006 new retirees
discovered that their pensions fell far below
the guaranteed threshold. One reason was
that expenses for managing the funds
consumed as much as 33 percent of workers'
contributions.

In March 1990, Chile returned to civilian rule for the first time in almost 17 years,
with the assumption of the presidency by
Patricio Aylwin. His years in power revealed that tensions still existed between
civilian politicians and the military. In
1993, for example, General Pinochet mobilized elements of the army in Santiago—a
move that, in the words of the independent
newspaper *La Época*, "marked the crystal-
lization of long-standing hostility" between the Aylwin government and the
army. The military had reacted both to in-
vestigations into human-rights abuses during the Pinochet dictatorship and proposed
legislation that would have subordinated
the military to civilian control. On the other
hand, the commanders of the navy and air
force as well as the two right-wing political
parties refused to sanction the actions of
the army.

President Aylwin regained the initiative
when he publicly chastised General Pinochet. Congress, in a separate action, affirmed its supremacy over the judiciary in
1993, when it successfully impeached a
Supreme Court justice for "notable derelic-
tion of duty." The court system had been
notorious for transferring human-rights
cases from civil to military courts, where
they were quickly dismissed. The impeachment augured well for further reform
of the judicial branch.

(United Nations photo/UN107005)

The rural areas of Chile have presented challenges for community development. Here, volunteers work on a road that will link the village of Tincnamar to a main road.

Further resistance to the legacy of General Pinochet was expressed by the people when, on December 11, 1993, the center-left coalition candidate Eduardo Frei Ruiz-Tagle won the Chilean presidential election, with 58 percent of the vote. As part of his platform, Frei had promised to bring the military under civilian rule. The parliamentary vote, however, did not give him the two-thirds majority needed to push through such a reform. The trend toward civilian government, though, seemed to be continuing.

Perhaps the final chapter in Pinochet's career began in November 1998, while the former dictator was in London for medical treatment. At that time, the British government received formal extradition requests from the governments of Spain, Switzerland, and France. The charges against Pinochet included attempted murder, conspiracy to murder, torture, conspiracy to torture, hostage taking, conspiracy to take hostages, and genocide, based on Pinochet's alleged actions while in power.

British courts ruled that the general was too ill to stand trial, and Pinochet returned to Chile. In May 2004 a Chilean appeals court revoked Pinochet's immunity from prosecution, a decision that renders a trial possible. Still, in November 2005 Pinochet was arrested on charges of tax fraud and passport forgery in connection with secret bank accounts he maintained under false names in other countries. Almost simultaneously a Chilean judge indicted him on human-rights abuses. Previously, the army

had accepted blame for human-rights abuses during the Pinochet era. As the army commander wrote in a Santiago newspaper: "The Chilean Army Chile has taken the difficult but irreversible decision to assume responsibility for all punishable and morally unacceptable acts in the past attributed to it as an institution…. Never and for no one can there be any ethical justification for violations of human rights." Importantly, the army's admissions is reassuring to those who wish to pursue human-rights issues but were fearful of the military's possible reaction.

THE ECONOMY

By 1998, the Chilean economy had experienced 13 consecutive years of strong growth. But the Asian financial crisis of that year hit Chile hard, in part because 33 percent of the nation's exports in 1997 went to Asian markets. Copper prices tumbled; and because the largest copper mine is government-owned, state revenues contracted sharply. Following a sharp recession in 1999, the economy once again began to grow. However, domestic recovery has been slow. Unemployment remains high at 9 percent of the workforce, and a growth rate of 5.5 percent did not produce sufficient revenue to finance President Lagos's planned social programs and education initiatives. The sluggish global economy in 2001 was partly to blame, as prices fell for copper, Chile's number-one export.

Although there is still a large gap between the rich and poor in Chile, those living in poverty has been reduced from 40

percent to 20 percent over the course of the last decade. The irony is that Chile's economic success story is built on the economic model imposed by the Pinochet regime. "Underlying the current prosperity", writes *New York Times* reporter Larry Rohter, "is a long trail of blood and suffering that makes the thought of reversing course too difficult to contemplate." Many Chileans want to bury the past and move on—but the persistence of memory will not allow closure at this time. Chile has chosen to follow its own course with respect to economic policy. While many of its neighbors in the Southern Cone—notably Argentina, Brazil, Bolivia, Peru, Ecuador, and Venezuela—have moved away from free trade and open markets, Chile remains firmly wed to both.

Newly elected President Michelle Bechelet, Chile's first woman president, who served in the outgoing Lagos government first as minister of health and then as minister of defense, remains committed to close ties to the United States and to free trade. As a Socialist she will strive to meet the needs of women and the poor—but she will also keep in place economic policies that have made the Chilean economy one of the most dynamic in the region.

Peruvian novelist and politician Mario Vargas Llosa observes that while Chile "is not paradise," it does have a "stability and economic dynamism unparalleled in Latin America." Indeed, "Chile is moving closer to Spain and Australia and farther from Peru or Haiti." He suggests that there has

ACHIEVEMENTS

Chile's great literary figures, such as Gabriela Mistrál and Pablo Neruda, have a great sympathy for the poor and oppressed. Other major Chilean writers, such as Isabel Allende and Ariel Dorfman, have won worldwide acclaim.

been a shift in Chile's political culture. "The ideas of economic liberty, a free market open to the world, and private initiative as the motor of progress have become embedded in the people of Chile."

Chilean novelist Ariel Dorfman has a different perspective: "Obviously it is better to be dull and virtuous than bloody and Pinochetista, but Chile has been a very gray country for many years now. Modernization doesn't always have to come with a lack of soul, but I think there is a degree of that happening."

SIGNS OF CHANGE

Although the Chilean Constitution was essentially imposed on the nation by the military in 1980, there are signs of change. The term for president was reduced from eight to six years in 1993; and in 1997, the Chamber of Deputies, the lower house of the Legislature, approved legislation to further reduce the term of a president to four years, with a prohibition on reelection. Military courts, which have broader peacetime jurisdiction than most other countries in the Western

Timeline: PAST

1541
The founding of Santiago de Chile

1818
Independence of Spain is proclaimed

1964–1970
Revolution in Liberty dramatically alters Chilean society

1973
A military coup ousts President Salvador Allende; General Augusto Pinochet becomes president

1988
Pinochet is voted out—and goes

1990s
Asian financial woes cut into Chilean economic growth

PRESENT

2000s
Ricardo Lagos, a moderate Socialist, wins the presidency in December 1999–January 2000 elections

Lagos government accelerates prosecution of human-rights abusers

2006
Chile elects its first woman president, Verónica Michelle Bechelet Jeria

Hemisphere, have also come under scrutiny by politicians. According to the *Revista*

Hoy, as summarized by *CHIP News*, military justice reaches far beyond the ranks. If, for example, several people are involved in the commission of a crime and one of the perpetrators happens to be a member of the military, all are tried in a military court. Another abuse noted by politicians is that the military routinely uses the charge of sedition against civilians who criticize it. A group of Christian Democrats wants to limit the jurisdiction of the military to military crimes committed by military personnel; eliminate the participation of the army prosecutor in the Supreme Court, where he sits on the bench in cases related to the military; grant civilian courts the authority to investigate military premises; and accord civilian courts jurisdiction over military personnel accused of civilian-related crimes. The military itself, in 2004, in an effort to improve its tarnished image has worked in the background to hold accountable those officers involved in human-rights abuses in the past.

Another healthy sign of change is a concerted effort by the Chilean and Argentine governments to discuss issues that have been a historical source of friction between the two nations. Arms escalation, mining exploration and exploitation in border areas, and trade and investment concerns were on the agenda. The Chilean foreign relations minister and the defense minister sat down with their Argentine counterparts in the first meeting of its kind in the history of Argentine–Chilean relations.

Colombia (Republic of Colombia)

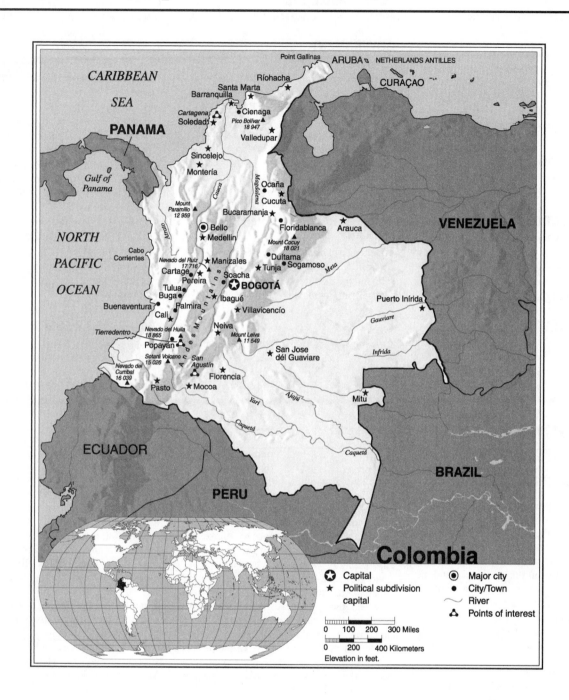

Colombia Statistics

GEOGRAPHY

Area in Square Miles (Kilometers):

440,000 (1,139,600) (about 3 times the size of Montana)

Capital (Population): Bogotá (6,005,000)

Environmental Concerns: deforestation; soil damage; air pollution
Geographical Features: flat coastal lowlands; central highlands; high Andes Mountains; eastern lowland plains
Climate: tropical on coast and eastern plains; cooler in highlands

PEOPLE

Population

Total: 42,310,775
Annual Growth Rate: 1.53%
Rural/Urban Population Ratio: 27/73
Major Language: Spanish

Ethnic Makeup: 58% Mestizo; 20% white; 14% mulatto; 4% African; 3% African Indian; 1% Indian
Religions: 95% Roman Catholic; 5% others

Health

Life Expectancy at Birth: 66 years (male); 74 years (female)
Infant Mortality Rate (Ratio): 24.7/1,000; Indians 233/1,000
Physicians Available (Ratio): 1/1,078

Education

Adult Literacy Rate: 91.3%
Compulsory (Ages): for 5 years between 6 and 12; free

COMMUNICATION

Telephones: 7.7 million main lines
Daily Newspaper Circulation: 55 per 1,000 people
Televisions: 188 per 1,000 people
Internet Users: 2 million

TRANSPORTATION

Highways in Miles (Kilometers): 69, 338 (115,564)

Railroads in Miles (Kilometers): 2,103 (3,386)
Usable Airfields: 1,101
Motor Vehicles in Use: 1,700,000

GOVERNMENT

Type: republic
Independence Date: July 10, 1810 (from Spain)
Head of State/Government: President Alvaro Uribe Velez is both head of state and head of government
Political Parties: Liberal Party; Conservative Party; New Democratic Force; Democratic Alliance M-19; Patriotic Union
Suffrage: universal at 18

MILITARY

Military Expenditures (% of GDP): 3.4%
Current Disputes: civil war; maritime boundary dispute with Venezuela; territorial disputes with Nicaragua

ECONOMY

Currency ($U.S. Equivalent): 2,877 pesos = $1

Per Capita Income/GDP: $6,300/$262.5 billion
GDP Growth Rate: 3.4%
Inflation Rate: 7.2%
Unemployment Rate: 13.6%
Labor Force: 16,800,000
Natural Resources: petroleum; natural gas; coal; iron ore; nickel; gold; copper; emeralds; hydropower
Agriculture: coffee; cut flowers; bananas; rice; tobacco; corn; sugarcane; cocoa beans; oilseed; vegetables; forest products; shrimp farming
Industry: textiles; food processing; petroleum; clothing and footwear; beverages; chemicals; cement; gold; coal; emeralds
Exports: $12.96 billion (primary partners United States, European Union, Andean Community)
Imports: $13.06 billion (primary partners United States, European Union, Andean Community)

SUGGESTED WEBSITE

http://www.cia.gov/cia/
publications/factbook/index.html

Colombia Country Report

COLOMBIA: THE VIOLENT LAND

Colombia has long been noted for its violent political history. The division of political beliefs in the mid-nineteenth century into conservative and liberal factions produced not only debate but also civil war. To the winner went the presidency and the spoils of office. That competition for office came to a head during the savage War of the Thousand Days (1899–1902). Nearly half a century later, Colombia was again plagued by political violence, which took perhaps 200,000 lives. Although on the surface it is distinct from the nineteenth-century civil wars, *La Violencia* ("The Violence," 1946–1958) offers striking parallels to the violence of the 1800s. Competing factions were again led by conservatives and liberals, and the presidency was the prize. Explanations for this phenomenon have tended to be at once simple and powerful. Colombian writers blame a Spanish heritage and its legacy of lust for political power.

Gabriel García Márquez, in his classic novel *One Hundred Years of Solitude*, spoofed the differences between liberals and conservatives. "The Liberals," said

Aureliano Buendia's father-in-law, "were Freemasons, bad people, wanting to hang priests, to institute civil marriage and divorce, to recognize the rights of illegitimate children as equal to those of legitimate ones, and to cut the country up into a federal system that would take power away from the supreme authority." On the other hand, "the Conservatives, who had received their power directly from God, proposed the establishment of public order and family morality. They were the defenders of the faith of Christ, of the principle of authority, and were not prepared to permit the country to be broken down into autonomous entities." Aureliano, when later asked if he was a Liberal or a Conservative, quickly replied: "If I have to be something I'll be a Liberal, because the Conservatives are tricky."

THE ROOTS OF VIOLENCE

The roots of the violence are far more complex than a simple quest for spoils caused by a flaw in national character. Historian Charles Bergquist has shown that "divisions within the upper class and the systematic philosophical and program-

matic positions that define them are not merely political manifestations of cultural traits; they reflect diverging economic interests within the upper class." These opposing interests developed in both the nineteenth and twentieth centuries. Moreover, to see Colombian politics solely as a violent quest for office ignores long periods of relative peace (1902–1935). But whatever the underlying causes of the violence, it has profoundly influenced contemporary Colombians.

La Violencia was the largest armed conflict in the Western Hemisphere since the Mexican Revolution (1910–1917). It was a civil war of ferocious intensity that cut through class lines and mobilized people from all levels of society behind the banner of either liberalism or conservatism. That elite-led parties were able to win popular support was evidence of their strong organization rather than their opponents' political weakness.

These multiclass parties still dominate Colombian political life, although the fierce interparty rivalry that characterized the civil wars of the nineteenth century as well as La Violencia has been stilled. In 1957, Colombia's social elite decided to bury partisan differences and devised a plan to end the widespread strife. Under this National Front agreement, the two parties agreed to divide legislative and bureaucratic positions equally and to alternate the presidency every four years from 1958 to 1974. This form of coalition government proved a highly successful means of elite compromise.

THE IMPACT OF LA VIOLENCIA

The violence has left its imprint on the people of Colombia in other ways. Some scholars have suggested that peasants now shun political action because of fear of renewed violence. Refugees from La Violencia generally experienced confusion and a loss of values. Usually, rising literacy rates, improved transportation and communications, and integration into the nation's life produce an upsurge of activism as people clamor for more rapid change. This has not been the case in rural Colombia. Despite guerrilla activity in the countryside—some of which is a spin-off from La Violencia, some of which until recently had a Marxist orientation, and some of which is banditry—the guerrillas have not been able to win significant rural support.

La Violencia also led to the professionalization and enlargement of the Colombian armed forces in the late 1950s and early 1960s. Never a serious participant in the nation's civil wars, the military acquired a new prestige and status unusual for Colombia. It must be considered an important factor in any discussion of Colombian politics today.

DEVELOPMENT

Drug-related crime has become the most common cause of death after cancer and has also contributed to a wave of kidnappings. This, together with continuing political violence, has had a damping effect on the nation's economy and deterred both tourists and investors. For example, petroleum exports have become significant for Colombia, but pipelines are vulnerable to sabotage by guerrillas.

A standoff between guerrillas and the military prompted the government of Virgilio Barco to engage reluctantly in a dialogue with the insurgents, with the ultimate goal of peace. In 1988, he announced a three-phase peace plan to end the violence, to talk about needed reforms, and ultimately to reincorporate guerrillas into society. This effort came to fruition in 1991, when the guerrilla movement M-19 laid down its arms after 16 years of fighting and engaged in political dialogue. Other guer-

rilla groups, notably the long-lived (since 1961) Colombian Revolutionary Armed Forces (FARC) and the National Liberation Army (ELN), led by a Spanish priest, chose to remain in the field.

Numbering perhaps 10,000, the guerrillas claim that their armed insurgency is about social change; but as *The Economist* has observed, lines between revolution and crime are increasingly blurred. Guerrillas ambush army units, attack oil pipelines, engage in blackmail, and kidnap rich ranchers and foreign oil executives for ransom. Some guerrillas are also apparently in the pay of the drug traffickers and collect a bounty for each helicopter they shoot down in the government's campaign to eradicate coca-leaf and poppy fields.

DRUGS AND DEATH

The guerrillas have a different perspective. One FARC leader asserted in an interview with the Colombian news weekly *Semana* that the guerrillas had both political and social objectives. Peace would come only if the government demilitarized large portions of the country and took action against the paramilitary organizations, some of them private and some of them supported by elements within the government. President Andrés Pastrana, who feared losing control of the country as well the credibility of his government, began to press for peace talks in January 1999 and, as a precondition to peace, agreed to demilitarize—that is, to withdraw government soldiers from a number of municipalities in southern Colombia. The United States objected that any policy of demilitarization would result in looser counter-narcotics efforts and urged a broader program to eradicate coca crops through aerial spraying. Critics of the policy claim that crop eradication plays into the hands of the guerrillas, who come to the support of the peasants who grow the coca. There is substance in the criticism, for by late 1999 FARC guerrillas controlled about 40 percent of the countryside.

FARC leaders, contrary to reports of foreign news media, disingenuously claim not to be involved in drug trafficking and have offered their own plan to counter the drug problem. It would begin with a government development plan for the peasants. In the words of a FARC leader: "Thousands of peasants need to produce and grow drugs to live, because they are not protected by the state." Eradication can succeed only if alternative crops can take the place of coca. Rice, corn, cacao, or cotton might be substituted. "Shooting the people, dropping bombs on them, dusting

their sown land, killing birds and leaving their land sterile" is not the solution.

The peace talks scheduled between the government and the guerrillas in 1999 stalled and then failed, in large measure because of distrust on the part of FARC. Although a large portion of southern Colombia was demilitarized, the activities of paramilitary organizations were not curbed, and the United States sought to intensify its eradication policy. In the meantime, the Colombian Civil War entered its fourth decade.

FREEDOM

Colombia continues to have the highest rate of violent deaths in Latin America. Guerrillas, the armed forces, right-wing vigilante groups and drug traffickers are responsible for many deaths. On the positive side, a 1993 law that accorded equal rights to black Colombians resulted in the 1995 election of Piedad de Castro, the first black woman to hold the position, to the Senate.

In addition to the deaths attributed to guerrilla warfare, literally hundreds of politicians, journalists, judges, and police officers have been murdered in Colombia. It has been estimated that 10 percent of the nation's homicides are politically motivated. Murder is the major cause of death for men between ages 15 and 45. The violence resulted in 250,000 deaths in the 1990s; 300,000 people have left the country; and, since the late 1980s, 1½ million have been internally displaced or become refugees. While paramilitary violence accounts for many deaths, drug trafficking and the unraveling of Colombia's fabric of law are responsible for most. As political scientist John D. Martz writes: "Whatever the responsibility of the military or the rhetoric of government, the penetration of Colombia's social and economic life by the drug industry [is] proving progressively destructive of law, security and the integrity of the political system." Colombian political scientist Juan Gabriel Tokatlian echoed these sentiments in 2001 when he wrote: "The state is losing sovereignty and legitimacy. The left-wing guerrillas and the right-wing paramilitaries control more territory than the government."

Drug traffickers, according to *Latin American Update*, "represent a new economic class in Colombia; since 1981 'narcodollars' have been invested in real estate and large cattle ranches." The newsmagazine *Semana* noted that drug cartels had purchased 2.5 million acres of land since 1984 and now own one-twelfth of the nation's productive farmland in the Magdalena River Basin. More than

100,000 acres of forest have been cut down to grow marijuana, coca, and opium poppies. Of particular concern to environmentalists is the fact that opium poppies are usually planted in the forests of the Andes at elevations above 6,000 feet. "These forests," according to Semana, "do not have great commercial value, but their tree cover is vital to the conservation of the sources of the water supply." The cartels also bought up factories, newspapers, radio stations, shopping centers, soccer teams, and bullfighters. The emergence of Medellín as a modern city of gleaming skyscrapers and expensive cars also reflects the enormous profits of the drug business.

Political scientist Francisco Leal Buitrago argues that while trafficking in narcotics in the 1970s was economically motivated, it had evolved into a social phenomenon by the 1980s. "The traffickers represent a new social force that wants to participate like other groups—new urban groups, guerrillas and peasant movements. Like the guerrillas, they have not been able to participate politically…."

HEALTH/WELFARE

Rape and other acts of violence against women are pervasive but seldom prosecuted. Spousal abuse was not considered a crime until 1996. Law 294 on family violence identifies as crimes violent acts committed within families, including spousal rape. Although the Constitution of 1991 prohibits it, discrimination against women persists in terms of access to employment and equal pay for equal work.

Domestic drug consumption has also emerged as a serious problem in Colombia's cities. *Latin American Regional Reports* notes that the increase in consumption of the Colombian form of crack, known as *bazuko*, "has prompted the growth of gangs of youths in slum areas running the bazuko business for small distributors." In Bogotá, police reported that more than 1,500 gangs operated from the city's slums.

URBANIZATION

As is the case in other Andean nations, urbanization has been rapid in Colombia. But the constantly spreading slums on the outskirts of the larger cities have not produced significant urban unrest or activism. Most of the migrants to the cities are first generation and are less frustrated and demanding than the general urban population. The new migrants perceive an improvement in their status and opportunities simply because they have moved into a more hopeful urban

environment. Also, since most of the migrants are poorly paid, their focus tends to be on daily survival, not political activism.

Migrants make a significant contribution to the parallel Colombian economy. As is the case in Peru and other South American countries, the informal sector amounts to approximately 30 percent of gross domestic product.

The Roman Catholic Church in Colombia has also tended to take advantage of rapid urbanization. Depending on the individual beliefs of local bishops, the Church has to a greater or lesser extent embraced the migrants, brought them into the Church, and created or instilled a sense of community where none existed before. The Church has generally identified with the expansion and change taking place and has played an active social role.

Marginalized city dwellers are often the targets of violence. Hired killers, called *sicarios*, have murdered hundreds of petty thieves, beggars, prostitutes, indigents, and street children. Such "clean-up" campaigns are reminiscent of the activities of the Brazilian death squads since the 1960s. An overloaded judicial system and interminable delays have contributed to Colombia's high homicide rate. According to government reports, lawbreakers have not been brought to justice in 97 to 99 percent of *reported* crimes. (Perhaps three-quarters of all crimes remain unreported to the authorities.) Increasingly, violence and murder have replaced the law as a way to settle disputes; private "justice" is now commonly resorted to for a variety of disputes.

SOCIAL CHANGE

Government has responded to calls for social change and reform. President Virgilio Barco sincerely believed that the eradication of poverty would help to eliminate guerrilla warfare and reduce the scale of violence in the countryside. Unfortunately, his policies lacked substance, and he was widely criticized for his indecisiveness.

President César Gaviria felt that political reform must precede social and economic change and was confident that Colombia's new Constitution would set the process of national reconciliation in motion. The constitutional debate generated some optimism about the future of liberal democracy in Colombia. As Christopher Abel writes, it afforded a forum for groups ordinarily denied a voice in policy formulation—"to civic and community movements in the 40 and more intermediate cities angry at the poor quality of basic public services; to indigenous movements…; and to cooperatives, blacks, women, pensioners, small businesses, consumer and sports groups."

ACHIEVEMENTS

Colombia has a long tradition in the arts and humanities and has produced international figures such as the Nobel Prize–winning author Gabriel García Márquez; the painters and sculptors Alejandro Obregón, Fernando Botero, and Edgar Negret; the poet León de Greiff; and many others well known in music, art, and literature.

Violence and unrest have thwarted all of these efforts. Since the mid-1980s, according to a former Minister of Defence writing in 2000, 200 car bombs had exploded in Colombian cities, an entire democratic left of center party (the Unión Patriotica) had been eliminated by right-wing paramilitaries, and 4 presidential candidates, 200 judges and investigators, half of the supreme court justices, 1,200 police, 151 journalists, and 300,000 ordinary Colombians had been murdered.

While some scholars have described Colombia as a "failed state" others perceptively note that the focus should be on what holds the nation together in the face of unprecedented assaults. In the words of political scientist Malcolm Deas, Colombia is more united than fragmented, ethnically and religiously homogeneous, and its regional differences, while real, are not especially divisive. President Alvaro Uribe, a tough-minded pragmatist, has worked hard to restore the rule of law to Colombia. His first year in office resulted in a significant reduction in murder and kidnapping and attacks by guerrillas, as well acreage devoted to coca cultivation. Economic recovery was underway, as is indicated by the increased amount of highway traffic. Colombians, for the first time in years, felt more secure and, in 2004, 80 percent of the voting population supported Uribe. A reflection of both his popularity and success was the decision of Colombia's Congress to pass an amendment to the Constitution that would allow Uribe to run for reelection in 2006. As of March 2006 polls indicated that Uribe maintained a high approval rate of 70 percent and success at the polls was expected.

ECONOMIC POLICIES

Colombia has a mixed economy. While state enterprises control domestic participation in the coal and oil industries and play a commanding role in the provision of electricity and communications, most of the economy is dominated by private business. At this point, Colombia is a moderate oil producer. A third of the nation's legal exports comes from the coffee industry, while exports of coal, cut flowers, seafood, and other nontraditional exports have experienced significant growth. In that Colombia is not saddled with an onerous foreign debt, its economy is relatively prosperous.

Contributing to economic success is the large informal sector. Also of tremendous importance are the profits from the illegal-drug industry. *The Economist* estimated that Colombia grossed perhaps $1.5 billion in drug sales in 1987, as compared to official export earnings of $5.5 billion. Indeed, over the past 20 years, profits from drug trafficking have grown to encompass between 25 and 35 percent of Colombia's legal exports. Perhaps half the profits are repatriated—that is, converted from dollars into local currency. An unfortunate side effect of the inflow of cash is an increase in the inflation rate.

FOREIGN POLICY

In the foreign-policy arena, President Barco's policies were attacked as low-profile, shallow, and too closely aligned to the policies of the United States. While Presidents Gaviria and Samper tried to adopt more independent foreign policy lines, especially in terms of the drug trade, Presidents Pastrana and Uribe have welcomed United States aid against drug trafficking and its attendant evils.

With an uneasy peace reigning in Central America, Colombia's focus has turned increasingly toward its neighbors and a festering territorial dispute with Venezuela over waters adjacent to the Guajira Peninsula. Colombia has proposed a multilateral solution to the problem, perhaps under the auspices of the International Court of Justice. Venezuela continues to reject a multilateral approach and seeks to limit any talks to the two countries concerned. It is likely that a sustained deterioration of in-

ternal conditions in either Venezuela or Colombia will keep the territorial dispute in the forefront. A further detriment to better relations with Venezuela is the justified Venezuelan fear that Colombian violence as a result of guerrilla activity, military sweeps, and drugs will cross the border. As it is, thousands of Colombians have fled to Venezuela to escape their violent homeland. Venezuela's president recently infuriated Colombia's government when he independently opened negotiations with guerrillas and implied that they had more power than did President Pastrana.

THE CLOUDED FUTURE

Francisco Leal Buitrago, a respected Colombian academic, argues forcefully that his nation's crisis is, above all, "political": "It is the lack of public confidence in the political regime. It is not a crisis of the state itself…, but in the way in which the state sets the norms—the rules for participation—for the representation of public opinion…."

Constitutional reforms have taken place in Colombia, but changes in theory must reflect the country's tumultuous realities. Many of those in opposition have looked for a political opening but in the meantime continue to wage an armed insurgency against the government. Other problems, besides drugs, that dog the government include corruption, violence, slow growth, high unemployment, a weak currency, inflation, and the need for major reforms in banking. To get the economy on track, the International Monetary Fund has recommended that Colombia broaden its tax base, enhance municipal tax collections, get tough on tax evasion, and reduce spending.

Endemic violence and lawlessness, the continued operation of guerrilla groups, the emergence of mini-cartels in the wake of the eclipse of drug kingpins, and the at-

titude of the military toward conditions in Colombia all threaten any kind of progress. The hard-line antidrug trafficking policy of the United States adds another complicated, and possibly counterproductive, dimension to the difficult task of governing Colombia.

Timeline: PAST

1525
The first Spanish settlement at Santa Marta

1810
Independence from Spain

1822
The creation of Gran Colombia (including Venezuela, Panama, and Ecuador)

1830
Independence as a separate country

1899–1902
War of the Thousand Days

1946–1958
La Violencia; nearly 200,000 lose their lives

1957
Women's suffrage

1980s
The drug trade becomes big business

1990s
Violence hampers progress; an earthquake kills or injures thousands in central Colombia

PRESENT

2000s
Colombia's violence threatens to involve its neighbors

Alvaro Uribe elected president in 2002

Presidential elections scheduled for 2006

Ecuador (Republic of Ecuador)

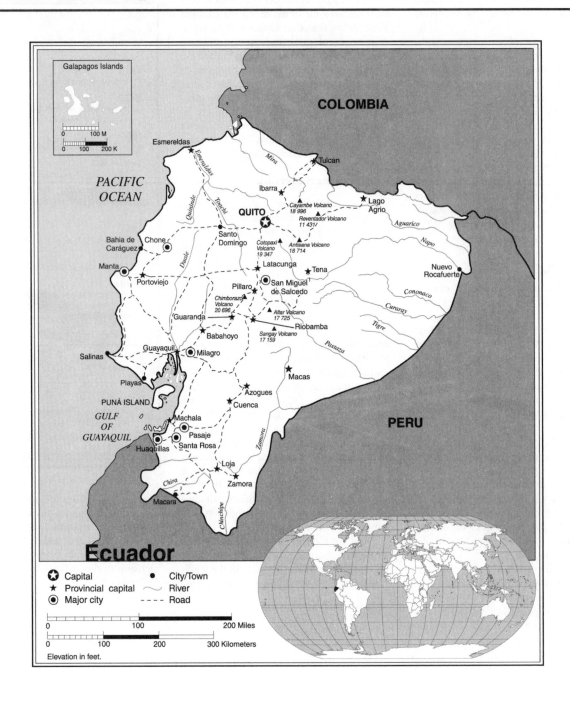

Ecuador Statistics

GEOGRAPHY

Area in Square Miles (Kilometers):
109,454 (283,560) (about the size of Nevada)

Capital (Population): Quito (1,445,000)

Environmental Concerns: deforestation; soil erosion; desertification; water pollution; pollution from petroleum wastes

Geographical Features: coastal plain; inter-Andean central highlands; flat to rolling eastern jungle

Climate: varied; tropical on the coast and in the inland jungle; cooler inland at higher elevations

PEOPLE

Population

Total: 13,212,742

Annual Growth Rate: 1.03%

Rural/Urban Population Ratio: 40/60

Major Languages: Spanish; Quechua and other Amerindian languages

Ethnic Makeup: 65% Mestizo; 25% Indian; 10% Spanish, black, and others
Religions: 95% Roman Catholic; 5% indigenous and others

Health

Life Expectancy at Birth: 73 years (male); 79 years (female)
Infant Mortality Rate (Ratio): 24.49/1,000
Physicians Available (Ratio): 1/904

Education

Adult Literacy Rate: 90%
Compulsory (Ages): for 6 years between 6 and 14; free

COMMUNICATION

Telephones: 1,426,200 main lines
Daily Newspaper Circulation: 72 per 1,000 people
Televisions: 79 per 1,000
Internet Users: 537,900

TRANSPORTATION

Highways in Miles (Kilometers): 26,858 (43,249)
Railroads in Miles (Kilometers): (812)

Usable Airfields: 182
Motor Vehicles in Use: 480,000

GOVERNMENT

Type: republic
Independence Date: May 24, 1822 (from Spain)
Head of State/Government: President Alfredo Palacio is both head of state and head of government
Political Parties: Democratic Left; Social Christian Party; Pachakutik; Popular Democracy; Popular Democratic Movement; others
Suffrage: universal and compulsory for literate people ages 18–65; optional for other eligible voters

MILITARY

Military Expenditures (% of GDP): 2.4%
Current Disputes: none

ECONOMY

Currency ($U.S. Equivalent): 1.00 dollar = $1

Per Capita Income/GDP: $3,300/$45.46 billion
GDP Growth Rate: 2.6%
Inflation Rate: 6.1%
Unemployment Rate: 9.8%; plus widespread underemployment
Labor Force: 4,200,000
Natural Resources: petroleum; fish; timber; hydropower
Agriculture: bananas; coffee; cocoa; rice; potatoes; manioc; plantains; sugarcane; livestock; balsa wood; fish; shrimp
Industry: petroleum; food processing; textiles; metalwork; paper products; wood products; chemicals; plastics; fishing; lumber
Exports: $6 billion (primary partners United States, Colombia, Italy)
Imports: $6.2 billion (primary partners United States, Colombia, Japan)

SUGGESTED WEBSITE

http://www.cia.gov/cia/
publications/factbook/
geos.ec.html

Ecuador Country Report

ECUADOR: A LAND OF CONTRASTS

Several of Ecuador's great novelists have had as the focus of their works the exploitation of the Indians. Jorge Icaza's classic *Huasipungo* (1934) describes the actions of a brutal landowner who first forces Indians to work on a road so that the region might be "developed" and then forces them, violently, from their plots of land so that a foreign company's operations will not be impeded by a troublesome Indian population.

That scenario, while possible in some isolated regions, is for the most part unlikely in today's Ecuador. In recent years, despite some political and economic dislocation, Ecuador has made progress in health care, literacy, human rights, freedom of the press, and representative government. Indigenous peoples have been particularly active and over the past decade have demanded cultural rights. An indigenous political party, Pachakutik, has identified with Ecuador's nonindigenous poor and won several seats in Congress. In protest against an economic program of austerity and reflecting ethnic and social conflict, several of these groups in league with midlevel army of-

ficers moved to topple President Jamil Mahuad from power in January 2000. It was South America's first successful coup in a quarter of a century. In April 2005 President Lucio Gutierrez, who was behind the coup, was himself ousted from the executive office. He lost the support of indigenous leaders, middle-class homemakers, and students who were angry both over his inability to deliver on promises made and widespread corruption. The new president, Alfredo Palacio, faces the same kinds of pressures that brought down previous governments. Austerity policies have hurt the indigenous poor and Ecuador's large public debt has hamstrung social programs.

Although Ecuador is still a conservative, traditional society, it has shown an increasing concern for the plight of its rural inhabitants, including the various endangered Indian groups inhabiting the Amazonian region. The new attention showered on rural Ecuador—traditionally neglected by policymakers in Quito, the capital city—reflects in part the government's concern with patterns of internal migration. Even though rural regions have won more attention from the state, social programs continue to be implemented only sporadically.

DEVELOPMENT

Petroleum has now become Ecuador's primary export and, after Venezuela, is Latin America's second most important supplier of oil to the United States. Throughout 2005 and 2006 oil protestors disrupted both production and delivery and demanded that oil companies invest more in the poor Amazonian communities where they operate.

Two types of migration are currently taking place: the move from the highlands to the coastal lowlands and the move from the countryside to the cities. In the early 1960s, most of Ecuador's population was concentrated in the mountainous central highlands. Today, the population is about equally divided between that area and the coast, with more than half the nation's people crowded into the cities. So striking and rapid has the population shift been that the director of the National Institute of Statistics commented that it had assumed "alarming proportions" and that the government had to develop appropriate policies if spreading urban slums were not to develop into "potential focal points for insurgency." What has emerged is a rough political parity between regions that

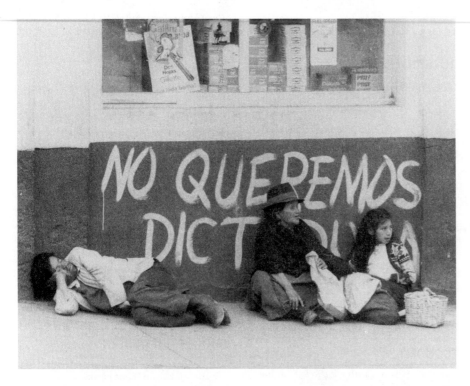

(United Nations photo/UN155089)

The migration of the poor to the urban areas of Ecuador has been very rapid and of great concern to the government. The increase in inner-city population can easily lead to political unrest. The graffiti in the photo says, "We don't want a dictatorship."

has led to parliamentary paralysis and political crisis.

The large-scale movement of people has not rendered the population more homogenous but, because of political parity, has instead fractured the nation. Political rivalry has always characterized relations between Quito, in the sierras, and cosmopolitan Guayaquíl, on the coast. The presidential election of 1988 illustrated the distinctive styles of the country. Rodrigo Borja's victory was regionally based, in that he won wide support in Ecuador's interior provinces. Usually conservative in its politics, the interior voted for the candidate of the Democratic Left, in part because of the extreme populist campaign waged by a former mayor of Guayaquíl, Abdalá Bucaram. Bucaram claimed to be a man of the people who was persecuted by the oligarchy. He spoke of his lower-class followers as the "humble ones," or, borrowing a phrase from former Argentine president Juan Perón, *los descamisados* ("the shirtless ones"). Bucaram, in the words of political scientist Catherine M. Conaghan, "honed a political style in the classic tradition of coastal populism. He combined promises of concrete benefits to the urban poor with a colorful anti-oligarchic style." Bucaram's style finally triumphed in 1996, when he won election to the presidency.

EDUCATION AND HEALTH

Central to the government's policy of development is education. Twenty-nine percent of the national budget was set aside for education in the early 1980s, with increases proposed for the following years. Adult literacy improved from 74 percent in 1974 to 87 percent by 1995. In the central highlands, however, illiteracy rates of more than 35 percent are still common, largely because Quechua is the preferred language among the Indian peasants.

FREEDOM

Ecuador's media, with the exception of two government-owned radio stations, are in private hands and represent a broad range of opinion. They are often critical of government policies, but they practice a degree of self-censorship because of defamation laws whose violation carry a three-year prison term.

The government has approached this problem with an unusual sensitivity to indigenous culture. Local Quechua speakers have been enlisted to teach reading and writing in both Quechua and Spanish. This approach has won the support of Indian leaders who are closely involved in planning local literacy programs built around indigenous values.

Health care has also shown steady improvement, but the total statistics hide sharp regional variations. Infant mortality and malnutrition are still severe problems in rural areas. In this sense, Ecuador suffers from a duality found in other Latin American nations with large Indian populations: Social and racial differences persist be-tween the elite-dominated capitals and the Indian hinterlands. Income, services, and resources tend to be concentrated in the capital cities. Ecuador, at least, is attempting to correct the imbalance.

The profound differences between Ecuador's highland Indian and its European cultures is illustrated by the story of an Indian peasant who, when brought to a clinic, claimed that he was dying as the result of a spell. He told the doctor, trained in Western medicine, that, while traveling a path from his highland village down to a valley, he passed by a sacred place, where a witch cast a spell on him. The man began to deteriorate, convinced that this had happened. The doctor, upon examination of the patient, could find no physical reason for the man's condition. Medicine produced no improvements. The doctor finally managed to save his patient, but only after a good deal of compromise with Indian culture. "Yes," he told the peasant, "a witch has apparently cast a spell on you and you are indeed dying." And then the doctor announced: "Here is a potion that will remove the spell." The patient's recovery was rapid and complete. Thus, though modern medicine can work miracles, health-care workers must also be sensitive to cultural differences.

THE ECONOMY

Between 1998 and 2000, the Ecuadoran economy was hit hard by two crises. Falling petroleum prices in combination with the ravages of the El Niño phenomenon transformed a $598 million surplus in 1997 into a troubling $830 million deficit in 1998. Petroleum revenues fell to third place, behind exports of bananas and shrimp, which themselves were devastated by bad weather (in the case of shrimp, due to the dramatic warming of waters in the eastern Pacific as a result of El Niño).

HEALTH/WELFARE

Educational and economic opportunities in Ecuador are often not made available to women, blacks, and indigenous peoples. Most of the nation's peasantry, overwhelmingly Indian or Mestizo, are poor. Infant mortality, malnutrition, and epidemic disease are common among these people.

President Jamil Mahuad was confronted from the outset of his administration with some daunting policy decisions. A projected growth rate for 1998 of only 1 percent and an inflation rate that soared to 40 percent resulted in budget austerity and an emergency request to Congress to cut spending and prepare legislation for the privatization of Ecuador's telecommunications and electrical industries. The privatization plans raised the ire of nationalists. In the mid-1990s, the government privatized more than 160 state-owned enterprises and, in an effort to modernize and streamline the economy, cut the number of public employees from 400,000 to 260,000.

The sharp economic downturn resulted in severe belt-tightening by the Mahuad government, threw people out of work, produced social and political upheaval, and led to a coup. The military quickly handed over power to the civilian vice president, Gustavo Noboa, to finish out Mahuad's term. Noboa took steps to restore Ecuador's economic viability and adopted some of Mahuad's unpopular policies, including "dollarization" of the economy and continued privatization of state enterprises.

Chronic political instability, which saw the removal of three presidents between 1997 and 2005, has had a negative impact on the government's ability to formulate policies and deliver needed programs on a consistent basis. One result is a continuous drumbeat of opposition from a broad range

of Ecuadorans, from the indigenous peoples of the Amazon to the slums around large cities to a large sector of the middle class. The climate for foreign investment has become troublesome and attacks on oil fields and facilities have tended to negate any benefits that might have accrued from rising petroleum prices.

BITTER NEIGHBORS

A long legacy of boundary disputes that reached back to the wars for independence created a strained relationship between Ecuador and Peru, which erupted in violence in July 1941. Ecuador initiated an undeclared war against Peru in an attempt to win territory along its southeastern border, in the Marañón River region, and, in the southwest, around the town of Zaramilla. In the 1942 Pact of Peace, Amity, and Limits, which followed a stunning Peruvian victory, Ecuador lost about 120,000 square miles of territory. The peace accord was guaranteed by Argentina, Brazil, Chile, and the United States. In January 1995, the usual tensions that grew each year as the anniversary of the conflict approached were given foundation when fighting again broke out between Peru and Ecuador; Peruvian soldiers patrolling the region had stumbled upon well-prepared and waiting Ecuadoran soldiers. Three weeks later, with the intervention of the guarantors of the original pact, the conflict ended. The Peruvian armed forces were shaken from their smug sense of superiority over the Ecuadorans, and the Ecuadoran defense minister used the fight to support his political pretensions.

ACHIEVEMENTS

Ecuadoran poets have often made their poetry an expression of social criticism. The so-called Tzántzicos group has combined avant-garde techniques with social commitment and has won a measure of attention from literary circles.

The border war sent waves of alarm through the rest of Latin America, in that it reminded more than a dozen nations of boundary problems with their neighbors. Of particular concern were revelations

made in 1998 and 1999 that individuals within the Argentine government and the military had sold arms to the Ecuadoran military during the conflict. Argentina was embarrassed because it was one of the original guarantors of the 1942 Pact of Peace.

On October 16, 1998, the Legislatures of Ecuador and Peru supported an agreement worked out by other governments in the region to end the border dispute. Under the terms of the agreement, Peru's sovereignty of the vast majority of the contested territory was affirmed. Ecuador won a major concession when it was granted navigation rights on the Amazon River and its tributaries within Peru and the right to establish trading centers on the river. In that both parties benefited from the negotiation, it is hoped that a lasting peace will have been effected.

Timeline: PAST

1528
First Spanish contact

1822
Ecuador is part of Gran Colombia (with Panama, Venezuela, and Colombia); independence as a separate state

1929
Women's suffrage

1941
A border war with Peru

1990s
Modernization laws aim to speed the privatization of the economy

Popular dissatisfaction with the government's handling of the economy rises

PRESENT

2000s
El Niño devastates the coastal economy; refugees and drug activity spill into Ecuador from Colombia

Lucio Gutierrez elected president in 2003 and ousted in 2005. Replaced by Alfredo Palacio

Guyana (Cooperative Republic of Guyana)

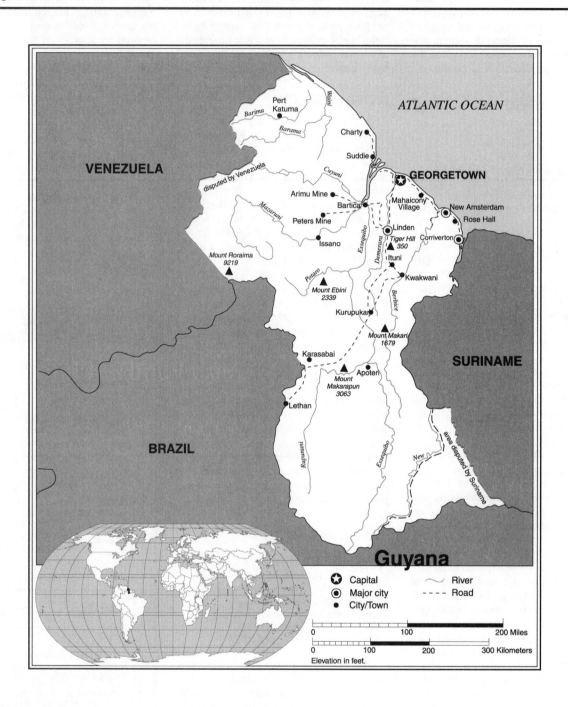

Guyana Statistics

GEOGRAPHY

Area in Square Miles (Kilometers): 82,990 (215,000) (about the size of Idaho)

Capital (Population): Georgetown (248,500)

Environmental Concerns: water pollution; deforestation

Geographical Features: mostly rolling highlands; low coastal plain; savannah in the south

Climate: tropical

PEOPLE*

Population

Total: 705,813

*Note: Estimates explicitly take into account the effects of excess mortality due to AIDS.

Annual Growth Rate: 0.61%
Rural/Urban Population Ratio: 74/36
Major Languages: English; indigenous
dialects; Creole; Hindi; Urdu
Ethnic Makeup: 51% East Indian, 30%
black; 14% mixed; 4% Amerindian; 2%
white and Chinese
Religions: 50% Christian; 33% Hindu; 9%
Muslim; 8% others

Health

Life Expectancy at Birth: 60 years (male);
64 (female)
Infant Mortality Rate (Ratio): 37.22/1,000
Physicians Available (Ratio): 1/3,000

Education

Adult Literacy Rate: 98%
Compulsory (Ages): 6–14; free

COMMUNICATION

Telephones: 80,400 main lines
Daily Newspaper Circulation: 97 per
1,000 people
Televisions: 1 per 26 people
Internet Users: 125,000

TRANSPORTATION

Highways in Miles (Kilometers): 4,949
(7,970)
Railroads in Miles (Kilometers): (187)
Usable Airfields: 1
Motor Vehicles in Use: 33,000

GOVERNMENT

Type: republic
Independence Date: May 26, 1966 (from
the United Kingdom)
Head of State/Government: President
Bharrat Jagdeo; Prime Minister Samuel
Hinds
Political Parties: People's National
Congress; Alliance for Guyana People's
Progressive Party; United Force;
Democratic Labour Movement; People's
Democratic Movement; National
Democratic Front; others
Suffrage: universal at 18

MILITARY

Military Expenditures (% of GDP): 0.8%
Current Disputes: territorial disputes with
Venezuela and Suriname

ECONOMY

Currency ($U.S. Equivalent):
190.672002) Guyanese dollars = $1
Per Capita Income/GDP: $4,000/$2.8
billion
GDP Growth Rate: 0.3%
Inflation Rate: 4.7%
Unemployment Rate: 9.1%
Natural Resources: bauxite; gold;
diamonds; hardwood timber; shrimp; fish
Agriculture: sugar; rice; wheat; vegetable
oils; livestock; potential for fishing and
forestry
Industry: bauxite; sugar; rice milling;
timber; fishing; textiles; gold mining
Exports: $5.12 million (primary partners
United States, Canada, United Kingdom)
Imports: $612 million (primary partners
United States, Trinidad and Tobago,
Netherland Antilles)

SUGGESTED WEBSITE

http://www.cia.gov/cia/
publications/factbook/geos/
gy.html

Guyana Country Report

GUYANA: RACIAL AND ETHNIC TENSIONS

Christopher Columbus, who cruised along what are now Guyana's shores in 1498, named the region *Guiana*. The first European settlers were the Dutch, who settled in Guyana late in the sixteenth century, after they had been ousted from Brazil by a resurgent Portuguese Crown. Dutch control ended in 1796, when the British gained control of the area. In 1815, as part of the treaty arrangements that brought the Napoleonic Wars to a close, the Dutch colonies of Essequibo, Demerera, and Berbice were officially ceded to the British. In 1831, the former Dutch colonies were consolidated as the Crown Colony of British Guiana.

DEVELOPMENT

Moderate economic growth continued into 2006. Important deals were concluded with Russian and German businesses to process and ship bauxite. The Russian company would process the ore into aluminum and a German company would provide facilities for shipping and barging the bauxite. Trade negotiations were continued with China on an accelerated basis.

Guyana is a society deeply divided along racial and ethnic lines. East Indians make up the majority of the population. They predominate in rural areas, constituting the bulk of the labor force on the sugar plantations, and they comprise nearly all of the rice-growing peasantry. They also dominate local businesses and are prominent in the professions. Blacks are concentrated in urban areas, where they are employed in clerical and secretarial positions in the public bureaucracy, in teaching, and in semiprofessional jobs. A black elite dominates the state bureaucratic structure.

Before Guyana's independence in 1966, plantation owners, large merchants, and British colonial administrators consciously favored some ethnic groups over others, providing them with a variety of economic and political advantages. The regime of President Forbes Burnham revived old patterns of discrimination for political gain.

Burnham, after ousting the old elite when he nationalized the sugar plantations and the bauxite mines, built a new regime that simultaneously catered to lower-class blacks and discriminated against East Indians. In an attempt to address the blacks' basic human needs, the Burnham government greatly expanded the number of blacks

holding positions in public administration. To demonstrate his largely contrived black-power ideology, Burnham spoke out strongly in support of African liberation movements. The government played to the fear of communal strife in order to justify its increasingly authoritarian rule.

FREEDOM

One of the priorities of the Jagan governments was the elimination of all forms of ethnic and racial discrimination, a difficult task in a country where political parties are organized along racial lines. It was hoped that Guyana's indigenous peoples would be offered accelerated development programs to enhance their health and welfare.

In the mid-1970s, a faltering economy and political mismanagement generated an increasing opposition to Burnham that cut across ethnic lines. The government increased the size of the military, packed Parliament through rigged elections, and amended the Constitution so that the president held virtually imperial power.

There has been some improvement since Burnham's death in 1985. The appearance of newspapers other than the government-controlled *Guyana Chronicle* and the public's dramatically increased access to television have served to curtail official control of the media. In politics, the election of Indo-Guyanese leader Cheddi Jagan to the presidency reflected deep-seated disfavor with the behavior and economic policies of the previous government of Desmond Hoyte. President Jagan identified the nation's foreign debt of $2 billion as a "colossally big problem, because the debt overhang impedes human development."

HEALTH/WELFARE

The government has initiated policies designed to lower the cost of living for Guyanese. Prices for essentials have been cut. Money has been allocated for school lunch programs and for a "food-for-work" plan. Pensions have been raised for the first time in years. The minimum wage, however, will not sustain an average family.

While president, Hoyte once pledged to continue the socialist policies of the late Forbes Burnham; but in the same breath, he talked about the need for privatization of the crucial sugar and bauxite industries. Jagan's economic policies, according to *Latin American Regional Reports*, outlined an uncertain course. During his campaign, Jagan stated that government should not be involved in sectors of the economy where private or cooperative ownership would be more efficient. In 1993, however, he backed away from the sale of the Guyana Electric Company and had some doubts about selling off the sugar industry. In Jagan's words: "Privatization and divestment must be approached with due care. I was not elected

president to preside over the liquidation of Guyana. I was mandated by the Guyanese people to rebuild the national economy and to restore a decent standard of living." Jagan's policies stimulated rapid socioeconomic progress as Guyana embarked on the road to economic recovery.

ACHIEVEMENTS

The American Historical Association selected Walter Rodney for the 1982 Beveridge Award for his study of the Guyanese working people. The award is for the best book in English on the history of the United States, Canada, or Latin America. Rodney, the leader of the Working People's Alliance, was assassinated in 1980.

Following Jagan's death, new elections were held in December 1997, and Janet Jagan, the ex-president's 77-year-old widow, was named president. In August 1999, she stepped down due to health reasons. She named Finance Minister Bharrat Jagdeo to succeed her.

Jagdeo's presidency has pushed infrastructure development and has promoted universal primary education. A five-year plan (2003–2007) promises to bring schools to the interior where educational opportunities have been minimal or nonexistent. He has also worked towards reducing the racial and ethnic enmity that has plagued the nation. Still, the Afro-Guyanese, who represent less than half of Guyana's population, tend to support the opposition People's National Congress party, which had held power from 1964 to 1992, and have responded to their lack of power by confronting the government on its policies, sometimes violently.

Timeline: PAST

1616
The first permanent Dutch settlements on Essequibo River

1815
The Netherlands cedes the territory to Britain

1966
Independence

1985
President Forbes Burnham dies

1990s
The government promises to end racial and ethnic discrimination

PRESENT

2000s
Territorial disputes with Suriname and Venezuela persist

Politics remains bitterly divided along ethnic lines

2006
Disastrous floods caused by high rainfall severely damage coastal agriculture

In the meantime, a divided Guyana may soon be confronted by an aggressive Venezuela, whose president seems intent on reigniting its long-standing border dispute with Guyana. With respect to rival offshore territorial claims between Guyana and Suriname, a UN tribunal has been established to settle the issue. The problem is particularly contentious because of the oil-producing potential of the disputed area.

Paraguay (Republic of Paraguay)

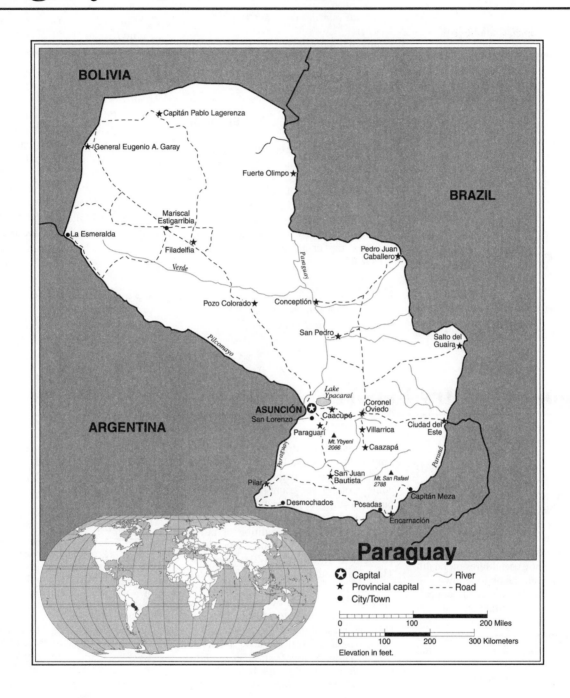

BOLIVIA

★ Capitán Pablo Lagerenza

★ General Eugenio A. Garay

Fuerte Olimpo ★

BRAZIL

La Esmeralda ●

Mariscal
Estigarribia ★

Verde

Filadelfia ★

Pedro Juan
Caballero ★

Paraguay

Pozo Colorado ★   Conceptión ★

San Pedro ★

Salto del
Guaira ★

Pilcomayo

Lake
Ypacaraí

ASUNCIÓN ✪
San Lorenzo

Caacupé ★

Coronel
Oviedo ★

Ciudad del
Este ★

ARGENTINA

Paraguarí ★
▲ Mt. Ybyeni
2066

Villarrica ★

Caazapá ★

Pilar ★

San Juan
Bautista ★

▲ Mt. San Rafael
2788

Paraná

Desmochados ●

Posadas ●

Capitán Meza ●

Encarnación ●

Paraguay

✪ Capital   〜 River
★ Provincial capital   - - - - Road
● City/Town

| 0 | 100 | 200 Miles |
| 0 | 100 | 200 | 300 Kilometers |

Elevation in feet.

Paraguay Statistics

GEOGRAPHY

Area in Square Miles (Kilometers): 157,048 (406,752) (about the size of California)
Capital (Population): Asunción (548,000)
Environmental Concerns: deforestation; water pollution; problems with waste disposal

Geographical Features: grassy plains and wooded hills east of Rio Paraguay; Gran Chaco region west of the river; mostly marshy plain near the river; dry forest and thorny scrub elsewhere

Climate: subtropical to temperate

PEOPLE

Population

Total: 6,191,368
Annual Growth Rate: 2.6%
Rural/Urban Population Ratio: 47/53

Major Languages: Spanish; Guaraní; Portuguese

Ethnic Makeup: 95% Mestizo; 5% white and Indian

Religions: 90% Roman Catholic; 10% Protestant

Health

Life Expectancy at Birth: 72 years (male); 77 years (female)

Infant Mortality Rate (Ratio): 26.67/1,000

Physicians Available (Ratio): 1/1,406

Education

Adult Literacy Rate: 94%

Compulsory (Ages): 6–12

COMMUNICATION

Telephones: 273,200 main lines

Daily Newspaper Circulation: 40 per 1,000 people

Televisions: 144 per 1,000

Internet Users: 100,000

TRANSPORTATION

Highways in Miles (Kilometers): 18,320 (29,500)

Railroads in Miles (Kilometers): 602 (970)

Usable Airfields: 937

Motor Vehicles in Use: 125,000

GOVERNMENT

Type: republic

Independence Date: May 14, 1811 (from Spain)

Head of State/Government: President Nicanor Duarte Frutos is both head of state and head of government

Political Parties: Colorado Party; Authentic Radical Liberal Party; Christian Democratic Party; Febrerist Revolutionary Party; National Encounter

Suffrage: universal and compulsory from 18 to 75

MILITARY

Military Expenditures (% of GDP): 0.9%

Current Disputes: none

ECONOMY

Currency ($U.S. Equivalent): 6,424 guaranis = $1

Per Capita Income/GDP: $4,600/$28.03 billion

GDP Growth Rate: 1.3%

Inflation Rate: 10.5%

Unemployment Rate: 16.4%

Labor Force: 1,700,000

Natural Resources: hydropower; timber; iron ore; manganese; limestone

Agriculture: cotton; sugarcane; soybeans; corn; wheat; tobacco; cassava (tapioca); fruits; vegetables; livestock; timber

Industry: sugar; cement; textiles; beverages; wood products

Exports: $2.7 billion (primary partners Brazil, Argentina, European Union)

Imports: $2.8 billion (primary partners Brazil, United States, Argentina)

SUGGESTED WEBSITE

http://www.cia.gov/cia/
publications/factbook/index.html

Paraguay Country Report

PARAGUAY

Paraguay is a country of paradox. Although there is little threat of foreign invasion and guerrilla activity is insignificant, a state of siege was in effect for 35 years, ending only in 1989 with the ouster of President (General) Alfredo Stroessner, who had held the reins of power since 1954. Government expenditures on health care in Paraguay are among the lowest in the Western Hemisphere, yet life expectancy is impressive, and infant mortality reportedly has fallen to levels comparable to more advanced developing countries. On the other hand, nearly a third of all reported deaths are of children under five years of age. Educational achievement, especially in rural areas, is low.

DEVELOPMENT

Paraguay's economy encountered severe difficulties in 2002 as a result of Argentina's financial crisis. Much of the economy is "underground" and is characterized by smuggling, money-laundering, drugs, and organized crime. Also problematic for development was the decision of the U.S. Congress to refuse Paraguay "certification" in the war against drug trafficking.

Paraguayan politics, economic development, society, and even its statistical base are comprehensible only within the context of its geography and Indo–Hispanic culture. Its geographic isolation in the midst of powerful neighbors has encouraged Paraguay's tradition of militarism and self-reliance—of being led by strongmen who tolerate little opposition. There is no tradition of constitutional government or liberal democratic procedures upon which to draw. Social values influence politics to the extent that politics is an all-or-nothing struggle for power and its accompanying prestige and access to wealth. These political values, in combination with a population that is largely poor and politically ignorant, contribute to the type of paternalistic, personal rule characteristic of a dictator such as Stroessner.

The paradoxical behavior of the Acuerdo Nacional—a block of opposition parties under Stroessner—was understandable within the context of a quest for power, or at least a share of power. Stroessner, always eager to divide and conquer, identified the Acuerdo Nacional as a fruitful field for new alliances. Leaping at the chance for patronage positions but anxious to demonstrate to Stroessner that they were a credible political force worthy of becom-

ing allies, Acuerdo members tried to win the support of unions and the peasantry. At the same time, the party purged its youth wing of leftist influences.

FREEDOM

Monolingual Guaraní speakers suffer from a marked disadvantage in the labor market. Where Guaraní speakers are employed, their wages are much lower than for monolingual Spanish speakers. This differential is accounted for by the "educational deficiencies" of the Guaraní speakers as opposed to those who speak Spanish.

Just when it seemed certain that Stroessner would rule until his death, Paraguayans were surprised in February 1989 when General Andrés Rodríguez—second-in-command of the armed forces, a member of the Traditionalist faction of the Colorado Party, which was in disfavor with the president, and a relative of Stroessner—seized power. Rodríguez's postcoup statements promised the democratization of Paraguay, respect for human rights, repudiation of drug trafficking, and the scheduling of presidential elections. Not surprisingly,

General Rodríguez emerged as President Rodríguez. When asked about voting irregularities, Rodríguez indicated that "real" democracy would begin with elections in 1993 and that his rule was a necessary "transition."

HEALTH/WELFARE

The Paraguayan government spends very little on human services and welfare. As a result, its population is plagued by health problems—including poor levels of nutrition, lack of drinkable water, absence of sanitation, and a prevalence of fatal childhood diseases.

"Real" democracy, following the 1993 victory of President Juan Carlos Wasmosy, had a distinct Paraguayan flavor. Wasmosy won the election with 40 percent of the vote; and the Colorado Party, which won most of the seats in Congress, was badly divided. When an opposition victory seemed possible, the military persuaded the outgoing government to push through legislation to reorganize the armed forces. In effect, they were made autonomous.

Political turmoil has continued to characterize Paraguayan politics. Assassination, an attempted coup in 2000, endemic corruption and back room deals are stock in trade. The victory of Paraguay's new president, Nicanor Duarte Frutos, will continue the Colorado's half-century lock on political power.

The problems he faces are serious. Corruption, counterfeiting, contraband, money laundering, and organized crime are entrenched. Despite campaign promises that "there will be no place for people who believe the party and state are there to be abused to the detriment of the country," few Paraguayans expect change. There are other issues that cloud the future. The commercialization of agriculture and high population growth have led to a dramatic increase in the number of landless families who have begun to migrate to urban areas where they resettle in shanty towns. Poverty effects nearly 60 percent of the population.

ACHIEVEMENTS

Paraguay has produced several notable authors, including Gabriel Casaccia and Augusto Roa Bastos. Roa Bastos makes extensive use of religious symbolism in his novels as a means of establishing true humanity and justice.

THE ECONOMY

It is difficult to acquire accurate statistics about the Paraguayan economy, in part because of the large informal sector and in part because of large-scale smuggling and drug trafficking. It is estimated that 20 percent of the nation's economy has been driven by illicit cross-border trafficking and that almost all of Paraguay's tobacco exports are illicit, counterfeit, or both. Officially, the country experienced negative

Timeline: PAST

1537
The Spanish found Asunción

1811
Independence is declared

1865–1870
War against the "Triple Alliance": Argentina, Brazil, and Uruguay

1954
General Alfredo Stroessner begins his rule

1961
Women win the vote

1989
Stroessner is ousted in a coup

1990s
A new Constitution is promulgated

PRESENT

2000s
Attempted coup in 2000

Nicanor Durate Frutos elected president in 2003

privatization plans, needed to raise revenue, must confront the military, which controls the most important state-owned enterprises. There is also concern about the "Brazilianization" of the eastern part of Paraguay, which has developed to the point at which Portuguese is heard as frequently as Spanish or Guaraní, the most common Indian language.

Peru (Republic of Peru)

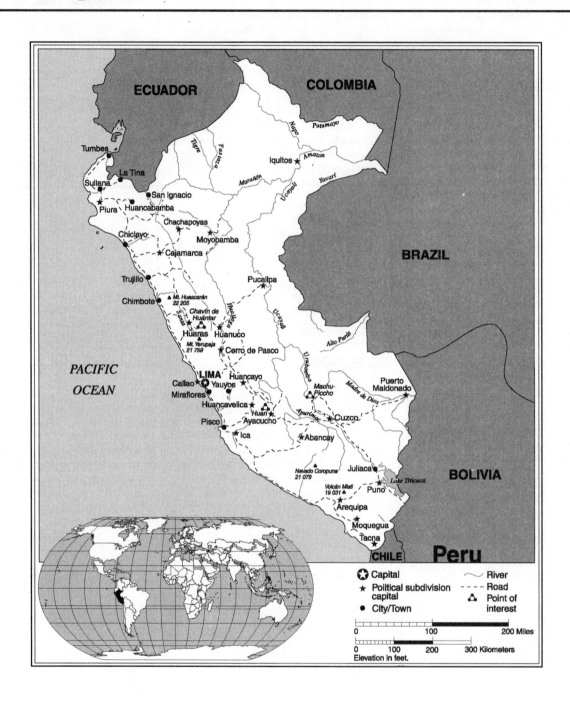

Peru Statistics

GEOGRAPHY

Area in Square Miles (Kilometers):

496,087 (1,285,200) (about the size of Alaska)

Capital (Population): Lima (6,743,000)

Environmental Concerns: deforestation; overgrazing; soil erosion; desertification; air and water pollution

Geographical Features: western coastal plain; high and rugged Andes Mountains in the center; eastern lowland jungle of Amazon Basin

Climate: temperate to tropical

PEOPLE

Population

Total: 27,544,305

Annual Growth Rate: 1.39%

98

Rural/Urban Population Ratio: 29/71

Major Languages: Spanish; Quechua; Aymara

Ethnic Makeup: 45% Indian; 37% Mestizo; 15% white, and others

Religions: more than 90% Roman Catholic; others

Health

Life Expectancy at Birth: 67 years (male); 71 years (female)

Infant Mortality Rate (Ratio): 33/1,000

Physicians Available (Ratio): 1/1,116

Education

Adult Literacy Rate: 90.9%

Compulsory (Ages): 6–11; free

COMMUNICATION

Telephones: 1,766,100 main lines

Daily Newspaper Circulation: 86 per 1,000 people

Televisions: 85 per 1,000

Internet Users: 2.5 million

TRANSPORTATION

Highways in Miles (Kilometers): 44,803 (72,146)

Railroads in Miles (Kilometers): 1,267 (2,041)

Usable Airfields: 234

Motor Vehicles in Use: 775,000

GOVERNMENT

Type: republic

Independence Date: July 28, 1821 (from Spain)

Head of State/Government: President Alejandro Toledo is both head of state and head of government

Political Parties: Change 90–New Majority; Union for Peru; Popular Action Party; Popular Christian Party; United Left; Civic Works Movement; Renovation Party; Alianza Popular Revolucionaria Americana (APRA); others

Suffrage: universal at 18

MILITARY

Military Expenditures (% of GDP): 1.3%

Current Disputes: a boundary dispute with Ecuador was resolved in 1999

ECONOMY

Currency ($U.S. Equivalent): 3.48 nuevo sols = $1

Per Capita Income/GDP: $5,200/$146.9 billion

GDP Growth Rate: 4%

Inflation Rate: 2.2%

Unemployment Rate: 13.4% (official rate); extensive underemployment

Labor Force: 7.5 million

Natural Resources: copper; silver; gold; petroleum; timber; fish; iron ore; coal; phosphate; potash

Agriculture: coffee; sugarcane; rice; wheat; potatoes; plantains; coca; livestock; wool; fish

Industry: mining; petroleum; fishing; textiles and clothing; food processing; cement; auto assembly; steel; shipbuilding; metal fabrication

Exports: $8.9 billion (primary partners United States, Japan, China)

Imports: $8.2 billion (primary partners United States, Colombia, Venezuela)

SUGGESTED WEBSITE

http://www.cia.org/cia/
publications/factbook/index.html

Peru Country Report

PERU: HEIR TO THE INCAS

The culture of Peru, from pre-Hispanic days to the present, has in many ways reflected the nation's variegated geography and climate. While 55 percent of the nation is covered with jungle, coastal Peru boasts one of the world's driest deserts. Despite its forbidding character, irrigation of the desert is made possible by run-offs from the Andes. This allows for the growing of a variety of crops in fertile oases that comprise about 5.5 percent of the land area.

Similarly, in the highlands, or *sierra*, there is little land available for cultivation. Because of the difficulty of the terrain, only about 7 percent of the land can produce crops. Indeed, Peru contains the lowest per capita amount of arable land in South America. The lack of fertile land has had—and continues to have—profound social and political repercussions, especially in the southern highlands near the city of Ayacucho.

THE SUPREMACY OF LIMA

Historically, coastal Peru and its capital city of Lima have attempted to dominate the sierra—politically, economically,

and, at times, culturally. Long a bureaucratic and political center, in the twentieth century Lima presided over the economic expansion of the coast. Economic opportunity in combination with severe population pressure in the sierra caused Lima and its port of Callao to grow tremendously in population, if not in services.

DEVELOPMENT

President Toledo's attempts to stimulate the economy with an infusion of foreign investments, privatization, a renegotiation of outstanding agreements with the IMF have been overshadowed by political scandal.

Ironically, the capital city has one of the worst climates for dense human settlement. Thermal inversions are common; between May and September, they produce a cloud ceiling and a pervasive cool fog.

Middle- and upper-class city dwellers have always been ignorant of the people of the highlands. Very few know either Quechua or Aymara, the Indian languages

spoken daily by millions of Peruvians. Yet this ignorance of the languages—and, by extension, of the cultures—has not prevented government planners or well-meaning intellectuals from trying to impose a variety of developmental models on the inhabitants of the sierra. In the late nineteenth century, for example, modernizers known collectively in Latin America as Positivists sought in vain to transform indigenous cultures by Europeanizing them. Other reformers sought to identify with the indigenous peoples. In the 1920s, a young intellectual named Victor Raúl Haya de la Torre fashioned a political ideology called APRISMO, which embraced the idea of an alliance of Indoamerica to recover the American states for their original inhabitants. While his broader vision proved to be too idealistic, the specific reforms he recommended for Peru were put into effect by reform-minded governments in the 1960s and 1970s. Sadly, reform continued to be developed and imposed from Lima, without an understanding of the rationale behind existing agrarian systems or an appreciation of a peasant logic that was based not on production of a surplus but on attaining a satisfying level of well-being. Much of the turmoil in rural Peru today stems from the agrarian reform of 1968–1979.

AGRARIAN REFORM

From the mid-1950s, rural laborers in the central and southern highlands and on the coastal plantations demonstrated an increasingly insistent desire for agrarian reform. Peasant communities in the sierra staged a series of land invasions and challenged the domination of the large estate, or *hacienda*, from outside. Simultaneously, tenants living on the estates pressured the hacienda system from within. In both cases, peasants wanted land.

The Peruvian government responded with both the carrot and the stick. A military regime, on the one hand, tried to crush peasant insurgency in 1962 and, on the other, passed agrarian reform legislation. The laws had no practical effect, but they did give legal recognition to the problem of land reform. In the face of continued peasant unrest in the south, the military enacted more substantial land laws in 1963, confiscating some property and redistributing it to peasants. The trend toward reform continued with the election of Francisco Belaunde Terry as president of a civilian government.

FREEDOM

President Toled's anti-corruption campaign ground to a halt in 2004 as the archaic court system proved totally incapable of handling the case load.

In the face of continued peasant militancy, Belaunde promised far-ranging reforms, but a hostile Congress refused to provide sufficient funds to implement the proposed reforms. Peasant unrest increased, and the government feared the development of widespread rural guerrilla warfare.

Against this backdrop of rural violence, the Peruvian military again seized power in 1968. To the astonishment of most observers, the military chose not to crush popular unrest but, rather, to embrace reforms. Clearly, the military had become sensitive to the political, social, and economic inequalities in Peru that had bred unrest. The military was intent on revolutionizing Peru from the top down rather than waiting for revolution from below.

In addition to land reform, the military placed new emphasis on Peru's Indian heritage. Tupac Amaru, an Incan who had rebelled against Spanish rule in 1780–1781, became a national symbol. In 1975, Quechua, the ancient language of the Inca, became Peru's second official language (along with Spanish). School curricula were revised and approached Peru's Indian heritage in a new and positive light.

NATIONALIZATION AND INTEGRATION

Behind the reforms, which were extended to industry and commerce and included the nationalization of foreign enterprises, lay the military's desire to provide for Peru a stable social and political order. The military leaders felt that they could provide better leadership in the quest for national integration and economic development than could "inefficient" civilians. Their ultimate goal was to construct a new society based on citizen participation at all levels.

As is so often the case, however, the reform model was not based on the realities of the society. It was naively assumed by planners that the Indians of the sierra were primitive socialists and wanted collectivized ownership of the land. In reality, each family's interests tended to make it competitive, rather than cooperative, with every other peasant family. Collectivization in the highlands failed because peasant communities outside the old hacienda structure clamored for the return of traditional lands that had been taken from them over the years. The Peruvian government found itself, awkwardly, attempting to defend the integrity of the newly reformed units from peasants who wanted their own land.

THE PATRON

Further difficulties were caused by the disruption of the patron–client relationship in the more traditional parts of the sierra. Hacienda owners, although members of the ruling elite, often enjoyed a tight bond with their tenants. Rather than a boss–worker relationship, the patron–client tie came close to kinship. Hacienda owners, for example, were often godparents to the children of their workers. A certain reciprocity was expected and given. But with the departure of the hacienda owners, a host of government bureaucrats arrived on the scene, most of whom had been trained on the coast and were ignorant of the customs and languages of the sierra. The peasants who benefited from the agrarian reform looked upon the administrators with a good deal of suspicion. The agrarian laws and decrees, which were all written in Spanish, proved impossible for the peasants to understand. Not surprisingly, fewer than half of the sierra peasants chose to join the collectives; and in a few places, peasants actually asked for the return of the hacienda owner, someone to whom they could relate. On the coast, the cooperatives did not benefit all agricultural workers equally, since permanent workers won the largest share of the benefits. In sum, the reforms had little impact on existing trends in agricultural production, failed to reverse income inequalities within the peasant population, and did not ease poverty.

The shortcomings of the reforms—in combination with drought, subsequent crop failures, rising food prices, and population pressure—created very difficult and tense situations in the sierra. The infant mortality rate rose 35 percent between 1978 and 1980, and caloric intake dropped well below the recommended minimum. More than half of the children under age six suffered from some form of malnutrition. Rural unrest continued.

RETURN TO CIVILIAN RULE

Unable to solve Peru's problems and torn by divisions within its ranks, the military stepped aside in 1980, and Belaunde was again elected as Peru's constitutional president. Despite the transition to civilian government, unrest continued in the highlands, and the appearance of a left-wing guerrilla organization known as Sendero Luminoso ("Shining Path") led the government to declare repeated states of emergency and to lift civil guarantees.

In an attempt to control the situation, the Ministry of Agriculture won the power to restructure and, in some cases, to liquidate the cooperatives and collectives established by the agrarian reform. Land was divided into small individual plots and given to the peasants. Because the plots can be bought, sold, and mortgaged, some critics argue that the undoing of the reform may hasten the return of most of the land into the hands of a new landed elite.

HEALTH/WELFARE

Peru's poor and the unemployed expect President Toledo to adopt policies that will stimulate the economy in ways that will generate employment and provide the revenue necessary for health care, social programs, and education.

Civilian rule, however, has not necessarily meant democratic rule for Peru's citizens. This helps to explain the spread of Sendero Luminoso despite its radical strategy and tactics of violence. By 1992, according to Diego García-Sayán, the executive director of the Andean Commission of Jurists, the Sendero Luminoso controlled "many parts of Peruvian territory. Through its sabotage, political assassinations, and terrorist actions, Sendero

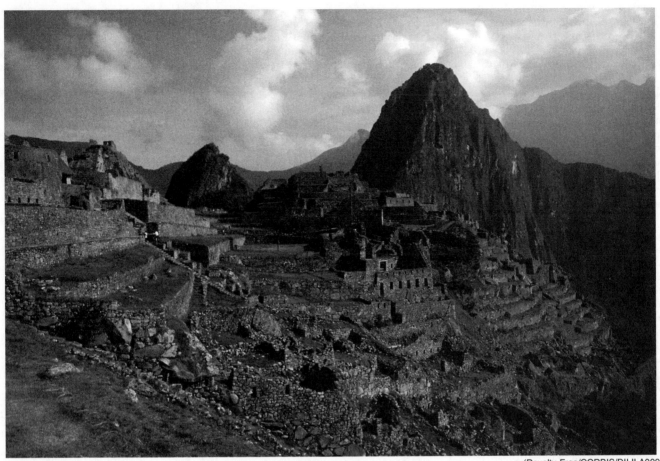

Machu Picchu, a famous Inca ruin, stands atop a 6,750-foot mountain in the Peruvian Andes.

Luminoso has helped to make political violence, which used to be rather infrequent, one of the main characteristics of Peruvian society."

Violence was not confined to the guerrillas of Sendero Luminoso or of the Tupac Amaru Revolutionary Movement (MRTA). Economist Javier Iguíñiz, of the Catholic University of Lima, argued that a solution to the violence required an understanding that it flowed from disparate, autonomous, and competing sources, including guerrillas, right-wing paramilitary groups, the Peruvian military and police forces, and cocaine traffickers, "particularly the well-armed Colombians active in the Huallaga Valley." Sendero Luminoso, until recently, was also active in the Huallaga Valley and profited from taxing drug traffickers. Raúl González, of Lima's Center for Development Studies, observed that as both the drug traffickers and the guerrillas "operate[d] outside the law, there has evolved a relationship of mutual convenience in certain parts of Huallaga to combat their common enemy, the state."

President Alan García vacillated on a policy toward the Sendero Luminoso in-

surgency. But ultimately, he authorized the launching of a major military offensive against Sendero Luminoso bases thought to be linked to drug trafficking. Later, determined to confront an insurgency that claimed 69,000 victims, President Alberto Fujimori armed rural farmers, known as *rondas campesinas,* to fight off guerrilla incursions. (The arming of peasants is not new to Peru; it is a practice that dates to the colonial period.) Critics correctly feared that the accelerated war against insurgents and drug traffickers would only strengthen the Peruvian military's political power.

A BUREAUCRATIC REVOLUTION?

Peruvian author Hernando DeSoto's best-selling and controversial book *The Other Path* (as opposed to Sendero Luminoso, or Shining Path), argues convincingly that both left- and right-wing governments in Latin America in general and in Peru in particular are neo-mercantile—that is, both intervene in the economy and promote the expansion of state activities. "Both strengthened the role of the government's bureaucracy until they made it the main ob-

stacle, rather than the main incentive, to progress, and together they produced, without consulting the electorate, almost 99 percent of the laws governing us." There are differences between left- and right-wing approaches: The left governs with an eye to redistributing wealth and well-being to the neediest groups, and the right tends to govern to serve foreign investors or national business interests. "Both, however, will do so with bad laws which explicitly benefit some and harm others. Although their aims may seem to differ, the result is that in Peru one wins or loses by political decisions. Of course, there is a big difference between a fox and a wolf but, for the rabbit, it is the similarity that counts."

DeSoto attacked the bureaucracy head-on when his private research center, the Institute for Liberty and Democracy, drafted legislation to abolish a collection of requirements built on the assumption that citizens are liars until proven otherwise. The law, which took effect in April 1989, reflected a growing rebellion against bureaucracy in Peru. Another law, which took effect in October 1989, radically simplified the process of gaining title to land. (DeSoto discovered that, to purchase a parcel of state-owned land in Peru, one had to invest 56 months of effort and 207 visits to 48 different offices). The legislation will have an important impact on the slum dwellers of Lima, for it will take much less time to regularize land titles as the result of invasions and seizures. Slum dwellers with land titles, according to DeSoto, invest in home improvements at a rate nine times greater than that of slum dwellers without titles. Slum dwellers who own property will be less inclined to turn to violent solutions to their problems.

The debureaucratization campaign has been paralleled by grassroots social movements that grew in response to a state that no longer could or would respond to the needs of its citizenry. Cataline Romero, director of the Bartolome de Las Cases Institute of Lima, said that "grass-roots social movements have blossomed into political participants that allow historically marginalized people to feel a sense of their own dignity and rights as citizens." Poor people have developed different strategies for survival as the government has failed to meet even their most basic needs. Most have entered the informal sector and have learned to work together through the formation of unions, mothers' clubs, and cooperatives. Concluded Romero: "As crisis tears institutions down, these communities are preparing the ground for building new institutions that are more responsive to the needs of the majority." DeSoto concurs and adds: "No one has ever considered that most poor Peruvians are a step ahead of the revolutionaries and are already changing the country's structures, and what politicians should be doing is guiding the change and giving it an appropriate institutional framework so that it can be properly used and governed."

By 2006 the advances made by the poor in the environs of the large cities was increasingly reflected in the sierras as well. Rolando Arellano, president of a large Peruvian marketing firm, noted: "Being called *serrano* is no longer an insult. That is a very important social change.... It is a vindication of the sierra tradition." Indeed, what is happening in Peru mirrors what is happening in indigenous communities in Ecuador and Bolivia. Formerly marginalized people have become a political, economic, and consumer force and now have the power to influence decisively elections at the national level.

DEMOCRACY AND THE "SELF-COUP"

In April 1992, President Fujimori, increasingly isolated and unable to effect economic

and political reforms, suspended the Constitution, arrested a number of opposition leaders, shut down Congress, and openly challenged the power of the judiciary. The military, Fujimori's staunch ally, openly supported the *autogolpe*, or "self-coup," as did business leaders and about 80 percent of the Peruvian people. In the words of political scientist Cynthia McClintock, writing in *Current History*, "Fujimori emerged a new caudillo, destroying the conventional wisdom that institutions, whether civilian or military, had become more important than individual leaders in Peru and elsewhere in Latin America." In 1993, a constitutional amendment allowed Fujimori to run for a second consecutive term.

In April 1995, Fujimori won a comfortable victory, with 64 percent of the vote. This was attributable to his successful economic policies, which saw the Peruvian economy grow by 12 percent—the highest in the world for 1994—and the campaign against Sendero Luminoso.

This represented the high point of Fujimori's administration. Increasingly dictatorial behavior and a fraudulent election in 2000, coupled with a severe economic slump precipitated by the crisis in Asian financial markets and the chaos wreaked on the infrastructure, coastal agriculture, and fishing industry by the phenomenon known as El Niño, undermined Fujimori's popularity. Rampant corruption was symbolized by one woman who, according to *The Christian Science Monitor*, "became so disgusted with her country's electoral fraud and corruption … that she undertook a simple but memorable political protest: handwashing the Peruvian flag in a public square for months on end."

ACHIEVEMENTS

Peru has produced a number of literary giants, including José Maria Mariategui, who believed that the "socialism" of the Indians should be a model for the rest of Peru; and Mario Vargas Llosa, always concerned with the complexity of human relationships.

Fujimori's decision to run for a third term, despite a constitutional prohibition, was followed by an election in April 2000 that observers characterized as "rife with fraud." Prodemocracy forces led by Alejandro Toledo, a one-time shoeshine boy, boycotted the run-off election and helped to organize a massive national protest march against Fujimori's swearing-in ceremony in July. Violence in the streets, press censorship, and revelations of massive corruption by Fujimori's intelligence

chief, Vladomiro Montesinos, forced Fujimori to resign from office and flee the country. Interim president Valentin Paniagua began the process of national reconstruction and created several commissions to investigate corruption and human-rights abuses.

Timeline: PAST

1500
The Inca Empire is at its height

1535
The Spanish found Lima

1821
Independence is proclaimed

1955
Women gain the right to vote

1968
A military coup: far-reaching reforms are pursued

1989
Debureaucratization campaign begins

1990s
El Niño spreads economic havoc and human misery; privatization

PRESENT

2000s
President Alberto Fujimori resigns
Reappearance of Sendero Luminoso in 2003

Toledo, elected president in 2001, has had a rough tenure in office. Despite solid economic growth that averaged 5 percent between 2001 and 2004 and rose to 6.7 percent in 2005, he has seen his popularity tumble. Persistent corruption and scandal in government, his failure to deliver on campaign promises of jobs, prosperity, and a return to democracy hamstrung his administration. Troubling also is the reappearance of Sendero Luminoso in 2003. Although small in number they have attacked security personnel, taken hostages, and initiated a rural campaign to win peasant support. They are well-financed because of their ties to Colombian cocaine traffickers. Indeed, former President Fujimori, whose supporters fondly refer to him as "El Chino"—and whose detractors call him "Chinochet"—still retains a large measure of popularity despite outstanding criminal charges. Many people support Fujimori because he is perceived as strong and decisive. A confident Fujimori, who had fled to Japan to escape criminal charges, appeared in Chile late in 2005 and fully expected to run as a candidate in the 2006 presidential election. But Chilean authorities, at the request of the Peruvian government, detained him while extradition papers were prepared.

The presidential campaign became particularly contentious when Ollanta Hu- mala, a nationalist former army officer, attended a news conference in Caracas, Venezuela, where he was praised by President Hugo Chavez for "joining the battle" against the Free Trade Area of the Americas supported by the United States. Outraged, the Peruvian government with- drew its ambassador from Venezuela for interfering with its election. Elections in April 2006 did not produce a clear winner and will necessitate a run-off between Ollanta Humala and former president Alan Garcia.

Suriname (Republic of Suriname)

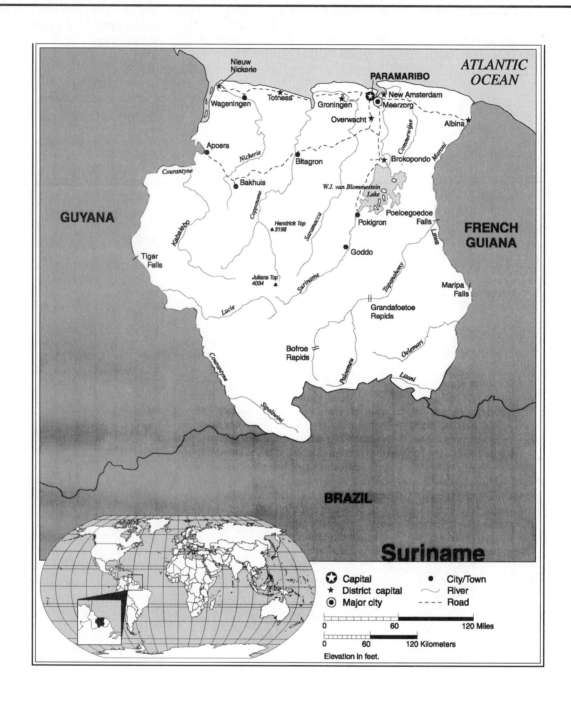

Suriname Statistics

GEOGRAPHY

Area in Square Miles (Kilometers): 63,037 (163,265) (about the size of Georgia)

Capital (Population): Paramaribo (216,000)

Environmental Concerns: deforestation; water pollution; threatened wildlife populations
Geographical Features: mostly rolling hills; a narrow coastal plain with swamps; mostly tropical rain forest
Climate: tropical

PEOPLE

Population

Total: 436,935
Annual Growth Rate: 0.31%
Rural/Urban Population Ratio: 50/50

Major Languages: Dutch; Sranantonga; English; Hindustani

Ethnic Makeup: 37% Hindustani (locally called East Indian); 31% Creole; 15% Javanese; 10% Bush Negro; 3% Amerindian; 3% Chinese

Religions: 27% Hindu; 25% Protestant; 23% Roman Catholic; 20% Muslim; 5% others

Health

Life Expectancy at Birth: 66 years (male); 71 years (female)

Infant Mortality Rate (Ratio): 25/1,000

Physicians Available (Ratio): 1/1,348

Education

Adult Literacy Rate: 93%

Compulsory (Ages): 6–16; free

COMMUNICATION

Telephones: 78,700 main lines

Daily Newspaper Circulation: 107 per 1,000 people

Televisions: 146 per 1,000 people

Internet Users: 20,000 (2002)

TRANSPORTATION

Highways in Miles (Kilometers): 2,813 (4,530)

Railroads in Miles (Kilometers): 103 (166)

Usable Airfields: 46

Motor Vehicles in Use: 66,000

GOVERNMENT

Type: constitutional democracy

Independence Date: November 25, 1975 (from the Netherlands)

Head of State/Government: President Runaldo Ronald Venetiaan is both head of state and head of government

Political Parties: New Front; Progressive Reform Party; National Democratic Party; National Party; others

Suffrage: universal at 18

MILITARY

Military Expenditures (% of GDP): 0.7%

Current Disputes: territorial disputes with Guyana and French Guiana

ECONOMY

Currency ($U.S. Equivalent): 2,346 guilders = $1

Per Capita Income/GDP: $3,500/$1.53 billion

GDP Growth Rate: 1.5%

Inflation Rate: 17%

Unemployment Rate: 17%

Labor Force: 100,000

Natural Resources: timber; hydropower; fish; kaolin; shrimp; bauxite; gold; nickel; copper; platinum; iron ore

Agriculture: paddy rice; bananas; palm kernels; coconuts; plantains; peanuts; livestock; forest products; shrimp

Industry: bauxite and gold mining; alumina and aluminum production; lumbering; food processing; fishing

Exports: $495 million (primary partners Norway, Netherlands, United States)

Imports: $604 million (primary partners United States, Netherlands, Trinidad and Tobago)

SUGGESTED WEBSITE

http://www.cia.gov/cia/
publications/factbook/index.html

Suriname Country Report

SURINAME: A SMALL-TOWN STATE

Settled by the British in 1651, Suriname, a small colony on the coast of Guiana, prospered with a plantation economy based on cocoa, sugar, coffee, and cotton. The colony came under Dutch control in 1667; in exchange, the British were given New Amsterdam (Manhattan, New York). The colony was often in turmoil because of Indian and slave uprisings, which took advantage of a weak Dutch power. When slavery was finally abolished, in 1863, plantation owners brought contract workers from China, India, and Java.

DEVELOPMENT

The bauxite industry, which had been in decline for 2 decades, now accounts for 15 percent of GDP and 70 percent of export earnings.

On the eve of independence from the Netherlands in 1975, Suriname was a complex, multiracial society. Although existing ethnic tensions were heightened as communal groups jockeyed for power in the new state, other factors cut across racial lines. Even though Creoles (native-born whites) were dominant in the bureaucracy as well as in the mining and industrial sectors, there was sufficient economic opportunity for all ethnic groups, so acute socioeconomic conflict was avoided.

THE POLITICAL FABRIC

Until 1980, Suriname enjoyed a parliamentary democracy that, because of the size of the nation, more closely resembled a small town or extended family in terms of its organization and operation. The various ethnic, political, and economic groups that comprised Surinamese society were united in what sociologist Rob Kroes describes as an "oligarchic web of patron–client relations" that found its expression in government. Through the interplay of the various groups, integration in the political process and accommodation of their needs were achieved. Despite the fact that most interests had access to the center of power, and despite the spirit of accommodation and cooperation, the military seized power early in 1980.

THE ROOTS OF MILITARY RULE

In Kroes's opinion, the coup originated in the army among noncommissioned officers, because they were essentially outside the established social and political system—they

were denied their "rightful" place in the patronage network. The officers had a high opinion of themselves and resented what they perceived as discrimination by a wasteful and corrupt government. Their demands for reforms, including recognition of an officers' union, were ignored. In January 1980, one government official talked of disbanding the army altogether.

FREEDOM

The Venetiaan government successfully brought to an end the Maroon insurgency of 8 years' duration. Under the auspices of the Organization of American States, the rebels turned in their weapons, and an amnesty for both sides in the conflict was declared.

The coup, masterminded and led by Sergeant Desire Bouterse, had a vague, undefined ideology. It claimed to be nationalist; and it revealed itself to be puritanical, in that it lashed out at corruption and demanded that citizens embrace civic duty and a work ethic. Ideological purity was maintained by government control or censorship of a once-free media. Wavering between left-wing radicalism and middle-of-the-road moderation, the rapid shifts in

Bouterse's ideological declarations suggest that this was a policy designed to keep the opposition off guard and to appease factions within the military.

The military rule of Bouterse seemed to come to an end early in 1988, when President Ramsewak Shankar was inaugurated. However, in December 1990, Bouterse masterminded another coup. The military and Bouterse remained above the rule of law, and the judiciary was not able to investigate or prosecute serious cases involving military personnel.

HEALTH/WELFARE

Amerindians and Maroons (the descendants of escaped African slaves) who live in the interior have suffered from the lack of educational and social services, partly from their isolation and partly from insurgency. With peace, however, it is hoped that the health, education, and general welfare of these peoples will improve.

With regard to Suriname's economic policy, most politicians see integration into Latin American and Caribbean markets as critical. The Dutch, who suspended economic aid after the 1990 coup, restored their assistance with the election of President Ronald Venetiaan in 1991. But civilian authorities were well aware of the roots of military rule and pragmatically allowed officers a role in government befitting their self-perceived status.

In 1993, Venetiaan confronted the military when it refused to accept his choice of officers to command the army. Army reform was still high on the agenda in 1995 and was identified by President Venetiaan as one of his government's three great tasks. The others were economic reform necessary to ensure Dutch aid and establish the country's eligibility for international credit; and the need to reestablish ties with the interior to consolidate an Organization of American States–brokered peace, after almost a decade of insurgency.

ACHIEVEMENTS

Suriname, unlike most other developing countries, has a small foreign debt and a relatively strong repayment capacity. This is substantially due to its export industry.

A loan negotiated with the Dutch in 2001 will help Suriname to develop agriculture, bauxite, and the gold-mining industry. Unfortunately the development policy also threatens deforestation, because of timber exports, and the pollution of waterways as a result of careless mining practices. Housing and health care also ranked highly on the government's list of priorities under President Jules Wijdenbosch. The government realized that it cannot forever depend on the largesse of the Netherlands. The planning and development minister stated that aid must be sought from other countries and that Suriname must increasingly rely on its own resources.

Parliamentary elections in 2005 were hotly contested between former President Ronald Venetiaan's New Front coalition and the National Democratic Party of former dictator Desi Bouterse. Ultimately a regional assembly reelected Venetiaan as president. His government faces some difficult problems. Inflation is high, the health system is close to collapse, and the government bureaucracy is filled with officeholders who owe their positions to patronage rather than need. Venetiaan has introduced austerity measures similar to those he implemented in 1991–96 with some success at that time.

Timeline: PAST

1651
British colonization efforts

1667
The Dutch receive Suriname from the British in exchange for New Amsterdam

1975
Independence of the Netherlands

1980s
A military coup

1990s
A huge drug scandal implicates high-level government officials

PRESENT

2000s
The Netherlands extends loan aid

2005
Ronald Venetiaan reelected president

Uruguay (Oriental Republic of Uruguay)

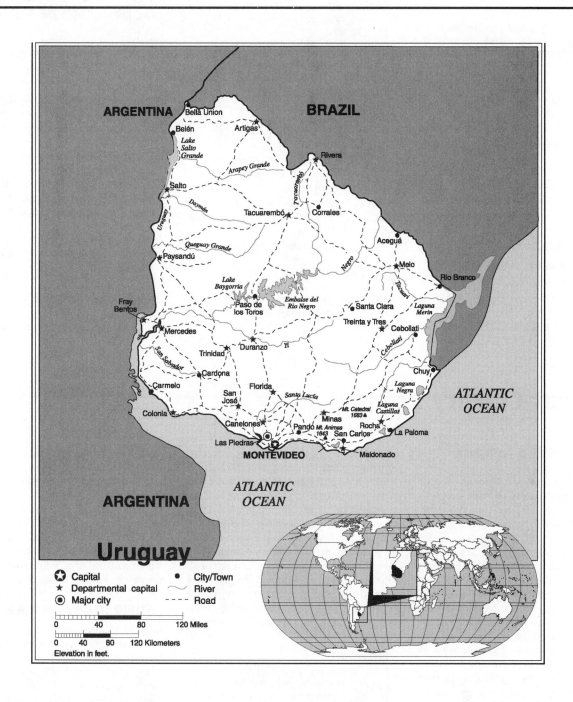

Uruguay Statistics

GEOGRAPHY

Area in Square Miles (Kilometers): 68,037 (176,215) (about the size of Washington State)

Capital (Population): Montevideo (1,304,000)

Environmental Concerns: transboundary pollution from Brazilian power plant; water pollution; waste disposal

Geographical Features: mostly rolling plains and low hills; fertile coastal lowland

Climate: warm temperate

PEOPLE

Population

Total: 3,399,237

Annual Growth Rate: 0.51%

Rural/Urban Population Ratio: 9/91

Major Languages: Spanish; Portunol:
  Brazilero
Ethnic Makeup: 88% white; 8% Mestizo;
  4% black
Religions: 66% Roman Catholic; 2%
  Protestant; 2% Jewish; 30%
  nonprofessing or others

Health

Life Expectancy at Birth: 72 years (male);
  79 years (female)
Infant Mortality Rate (Ratio): 15.2/1,000
Physicians Available (Ratio): 1/282

Education

Adult Literacy Rate: 97.3%
Compulsory (Ages): for 6 years between 6
  and 14; free

COMMUNICATION

Telephones: 946,500 main lines
Daily Newspaper Circulation: 241 per
  1,000 people
Televisions: 191 per 1,000
Internet Users: 400,000 (2002)

TRANSPORTATION

Highways in Miles (Kilometers): 5,390
  (8,983)
Railroads in Miles (Kilometers): 1,243
  (2,073)
Usable Airfields: 65
Motor Vehicles in Use: 525,000

GOVERNMENT

Type: republic
Independence Date: August 25, 1828
  (from Brazil)
Head of State/Government: President
  Tabaré Vázquez is both head of state and
  head of government
Political Parties: National (Blanco) Party
  factions; Colorado Party factions; Broad
  Front Coalition; others
Suffrage: universal and compulsory at 18

MILITARY

Military Expenditures (% of GDP): 2%
Current Disputes: boundary disputes with
  Brazil

ECONOMY

Currency ($U.S. Equivalent): 28.21 pesos
  = $1
Per Capita Income/GDP: $12,600/$42.94
  billion
GDP Growth Rate: 0.3%
Inflation Rate: 10.2%
Unemployment Rate: 16.1%
Labor Force: 1,380,000
Natural Resources: arable land;
  hydropower; minor minerals; fisheries
Agriculture: wheat; rice; corn; sorghum;
  livestock; fish
Industry: food processing; textiles;
  chemicals; beverages; transportation
  equipment; petroleum products
Exports: $2.1 billion (primary partners
  Mercosur, European Union, United
  States)
Imports: $1.9 billion (primary partners
  Mercosur, European Union, United
  States)

SUGGESTED WEBSITE

http://www.cia.gov/cia/
  publications/factbook/index.html

Uruguay Country Report

URUGUAY: ONCE A PARADISE

The modern history of Uruguay begins with the administration of President José Batlle y Ordoñez. Between 1903 and 1929, Batlle's Uruguay became one of the world's foremost testing grounds for social change, and it eventually became known as the "Switzerland of Latin America." Batlle's Colorado Party supported a progressive role for organized labor and formed coalitions with the workers to challenge the traditional elite and win benefits. Other reforms included the formal separation of church and state, nationalization of key sectors of the economy, and the emergence of mass-based political parties. Batlle's masterful leadership was facilitated by a nation that was compact in size; had a small, educated, and homogeneous population; and had rich soil and a geography that facilitated easy communication and national integration.

DEVELOPMENT

Uruguay's people, in an assertion of their independence, in 2003 rejected recommendations made by the IMF with regard to economic reform.

Although the spirit of Batllismo eventually faded after his death in 1929, Batlle's legacy is still reflected in many ways. Reports on income distribution reveal an evenness that is uncommon in developing countries. Extreme poverty is unusual in Uruguay, and most of the population enjoy an adequate diet and minimal standards of living. Health care is within the reach of all citizens. And women in Uruguay are granted equality before the law, are present in large numbers at the national university, and have access to professional careers.

FREEDOM

Uruguay's military is constitutionally prohibited from involvement in issues of domestic security unless ordered to do so by civilian authorities. The press is free and unrestricted, as is speech. The political process is open, and academic freedom is the norm in the national university.

But this model state fell on bad times beginning in the 1960s. Runaway inflation, declining agricultural production, a swollen bureaucracy, official corruption, and bleak prospects for the future led to the appearance of youthful middle-class urban guerrillas. Known as Tupamaros, they first attempted to jar the nation to its senses with a Robin Hood–style approach to reform. When that failed, they turned increasingly to terrorism in an effort to destroy a state that resisted reform. The Uruguayan government was unable to quell the rising violence. It eventually called on the military, which crushed the Tupamaros and then drove the civilians from power in 1973.

RETURN TO CIVILIAN RULE

In 1980, the military held a referendum to try to gain approval for a new constitution. Despite extensive propaganda, 60 percent of Uruguay's population rejected the military's proposals and forced the armed forces to move toward a return to civilian government. Elections in 1984 returned the Colorado Party to power, with Julio Maria Sanguinetti as president.

By 1989, Uruguay was again a country of laws, and its citizens were anxious to heal the wounds of the 1970s. A test of the nation's democratic will involved the highly controversial 1986 Law of Expiration, which effectively exempted military and police personnel from prosecution for alleged human-rights abuses committed under orders during the military regime.

Many Uruguayans objected and created a pro-referendum commission. They invoked a provision in the Constitution that is unique to Latin America: *Article 79* states that if 25 percent of eligible voters sign a petition, it will initiate a referendum, which, if passed, will implicitly annul the Law of Expiration. Despite official pressure, the signatures were gathered. The referendum was held on April 16, 1989. It was defeated by a margin of 57 to 43 percent.

HEALTH/WELFARE

Uruguay compares favorably with all of Latin America in terms of health and welfare. Medical care is outstanding, and the quality of public sanitation equals or exceeds that of other developing countries. Women, however, still experience discrimination in the workplace.

The winds of free-market enterprise and privatization then started to blow through the country. When Sanguinetti regained the presidency in 1994, he was expected, as the leader of the Colorado Party—the party of José Batlle—to maintain the economic status quo. But in 1995, he said that his first priority would be to reform the social-security system, which cannot pay for itself, in large part because people in Uruguay are allowed to retire years earlier than in other countries. Reform was also begun in other sectors of the economy. Government employees were laid off, tariffs were reduced, and a program to privatize state industries was inaugurated. The new policies, according to officials, would produce "a change of mentality and culture" in public administration.

In his first two years in power, Sanguinetti's successor, Jorge Batlle, has been unable to bring recession to an end. Low prices for agricultural exports, Argentina's economic malaise, and a public debt that stood at 45 percent of gross domestic prod-

Timeline: PAST

1624
Jesuits and Franciscans establish missions in the region

1828
Uruguay is established as a buffer state between Argentina and Brazil

1903–1929
The era of President José Batlle y Ordoñez; social reform

1932
Women win the right to vote

1963–1973
Tupamaro guerrillas wage war against the government

1990s
The government endorses sweeping economic and social reforms

PRESENT

2000s
President Battle struggles with the economy

Presidential elections scheduled for October 2004

2004
Tabaré Vázquez becomes president and promises a social transformation

uct presented the government with difficult policy decisions. To add to these woes, the appearance of hoof-and-mouth disease in southern Brazil in mid-2001 threatened Uruguay's important beef and wool industries. Once again there was talk of privatization, but a referendum held in December 2003 on the future of ANCAP, the national oil company showed that 62 percent of the electorate wanted no change. Interestingly, these same respondents also oppose monopolies. The failure of the referendum was seen by some political observers as a

signal that Batlle would not win reelection in October 2004. That is exactly what happened. What was surprising was neither traditional party won the presidential election. Rather the victor, Tabaré Vázquez, headed up a broad front of political factions that ranged from Communists to Christian Democrats. During the campaign Vázquez's rhetoric promised far-reaching changes that suggested a social transformation of the country. Uruguay's reality, however, is that it does not have the financial resources necessary to support the kinds of domestic programs that featured prominently in campaign speeches. The president has recently indicated that $100 million will be earmarked for the poor. He has also indicated that his government will reopen investigations into the disappearance of people during the years of military rule. On the foreign policy front he has re-established relations with Cuba, raised questions about the wisdom of free-trade agreements, and moved closer to populist leaders such as Brazil's Lula and Venezuela's Chavez.

ACHIEVEMENTS

Of all the small countries in Latin America, Uruguay has been the most successful in creating a distinct culture. High levels of literacy and a large middle class have allowed Uruguay an intellectual climate that is superior to many much-larger nations.

People expect results and not rhetoric. One woman who has seen her pension drastically reduced by Uruguay's economic malaise told a *New York Times* reporter: "The front has to carry out the program it promised us. If not, the people will protest, and when it comes time to vote again, we will throw them out. We're not going to accept another neoliberal government, indifferent to people's social needs."

Venezuela (Bolivarian Republic of Venezuela)

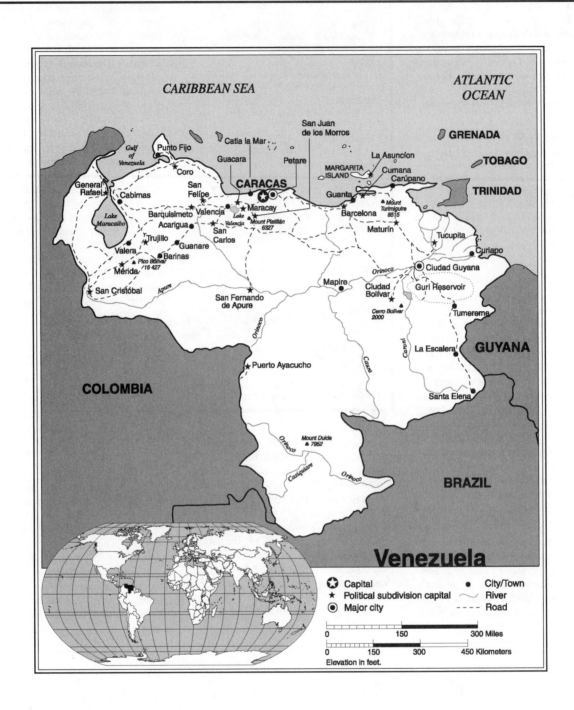

CARIBBEAN SEA

ATLANTIC OCEAN

GRENADA

TOBAGO

TRINIDAD

San Juan de los Morros

Catia la Mar

Punto Fijo

Gulf of Venezuela

Guacara

Petare

La Asunción

MARGARITA ISLAND

Cumana

Carúpano

Coro

General Rafael

Cabimas

San Felípe

CARACAS

Guanta

Lake Maracaibo

Barquisimeto

Valencia

Maracay

Lake Valencia

Barcelona

Mount Turimiguire 8515

Acarigua

San Carlos

Mount Platillán 6327

Maturín

Tucupita

Trujillo

Guanare

Curiapo

Valera

Barinas

Ciudad Guyana

Pico Bolívar 16 427

Orinoco

Mérida

Mapire

Ciudad Bolívar

Guri Reservoir

San Cristóbal

Apure

Tumeremo

San Fernando de Apure

Cerro Bolívar 2000

Caura

Caroní

La Escalera

GUYANA

COLOMBIA

Puerto Ayacucho

Orinoco

Santa Elena

Mount Duida 7952

Orinoco

Casiquiare

Orinoco

BRAZIL

Venezuela

- ✪ Capital
- ★ Political subdivision capital
- ◎ Major city
- ● City/Town
- ～ River
- - - - Road

| 0 | 150 | 300 Miles |
| 0 | 150 | 300 | 450 Kilometers |

Elevation in feet.

Venezuela Statistics

GEOGRAPHY

Area in Square Miles (Kilometers):
352,143 (912,050) (about twice the size of California)
Capital (Population): Caracas (3,700,000)

Environmental Concerns: water, sewage, air, oil, and urban pollution; deforestation; soil degradation

Geographical Features: a flat coastal plain and the Orinoco Delta are bordered by

Andes Mountains and hills; plains (llanos) extend between the mountains and the Orinoco; Guyana Highlands and plains are south of the Orinoco

Climate: varies from tropical to temperate

PEOPLE

Population

Total: 25,017,387
Annual Growth Rate: 1.44%
Rural/Urban Population Ratio: 14/86
Major Languages: Spanish; indigenous
dialects
Ethnic Makeup: 67% Mestizo; 21% white;
10% black; 2% Indian
Religions: 96% Roman Catholic; 4%
Protestant and others

Health

Life Expectancy at Birth: 70 years (male);
76 years (female)
Infant Mortality Rate (Ratio): 23/1,000
Physicians Available (Ratio): 1/576

Education

Adult Literacy Rate: 93%
Compulsory (Ages): 5–15; free

COMMUNICATION

Telephones: 2,841,800 main lines
Daily Newspaper Circulation: 215 per
1,000 people
Televisions: 183 per 1,000

Internet Users: 1,274,400 (2002)

TRANSPORTATION

Highways in Miles (Kilometers): 57,693
(96,155)
Railroads in Miles (Kilometers): 363 (584)
Usable Airfields: 366
Motor Vehicles in Use: 2,025,000

GOVERNMENT

Type: republic
Independence Date: July 5, 1811 (from
Spain)
Head of State/Government: President
Hugo Chavez Frias is both head of state
and head of government
Political Parties: National Convergence;
Social Christian Party; Democratic
Action; Movement Toward Socialism;
Radical Cause; Homeland for All
Suffrage: universal at 18

MILITARY

Military Expenditures (% of GDP): 1.3%
Current Disputes: territorial disputes with
Guyana and Colombia

ECONOMY

Currency ($ U.S. Equivalent): 1,607
bolívars = $1
Per Capita Income/GDP: $4,800/$117.9
billion
GDP Growth Rate: –9.2%
Inflation Rate: 31.1%
Unemployment Rate: 18%
Labor Force: 9,900,000
Natural Resources: petroleum; natural
gas; iron ore; gold; bauxite; other
minerals; hydropower; diamonds
Agriculture: corn; sorghum; sugarcane;
rice; bananas; vegetables; coffee;
livestock; fish
Industry: petroleum; mining; construction
materials; food processing; textiles;
steel; aluminum; motor-vehicle
assembly
Exports: $25.86 billion (primary partners
United States, Colombia, Brazil)
Imports: $10.71 billion (primary partners
United States, Japan, Colombia)

SUGGESTED WEBSITE

http://www.cia.org/cia/
publications/factbook/index.html

Venezuela Country Report

VENEZUELA: CHANGING TIMES

Venezuela is a country in transition. After decades of rule by a succession of *caudillos* (strong, authoritarian rulers), national leaders can now point to four decades of unbroken civilian rule and peaceful transfers of presidential power. Economic growth—stimulated by mining, industry, and petroleum—has, until recently, been steady and, at times, stunning. With the availability of better transportation; access to radio, television, newspapers, and material goods; and the presence of the national government in once-isolated towns, regional diversity is less striking now than a decade ago. Fresh lifestyles and perspectives, dress and music, and literacy and health care are changing the face of rural Venezuela.

THE PROBLEMS OF CHANGE

Such changes have not been without problems—significant ones. Venezuela, despite its petroleum-generated wealth, remains a nation plagued by huge imbalances, in-equalities, contradictions, and often bitter debate over the meaning and direction of national development. Some critics note the danger of the massive rural-

to-urban population shift and the influx of illegal immigrants (from Colombia and other countries), both the result of Venezuela's rapid economic development. Others warn of the excessive dependence on petroleum as the means of development and are concerned about the agricultural output at levels insufficient to satisfy domestic requirements. Venezuela, once a food exporter, periodically has had to import large amounts of basic commodities—such as milk, eggs, and meat—to feed the expanding urban populations. Years of easy, abundant money also promoted undisciplined borrowing abroad to promote industrial expansion and has saddled the nation with a serious foreign-debt problem. Government corruption was rampant and, in fact, led to the impeachment of President Carlos Andrés Pérez in 1993.

THE CHARACTER OF MODERNIZATION

The rapid changes in Venezuelan society have produced a host of generalizations as to the nature of modernization in this Andean republic. Commentators who speak of a revolutionary break with the past—of a "new" Venezuela completely severed from its historic roots reaching back to the

sixteenth century—ignore what is enduring about Venezuela's Hispanic culture.

Even before it began producing petroleum, Venezuela was not a sleepy backwater. Its Andean region was always the most prosperous area in the South American continent and was a refuge from the civil wars that swept other parts of the country. There were both opportunity and wealth in the coffee-growing trade. With the oil boom and the collapse of coffee prices in 1929, the Andean region experienced depopulation as migrants left the farms for other regions or for the growing Andean cities. In short, Venezuela's rural economy should not be seen as a static point from which change began but as a part of a dynamic process of continuing change, which now has the production of petroleum as its focus.

CULTURAL IDENTITY

Historian John Lombardi identifies language, culture, and an urban network centered on the capital city of Caracas as primary forces in the consolidation of the nation. "Across the discontinuities of civil war and political transformation, agricultural and industrial economies, rural life styles and urban agglomerations, Venezuela

(United States Dept. of the Interior, Bureau of Mines/DILmhhe001875)

When oil was discovered in Venezuela, rapid economic growth caused many problems in national development. By depending on petroleum as the major source of wealth, Venezuela was at the mercy of the fickle world energy market.

has functioned through the stable network of towns and cities whose interconnections defined the patterns of control, the directions of resource distribution, and the country's identity."

One example of the country's cultural continuity can be seen by looking into one dimension of Venezuelan politics. Political parties are not organized along class lines but tend to cut across class divisions. This is not to deny the existence of class consciousness—which is certainly ubiquitous in Venezuela—but it is not a major *political* force. Surprisingly, popular support for elections and strong party affiliations are more characteristic of rural areas than of cities. The phenomenon cannot be explained as a by-product of modernization. Party membership and electoral participation are closely linked to party organization, personal ties and loyalties, and charismatic leadership. The party, in a sense, becomes a surrogate *patrón* that has power and is able to deliver benefits to the party faithful.

IMPACTS OF URBANIZATION

Another insight into Hispanic political culture can be found in the rural-to-urban shift in population that has often resulted in large-scale seizures of land in urban areas by peasants. Despite the illegality of the

seizures, such actions are frequently encouraged by officials because, they argue, it provides the poor with enough land to maintain political stability and to prevent peasants from encroaching on richer neighborhoods. Pressure by the new urban dwellers at election time usually results in their receiving essential services from government officials. In other words, municipal governments channel resources in return for expected electoral support from the migrants. Here is a classic Hispanic response to challenge from below—to bend, to cooperate.

Cultural values also underlie both the phenomenon of internal migration and the difficulty of providing adequate skilled labor for Venezuela's increasingly technological economy. While the attraction of the city and its many opportunities is one reason for the movement of population out of rural areas, so too is that segment of Venezuelan culture, which belittles the peasant and rural life in general. Similarly, the shortage of skilled labor is the result not only of inadequate training but also of social values that neither reward nor dignify skilled labor.

DEVELOPMENT

The populist Chavez government, under the ideological umbrella of "21st century Socialism," is in the process of reorganizing the nation's oil industry and takes a larger share from private multinational companies. The banks are also being reorganized with strict limits placed on lending. Internationally, Venezuela has developed a state-to-state barter system and trades items as diverse as cattle, oil, and cement.

THE SOCIETY

The rapid pace of change has contributed to a reexamination of the roles and rights of women in Venezuela. In recent years, women have occupied positions in the cabinet and in the Chamber of Deputies; several women deputies have held important posts in political parties.

Yet while educated women are becoming more prominent in the professions, there is a reluctance to employ women in traditional "men's" jobs, and blatant inequality still blemishes the workplace. Women, for example, are paid less than men for similar work. And although modern feminist goals have become somewhat of a social and economic force, at least in urban centers, the traditional roles of wife and mother continue to hold the most prestige, and physical beauty is still often viewed as a woman's most precious asset. In addition, many men seek deference from

women rather than embracing social equality. Nevertheless, the younger generations of Venezuelans are experiencing the social and cultural changes that have tended to follow women's liberation in Western industrialized nations: higher levels of education and career skills; broadened intellectualism; increasing freedom and equality for both men and women; relaxed social mores; and the accompanying personal turmoil, such as rising divorce and single-parenthood rates.

FREEDOM

Freedom of the press has experienced some erosion under the current government. Media watchdogs have accused Chavez for, in the words of *BBC News*, "creating a hostile and intimidatory climate for journalists, while some major private media outlets have been have been criticised for playing a direct role in the opposition movement against him...." A controversial media law passed in 2005, ostensibly aimed at improving broadcast standards, also "bans material deemed to harm national security" and is seen by some as an attempt to silence media criticism.

Venezuelans generally enjoy a high degree of individual liberty. Civil, personal, and political rights are protected by a strong and independent judiciary. Citizens generally enjoy a free press. There exists the potential for governmental abuse of press freedom, however. Several laws leave journalists vulnerable to criminal charges, especially in the area of libel. Journalists must be certified to work, and certification may be withdrawn by the government if journalists are perceived to stray from the "truth," misquote sources, or refuse to correct "errors." But as a rule, radio, television, and newspapers are free and are often highly critical of the government.

The civil and human rights enjoyed by most Venezuelans have not necessarily extended to the nation's Indian population in the Orinoco Basin. For years, extra-regional forces—in the form of rubber gatherers, missionaries, and developers—have to varying degrees undermined the economic self-sufficiency, demographic viability, and tribal integrity of indigenous peoples. A government policy that stressed the existence of only one Venezuelan culture posed additional problems for Indians.

In 1991, however, President Pérez signed a decree granting a permanent homeland, encompassing some 32,000 square miles in the Venezuelan Amazon forest, to the country's 14,000 Yanomamö Indians. Venezuela will permit no mining

Caracas, Venezuela, an ultra-modern city of 3.7 million exemplifying the extremes of poverty and wealth that exist in Latin America, sprawls for miles over mountains and valleys.

or farming in the territory and will impose controls on existing religious missions. President Pérez stated that "the primary use will be to preserve and to learn the traditional ways of the Indians." As James Brooke reported in *The New York Times,* "Venezuela's move has left anthropologists euphoric."

Race relations are outwardly tranquil in Venezuela, but there exists an underlying racism in nearly all arenas. People are commonly categorized by the color of their skin, with white being the most prized. Indeed, race, not economic level, is still a major social-level determinant. This unfortunate reality imparts a sense of frustration and a measure of hopelessness to many of Venezuela's people, in that even those who acquire a good education and career training may be discriminated against in the workplace because they are "of color." Considering that only one-fifth of the population are of white extraction, with 67 percent Mestizos and 10 percent blacks, this is indeed a widespread and debilitating problem.

President Chavez is of mixed racial ancestry and has won broad support among the disadvantaged because he has moved to remove, in the words of Benjamin Keene and Keith Haynes, "the social stigma historically attached to the terms *mulatto, mestizo,* and *black.* This new sense of dignity, not just the hope for improvement in economic status, helped to explain the fierce loyalty of these masses toward their leader." Indicative of an underlying racism among some of those opposed to Chavez are the terms of opprobrium used to describe him, including *el Mono* (the monkey) or *el Negro* (the black).

A VIGOROUS FOREIGN POLICY

Venezuela has always pursued a vigorous foreign policy. In the words of former president Luis Herrera Campins: "Effective action by Venezuela in the area of international affairs must take certain key facts into account: economics—we are a producer-exporter of oil; politics—we have a stable, consolidated democracy; and geopolitics—we are at one and the same time a Caribbean, Andean, Atlantic, and Amazonian country." Venezuela has long assumed that it should be the guardian of Simón Bolívar's ideal of creating an independent and united Latin America. The nation's memory of its continental leadership, which developed during the Wars for Independence (1810–1826), has been rekindled in Venezuela's desire to promote the political and economic integration of both the continent and the Caribbean. Venezuela's foreign policy remains true to the Bolivarian ideal of an independent Latin America and it should come as no surprise that President Chavez has adopted the term "Bolivarian Revolution" for his movement. In the Caribbean Venezuela has invested in industry and provided cut-rate petroleum to many microstates. In South America he has established close relations with other populist governments, including those in Brazil, Bolivia, Argentina, and Uruguay. And he has openly challenged the United States with his strong stand against free-trade agreements.

PROMISING PROSPECTS TURN TO DISILLUSIONMENT

The 1980s brought severe turmoil to Venezuela's economy. The boom times of the 1970s turned to hard times as world oil prices dropped. Venezuela became unable to service its massive foreign debt (currently $34 billion) and to subsidize the "common good," in the form of low gas and transportation prices and other amenities. In 1983, the currency, the bolívar, which had remained stable and strong for many years at 4.3 to the U.S. dollar, was devalued, to an official rate of 14.5 bolívars to the dollar. This was a boon to foreign visitors to the country, which became known as one of the world's greatest travel bargains, but a catastrophe for Venezuelans. (In June 2004, the exchange rate was about 1,116 bolívars to the dollar on the free market.)

President Jaime Lusinchi of the Democratic Action Party, who took office early in 1984, had the unenviable job of trying to cope with the results of the preceding years of free spending, high expectations, dependence on oil, and spiraling foreign debt. Although the country's gross national product grew during his tenure (agriculture growth contributed significantly, rising from 0.4 percent of gross national product in 1983 to 6.8 percent in 1986), austerity measures were in order. The Lusinchi government was not up to the challenge. Indeed, his major legacy was a corruption scandal at the government agency Recadi, which was responsible for allocating foreign currency to importers at the official rate of 14.5 bolívars to the dollar. It was alleged that billions of dollars were skimmed, with a number of high-level government officials, including three finance ministers, implicated. Meanwhile, distraught Venezuelans watched inflation and the devalued bolívar eat up their savings; the once-blooming middle class started getting squeezed out.

HEALTH/WELFARE

A 1997 survey of children working in the informal sector revealed that 25 percent were between ages 5 and 12; that they worked more than 7 hours a day and earned about $2; and that their "jobs" included garbage collection, lotteries and gambling, and selling drugs. Fewer than half attended school. President Chavez has created 6,840 cooperatives that now employ 210,000 people, many of them who previously were unemployed or underemployed.

In the December 1988 national elections, another Democratic Action president, Carlos Andrés Pérez, was elected. Pérez, who had served as president from 1974 to 1979, was widely rumored to have stolen liberally from Venezuela's coffers during that tenure. Venezuelans joked at first that "Carlos Andrés is coming back to get what he left behind," but as the campaign wore on, some political observers were dismayed to hear the preponderance of the naive sentiment that "now he has enough and will really work for Venezuela this time."

One of Pérez's first acts upon reentering office was to raise the prices of government-subsidized gasoline and public transportation. Although he had warned that tough austerity measures would be implemented, the much-beleaguered and disgruntled urban populace took to the streets in February 1989 in the most serious rioting to have occurred in Venezuela since it became a democracy. Army tanks rolled down the

major thoroughfares of Caracas, the capital; skirmishes between the residents and police and military forces were common; looting was widespread. The government announced that 287 people had been killed. Unofficial hospital sources charge that the death toll was closer to 2,000. A stunned Venezuela quickly settled down in the face of the violence, mortified that such a debacle, widely reported in the international press, should take place in this advanced and peaceable country. But tourism, a newly vigorous and promising industry as a result of favorable currency-exchange rates, subsided immediately; it has yet to recover fully.

On February 4, 1992, another ominous event highlighted Venezuela's continuing political and economic weaknesses. Rebel military paratroopers, led by Hugo Chavez, attacked the presidential palace in Caracas and government sites in several other major cities. The coup attempt, the first in Venezuela since 1962, was rapidly put down by forces loyal to President Pérez, who escaped what he described as an assassination attempt. Reaction within Venezuela was mixed, reflecting widespread discontent with Pérez's tough economic policies, government corruption, and declining living standards. A second unsuccessful coup attempt, on November 27, 1992, followed months of public demonstrations against Pérez's government.

Perhaps the low point was reached in May 1993, when Pérez was suspended from office and impeachment proceedings initiated. Allegedly the president had embezzled more than $17 million and had facilitated other irregularities. Against a backdrop of military unrest, Ramón José Velásquez was named interim president.

ACHIEVEMENTS

Venezuela's great novelists, such as Rómulo Gallegos and Artúro Uslar Pietri, have been attracted by the barbarism of the backlands and the lawlessness native to rural regions. Gallegos's classic *Doña Barbara*, the story of a female regional chieftain, has become world-famous.

In December 1993, Venezuelans elected Rafael Caldera, who had been president in a more prosperous and promising era (1969–1974). Caldera's presidency too was fraught with problems. In his first year, he had to confront widespread corruption in official circles, the devaluation of the bolívar, drug trafficking, a banking structure in disarray, and a high rate of violent crime in Caracas. Indeed, in 1997, a relative of President Caldera was mugged and a Spanish diplo-

mat who had traveled to Caracas to negotiate a trade agreement with Venezuela was robbed in broad daylight.

In an attempt to restore order from chaos, President Caldera inaugurated his "Agenda Venezuela" program to address the difficult problems created by deep recession, financial instability, deregulation, privatization, and market reforms. The plan was showing signs of progress when it was undercut by the collapse of petroleum prices.

Timeline: PAST

1520
The first Spanish settlement at Cumaná

1822–1829
Venezuela is part of Gran Colombia

1829
Venezuela achieves independence as a separate country

1922
The first productive oil well

1947
Women win the right to vote

1976
Foreign oil companies are nationalized

1980s
Booming public investment fuels inflation; Venezuela seeks renegotiation of foreign debt

1990s
Social and economic crisis grips the nation; Hugo Chavez wins the presidency and sets about to redraft the Constitution; Chavez's government is challenged by massive flooding that leaves more than 30,000 people dead and many more homeless

PRESENT

2000s
A new Constitution is approved

Chavez strengthens executive power; Chavez is reelected

2006
Presidential elections scheduled

The stage was thus set for the emergence of a "hero" who would promise to solve all of Venezuela's ills. In the presidential election of 1998, the old parties were swept from power and a populist—the same Hugo Chavez who had attempted a coup in 1992—won with 55 percent of the popular vote. Those who expected change were not disappointed, although some of Chavez's actions have raised concerns about the future of democracy in Venezuela. A populist and a pragmatist, it is difficult to ascertain where Chavez's often contradictory policies will lead. Since taking power in February 1999, he has placed the army in control of the operation of medical clinics and has put soldiers to work on road and sewer repairs and in school and hospital construction. He has talked about the need to cut costs and uproot what he perceives as a deeply corrupt public sector—but he has refused to downsize the bureaucracy. Chavez supports privatization of the nation's pension fund and electric utilities, but he wants to maintain state control over health care and the petroleum industry.

Perhaps of greater concern is Chavez's successful bid to redraft Venezuela's Constitution, to provide "a better version." He claimed that the document had eroded democracy by allowing a political elite to rule without restraint for decades. Chavez's "democratic" vision demands special powers to revamp the economy without congressional approval. Through clever manipulation of the people by means of his own radio and television shows, and newspaper, Chavez intimidated Congress into granting him almost all the power he wanted to enact financial and economic legislation by decree. A referendum in April 1999 gave him a huge majority supporting the creation of an assembly to redraft the Constitution. A draft was completed in November. The political opposition was convinced that the new document would allow Chavez to seek a second consecutive term in office, which had been prohibited in Venezuela, and that

he was doing nothing less than creating a dictatorship under the cover of democracy and the law. Their fears have been realized, as the new Constitution allows for consecutive six-year terms.

The trend towards more centralized executive authority continued in 2000 and 2001. When the new 1999 Constitution was "reprinted" in March 2000, critics noted substantial changes from the original—changes that enhanced presidential power. In the same month, a group of retired military officers called on President Chavez to halt the politicization of the armed forces. The president's response was to appoint active-duty officers to a range of important positions in the government, including the state-owned petroleum company and foreign ministry. Organized labor complained that Chavez has attempted to transform the labor movement into an appendage of the ruling political party and has ignored union leadership in direct appeals by the government to rank-and-file workers. He has alienated the Catholic hierarchy over abortion and education issues; and the media, while legally free to criticize the government, have felt the need to exercise self-censorship. Perhaps most ominously, Chavez asked for and received from a compliant Legislature permission to rule by decree on a broad spectrum of issues, from the economy to public security. The *Ley Habilitante* al-

lows him to enact legislation without parliamentary debate or even approval.

Equally radical and unpredictable is Chavez's policy toward neighboring Colombia. Chavez opened a dialogue with Colombia's guerrillas and dismissed Colombia's protests with the statement that the guerrillas held effective power.

Chavez clearly sees himself as a major player in the region and seems to enjoy annoying the United States. He is friends with Fidel Castro, met with Saddam Hussein in Baghdad, and strengthened relations with a number of Caribbean, Central American, and South American states. Venezuela's long-standing boundary dispute with neighboring Guyana has also been resurrected.

Venezuela's future is wholly unpredictable in large measure because its current government is unpredictable. Growing dissatisfaction with Chavez's strong-arm rule precipitated street violence in early April 2002. For four days he was apparently forced from power by elements in the military, but demonstrations by Chavez's supporters resulted in his return to office. The political opposition mounted a campaign to gather the signatures necessary to force a recall vote in August 2004. Chavez emerged as the winner and announced that he will run for another six-year term in elections in 2006. Given the repeated failures of the opposition to challenge Chavez, it is almost a certainty that he will win.

The Caribbean

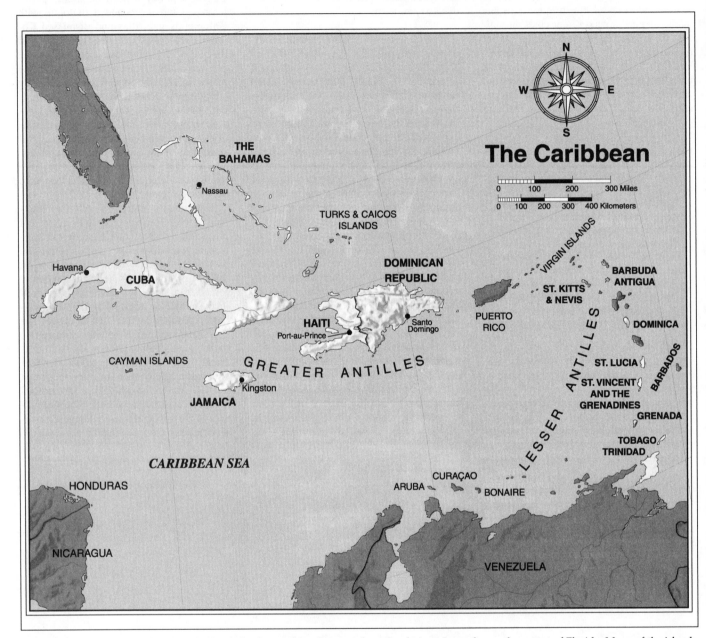

The Caribbean

THE BAHAMAS

Nassau

TURKS & CAICOS ISLANDS

Havana

CUBA

DOMINICAN REPUBLIC

HAITI
Port-au-Prince

Santo Domingo

PUERTO RICO

VIRGIN ISLANDS

ST. KITTS & NEVIS

BARBUDA
ANTIGUA

DOMINICA

CAYMAN ISLANDS

GREATER ANTILLES

Kingston

JAMAICA

ST. LUCIA

ST. VINCENT AND THE GRENADINES

BARBADOS

GRENADA

LESSER ANTILLES

TOBAGO
TRINIDAD

CARIBBEAN SEA

HONDURAS

CURAÇAO

ARUBA

BONAIRE

NICARAGUA

VENEZUELA

The Caribbean region consists of hundreds of islands stretching from northern South America to the southern part of Florida. Many of the islands cover just a few square miles and are dominated by a central range of mountains; only Cuba has any extensive lowlands. Almost every island has a ring of coral, making approaches very dangerous for ships. The land that can be used for agriculture is extremely fertile; but many islands grow only a single crop, making them vulnerable to fluctuations in the world market in that particular commodity.

The Caribbean Sea of Diversity

To construct a coherent overview of the Caribbean is an extremely difficult task because of the region's profound geographical and cultural diversity. "The history of the Caribbean is the examination of fragments, which, like looking at a broken vase, still provides clues to the form, beauty, and value of the past." So writes historian Franklin W. Knight in his study of the Caribbean. Other authors have drawn different analogies: Geographer David Lowenthal and anthropologist Lambros Comitas note that the West Indies "is a set of mirrors in which the lives of black, brown, and white, of American Indian and East Indian, and a score of other minorities continually interact."

For the geographer, the pieces fall into a different pattern, consisting of four distinct geographical regions. The first contains the Bahamas as well as the Turks and Caicos Islands. The Greater Antilles—consisting of Cuba, Hispaniola (Haiti and the Dominican Republic), Jamaica, the Cayman Islands, Puerto Rico, and the Virgin Islands—make up the second region. Comprising the third region are the Lesser Antilles—Antigua and Barbuda, Dominica, St. Lucia, St. Vincent and the Grenadines, Grenada, and St. Kitts and Nevis as well as various French departments and British and Dutch territories. The fourth group consists of islands that are part of the South American continental shelf: Trinidad and Tobago, Barbados, and the Dutch islands of Aruba, Curaçao, and Bonaire. Within these broad geographical regions, each nation is different. Yet on each island there often is a firmly rooted parochialism—a devotion to a parish or a village, a mountain valley or a coastal lowland.

CULTURAL DIVERSITY

To break down the Caribbean region into culture groups presents its own set of problems. The term "West Indian" inadequately describes the culturally Hispanic nations of Cuba and the Dominican Republic. On the other hand, "West Indian" does capture the essence of the cultures of Belize, the Caribbean coast of Central America, and Guyana, Suriname, and Cayenne (French Guiana). In Lowenthal's view: "Alike in not being Iberian [Hispanic], the West Indies are not North American either, nor indeed do they fit any ordinary regional pattern. Not so much undeveloped as overdeveloped, exotic without being traditional, they are part of the Third World yet ardent emulators of the West."

EFFORTS AT INTEGRATION

To complicate matters further, few West Indians would identify themselves as such. They are Jamaicans, or Bajans (people from Barbados), or Grenadans. Their economic, political, and social worlds are usually confined to the islands on which they live and work. In the eyes of its inhabitants, each island, no matter how small, is—or should be—sovereign. Communications by air, sea, and telephone with the rest of the world are ordinarily better than communications within the Caribbean region itself. Trade, even between neighboring islands, has always been minimal. Economic ties with the United States or Europe, and in some cases with Venezuela, are more important.

A British attempt to create a "West Indies Federation" in 1958 was reduced to a shambles by 1962. Member states had the same historical background; spoke the same languages; had similar economies; and were interested in the same kinds of food, music, and sports. But their spirit of independence triumphed over any kind of regional federation that "threatened" their individuality. In the words of a former Bajan prime minister, "We live together very well, but we don't like to live together." A Trinidadian explanation for the failure of the federation is found in a popular calypso verse from the early 1960s:

> Plans was moving fine
> When Jamaica stab we from behind
> Federation bust wide open
> But they want Trinidad to bear the burden.

Recently, however, the Windward Islands (Dominica, Grenada, St. Lucia, and St. Vincent and the Grenadines) have discussed political union. While each jealously guards its sovereignty, leaders are nevertheless aware that some integration is necessary if they are to survive in a changing world. The division of the world into giant economic blocs points to political union and the creation of a Caribbean state with a combined population of nearly half a million. Antigua and Barbuda resist because they believe that, in the words of former prime minister Vere Bird, "political union would be a new form of colonialism and undermine sovereignty."

While political union remains problematic, the 15 members of the Caribbean Community and Common Market (CARICOM, a regional body created in 1973) began long-term negotiations with Cuba in 1995 with regard to a free-trade agreement. CARICOM leaders informed Cuba that "it needs to open up its economy more." The free-market economies of CARICOM are profoundly different from Cuba's rigid state controls. "We need to assure that trade and investment will be mutually beneficial." Caribbean leaders have pursued trade with Cuba in the face of strong opposition from the United States. In general, CARICOM countries are convinced that "constructive engagement" rather than a policy of isolation is the best way to transform Cuba.

Political problems also plague the Dutch Caribbean. Caribbean specialist Aaron Segal notes that the six-island Netherlands Antilles Federation has encountered severe internal difficulties. Aruba never had a good relationship with the larger island of Curaçao and, in 1986, became a self-governing entity, with its own flag, Parliament, and currency, but still within the Netherlands. "The other Netherlands Antillean states have few complaints about their largely autonomous relations with the Netherlands but find it hard to get along with one another."

Interestingly, islands that are still colonial possessions generally have a better relationship with their "mother" countries than with one another. Over the past few decades, smaller islands—

(©Iconotec.com/DILF0006769)

The weekly open-air market in St. Lucia provides a variety of local produce.

populations of about 50,000 or less—have learned that there are advantages to a continued colonial connection. The extensive subsidies paid by Great Britain, France, or the Netherlands have turned dependency into an asset. Serving as tax-free offshore sites for banks and companies as well as encouraging tourism and hotel investments have led to modest economic growth.

CULTURAL IDENTIFICATION

Despite the local focus of the islanders, there do exist some broad cultural similarities. To the horror of nationalists, who are in search of a Caribbean identity that is distinct from Western civilization, most West Indians identify themselves as English or French in terms of culture. Bajans, for example, take a special pride in identifying their country as the "Little England of the Caribbean." English or French dialects are the languages spoken in common.

Nationalists argue that the islands will not be wholly free until they shatter the European connection. In the nationalists' eyes, that connection is a bitter reminder of slavery. After World War II, several Caribbean intellectuals attacked the strong European orientation of the islands and urged the islanders to be proud of their black African heritage. The shift in focus was most noticeable in the French Caribbean, although this new ethnic consciousness was echoed in the English-speaking islands as well in the form of a black-power movement during the 1960s and 1970s. It was during those years,

when the islands were in transition from colonies to associated states to independent nations, that the Caribbean's black majorities seized political power by utilizing the power of their votes.

It is interesting to note that at the height of the black-power and black-awareness movements, sugar production was actually halted on the islands of St. Vincent, Antigua, and Barbuda —not because world-market prices were low, but because sugar cultivation was associated with the slavery of the past.

African Influences

The peoples of the West Indies are predominantly black, with lesser numbers of people of "mixed blood" and small numbers of whites. Culturally, the blacks fall into a number of groups. Throughout the nineteenth century, in Haiti, blacks strove to realize an African-Caribbean identity. African influences have remained strong on the island, although they have been blended with European Christianity and French civilization. Mulattos, traditionally the elite in Haiti, have strongly identified with French culture in an obvious attempt to distance themselves from the black majority, who comprise about 95 percent of the population. African-Creoles, as blacks of the English-speaking islands prefer to be called, are manifestly less "African" than the mass of Haitians. An exception to this generalization is the Rastafarians, common in Jamaica and found in lesser numbers on some of the other islands. Convinced that they are Ethiopians, the Rastafarians hope to return to Africa.

Racial Tension

The Caribbean has for years presented an image of racial harmony to the outside world. Yet, in actuality, racial tensions are not only present but also have become sharper during the past few decades. Racial unrest broke to the surface in Jamaica in 1960 with riots in the capital city of Kingston. Tensions heightened again in 1980–1981 and in 1984, to the point that the nation's tourist industry drastically declined. A recent slogan of the Jamaican tourist industry, "Make It Jamaica Again," was a conscious attempt to downplay racial antagonism. The black-power movement in the 1960s on most of the islands also put to the test notions of racial harmony.

Most people of the Caribbean, however, believe in the myth of racial harmony. It is essential to the development of nationalism, which must embrace all citizens. Much racial tension is officially explained as class difference rather than racial prejudice. There is some merit to the class argument. A black politician on Barbuda, for example, enjoys much more status and prestige than a poor white "Redleg" from the island's interior. Yet if a black and a Redleg competed for the job of plantation manager, the white would likely win out over the black. In sum, race does make a difference, but so too does one's economic or political status.

East Indians

The race issue is more complex in Trinidad and Tobago, where there is a large East Indian (i.e., originally from India) minority. The East Indians, for the most part, are agricultural workers. They were originally introduced by the British between 1845 and 1916 to replace slave labor on the plantations. While numbers of East Indians have moved to the cities, they still feel that they have little in common with urban blacks. Because of their large numbers, East Indians are able to preserve a distinctive, healthy culture and community and to compete with other groups for political office and status.

East Indian culture has also adapted, but not yielded, to the West Indian world. In the words of Trinidadian-East Indian author V. S. Naipaul: "We were steadily adopting the food styles of others: The Portuguese stew of tomato and onions ... the Negro way with yams, plantains, breadfruit, and bananas," but "everything we adopted became our own; the outside was still to be dreaded...." The East Indians in Jamaica, who make up about 3 percent of the population, have made even more accommodations to the cultures around them. Most Jamaican-East Indians have become Protestant (the East Indians of Trinidad have maintained their Hindu or Islamic faith).

East Indian conformity and internalization, and their strong cultural identification, have often made them the targets of the black majority. Black stereotypes of the East Indians describe them in the following terms: "secretive," "greedy," and "stingy." And East Indian stereotypes describing blacks as "childish," "vain," "pompous," and "promiscuous" certainly do not help to ease ethnic tensions.

REVOLUTIONARY CUBA

In terms of culture, the Commonwealth Caribbean (former British possessions) has little in common with Cuba or the Dominican Republic. But Cuba has made its presence felt in other ways. The Cuban Revolution, with the social progress that it entailed for many of its people and the strong sense of nationalism that it stimulated, impressed many West Indians. For new nation-states still in search of an identity, Cuba offered some clues as to how to proceed. For a time, Jamaica experimented with Cuban models of mass mobilization and programs designed to bring social services to the majority of the population. Between 1979 and 1983, Grenada saw merit in the Cuban approach to social and economic problems. The message that Cuba seemed to represent was that a small Caribbean state could shape its own destiny and make life better for its people.

The Cuba of Fidel Castro, while revolutionary, is also traditional. Hispanic culture is largely intact. The politics are authoritarian and personality-driven, and Castro himself easily fits into the mold of the Latin American leader, or caudillo, whose charisma and benevolent paternalism win him the widespread support of his people. Castro's relationship with the Roman Catholic Church is also traditional and corresponds to notions of a dualistic culture that has its roots in the Middle Ages. In Castro's words: "The same respect that the Revolution ought to have for religious beliefs, ought also to be had by those who talk in the name of religion for the political beliefs of others. And, above all, to have present that which Christ said: 'My kingdom is not of this world.' What are those who are said to be the interpreters of Christian thought doing meddling in the problems of this world?" Castro's comments should not be interpreted as a Communist assault on religion. Rather, they express a time-honored Hispanic belief that religious life and everyday life exist in two separate spheres.

The social reforms that have been implemented in Cuba are well within the powers of all Latin American governments to enact. Those governments, in theory, are duty-bound to provide for the welfare of their peoples. Constitutionally, the state is infallible and all-powerful. Castro has chosen to identify with the needs of the majority of Cubans, to be a "father" to his people. Again, his actions are not so much Communistic as Hispanic.

Where Castro has run against the grain is in his assault on Cuba's middle class. In a sense, he has reversed a trend that is evident in much of the rest of Latin America—the slow, steady progress of a middle class that is intent on acquiring a share of the power and prestige traditionally accorded to elites. Cuba's middle class was effectively shattered—people were deprived of much of their property; their livelihood; and, for those who fled into exile, their citizenship. Many expatriate Cubans remain bitter toward what they perceive as Castro's betrayal of the Revolution and the middle class.

EMIGRATION AND MIGRATION

Throughout the Caribbean, emigration and migration are a fact of life for hundreds of thousands of people. These are not new phenomena; their roots extend to the earliest days of European settlement. The flow of people looking for work is deeply rooted in history, in contemporary political economy, and even in Caribbean island culture. The Garifuna (black-Indian mixture) who settled in Belize and coastal parts of Mexico, Guatemala, Honduras, and Nicaragua originally came from St. Vincent. There, as

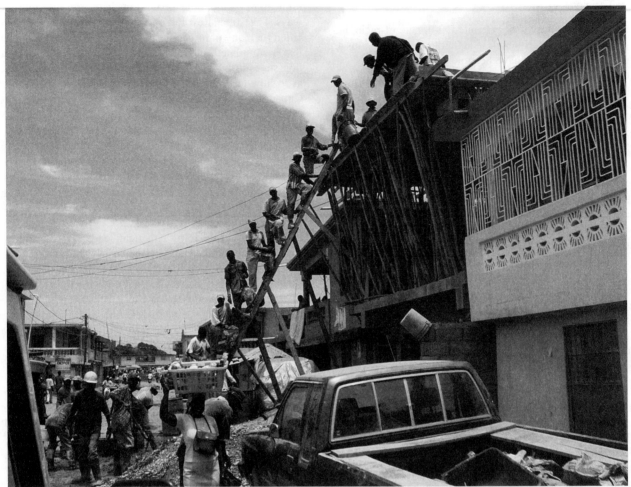

(Courtesy of Robert Buss/BussHaiti14)

These workers in Port-de-Paix, Haiti are hand-carrying building materials up a ladder to add a second story to an existing home. Most people build with the intent of someday putting on a second story. When they get a little money they buy a few cinder/cement blocks until they have enough to build. Here they are hauling gravel to make concrete bucket by bucket. The roof is supported by many sticks that will remain there until the work is completed.

escaped slaves, they intermixed with remnants of Indian tribes who had once peopled the islands, and they adopted many of their cultural traits. Most of the Garifuna (or Black Caribs, as they are also known) were deported from St. Vincent to the Caribbean coast of Central America at the end of the eighteenth century.

From the 1880s onward, patois-speaking (French dialect) Dominicans and St. Lucians migrated to Cayenne (French Guiana) to work in the gold fields. The strong identification with Europe has drawn thousands more to what many consider their cultural homes.

High birth rates and lack of economic opportunity have forced others to seek their fortunes elsewhere. Many citizens of the Dominican Republic have moved to New York, and Haitian refugees have thrown themselves on the coast of Florida by the thousands. Other Haitians seek seasonal employment in the Dominican Republic or the Bahamas. There are sizable Jamaican communities in the Dominican Republic, Haiti, the Bahamas, and Belize.

On the smaller islands, stable populations are the exception rather than the rule. The people are constantly migrating to larger places in search of higher pay and a better life. Such emigrants moved to Panama when the canal was being cut in the early 1900s or sought work on the Dutch islands of Curaçao and

Aruba when oil refineries were built there in the 1920s. They provided much of the labor for the banana plantations in Central America. Further contributing to out-migration is the changing character of some island economies. Many islands can no longer compete in world markets for sugar or bananas and have been forced to diversify. In 2005 St. Kitts closed its last sugar mills, ending a 350-year relationship with what had been the island's main industry. Now hope has been placed in tourism. For agricultural workers the alternatives are retraining or emigration.

The greatest number of people by far have left the Caribbean region altogether and emigrated to the United States, Canada, and Europe. Added to those who have left because of economic or population pressures are political refugees. The majority of these are Cubans, most of whom have resettled in Florida.

Some have argued that the prime mover of migration from the Caribbean lies in the *ideology* of migration—that is, the expectation that all nonelite males will migrate abroad. Sugarcane slave plantations left a legacy that included little possibility of island subsistence; and so there grew the need to migrate to survive, a reality that was absorbed into the culture of lower-class blacks. But for these blacks, there has also existed the expectation to return. (In contrast, middle- and upper-class migrants have historically departed permanently.) Historian Bonham Richardson writes: "By traveling away and returning the people have been able to cope more successfully with the vagaries of man and nature than they would have by staying at home. The small islands of the region are the most vulnerable to environmental and economic uncertainty. Time and again in the Lesser Antilles, droughts, hurricanes, and economic depressions have diminished wages, desiccated provision grounds, and destroyed livestock, and there has been no local recourse to disease or starvation." Hence, men and women of the small West Indian islands have been obliged to migrate. "And like migrants everywhere, they have usually considered their travels temporary, partly because they have never been greeted cordially in host communities."

On the smaller islands, such as St. Kitts and Nevis, family and community ceremonies traditionally reinforce and sustain the importance of emigration and return. Funerals reunite families separated by vast distances; Christmas parties and carnival celebrations are also occasions to welcome returning family and friends.

Monetary remittances from relatives in the United States, England, Canada, or the larger islands are a constant reminder of the importance of migration. According to Richardson: "Old men who have earned local prestige by migrating and returning exhort younger men to follow in their footsteps…. Learned cultural responses thereby maintain a migration ethos … that is not only valuable in coping with contemporary problems, but also provides continuity with the past."

The Haitian diaspora (dispersion) offers some significant differences. While Haitian migration is also a part of the nation's history, a return flow is noticeably absent. One of every six Haitians now lives abroad—primarily in Cuba, the Dominican Republic, Venezuela, Colombia, Mexico, and the Bahamas. In French Guiana, Haitians comprise more than 25 percent of the population. They are also found in large numbers in urban areas of the United States, Canada, and France. The typical Haitian emigrant is poor, has little education, and has few skills or job qualifications.

Scholar Christian A. Girault remarks that although "ordinary Haitian migrants are clearly less educated than the Cubans, Dominicans, Puerto Ricans and even Jamaicans, they are not Haiti's most miserable; the latter could never hope to buy an air ticket or boat passage, or to pay an agent." Those who establish new roots in host countries tend to remain, even though they experience severe discrimination and are stereotyped as "undesirable" because they are perceived as bringing with them "misery, magic and disease," particularly AIDS.

There is also some seasonal movement of the population on the island itself. Agricultural workers by the tens of thousands are found in neighboring Dominican Republic. *Madames sara*, or peddlers, buy and sell consumer goods abroad and provide "an essential provisioning function for the national market."

AN ENVIRONMENT IN DANGER

When one speaks of soil erosion and deforestation in a Caribbean context, Haiti is the example that usually springs to mind. While that image is accurate, it is also too limiting, for much of the Caribbean is threatened with ecological disaster. Part of the problem is historical, for deforestation began with the development of sugarcane cultivation in the seventeenth century. But

(Photo Lisa Clyde/Carir5)

These lush mountain peaks in St. Lucia are volcanic in origin.

now, soil erosion and depletion as well as the exploitation of marginal lands by growing populations perpetuate a vicious cycle between inhabitants and the land on which they live. Cultivation of sloping hillsides, or denuding the slopes in the search of wood to make charcoal, creates a situation in which erosion is constant and an ecological and human disaster likely. In 2004 days of heavy rain on the island of Hispaniola generated thousands of mudslides and killed an estimated 2,000 people in Haiti and the Dominican Republic.

A 1959 report on soil conditions in Jamaica noted that, in one district of the Blue Mountains, on the eastern end of that island, the topsoil had vanished, a victim of rapid erosion. The problem is not unique to the large islands, however. Bonham Richardson observes that ecological degradation on the smallest islands is acute. Thorn scrub and grasses have replaced native forest. "A regional drought in 1977, leading to starvation in Haiti and producing crop and livestock loss south to Trinidad, was severe only partly because of the lack of rain. Grasses and shrubs afford little protection against the sun and thus cannot help the soil to retain moisture in the face of periodic drought. Neither do they inhibit soil loss."

Migration of the islands' inhabitants has at times exacerbated the situation. In times of peak migration, a depleted labor force on some of the islands has resulted in landowners resorting to the raising of livestock, which is not labor-intensive. But livestock contribute to further ecological destruction. "Emigration itself has thus indirectly fed the ongoing devastation of island environments, and some of the changes seem irreversible. Parts of the smaller islands already resemble moonscapes. They seem simply unable to sustain their local resident populations, not to mention future generations or those working abroad who may someday be forced to return for good."

MUSIC, DANCE, FOLKLORE, AND FOOD

Travel accounts of the Caribbean tend to focus on local music, dances, and foods. Calypso, the limbo, steel bands, reggae, and African–Cuban rhythms are well known. Much of the music derives from Amerindian and African roots.

Calypso music apparently originated in Trinidad and spread to the other islands. Calypso singers improvise on any theme; they are particularly adept at poking fun at politicians and their shortcomings. Indeed, governments are as attentive to the lyrics of a politically inspired calypso tune as they are to the opposition press. On a broader scale, calypso is a mirror of Caribbean society.

Some traditional folkways, such as storytelling and other forms of oral history, are in danger of being replaced by electronic media, particularly radio, tape recorders, and jukeboxes. The new entertainment is both popular and readily available.

Scholar Laura Tanna has gathered much of Kingston, Jamaica's, oral history. Her quest for storyteller Adina Henry took her to one of the city's worst slums, the Dungle, and was reprinted in *Caribbean Review*: "We walked down the tracks to a Jewish cemetery, with gravestones dating back to the 1600s. It, too, was covered in litter, decaying amid the rubble of broken stones. Four of the tombs bear the emblem of the skull and crossbones. Popular belief has it that Spanish gold is buried in the tombs, and several of them have been desecrated by treasure seekers. We passed the East Indian shacks, and completed our tour of Majesty Pen amidst greetings of 'Love' and 'Peace' and with the fragrance of ganja [marijuana] wafting across the way. Everywhere, people were warm and friendly, shaking hands, chatting, drinking beer, or playing dominos. One of the shacks had a small bar and jukebox inside. There, in the midst of pigs grunting at one's feet in the mud and slime, in the dirt and dust, people had their own jukeboxes, tape recorders, and radios, all blaring out reggae, the voice of the ghetto." Tanna found Miss Adina, whose stories revealed the significant African contribution to West Indian folk culture.

In recent years, Caribbean foods have become more accepted, and even celebrated, within the region as well as internationally. Part of the search for an identity involves a new attention to traditional recipes. French, Spanish, and English recipes have been adapted to local foods—iguana, frogs, seafood, fruits, and vegetables. Cassava, guava, and mangos figure prominently in the islanders' diets.

The diversity of the Caribbean is awesome, with its potpourri of peoples and cultures. Its roots lie in Spain, Portugal, England, France, the Netherlands, Africa, India, China, and Japan. There has emerged no distinct West Indian culture, and the Caribbean peoples' identities are determined by the island—no matter how small—on which they live. For the Commonwealth Caribbean, nationalist stirrings are still weak and lacking in focus; while people in Cuba and the Dominican Republic have a much surer grasp on who they are. Nationalism is a strong integrating force in both of these nations. The Caribbean is a fascinating and diverse corner of the world that is far more complex than the travel posters imply.

Antigua and Barbuda

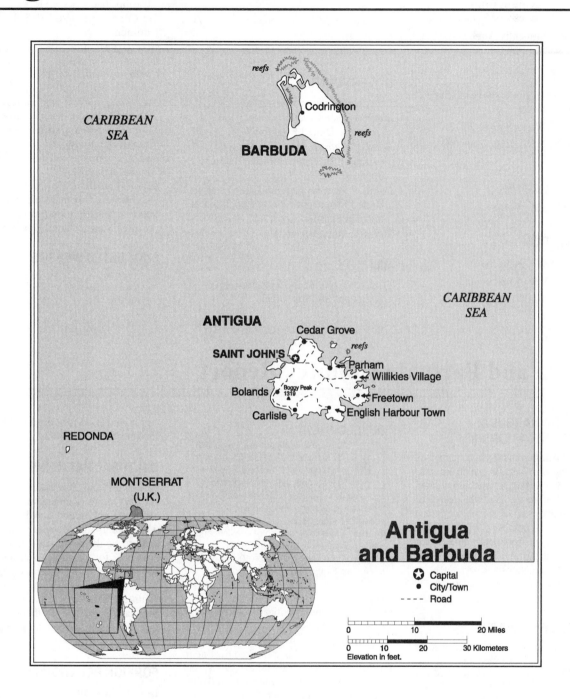

Antigua and Barbuda Statistics

GEOGRAPHY

Area in Square Miles (Kilometers): 171 (442) (about 2 1/2 times the size of Washington, D.C.)

Capital (Population): Saint John's (35,700)

Environmental Concerns: water management; clearing of trees

Geographical Features: mostly low-lying limestone and coral islands, with some higher volcanic areas

Climate: tropical marine

PEOPLE

Population

Total: 68,320

Annual Growth Rate: 0.06%

Rural/Urban Population Ratio: 64/36

GLOBAL STUDIES

Major Languages: English; Creole

Ethnic Makeup: almost entirely black African origin; some of British, Portuguese, Lebanese, or Syrian origin

Religions: predominantly Anglican; other Protestant sects; some Roman Catholic

Health

Life Expectancy at Birth: 69 years (male); 74 years (female)

Infant Mortality Rate (Ratio): 20/1,000

Physicians Available (Ratio): 1/1,083

Education

Adult Literacy Rate: 89%

Compulsory (Ages): 5–16

COMMUNICATION

Telephones: 38,000 main lines

Televisions: 435 per 1,000 people

Internet Users: 10,000 (2002)

TRANSPORTATION

Highways in Miles (Kilometers): 150 (240)

Railroads in Miles (Kilometers): 48 (77)

Usable Airfields: 3

Motor Vehicles in Use: 14,700

GOVERNMENT

Type: parliamentary democracy

Independence Date: November 1, 1981 (from the United Kingdom)

Head of State/Government: Queen Elizabeth II; Prime Minister Baldwin Spencer

Political Parties: Antigua Labour Party; United Progressive Party; a coalition of opposing parties

Suffrage: universal at 18

MILITARY

Current Disputes: tensions between Antiguans and Barbudans

ECONOMY

Currency ($U.S. Equivalent): 2.67 East Caribbean dollars = $1

Per Capita Income/GDP: $11,000/$750 million

GDP Growth Rate: 3%

Inflation Rate: 0.4%

Unemployment Rate: 11%

Labor Force: 30,000

Natural Resources: negligible; the pleasant climate fosters tourism

Agriculture: cotton; fruits; vegetables; sugarcane; livestock

Industry: tourism; construction; light manufacturing

Exports: $689 million (primary partners Caribbean, Guyana, United States)

Imports: $692 million (primary partners United States, United Kingdom, Canada)

SUGGESTED WEBSITE

http://www.cia.gov/cia/ publications/factbook/geos/ ac.html

Antigua and Barbuda Country Report

ANTIGUA AND BARBUDA: A STRAINED RELATIONSHIP

The nation of Antigua and Barbuda gained its independence from Great Britain on November 1, 1981. Both islands, tenuously linked since 1967, illustrate perfectly the degree of localism characteristic of the West Indies. Barbudans—who number approximately 1,200—culturally and politically believe that they are not Antiguans; indeed, since independence of Britain, they have been intent on secession. Barbudans view Antiguans as little more than colonial masters.

MEMORIES OF SLAVERY

Antigua was a sugar island for most of its history. This image changed radically in the 1960s, when the black-power movement then sweeping the Caribbean convinced Antiguans that work on the sugar plantations was "submissive" and carried the psychological and social stigma of historic slave labor. In response to the clamor, the government gradually phased out sugar production, which ended entirely in 1972. The decline of agriculture resulted in a strong rural-to-urban flow of people. To replace lost revenue from the earnings of sugar, the government promoted tourism.

Tourism produced the unexpected result of greater freedom for women, in that they gained access to previously unavailable

DEVELOPMENT

Land-use patterns in the islands show that 37 percent of the land is devoted to grazing, 34 percent to woodlands, 11 percent to settlements, 3 percent to tourist areas, and 3 percent to airports. Agricultural use accounts for only 8 percent of the land. Tourism, the leading source of employment, has replaced agriculture as the prime generator of revenue. Perhaps 50 percent of foreign exchange derives from tourism.

employment opportunities. Anthropologist W. Penn Handwerker has shown that a combination of jobs and education for women has resulted in a marked decline in fertility. Between 1965 and the 1980s, real wages doubled, infant mortality fell dramatically, and the proportion of women ages 20 to 24 who completed secondary school rose from 3 percent to about 50 percent. "Women were freed from dependency on their children" as well as their men and created "conditions for a revolution in gender relations." Men outmigrated as the economy shifted, and women took the new jobs in tourism. Many of the jobs demanded higher skills, which in turn resulted in more education for women, followed by even better jobs. And notes Handwerker: "Women empowered by edu-

cation and good jobs are less likely to suffer abuse from partners."

CULTURAL PATTERNS

Antiguans and Barbudans are culturally similar. Many islanders still have a strong affinity for England and English culture, while others identify more with what they hold to be their African–Creole roots. On Antigua, for example, Creole, which is spoken by virtually the entire population, is believed to reflect what is genuine and "natural" about the island and its culture. Standard English, even though it is the official language, carries in the popular mind an aura of falseness.

FOREIGN RELATIONS

Despite the small size of the country, Antigua and Barbuda are actively courted by regional powers. The United States maintains a satellite-tracking station on Antigua, and Brazil has provided loans and other assistance. A small oil refinery, jointly supported by Venezuela and Mexico, began operations in 1982.

FAMILY POLITICS

From 1951 to 2004, with one interruption, Antiguan politics has been dominated by the family of Vere Bird and his Antigua

124

Labour Party (ALP). Charges of nepotism, corruption, drug smuggling, and money laundering dogged the Vere Bird administration for years. Still, in 1994, Lester Bird managed to succeed his 84-year-old father as prime minister, and the ALP won 11 of 17 seats in elections. Lester admitted that his father had been guilty of some "misjudgments" and quickly pledged that the ALP would improve education, better the status of women, and increase the presence of young people in government.

The younger Bird, in his State of the Nation address early in 1995, challenged Antiguans to transform their country on their own terms, rather than those dictated by the International Monetary Fund. His government would take "tough and unpopular" measures to avoid the humiliation of going "cap in hand" to foreign financial institutions. Those tough measures included increases in contributions for medical benefits, property and personal taxes, and business and motor-vehicle licenses.

In 2003, however, the government angered public employees, who constitute one-third of the labor force, when it failed to pay salaries on time. Tourism was stagnant and the public debt was a very high 140 percent of GDP. Economic difficulties when coupled with persistent scandal and corruption brought 90 percent of the electorate to the polls in 2004 and Bird's ALP was soundly defeated. Prime Minister Baldwin Spencer's government must now live up to the expectations of the electorate. Tourism, the earnings from which slipped from 80 percent of GDP in 1994 to only 50 percent in 2004, is a major area of concern. Internet gambling sites have emerged as a revenue supplement to tourism, but this has embroiled Antigua in a trade dispute with the United States, which places restrictions on the business. Agricultural production, consisting primarily of fruits and vegetables, concentrates on the domestic market and does not generate significant foreign exchange earnings. Spencer's administration must make some difficult choices in the near future.

Timeline: PAST

1632
The English settle Antigua

1834
Antigua abolishes slavery

1958–1962
Antigua becomes part of the West Indies Federation

1981
Independence from Great Britain

1990s
Barbuda talks of secession; Hurricane Luis devastates the islands

PRESENT

2000s
The Bird government announces a "zero tolerance" drug policy
Bird political dynasty comes to an end in 2004

The Bahamas (Commonwealth of the Bahamas)

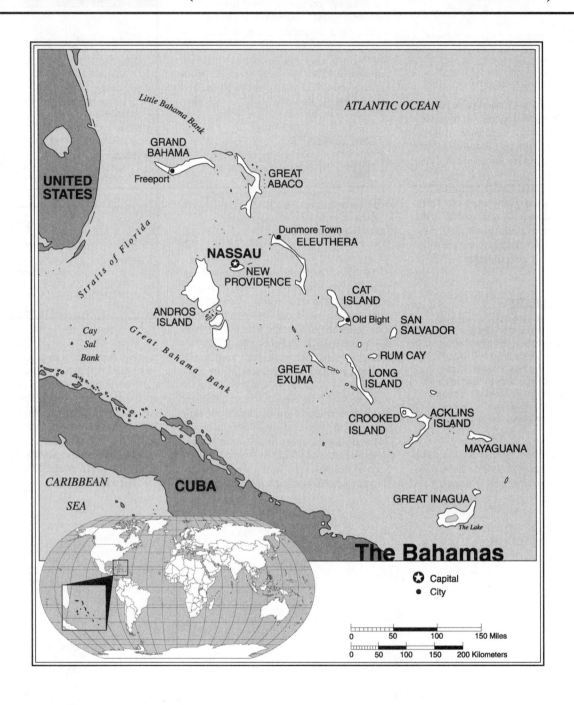

The Bahamas Statistics

GEOGRAPHY

Area in Square Miles (Kilometers): 5,380 (13,934) (about the size of Connecticut)

Capital (Population): Nassau (172,300)

Environmental Concerns: coral-reef decay; waste disposal

Geographical Features: long, flat coral formations with some low, rounded hills

Climate: tropical marine

PEOPLE

Population

Total: 299,697

Annual Growth Rate: 0.72%

Rural/Urban Population Ratio: 13/87

Ethnic Makeup: 85% black; 15% white

Major Language: English

Religions: 32% Baptist; 22% Protestant; 20% Anglican; 19% Roman Catholic; 7% unaffiliated or unknown

Health
Life Expectancy at Birth: 62 years (male); 69 years (female)
Infant Mortality Rate (Ratio): 25/1,000
Physicians Available (Ratio): 1/709

Education
Adult Literacy Rate: 95.6%
Compulsory (Ages): 5–14; free

COMMUNICATION
Telephones: 126,600 main lines
Daily Newspaper Circulation: 126 per 1,000 people
Televisions: 179 per 1,000 people
Internet Users: 60,000 (2002)

TRANSPORTATION
Highways in Miles (Kilometers): 1,672 (2,693)
Railroads in Miles (Kilometers): none

Usable Airfields: 62
Motor Vehicles in Use: 83,000

GOVERNMENT
Type: constitutional parliamentary democracy
Independence Date: July 10, 1973 (from the United Kingdom)
Head of State/Government: Queen Elizabeth II; Prime Minister Perry Christie
Political Parties: Free National Movement; Progressive Liberal Party
Suffrage: universal at 18

MILITARY
Current Disputes: none

ECONOMY
Currency ($U.S. Equivalent): 1.00 Bahamian dollar = $1

Per Capita Income/GDP: $16,800/$5.09 billion
GDP Growth Rate: 1%
Inflation Rate: 1.7%
Unemployment Rate: 7%
Labor Force: 156,000
Natural Resources: salt; aragonite; timber
Agriculture: citrus fruits; vegetables; poultry
Industry: tourism; banking; cement; oil refining and transshipment; salt production; rum; aragonite; pharmaceuticals; steel pipe
Exports: $361 million (primary partners United States, Switzerland, United Kingdom)
Imports: $1.61 billion (primary partners United States, Italy, Japan)

SUGGESTED WEBSITE
http://www.cia.gov/cia/publications/factbook/index.html

The Bahamas Country Report

BAHAMAS: A NATION OF ISLANDS
Christopher Columbus made his first landfall in the Bahamas in 1492, when he touched ashore on the island of San Salvador. Permanent settlements on the islands were not established by the British until 1647, when the Eleutheran Adventurers, a group of English and Bermudan religious dissidents, landed. The island was privately governed until 1717, when it became a British Crown colony. During the U.S. Civil War, Confederate blockade runners used the Bahamas as a base. The tradition continued in the years after World War I, when Prohibition rum runners used the islands as a base. Today, drug traffickers utilize the isolation of the out-islands for their illicit operations.

DEVELOPMENT

Together manufacturing and agriculture account for only 10 percent of GDP. There has been little growth in either sector. Offshore banking is important.

Although the Bahamas are made up of almost 700 islands, only 10 have populations of any significant size. Of these, New Providence and Grand Bahama contain more than 75 percent of the Bahamian population. Because most economic and cultural activities take place on the larger islands, other islands—particularly those in the southern region—have suffered depopulation over the years as young men and women have moved to the two major centers of activity.

FREEDOM

Women participate actively in all levels of government and business. The Constitution does, however, make some distinctions between males and females with regard to citizenship and permanent-resident status.

Migrants from Haiti and Jamaica have also caused problems for the Bahamian government. There are an estimated 60,000 illegal Haitians now resident in the Bahamas—equivalent to nearly one-fifth of the total Bahamian population of 300,000. The Bahamian response was tolerance until late 1994, when the government established tough new policies that reflected a fear that the country would be "overwhelmed" by Haitian immigrants. In the words of one official, the large numbers of Haitians would "result in a very fundamental economic and social transformation that even the very naïve would understand to be undesirable." Imprisonment, marginalization, no legal right to work, and even the denial of access to schools and hospitals are now endured by the immigrants.

Bahamian problems with Jamaicans are rooted differently. The jealous isolation of each of the island nations is reflected in the peoples' fears and suspicions of the activities of their neighbors. As a result, interisland freedom of movement is subject to strict scrutiny.

The Bahamas were granted their independence from Great Britain in 1973 and established a constitutional parliamentary democracy governed by a freely elected prime minister and Parliament. Upon independence, there was a transfer of political power from a small white elite to the black majority, who comprise 85 percent of the population. Whites continue to play a role in the political process, however, and several hold high-level civil-service and political posts.

The country has enjoyed a marked improvement in health conditions over the past few decades. Life expectancy has risen, and infant mortality has declined. Virtually all people living in urban areas have access to good drinking water, although the age and dilapidated condition of the capital's (Nassau) water system could present problems in the near future.

HEALTH/WELFARE

Cases of child abuse and neglect in the Bahamas rose in the 1990s. The Government and Women's Crisis Centre focused on the need to fight child abuse through a public-awareness program that had as its theme: "It shouldn't hurt to be a child."

The government has begun a program to restructure education on the islands. The authorities have placed a new emphasis on technical and vocational training so that skilled jobs in the economy now held by foreigners will be performed by Bahamians. But while the literacy rate has remained high, there is a shortage of teachers, equipment, and supplies.

ACHIEVEMENTS

The natural beauty of the islands has had a lasting effect on those who have visited them. As a result of his experiences in the waters off Bimini, Ernest Hemingway wrote his classic *The Old Man and the Sea*.

The government of Prime Minister Hubert A. Ingraham and his Free National Movement won a clear mandate in 1997 over the opposition Progressive Liberal Party to continue the policies and programs it initiated in 1992. *The Miami Herald* reported that the election "marked a watershed in Bahamian politics, with many new faces on the ballot and both parties facing leadership succession struggles before the next vote is due in 2002."

Ideologically, the two contending political parties were similar; thus, voters made their decisions on the basis of who they felt would provide jobs and bring crime under control. In 2002 voters decided that the Progressive Liberal Party would do a better job and elected Perry Christie as prime minister.

Honest government and a history of working effectively with the private sector to improve the national economy have dramatically increased foreign investment in the Bahamas. Rapid growth in the service sector of the economy has stimulated the migration of people from fishing and farming villages to the commercial tourist centers in New Providence Island, Grand Bahama, and Great Abaco. It is estimated that tourism now accounts for 60 percent of GDP and absorbs half of the labor force. Importantly, today there are more companies owned by Bahamians than ever before.

Despite new investments, many young Bahamians out-migrate. The thousands of illegal Haitian immigrants have added pressure to the job market and still worry some Bahamians that their own sense of identity may be threatened. But in general, there is a sense of optimism in the islands.

Timeline: PAST

1492
Christopher Columbus first sights the New World at San Salvador Island

1647
The first English settlement in the Bahamas

1967
Black-power controversy

1973
Independence from Great Britain

1980s
Violent crime, drug trafficking, and narcotics addiction become serious social problems

1990s
New investments create jobs and cut the unemployment rate

PRESENT

2000s
Employment is up, and so is many Bahamians' sense of optimism

Perry Christie elected prime minister in 2002

Barbados

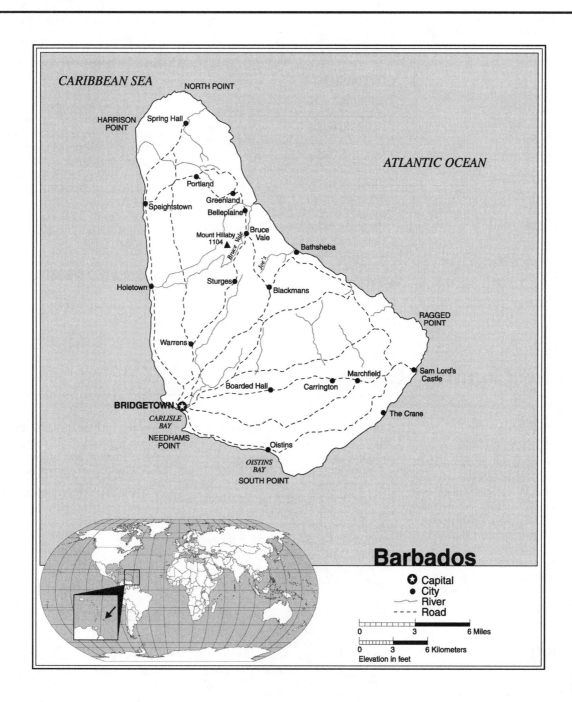

Barbados Statistics

GEOGRAPHY

Area in Square Miles (Kilometers): 166
(431) (about 2½ times the size of
Washington, D.C.)

Capital (Population): Bridgetown (6,000)

Environmental Concerns: pollution of
coastal waters from waste disposal by
ships; soil erosion; illegal solid-waste
disposal
Geographical Features: relatively flat;
rises gently to central highland region
Climate: tropical marine

PEOPLE

Population

Total: 278,289
Annual Growth Rate: 0.36%
Rural/Urban Population Ratio: 52/48
Major Language: English

Ethnic Makeup: 80% black; 16% mixed or other; 4% white

Religions: 67% Protestant (Anglican, Pentecostal, Methodist, others); 4% Roman Catholic; 17% unaffiliated; 12% others or unknown

Health

Life Expectancy at Birth: 70 years (male); 73 years (female)
Infant Mortality Rate (Ratio): 12.3/1,000
Physicians Available (Ratio): 1/842

Education

Adult Literacy Rate: 97.4%
Compulsory (Ages): 5–16

COMMUNICATION

Telephones: 133,000 main lines
Daily Newspaper Circulation: 157 per 1,000 people
Televisions: 287 per 1,000 people
Internet Users: 30,000 (2002)

TRANSPORTATION

Highways in Miles (Kilometers): 1,025 (1,650)
Railroads in Miles (Kilometers): none
Usable Airfields: 1
Motor Vehicles in Use: 48,500

GOVERNMENT

Type: parliamentary democracy; independent sovereign state within Commonwealth
Independence Date: November 30, 1966 (from the United Kingdom)
Head of State/Government: Queen Elizabeth II; Prime Minister Owen Seymour Arthur
Political Parties: Democratic Labour Party; Barbados Labour Party; National Democratic Party
Suffrage: universal at 18

MILITARY

Current Disputes: none

ECONOMY

Currency ($U.S. Equivalent): 2.00 Bajan dollars = $1
Per Capita Income/GDP: $16,200/$4.49 billion
GDP Growth Rate: -0.6%
Inflation Rate: 2.5%
Unemployment Rate: 9%
Labor Force: 128,500
Natural Resources: petroleum; fish; natural gas
Agriculture: sugarcane; vegetables; cotton
Industry: tourism; light manufacturing; sugar; component assembly
Exports: $206 million (primary partners United Kingdom, United States, Trinidad and Tobago)
Imports: $1.01 billion (primary partners United States, Trinidad and Tobago, Japan)

SUGGESTED WEBSITE

http://www.cia.gov/cia/ publications/factbook/index.html

Barbados Country Report

THE LITTLE ENGLAND OF THE CARIBBEAN

A parliamentary democracy that won its independence from Britain in 1966, Barbados boasts a House of Assembly that is the third oldest in the Western Hemisphere, after Bermuda's and Virginia's. A statement of the rights and privileges of Bajans (as Barbadians are called), known as the Charter of Barbados, was proclaimed in 1652 and has been upheld by those governing the island. The press is free, labor is strong and well organized, and human rights are respected.

DEVELOPMENT

Between 1971 and 1999, there was an approximate 30 percent decrease in the amount of land used for agriculture. Formerly agricultural land has been transformed into golf courses, residential areas, commercial developments, tourist facilities, or abandoned. Additionally, there are offshore reserves of oil and natural gas.

While the majority of the populations of the English-speaking West Indies still admire the British, this admiration is carried to extremes in Barbados. In 1969, for example, Bajan soccer teams chose English names and colors—Arsenal, Tottenham Hotspurs, Liverpool, and Coventry City. Among the primary religions are Anglican and Methodist Protestantism.

Unlike most of the other islands of the Caribbean, European sailors initially found Barbados uninhabited. It has since been determined that the island's original inhabitants, the Arawak Indians, were destroyed by Carib Indians who overran the region and then abandoned the islands. Settled by the English, Barbados was always under British control until its independence.

FREEDOM

Barbados has maintained an excellent human-rights record. The government officially advocates strengthening the human-rights machinery of the United Nations and the Organization of American States. Women are active participants in the country's economic, political, and social life.

A DIVERSIFYING ECONOMY

In terms of wealth, as compared to other West Indian nations, Barbados is well off. One important factor is that Barbados has been able to diversify its economy; thus, the country is no longer dependent solely on sugar and its by-products rum and molasses. Manufacturing and high-technology industries now contribute to economic growth, and tourism has overtaken agriculture as a generator of foreign exhange. Offshore finance and information services have also become important.

The Constitution of 1966 authorized the government to promote the general welfare of the citizens of the island through equitable distribution of wealth. While governments have made a sincere effort to wipe out pockets of poverty, a great disparity in wealth still exists.

RACE AND CLASS

Barbados is a class- and race-conscious society. One authority noted that there are three classes (elite, middle class, and masses) and two colors (white/light and black). Land is highly concentrated in the hands of a few; 10 percent of the population own 95 percent of the land. Most of the nation's landed estates and businesses are

HEALTH/WELFARE

By 2000, unemployment had dropped to 9 percent, from the 1993 high of 26 percent. Although prices have risen, a sound economy has given people more money to spend on consumer goods, durables, and housing.

owned by whites, even though they comprise a very small percentage of the population (4 percent).

While discrimination based on color is legally prohibited, color distinctions continue to correlate with class differences and dominate most personal associations. Although whites have been displaced politically, they still comprise more than half of the group considered "influential" in the country.

ACHIEVEMENTS

 Bajan George Lamming has won attention from the world's literary community for his novels, each of which explores a stage in or an aspect of the colonial experience. Through his works, he explains what it is to be simultaneously a citizen of one's island and a West Indian.

Even though Barbados's class structure is more rigid than that of other West Indian states, there is upward social mobility for all people, and the middle class has been growing steadily in size. Poor whites, known as "Redlegs," have frequently moved into managerial positions on the estates. The middle class also includes a fairly large percentage of blacks and mulattos. Bajans have long enjoyed access to public and private educational systems, which have been the object of a good deal of national pride. Adequate medical care is available to all residents through local clinics and hospitals under a government health program. All Bajans are covered under government health insurance programs.

Timeline: PAST

1625
Barbados is occupied by the English

1647
The first sugar from Barbados is sent to England

1832
Full citizenship is granted to nonwhites

1951
Universal suffrage

1966
Independence from Great Britain

1990s
Barbados develops an offshore banking industry

PRESENT

2000s
The Arthur government continues its policy of economic diversification

Inflation falls to 2.5 percent in 2003

SEEKING A LEADERSHIP ROLE

Given the nation's relative wealth and its dynamism, Bajans have been inclined to seek a strong role in the region. In terms of Caribbean politics, economic development, and defense, Bajans feel that they have a right and a duty to lead.

The Labour Party has continued to push privatization policies. In 1993, an important step was taken toward the greater diversification of the nation's economic base with the creation of offshore financial services. By 1995, the new industry had created many new jobs for Bajans and had significantly reduced the high unemployment rate. Recent discussions on the Free Trade Area of the Americas (FTAA) has stimulated much debate among the smaller Caribbean states. While the Barbados government sees the possibilities of tying into a market of 800 million consumers, it also feels that the larger states must afford smaller nations special and differential treatment. Others are concerned about maintaining the "Bajan way of life" and worry that "the world is falling in on us." Critics charge that any new wealth would be skewed saying, it has the attributes of "fancy molasses." "Very little trickles down, the rich get richer while the poor become marginalized." Other concerns have been expressed about pollution and the possible loss, because of FTAA, of offshore financial privileges.

Cuba (Republic of Cuba)

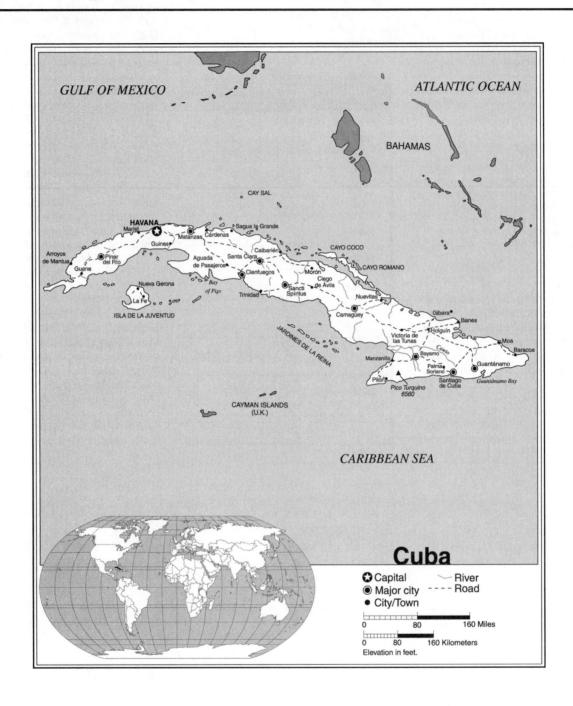

GULF OF MEXICO

ATLANTIC OCEAN

BAHAMAS

CAY SAL

HAVANA
Mariel
Guines
Matanzas
Cárdenas
Sagua la Grande
CAYO COCO
Arroyos
de Mantua
Pinar
del Río
Guane
Aguada
de Pasajeros
Santa Clara
Caibarién
CAYO ROMANO
Nueva Gerona
Bay
of Pigs
Clenfuegos
Morón
Ciego
de Ávila
La Fe
Trinidad
Sancti
Spíritus
Nuevitas
ISLA DE LA JUVENTUD
Camagüey
Gibara
Banes
JARDINES DE LA REINA
Victoria de
las Tunas
Holguín
Moa
Baracoa
Manzanillo
Bayamo
Canto
Pilón
Palma
Soriano
Guantánamo
Pico Turquino
6560
Santiago
de Cuba
Guantánamo Bay

CAYMAN ISLANDS
(U.K.)

CARIBBEAN SEA

Cuba

⊕ Capital   River
◉ Major city   - - - - Road
● City/Town

0   80   160 Miles
0   80   160 Kilometers
Elevation in feet.

Cuba Statistics

GEOGRAPHY

Area in Square Miles (Kilometers): 44,200
(114,471) (about the size of
Pennsylvania)

Capital (Population): Havana (2,185,000)

Environmental Concerns: pollution of
Havana Bay; threatened wildlife
populations; deforestation
Geographical Features: mostly flat to
rolling plains; rugged hills and
mountains in the southeast
Climate: tropical

PEOPLE

Population

Total: 11,308,764

Annual Growth Rate: 0.34%

Rural/Urban Population Ratio: 24/76

Ethnic Makeup: 51% mulatto; 37% white; 11% black; 1% Chinese
Major Language: Spanish
Religion: 85% Roman Catholic before Castro assumed power

Health

Life Expectancy at Birth: 74 years (male); 79 years (female)
Infant Mortality Rate (Ratio): 7.5/1,000
Physicians Available (Ratio): 1/231

Education

Adult Literacy Rate: 95.7%
Compulsory (Ages): 6–11; free

COMMUNICATION

Telephones: 574,400 main lines
Daily Newspaper Circulation: 122 per 1,000 people
Televisions: 200 per 1,000 people
Internet Users: 120,000

TRANSPORTATION

Highways in Miles (Kilometers): 37,793 (60,858)

Railroads in Miles (Kilometers): 2,985 (4,807)
Usable Airfields: 170

GOVERNMENT

Type: Communist state
Independence Date: May 20, 1902 (from Spain)
Head of State/Government: President Fidel Castro Ruz is both head of state and head of government
Political Parties: Cuban Communist Party
Suffrage: universal at 16

MILITARY

Military Expenditures (% of GDP): 1.8% (est.)
Current Disputes: U.S. Naval Base at Guantanamo Bay is leased to the United States

ECONOMY

Currency ($U.S. Equivalent): 1.000 Cuban pesos = $1 (official rate)

Per Capita Income/GDP: $2,800/$31.59 billion
GDP Growth Rate: 1.3%
Inflation Rate: 5%
Unemployment Rate: 3.2%
Labor Force: 4,500,000
Natural Resources: cobalt; nickel; iron ore; copper; manganese; salt; timber; silica; petroleum; arable land
Agriculture: sugarcane; tobacco; citrus fruits; coffee; rice; potatoes; beans; livestock
Industry: sugar; petroleum; food; textiles; tobacco; chemicals; paper and wood products; metals; cement; fertilizers; consumer goods; agricultural machinery
Exports: $1.4 billion (primary partners Russia, the Netherlands, Canada)
Imports: $4.5 billion (primary partners Spain, Venezuela, Mexico)

SUGGESTED WEBSITE

http://www.cia.gov/cia/
publications/factbook/index.html

Cuba Country Report

REFLECTIONS ON A REVOLUTION

Cuba, which contains about half the land area of the West Indies, has held the attention of the world since 1959. In that year, Fidel Castro led his victorious rebels into the capital city of Havana and began a revolution that has profoundly affected Cuban society. The Cuban Revolution had its roots in the struggle for independence of Spain in the late nineteenth century, in the aborted Nationalist Revolution of 1933, and in the Constitution of 1940. It grew from Cuba's history and must be understood as a Cuban phenomenon.

The Revolution in some respects represents the fulfillment of the goals of the Cuban Constitution of 1940, a radically nationalist document that was never fully implemented. It banned *latifundia* (the ownership of vast landed estates) and discouraged foreign ownership of the land. It permitted the confiscation of property in the public or social interest. The state was authorized to provide full employment for its people and to direct the course of the national economy. Finally, the Constitution of 1940 gave the Cuban state control of the sugar industry, which at the time was controlled by U.S. companies.

The current Constitution, written in 1976, incorporates 36 percent of the articles of the 1940 Constitution. In other words, many of Castro's policies and programs are founded in Cuban history and the aspirations of the Cuban people. Revolutionary Cuba—at least in its earlier years—was very successful in solving the nation's most pressing problems of poverty. But those successes must be balanced against the loss of basic freedoms imposed by a strong authoritarian state.

ACHIEVEMENTS OF THE REVOLUTION

Education

One of the Revolution's most impressive successes has been in the area of education. In 1960, the Castro regime decided to place emphasis on raising the minimum level of education for the whole population. To accomplish this, some 200,000 Cubans were mobilized in 1961 under the slogan "Let those who know more teach those who know less." In a single year, the literacy rate rose from 76 to 96 percent. Free education was made available to all Cubans. The literacy campaign involved many Cu-

bans in an attempt to recognize and attack the problems of rural impoverishment. It was the first taste of active public life for many women who were students or teachers and because of their involvement, they began to redefine sex roles and attitudes.

While the literacy campaign was a resounding triumph, long-term educational policy was less satisfactory. Officials blamed the high dropout rate in elementary and junior high schools on poor school facilities and inadequate teacher training. Students also apparently lacked enthusiasm, and Castro himself acknowledged that students needed systematic, constant, daily work and discipline.

"Scholarship students and students in general," in Castro's words, "are willing to do anything, except to study hard."

Health Care

The Revolution took great strides forward in improving the health of the Cuban population, especially in rural regions. Success in this area is all the more impressive when one considers that between one-third and one-half of all doctors left the country between 1959 and 1962. Health care initially declined sharply, and the infant mortality rate rose rapidly. But with the training of new health-care professionals, the gaps were filled. The infant mortality rate in Cuba is now at a level comparable to that of developed countries.

DEVELOPMENT

Vladimir Putin, president of Russia, visited Cuba in 2000 and promised a stronger economic relationship between the two countries. After Brazil, Cuba is Russia's largest trading partner in the region. Venezuela has provided cut-rate oil.

From the outset, the government decided to concentrate on rural areas, where the need was the greatest. Medical treatment was free, and newly graduated doctors had to serve in the countryside for at least two years. The Cuban health service was founded on the principle that good health for all, without discrimination, is a birthright of Cubans. All Cubans were included under a national health plan.

The first national health standards were developed between 1961 and 1965, and eight priority areas were identified: infant and maternal care, adult health care, care for the elderly, environmental health, nutrition, dentistry, school health programs, and occupational health. A program of insect spraying and immunization eradicated malaria and poliomyelitis. Cuban life expectancy became one of the highest in the world, and Cuba's leading causes of death became the same as in the United States—heart disease, cancer, and stroke.

Before the Revolution of 1959, there was very little health and safety regulation for workers. Afterward, however, important advances were made in the training of specialized inspectors and occupational physicians. In 1978, a Work Safety and Health Law was enacted, which defined the rights and responsibilities of government agencies, workplace administrators, unions, and workers.

Cuba also exported its health-care expertise. It has had medical teams in countries from Nicaragua to Yemen and more doctors overseas than the World Health Organization. From 2003 to the present Cuban medical personnel provided health care to Venezuela, which in turn provided Cuba with cheap petroleum.

Redistribution of Wealth

The third great area of change presided over by the Revolution was income redistribution. The Revolution changed the lives of rural poor and agricultural workers. They gained the most in comparison to

other groups in Cuban society—especially urban groups. From 1962 to 1973, for example, agricultural workers saw their wages rise from less than 60 percent to 93 percent of the national average.

Still, Cuba's minimum wage was inadequate for most families. Many families needed two wage earners to make ends meet. All wages were enhanced by the so-called social wage, which consisted of free medical care and education, subsidized housing, and low food prices. Yet persistent shortages and tight rationing of food undermined a good portion of the social wage. Newly married couples found it necessary to live with relatives, sometimes for years, before they could obtain their own housing, which was in short supply. Food supplies, especially those provided by the informal sector, were adversely affected by a 1986 decision to eliminate independent producers because an informal private sector was deemed antithetical to "socialist morality" and promoted materialism.

FREEDOM

The Committee to Protect Journalists noted that those who try to work outside the confines of the state media face tremendous obstacles. "The problems of a lack of basic supplies ... are dwarfed by Fidel Castro's campaign of harassment and intimidation against the fledgling free press."

Women in Cuba

From the outset of the Revolution, Fidel Castro appealed to women as active participants in the movement and redefined their political roles. Women's interests were protected by the Federation of Cuban Women, an integral part of the ruling party. The Family Code of 1975 equalized pay scales, reversed sexual discrimination against promotions, provided generous maternity leave, and gave employed women preferential access to goods and services. Although women comprised approximately 30 percent of the Cuban workforce, most were still employed in traditionally female occupations; the Third Congress of the Cuban Communist Party admitted in 1988 that both racial minorities and women were underrepresented in responsible government and party positions at all levels. This continues to be a problem.

SHORTCOMINGS

Even at its best, the new Cuba had significant shortcomings. Wayne Smith, a former chief of the U.S. Interest Section in Havana who was sympathetic to the Revolution,

wrote: "There is little freedom of expression and no freedom of the press at all. It is a command society, which still holds political prisoners, some of them under deplorable conditions. Further, while the Revolution has provided the basic needs of all, it has not fulfilled its promise of a higher standard of living for the society as a whole. Cuba was, after all, an urban middle-class society with a relatively high standard of living even before the Revolution.... The majority of Cubans are less well off materially."

Castro, to win support for his programs, did not hesitate to take his revolutionary message to the people. Indeed, the key reason why Castro enjoyed such widespread support in Cuba was because the people had the sense of being involved in a great historical process.

Alienation

Not all Cubans identified with the Revolution, and many felt a deep sense of betrayal and alienation. The elite and most of the middle class strongly resisted the changes that robbed them of influence, prestige, and property. Some were particularly bitter, for at its outset, the Revolution had been largely a middle-class movement. For them, Castro was a traitor to his class. Thousands fled Cuba, and some formed the core of an anti-Castro guerrilla movement based in South Florida.

(Corbis, Inc./OF016656)

Fidel Castro has been the prime minister of Cuba since he seized power in 1959. Pictured above is Castro at the United Nations, as he looked in 1960.

There are many signs that Castro's government, while still popular among many people, has lost the widespread acceptance it enjoyed in the 1960s and 1970s. While Castro still has the support of the older generation and those in rural areas who benefited from the social transformation of the island, limited economic growth has led to dissatisfaction among urban workers and youth, who are less interested in Castro as a revolutionary hero and more interested in economic gains.

HEALTH/WELFARE

In August 1997, the Cuban government reported 1,649 HIV cases, 595 cases of full-blown AIDS, and 429 deaths, a significant increase over figures for 1996. Cuban medical personnel are working on an AIDS vaccine. AIDS has been spread in part because of an economic climate that has driven more women to prostitution.

More serious disaffection may exist in the army. Journalist Georgie Anne Geyer, writing in *World Monitor*, suggests that the 1989 execution of General Arnaldo Ochoa, ostensibly for drug trafficking, was actually motivated by Castro's fears of an emerging competitor for power. "The 1930s-style show trial effectively revealed the presence of an 'Angola generation' in the Cuban military.... That generation, which fought in Angola between 1974 and 1989, is the competitor generation to Castro's own Sierra Maestra generation." The condemned officers argued that their dealings with drug traffickers were not for personal enrichment but were designed to earn desperately needed hard currency for the state. Some analysts are convinced that Castro knew about drug trafficking and condoned it; others claim that it took place without his knowledge. But the bottom line is that the regime had been shaken at the highest levels, and the purge was the most far-reaching since the 1959 Revolution.

The Economy

The state of the Cuban economy and the future of the Cuban Revolution are inextricably linked. Writing in *World Today*, James J. Guy predicted that, given the economic collapse of the former Soviet Union and its satellites, "Cuba is destined to face serious structural unemployment: its agrarian economy cannot generate the white-collar, technical jobs demanded by a swelling army of graduates.... The entire system is deteriorating—the simplest services take months to deliver, water and electricity are constantly interrupted...," and there is widespread corruption and black-marketeering.

Oil is particularly nettlesome. For years after the collapse of the Soviet Union Cuba had no access to affordable petroleum, at great cost to the economy. That changed in 2003 when Venezuela provided Cuba with discounted oil in exchange for Cuban expertise in the areas of health and sports.

Although Castro prides Cuba on being one of the last bulwarks of untainted Marxism-Leninism, in April 1991 he said: "We are not dogmatic ... we are realistic ... Under the special conditions of this extraordinary period we are also aware that different forms of international cooperation may be useful." He noted that Cuba had contacted foreign capitalists about the possibility of establishing joint enterprises and remarked that more than 49 percent foreign participation in state businesses was a possibility.

In 1993, Castro called for economic realism. Using the rhetoric of the Revolution, he urged the Legislative Assembly to think seriously about the poor condition of the Cuban economy: "It is painful, but we must be sensible.... It is not only with decisiveness, courage and heroism that one saves the Revolution, but also with intelligence. And we have the right to invent ways to survive in these conditions without ever ceasing to be revolutionaries."

ACHIEVEMENTS

A unique cultural contribution of Cuba to the world was the Afro-Cuban movement, with its celebration of black song and dance rhythms. The work of contemporary prize-winning Cuban authors such as Alejo Carpentier and Edmundo Desnoes has been translated into many languages.

A government decree in September 1993 allowed Cubans to establish private businesses; today, Cubans in some 140 professions can work on their own for a profit. At about the same time, the use of dollars was decriminalized, the Cuban currency became convertible, and, in the agricultural sector, the government began to transform state farms into cooperatives. Farmers are now allowed to sell some of their produce in private markets and, increasingly, market forces set the prices of many consumer goods. Managers in state-owned enterprises have been given unprecedented autonomy; and foreign investment, in contrast with past practice, is now encouraged.

Still, the Cuban economy has continued its decline. Mirta Ojito, writing in *The New York Times*, sees older revolutionaries "coming to terms with the failure of their dreams." Cuba now resembles most other underdeveloped countries, with "many

needy, unhappy, sad people." The Revolution was supposed to make Cuba prosperous, "not merely survive," and end the country's dependence on the U.S. dollar. By 1999, dollars in circulation in Cuba had created a parallel speculative economy.

So pervasive had the parallel dollar economy become that in October 2004 Castro decreed that dollars would no longer be accepted for commercial transactions anywhere on the island, although dollar bank accounts would still be legal. Expatriate Cubans, who remit perhaps $1 billion annually to relatives on the island, were told to send euros, British pounds, or Canadian dollars. There is certainly a pragmatic side to Castro's decision. By encouraging people to convert their dollars to what was called the "convertible peso" (after a period of grace the government would charge 10 percent to exchange dollars for pesos; there would be no exchange charge for other currencies), Castro was able to provide his government with the dollars needed to purchase critical inputs for Cuba's economy. In the words of Mexico's former ambassador to Cuba, as reported in the *New York Times*, "I don't think this is a political decision at all. It's a pragmatic move." Cuba had to buy more oil than it had planned, and so it urgently needed dollars. Castro was also responding to United States efforts to strengthen economic sanctions against Cuba by setting limits on the amount of money that people could send to relatives on the island.

With the new millennium, Cuba's infrastructure continued to crumble. In 2001, salaries averaged just $15 per month, and the weekly ration card given to each family provides one chicken, just over three pounds of rice and beans, sugar, and two pints of cooking oil. With rising prices, it is not surprising that prostitution, moonlighting, black-marketeering, and begging have rapidly increased. Castro has talked with CARICOM states about the possibilities of free trade, but the stifling bureaucracy makes it much easier to export *from* rather than export *to* Cuba.

Freedom Issues

Soon after the Revolution, the government assumed total control of the media. No independent news organization is allowed, and all printed publications are censored by the government or the Communist Party. The arts are subject to strict censorship, and even sports must serve the purposes of the Revolution. As Castro noted: "Within the Revolution everything is possible. Outside it, nothing."

In many respects, there is less freedom now in Cuba than there was before the Revolution. Cuba's human-rights record is not

Timeline: PAST

1492
The island is discovered by Christopher Columbus

1511
The founding of Havana

1868–1878
The Ten Years' War in Cuba

1895–1898
The Cuban War of Independence

1902
The Republic of Cuba is established

1940
Cuba writes a new, progressive Constitution

1959
Fidel Castro seizes power

1961
An abortive U.S.–sponsored invasion at the Bay of Pigs

1980s
Mass exodus from Cuba; trial and execution of top military officials for alleged dealing in drugs

1990s
The economy rapidly deteriorates; Castro pursues Economic Liberalization Tensions flare between Cuba and the United Sates over the disposition of a young Cuban refugee, Elián González

PRESENT

2000s
The U.S. trade embargo, supported only by Israel, continues to make life difficult for the Cuban people

good. There are thousands of political prisoners, and rough treatment and torture—physical and psychological—occur. The Constitution of 1976 allows the repression of all freedoms for all those who oppose the Revolution. U.S. political scientist William LeGrande, who was sympathetic to the Revolution, nevertheless noted that "Cuba is a closed society. The Cuban Communist Party does not allow dissenting views on fundamental policy. It does not allow people to challenge the basic leadership of the regime." But here, too, there are signs of change. In 1995, municipal elections were held under a new system that provides for run-offs if none of the candidates gains a clear majority. In an indication of a new competitiveness in Cuban politics, 326 out of 14,229 positions were subject to the run-off rule.

THE FUTURE

It will be difficult for Castro to maintain the unquestioned support of the Cuban population. There must be continued positive accomplishments in the economy. Health and education programs are successful and will continue to be so. "Cubans get free health care, free education and free admission to sports and cultural events [and] 80 percent of all Cubans live in rent-free apartments, and those who do pay rent pay only between 6 and 10 percent of their salaries," according to James J. Guy.

But there must be a recovery of basic political and human freedoms. Criticism of the government must not be the occasion for jail terms or exile. The Revolution must be more inclusive and less exclusive.

Although Castro has never been effectively challenged, there are signs of unrest on the island. The military, as noted, is a case in point. Ironically, although Castro lost a good deal of luster internationally as a result of statist economic policies, recent trends in the region away from free trade and toward more authoritarian forms of government has given him strong allies in South America.

Still, many Cubans are frustrated with their lives and continue to take to the sea in an attempt to reach the United States. Thousands have been intercepted by the United States Coast Guard and have been interned.

The question is increasingly asked, What will happen once Fidel, through death or retirement, is gone from power? Castro's assumption is that the new Constitution, which institutionalizes the Revolution, will provide a mechanism for succession. Over the past few years, he has made some effort to depersonalize the Revolution; his public appearances are fewer and he does less traveling around the countryside. But there is no transition plan, and Castro continues to behave as if he is the embodiment of the Revolution. As for his staying power, a recent anecdote is revealing. When presented with a gift of a Galapagos tortoise, Castro asked how long they lived. The reply, "More than a hundred years," prompted Castro to say, "How sad it is to outlive one's pets."

Change must come to Cuba. More than half of all Cubans alive today were born after the Revolution. They are not particularly attuned to the rhetoric of revolution and seem more interested in the attainment of basic freedoms and consumer goods. In January 1999, *The Economist* asked: "What will follow Fidel?" The magazine suggested that Cubans could be faced with violence and political turmoil, for there were "no plausible political heirs in sight, no credible opposition, and an exile community eager not only for return but also revenge."

Dominica (Commonwealth of Dominica)

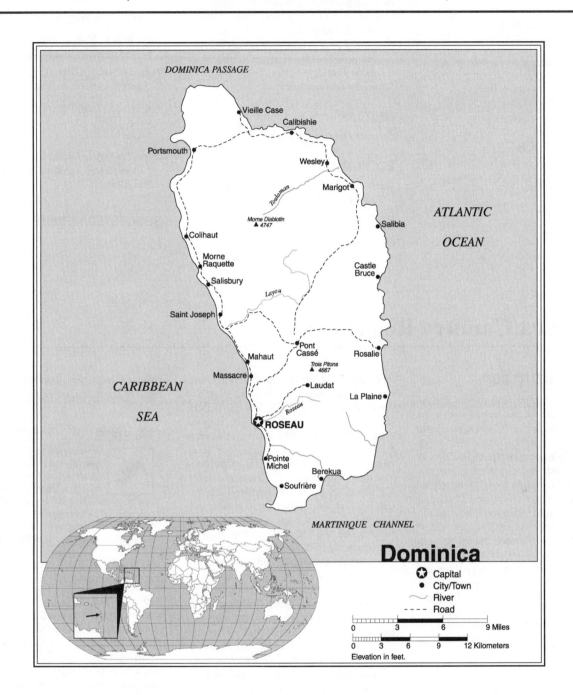

Dominica Statistics

GEOGRAPHY

Area in Square Miles (Kilometers): 289
(752) (about 4 times the size of
Washington, D.C.)
Capital (Population): Roseau (16,000)
Geographical Features: rugged
mountains of volcanic origin
Climate: tropical

PEOPLE

Population

Total: 69,278
Annual Growth Rate: –0.45%
Rural/Urban Population Ratio: 30/70
Major Languages: English; French Creole

Ethnic Makeup: mostly black; some Carib
Indians
Religions: 77% Roman Catholic; 15%
Protestant; 8% other or unaffiliated

Health

Life Expectancy at Birth: 71 years (male);
76 years (female)

Infant Mortality Rate (Ratio): 14/1,000
Physicians Available (Ratio): 1/2,112

Education

Adult Literacy Rate: 94%
Compulsory (Ages): 5–15; free

COMMUNICATION

Telephones: 23,700 main lines
Televisions: 1 per 13 people
Internet Users: 12,500

TRANSPORTATION

Highways in Miles (Kilometers): 484 (780)
Railroads in Miles (Kilometers): none
Usable Airfields: 2
Motor Vehicles in Use: 13,000

GOVERNMENT

Type: parliamentary democracy

Independence Date: November 3, 1978
  (from the United Kingdom)
Head of State/Government: President
  Nicholas J. O. Liverpool; Prime Minister
  Roosevelt Skerrit
Political Parties: United Workers Party;
  Dominica Freedom Party; Dominica
  Labour Party
Suffrage: universal at 18

MILITARY

Current Disputes: none

ECONOMY

Currency ($U.S. Equivalent): 2.67 East
  Caribbean dollars = $1
Per Capita Income/GDP: $5,400/$380
  million
GDP Growth Rate: -1%
Inflation Rate: 1.1%

Unemployment Rate: 23%

Labor Force: 25,000

Natural Resources: timber

Agriculture: fruits; cocoa; root crops;
  forestry and fishing potential

Industry: soap; coconut oil; tourism;
  copra; furniture; cement blocks; shoes

Exports: $39 million (primary partners
  CARICOM, United Kingdom, United
  States)

Imports: $98.2 million (primary partners
  United States, CARICOM, United
  Kingdom)

SUGGESTED WEBSITE

http://www.cia.gov/cia/
  publications/factbook/index.html

Dominica Country Report

A FRAGMENTED NATION

Christopher Columbus discovered the island of Dominica on his second voyage to the New World in 1493. Because of the presence of Carib Indians, who were known for their ferocity, Spanish efforts to settle the island were rebuffed. It was not until 1635 that France took advantage of Spanish weakness and claimed Dominica as its own. French missionaries became the island's first European settlers. Because of continued Carib resistance, the French and English agreed in 1660 that both Dominica and St. Vincent should be declared neutral and left to the Indians. Definitive English settlement did not occur until the eighteenth century, and the island again became a bone of contention between the French and English. It became Britain's by treaty in 1783.

DEVELOPMENT

In 2004 the Dominican government severed relations with Taiwan in favor of China. As a reward China reportedly offered to give more than $100 million in aid to bolster the island's fragile economy.

Dominica is a small and poor country that gained its independence from Great Britain in 1978. Culturally, the island reflects a number of patterns. Ninety percent of the population speak French patois (dia-

lect), and most are Roman Catholic, while only a small minority speak English and are Protestant. Yet English is the official language. Descendants of the original Carib inhabitants still live in a reserve in the northern part of the island. For years many in the non-indigenous population saw them as drunken, lazy, and dishonest. But others see them as symbolically important because they represent an ancient culture and fit into the larger Caribbean search for cultural and national identity. In 2004 the newly elected chief of the Caribs told the *Chronicle*, a Dominican weekly newspaper, that "…we are the rightful owners of this country and we deserve much more than we get…. '[We]…need a bigger share of development.'" A significant step was taken in this direction in 2005 when the Carib Indians were given a cabinet position in the government of the ruling Dominica Labour Party. There is also a small number of Rastafarians who identify with their black African roots.

Today, Dominica's population is broken up into sharply differentiated regions. The early collapse of the plantation economy left pockets of settlements, which are still isolated from one another. A difficult topography and poor communications exaggerate the differences between these small communities. This contrasts with nations such as Jamaica and Trinidad and Tobago, which have a greater sense of national awareness because there are good communications and mass media that

reach most citizens and foster the development of a national perception.

FREEDOM

Freedom House, an international human-rights organization, listed Dominica as "free." It also noted that "the rights of the native Caribs may not be fully respected." The example set by former prime minister Mary Eugenia Charles led to greater participation by women in the island's political life.

EMIGRATION

Although Dominica has a high birth rate and its people's life expectancy has measurably increased over the past few years, the growth rate has been dropping due to significant out-migration. Out-migration is not a new phenomenon. From the 1880s until well into the 1900s, many Dominicans sought economic opportunity in the gold fields of French Guiana. Today, most move to the neighboring French departments of Guadeloupe and Martinique.

THE ECONOMY

Dominica's chief export, bananas, has suffered for some years from natural disasters and falling prices. Hurricanes blew down the banana trees in 1979, 1980, 1989, and 1995, and banana exports fell dramatically. A drop in banana prices in 1997 prompted the opposition Dominica Freedom Party to

HEALTH/WELFARE

With the assistance of external donors, Dominica has rebuilt many primary schools destroyed in Hurricane Hugo in 1989. A major restructuring of the public health administration has improved the quality of health care, even in the previously neglected rural areas.

ACHIEVEMENTS

Traditional handcrafts—especially intricately woven baskets, mats, and hats—have been preserved in Dominica. Schoolchildren are taught the techniques to pass on this dimension of Dominican culture.

demand that Dominica become part of a single market in order to take advantage of set prices enjoyed by the producers of Martinique and Guadeloupe. Recent talks among producers, Windward Island governments, and the European Union focused on the need for radical changes in the banana industry. The head of the Windward Islands Banana Development and Exporting Company said that the industry should be "market-led rather than production-led." He also noted that the industry was too fragmented, with 10,000 growers all over the islands. This was one reason why costs were high and yields low. With new technology, an acre should produce 20 tons of fruit instead of the four tons now harvested. Together with other banana-producing small states in the Caribbean, Dominica has increasingly turned to nontraditional crops, including root crops, cucumbers, flowers, hot peppers, tomatoes, and nonbanana tropical fruits.

Hard-pressed for revenue, the *Economist* reports that Dominica has traded on its sovereignty for cash. It has sold passports to foreigners, hosted off-shore banks, and voted with Japan in favor of commercial whaling. The "favorite local game" involves playing off China and Taiwan for economic gain.

POLITICAL FREEDOM

Despite economic difficulties and several attempted coups, Dominica still enjoys a parliamentary democracy patterned along British lines. The press is free and has not been subject to control—save for a brief state of emergency in 1981, which corresponded to a coup attempt by former prime minister Patrick John and unemployed members of the disbanded Defense Force. Political parties and trade unions are free to organize. Labor unions are small but enjoy the right to strike. Women have full rights under the law and are active in the political system; former prime minister Mary Eugenia Charles was the Caribbean's first woman to become a head of government.

Dominican Republic

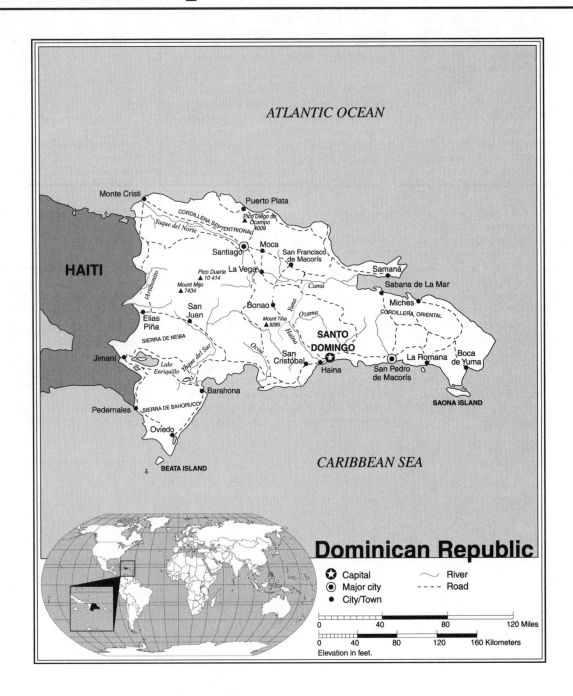

Dominican Republic Statistics

GEOGRAPHY

Area in Square Miles (Kilometers): 18,712 (48,464) (about twice the size of New Hampshire)

Capital (Population): Santo Domingo (3,166,000)

Environmental Concerns: water shortages; soil erosion; damage to coral reefs; deforestation; damage from Hurricane Georges

Geographical Features: rugged highlands and mountains with fertile valleys interspersed

Climate: tropical maritime

PEOPLE

Population

Total: 8,833,634

Annual Growth Rate: 1.33%

Rural/Urban Population Ratio: 37/63

Major Language: Spanish

Ethnic Makeup: 73% mixed; 16% white; 11% black
Religions: 95% Roman Catholic; 5% others

Health

Life Expectancy at Birth: 65 years (male); 69 years (female)
Infant Mortality Rate (Ratio): 36/1,000
Physicians Available (Ratio): 1/1,076

Education

Adult Literacy Rate: 84.7%
Compulsory (Ages): 6–14

COMMUNICATION

Telephones: 909,000 main lines
Daily Newspaper Circulation: 35 per 1,000 people
Televisions: 97 per 1,000 people
Internet Users: 300,000

TRANSPORTATION

Highways in Miles (Kilometers): 7,825 (12,600)

Railroads in Miles (Kilometers): 470 (757)
Usable Airfields: 28
Motor Vehicles in Use: 206,000

GOVERNMENT

Type: republic
Independence Date: February 27, 1844 (from Haiti)
Head of State/Government: President Leonel Fernández is both head of state and head of government
Political Parties: Dominican Revolutionary Party; Social Christian Reformist Party; Dominican Liberation Party; Independent Revolutionary Party; others
Suffrage: universal and compulsory at 18, or at any age if married; members of the armed forces or the police cannot vote

MILITARY

Military Expenditures (% of GDP): 1.1%
Current Disputes: none

ECONOMY

Currency ($U.S. Equivalent): 30.83 Dominican pesos = $1
Per Capita Income/GDP: $6,000/$52.16 billion
GDP Growth Rate: -1.8%
Inflation Rate: 21.2%
Unemployment Rate: 15.5%
Labor Force: 2,300,000–2,600,000
Natural Resources: nickel; bauxite; gold; silver; arable land
Agriculture: sugarcane; coffee; cotton; cocoa; tobacco; rice; beans; potatoes; corn; bananas; livestock
Industry: tourism; sugar processing; ferronickel and gold mining; textiles; cement; tobacco
Exports: $5.1 billion (primary partners United States, Belgium, Asia)
Imports: $7.9 billion (primary partners United States, Venezuela, Mexico)

SUGGESTED WEBSITE

http://www.cia.org/cia/
publications/factbook/index.html

Dominican Republic Country Report

DOMINICAN REPUBLIC: RACIAL STRIFE

Occupying the eastern two-thirds of the island of Hispaniola (Haiti comprises the western third), the Dominican Republic historically has feared its neighbor to the west. Much of the fear has its origins in race. From 1822 until 1844, the Dominican Republic—currently 73 percent mixed, or mulatto—was ruled by a brutal black Haitian regime. One authority noted that the Dominican Republic's freedom from Haiti has always been precarious: "Fear of reconquest by the smaller but more heavily populated (and, one might add, black) neighbor has affected Dominican psychology more than any other factor."

DEVELOPMENT

The U.S. decision to grant the Dominican Republic NAFTA parity with regard to textiles will allow these goods to enter the U.S. market at prices close to those of Mexico. The Dominican government is generally supportive of recent FTAA initiatives because of market accessibility and job creation.

In the 1930s, for example, President Rafael Trujillo posed as the defender of Catholic values and European culture

against the "barbarous" hordes of Haiti. Trujillo ordered the massacre of from 12,000 to 20,000 Haitians who had settled in the Dominican Republic in search of work. For years, the Dominican government had encouraged Haitian sugarcane cutters to cross the border to work on the U.S.–owned sugar plantations. But with the world economic depression in the 1930s and a fall in sugar prices and production, many Haitians did not return to their part of the island; in fact, additional thousands continued to stream across the border. The response of the Dominican government was wholesale slaughter.

Since 1952, a series of five-year agreements have been reached between the two governments to regularize the supply of Haitian cane cutters. An estimated 20,000 cross each year into the Dominican Republic legally, and an additional 60,000 enter illegally. Living and working conditions are very poor for these Haitians, and the migrants have no legal status and no rights. Planters prefer the Haitian workers because they are "cheaper and more docile" than Dominican laborers, who expect reasonable food, adequate housing, electric lights, and transportation to the fields. Today, as in the 1930s, economic troubles have gripped the Dominican Republic; the government has promised across-the-board sacrifices.

There is a subtle social discrimination against darker-skinned Dominicans, although this has not proved to be an insurmountable obstacle, as many hold elected political office. Discrimination is in part historical, in part cultural, and must be set against a backdrop of the sharp prejudice against Haitians. This prejudice is also directed against the minority in the Dominican population who are of Haitian descent. For example, during the contested presidential election of 1994, President Joaquín Balaguer Ricardo introduced the issue of race when questions were raised about his opponent's rumored Haitian origins. President Leonel Fernández has worked hard for better relations with Haitians, but the bitter memories and policies of the past undercut his efforts.

FREEDOM

Dominican politics remain volatile even as the country returns to economic stability. The media are generally free, but from time to time the government reveals a degree of intolerance against its critics.

WOMEN'S RIGHTS

Women in the Dominican Republic have enjoyed political rights since 1941. While in office, President Balaguer, in an unprecedented move, named women governors for eight of the country's 29 provinces. Sexual discrimination is prohibited by law, but women have not shared equal social or economic status or opportunity with men. Divorce, however, is easily obtainable, and women can hold property in their own names. A 1996 profile of the nation's population and health noted that 27 percent of Dominican households were headed by women. In urban areas, the percentage rose to 31 percent.

HEALTH/WELFARE

Sociologist Laura Raynolds notes that a restructuring of labor that moved thousands of women into nontraditional agriculture and manufacturing for export has reduced them to a "cheap and disciplined" workforce. Their work is undervalued to enhance profits. In that the majority of these workers are mothers, there has been a redefinition of family identity and work.

AN AIR OF CHANGE

Progress toward a political scene free of corruption and racism has been fitful. The 1994 presidential election was marred by what multinational observers called massive fraud. The opposition claimed that Balaguer not only "stole the election" but also employed racist, anti-Haitian rhetoric that "inflamed stereotypes of Haitians in the Dominican Republic." Widespread unrest in the wake of the election, together with pressure from the Roman Catholic Church, the Organization of American States, and the United States, resulted in the "Pact for Democracy," which forced Balaguer to serve a shortened two-year term as president. New elections in 1996 returned Leonel Fernández to the presidency.

ACHIEVEMENTS

Some of the best baseball in the hemisphere is played in the Dominican Republic. Three of its citizens, pitcher Pedro Martínez and sluggers Sammy Sosa and David Ortíz, have become stars in major-league baseball in the United States. They have raised awareness of their country and have contributed to the welfare of Dominicans.

A brief economic recovery has been followed by sharp recession. Inflation soared to 10 percent a month in 2003, the slowdown in the global economy cut into the tourist industry, and assembly plants in the free trade zone were forced to cut back. Many of the problems were blamed on President Hipólito Mejía's economic policies, which included a $2.4 billion bail-out of the nation's third largest commercial bank—bankrupted by massive fraud. In elections in 2004 Mejía resorted to demagoguery, distributed motorcycles at cut rates, and promised a 30 percent raise to public employees. He lost the

Timeline: PAST

1496
The founding of Santo Domingo, the oldest European city in the Americas

1821
Independence from Spain is declared

1822–1844
Haitian control

1844
Independence as a separate state

1930–1961
The era of General Rafael Trujillo

1965
Civil war and U.S. intervention

1990s
Diplomatic relations are restored with Cuba

Hurricane Georges slams into the nation, killing many and causing $1.3 billion in damage

PRESENT

2000s
Leonel Fernández elected president in May 2004

election to former president Leonel Fernández, who has pledged to cut inflation, stabilize the exchange rate, and restore investor confidence.

Grenada

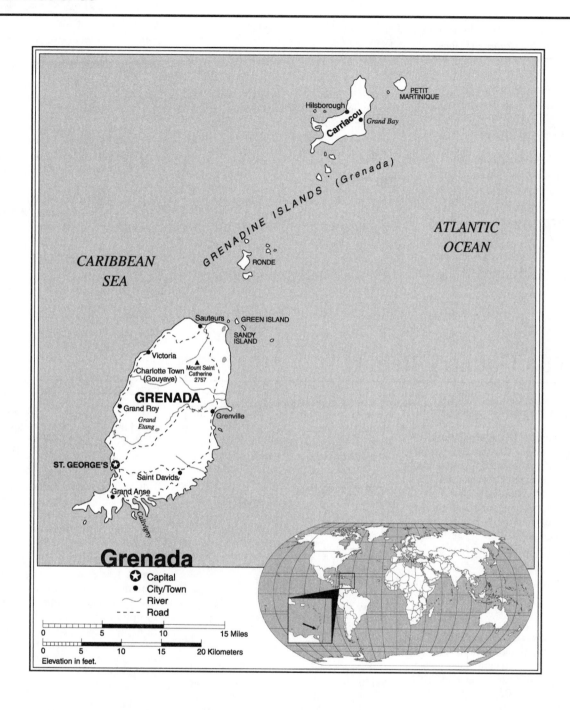

Grenada

- ⊛ Capital
- ● City/Town
- ⌇ River
- --- Road

0 ___ 5 ___ 10 ___ 15 Miles

0 ___ 5 ___ 10 ___ 15 ___ 20 Kilometers

Elevation in feet.

Grenada Statistics

GEOGRAPHY

Area in Square Miles (Kilometers): 133
(340) (about twice the size of
Washington, D.C.)
Capital (Population): St. George's (4,500)
Geographical Features: volcanic in
origin, with central mountains

Climate: tropical

PEOPLE

Population

Total: 89,357
Annual Growth Rate: 0.14%

Rural/Urban Population Ratio: 64/36

Major Languages: English; French patois

Ethnic Makeup: mainly black

Religions: largely Roman Catholic;
Church of England; other Protestant
sects

Health

Life Expectancy at Birth: 63 years (male);
  66 years (female)
Infant Mortality Rate (Ratio): 14.6/1,000
Physicians Available (Ratio): 1/2,045

Education

Adult Literacy Rate: 98%
Compulsory (Ages): 5–6; free

COMMUNICATION

Telephones: 33,500 main lines
Televisions: 154 per 1,000 people
Internet Users: 15,000 (2002)

TRANSPORTATION

Highways in Miles (Kilometers): 646
  (1,040)
Railroads in Miles (Kilometers): none
Usable Airfields: 3

GOVERNMENT

Type: parliamentary democracy
Independence Date: February 7, 1974
  (from the United Kingdom)
Head of State/Government: Queen
  Elizabeth II; Prime Minister Keith
  Mitchell
Political Parties: New National Party;
  Grenada United Labour Party; The
  National Party; National Democratic
  Congress; Maurice Bishop Patriotic
  Movement; Democratic Labour Party
Suffrage: universal at 18

MILITARY

Current Disputes: none

ECONOMY

Currency ($U.S. Equivalent): 2.67 East
  Caribbean dollars = $1
Per Capita Income/GDP: $5,000/$440
  million

GDP Growth Rate: 2.5%
Inflation Rate: 2.8%
Unemployment Rate: 12.5%
Labor Force: 42,300
Natural Resources: timber; tropical fruit;
  deepwater harbors
Agriculture: bananas; cocoa; nutmeg;
  mace; citrus fruits; avocados; root crops;
  sugarcane; corn; vegetables
Industry: food and beverages; spice
  processing; textiles; light assembly
  operations; tourism; construction
Exports: $46 million (primary partners
  CARICOM, United Kingdom, United
  States)
Imports: $208 million (primary partners
  United States, CARICOM, United
  Kingdom)

SUGGESTED WEBSITE

http://www.cia.gov/cia/
publications/factbook/index.html

Grenada Country Report

GRENADA: A FRESH BEGINNING

On his third voyage to the New World in 1498, Christopher Columbus sighted Grenada, which he named Concepción. The origin of the name Grenada cannot be clearly established, although it is believed that the Spanish renamed the island for the Spanish city of Granada. Because of a fierce aboriginal population of Carib Indians, the island remained uncolonized for 100 years.

Grenada, like most of the Caribbean, is ethnically mixed. Its culture draws on several traditions. The island's French past is preserved among some people who still speak patois (a French dialect). There are few whites on the island, save for a small group of Portuguese who immigrated earlier in the century. The primary cultural identification is with Great Britain, from which Grenada won its independence in 1974.

Grenada's political history has been tumultuous. The corruption and violent tactics of Grenada's first prime minister, Eric Gairy, resulted in his removal in a bloodless coup in 1979. Even though this action marked the first extra-constitutional change of government in the Commonwealth Caribbean (former British colonies), most Grenadians supported the coup, led by Maurice Bishop and his New Joint Endeavor for Welfare, Education, and Liberation (JEWEL) movement. Prime Minis-

ter Bishop, like Jamaica's Michael Manley before him, attempted to break out of European cultural and institutional molds and mobilize Grenadians behind him.

DEVELOPMENT

Prime Minister Mitchell has moved to end what Grenadians call "barter trade" and the government calls "smuggling." For years, Grenadian fishermen have exchanged their fish in Martinique for beer, cigarettes, and appliances. The cash-strapped treasury desperately needs the tariff revenues and has used drug interdiction as a means to end the contraband trade.

Bishop's social policies laid the foundation for basic health care for all Grenadians. With the departure of Cuban medical doctors in 1983, however, the lack of trained personnel created a significant health-care problem. Moreover, although medical-care facilities exist, these are not always in good repair, and equipment is aging and not reliable. Methods of recording births, deaths, and diseases lack systemization in Grenada, so it is risky to rely on local statistics to estimate the health needs of the population. There has also been some erosion from Bishop's campaign to accord women equal pay, status, and treatment. Two women were elected to Parliament, but skilled em-

ployment for women tends to be concentrated in the lowest-paid sector.

On October 19, 1983, Bishop and several of his senior ministers were killed during the course of a military coup. Six days later, the United States, with the token assistance of soldiers and police from states of the Eastern Caribbean, invaded Grenada, restored the 1974 Constitution, and prepared the way for new elections (in 1984).

According to one scholar, the invasion was a "lesson in a peacemaker's role in rebuilding a nation. Although Grenada has a history of parliamentary democracy, an atmosphere of civility, fertile soil, clean drinking water, and no slums, continued aid has not appreciably raised the standard of living and the young are resentful and restless."

FREEDOM

Grenadians are guaranteed full freedom of the press and speech. Newspapers, most of which are published by political parties, freely criticize the government without penalty. The OAS reported ballot fraud in the elections of November 2003, thus giving PM Keith Mitchell yet another term.

Grenada's international airport, the focus of much controversy, has pumped new blood into the tourist industry. Moves have

Timeline: PAST

1498
Grenada is discovered by Christopher Columbus

1763
England acquires the island from France by treaty

1834
Slavery is abolished

1958–1962
Member of the West Indies Federation

1974
Independence from Great Britain

1979
A coup brings Maurice Bishop to power

1983
Prime Minister Bishop is assassinated; U.S. troops land

1995
Former mathematics professor Keith Mitchell is elected prime minister

PRESENT

2000s
Venezuela experiments with new shipping routes to Grenada to expand markets in both nations

also been made by the Grenadian government to promote private-sector business and to diminish the role of the government in the economy. Large amounts of foreign aid, especially from the United States, have helped to repair the infrastructure.

In recent years, foreign governments such as Kuwait, attracted by the power of Grenada's vote in the United Nations, have committed millions of dollars to Grenada's infrastructure. Some of these partnerships, particularly that involving Japan's access to Caribbean fish stocks, may have severe consequences for Grenadians in the future.

HEALTH/WELFARE

Grenada still lacks effective legislation for regulation of working conditions, wages, and occupational-safety and health standards. Discrimination is prohibited by law, but women are often paid less than men for the same work.

Significant problems remain. Unemployment has not significantly decreased; it remains at 15 percent of the workforce. Not surprisingly, the island has experienced a rising crime rate.

Prime Minister Keith Mitchell of the New National Party has promised to create more jobs in the private sector and to cut taxes to stimulate investment in small, high-technology businesses. He also stated that government would become smaller and leaner.

Just as the economy had begun to experience its first significant growth in de-

ACHIEVEMENTS

A series of public consultations have been held with respect to the reestablishment of local government in the villages. Some 52 village councils work with the government in an effort to set policies that are both responsive and equitable.

cades, Hurricane Ivan struck the island a direct hit in 2004. It killed many people, destroyed or damaged 90 percent of the island's structures, and devastated the nutmeg crop, dealing the economy a serious blow. Privatization has continued, attracting foreign capital. As is the case in much of the Caribbean, tourism has become an important source of revenue and employment in Grenada, with a rapid expansion of the service sector. Despite the decline of agricultural exports, Grenada has maintained its position as the world's second-largest exporter of nutmeg. To protect forested areas and what remains of its agricultural base, in 2001 the government developed a "Land Bank" policy. Designed to promote the efficient use and management of all agricultural lands, the government helps those who want to engage in agricultural pursuits but lack access to land, and pressures landowners who have not maintained prime agricultural land in a productive state.

Haiti (Republic of Haiti)

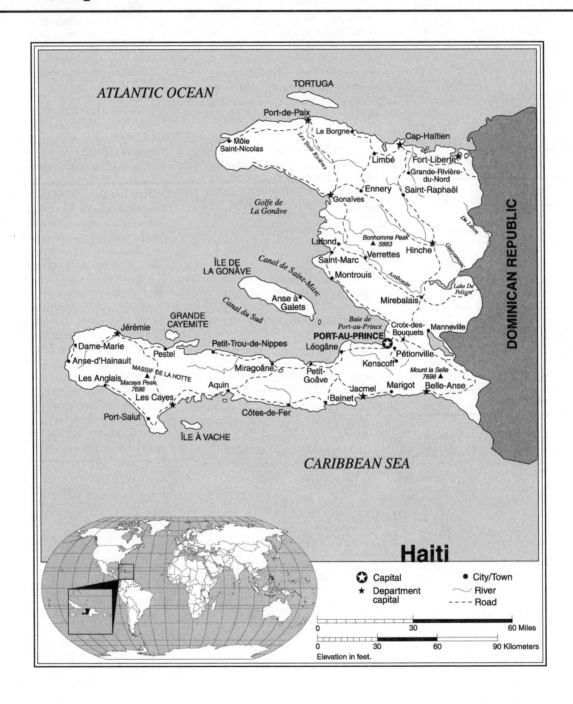

Haiti Statistics

GEOGRAPHY

Area in Square Miles (Kilometers):
10,714 (27,750) (about the size of Maryland)

Capital (Population): Port-au-Prince (845,000)

Environmental Concerns: extensive deforestation; soil erosion; inadequate potable water

Geographical Features: mostly rough and mountainous

Climate: tropical to semiarid

PEOPLE*

Population

Total: 7,656,166

*Note: Estimates explicitly take into account the effects of excess mortality due to AIDS.

146

Annual Growth Rate: 1.71%

Rural/Urban Population Ratio: 68/32

Major Languages: French; Creole

Ethnic Makeup: 95% black; 5% mulatto and white

Religions: 80% Roman Catholic (of which the majority also practice Vodun); 16% Protestant; 4% others

Health

Life Expectancy at Birth: 50 years (male); 53 years (female)

Infant Mortality Rate (Ratio): 95.2/1,000

Physicians Available (Ratio): 1/9,846

Education

Adult Literacy Rate: 52.9%

COMMUNICATION

Telephones: 130,000 main lines

Daily Newspaper Circulation: 7 per 1,000 people

Televisions: 4 per 1,000 people

Internet Users: 80,000

TRANSPORTATION

Highways in Miles (Kilometers): 2,588 (4,160)

Railroads in Miles (Kilometers): privately owned industrial line

Usable Airfields: 13

Motor Vehicles in Use: 53,000

GOVERNMENT

Type: republic

Independence Date: January 1, 1804 (from France)

Head of State/Government: Interim President René Preval

Political Parties: National Front for Change and Democracy; National Congress of Democratic Movements; Movement for the Installation of Democracy in Haiti; National Progressive Revolutionary Party; Lavalas Family; Haitian Christian Democratic Party; others

Suffrage: universal at 18

MILITARY

Current Disputes: claims U.S.– administered Navassa Island

ECONOMY

Currency ($U.S. Equivalent): 40.5 gourde = $1

Per Capita Income/GDP: $1,600/$12.8 billion

GDP Growth Rate: -1%

Inflation Rate: 37.3%

Unemployment Rate: 65%

Labor Force: 3,600,000; unskilled labor abundant

Natural Resources: bauxite; copper; calcium carbonate; gold; marble; hydropower

Agriculture: coffee; mangoes; sugarcane; rice; corn; sorghum; wood

Industry: sugar refining; flour milling; textiles; cement; tourism; light assembly based on imported parts

Exports: $321 million (primary partners United States, European Union)

Imports: $1.2 billion (primary partners United States, European Union)

SUGGESTED WEBSITE

http://www.cia.gov/cia/
publications/factbook/geos/
ha.html

Haiti Country Report

HAITI

Haiti, which occupies the western third of the island of Hispaniola (the Dominican Republic comprises the other two-thirds), was the first nation in Latin America to win independence from its mother country—in this instance, France. It is the poorest country in the Western Hemisphere and one of the least developed in the world. Agriculture, the main employer of the population, is pressed beyond the limits of the available land; the result has been catastrophic deforestation and erosion. While only roughly 30 percent of the land is suitable for planting, 50 percent is actually under cultivation. Haitians are woefully poor, suffer from poor health and lack of education, and seldom find work. Even when employment is found, wages are miserable, and there is no significant labor movement to intercede on behalf of the workers.

A persistent theme in Haiti's history has been a bitter rivalry between a small mulatto elite, consisting of 3 to 4 percent of the population, and the black majority. When François Duvalier, a black country doctor, was president (1957–1971), his avowed aim was to create a "new equilibrium" in the country—by which he meant a major shift in power from the established, predominantly mulatto, elite to a new, black middle class. Much of Haitian culture explicitly rejects Western civilization, which is identified with the mulattos. The Creole language of the masses and their practice of Vodun (voodoo), a combination of African spiritualism and Christianity, has not only insulated the population from the "culturally alien" regimes in power but has also given Haitians a common point of identity.

DEVELOPMENT

 Haiti's agricultural sector, where the vast majority of people earn a living, continues to suffer from massive soil erosion caused by deforestation, poor farming techniques, overpopulation, and low investment.

Haitian intellectuals have raised sharp questions about the nation's culture. Modernizers would like to see the triumph of the French language over Creole and Roman Catholicism over Vodun. Others argue that significant change in Haiti can come only from within, from what is authentically Haitian. The refusal of Haitian governments to recognize Creole as the official language has only added to the determination of the mulatto elite and the black middle class to exclude the rest of the population from effective participation in political life.

FREEDOM

 Demobilized soldiers and armed political factions are responsible for much of the violence in Haiti and have come to dominate drug trafficking. The rule of law cannot be maintained in the face of judicial corruption and a dysfunctional legal system.

For most of its history, Haiti has been run by a series of harsh authoritarian regimes. The ouster in 1986 of President-for-Life Jean-Claude Duvalier promised a more democratic opening as the new ruling National Governing Council announced as its primary goal the transition to a freely

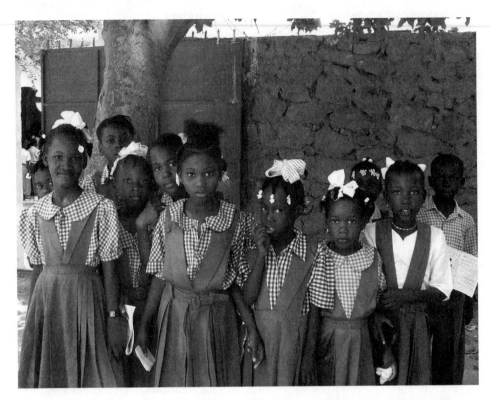

(Courtesy of Robert Buss/BussHaiti24)

These children in Port-de-Paix are dressed in their school uniforms, a requirement, whether in public or private school. Since it is a privilege for children to attend and there is a cost, only 50 percent of children are registered for school. They have little to no materials to work with and most learning is done through memorization.

elected government. Political prisoners were freed; the dreaded secret police, the Tontons Macoute, were disbanded; and the press was unmuzzled.

HEALTH/WELFARE

Until 30 years ago, Haiti was self-sufficient in food production. It must now import about a third of its food needs. Nevertheless, the country has a rapidly expanding population, with a doubling time of 35 years overall, far faster than the Caribbean average of 52 years.

The vacuum left by Duvalier's departure was filled by a succession of governments that were either controlled or heavily influenced by the military. Significant change was heralded in 1990 with the election to power of an outspoken Roman Catholic priest, Jean-Bertrand Aristide. By the end of 1991, he had moved against the military and had formulated a foreign policy that sought to move Haiti closer to the nations of Latin America and the Caribbean. Aristide's promotion of the "church of the poor," which combined local beliefs with standard Catholic instruction, earned him the enmity of both conservative Church leaders and Vodun priests. The radical language of his Lavalas (Floodtide) movement, which promised sweeping economic and social changes, made business leaders and rural landowners uneasy.

Timeline: PAST

1492
The island is discovered by Christopher Columbus; named Hispaniola

1697
The western portion of Hispaniola is ceded to France

1804
Independence from France

1957–1971
The era of President François Duvalier

1971
Jean-Claude Duvalier is named president-for-life

1986
Jean-Claude Duvalier flees into exile

1991
A military coup ousts President Jean-Bertrand Aristide

PRESENT

2000s
The suffering of millions continues

Aristide ousted in February 2004

2006
René Préval elected president

Perhaps not surprisingly in this coup-ridden nation, the army ousted President Aristide in 1991. It took tough economic

sanctions and the threat of an imminent U.S. invasion to force the junta to relinquish power. Aristide, with the support of U.S. troops, was returned to power in 1994. Once an uneasy stability was restored to the country, U.S. troops left the peacekeeping to UN soldiers.

Although there was a period of public euphoria over Aristide's return, the assessment of the *Guardian*, a British newspaper, was somber: Crime rates rose precipitously, political violence continued, and Aristide's enemies were still in Haiti—and armed. Haitians, "sensing a vacuum," took the law "into their own hands."

ACHIEVEMENTS

In the late 1940s, Haitian "primitive" art created a sensation in Paris and other art centers. Although the force of the movement has now been spent, it still represents a unique, colorful, and imaginative art form.

René Préval, who had served briefly as Aristide's prime minister, was himself elected to the presidency in 1996. According to *Caribbean Week*, Préval was caught between "a fiercely independent Parliament [and] an externally-imposed structural adjustment programme...." Préval, presiding over a divided party, was unable to have his choices for cabinet posts approved by the Legislature, which left Haiti without an effective government from 1997 to 1999.

Aristide was reelected in 2000 in a vote characterized by irregularities and fraud. The result was parliamentary paralysis, as the opposition effectively boycotted Aristide's few initiatives, and a country where virtually every institution failed to function. Violent protests and equally violent government repression finally forced Aristide from power at the end of February, 2004. Meanwhile, the suffering of Haiti's people continued unabated, compounded by heavy spring rains and mudslides that killed perhaps 2,000 people.

For the next year and a half a bitterly divided nation attempted to lay the groundwork for new elections in the midst of rampant crime, gang violence, politically motivated attacks and murders, and widespread police corruption. Some 7,000 United Nations peacekeepers themselves came under assault. Political scientists began to use Haiti as an example of a "failed state." Elections were finally held in February 2006 and René Préval won with 51 percent of a contested vote. He has promised to come to the aid of Haiti's poor—but many have made that promise before. Particularly worrisome have been statements by exiled president Jean-Bertrand Aristide that he intends to return to Haiti.

Jamaica

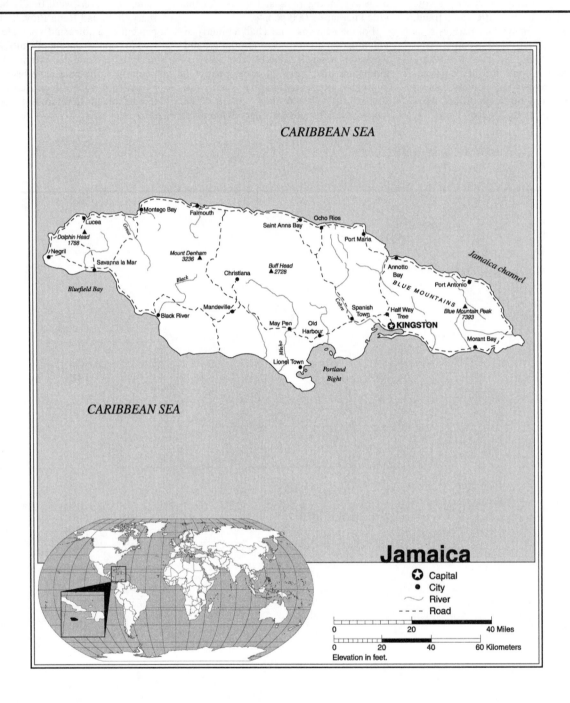

Jamaica Statistics

GEOGRAPHY

Area in Square Miles (Kilometers): 4,244 (10,991) (slightly smaller than Connecticut)

Capital (Population): Kingston (104,000)

Environmental Concerns: deforestation; damage to coral reefs; water and air pollution

Geographical Features: Mostly mountains, with a narrow, discontinuous coastal plain

Climate: tropical; temperate interior

PEOPLE

Population

Total: 2,713,130

Annual Growth Rate: 0.66%

Rural/Urban Population Ratio: 46/54

Major Languages: English; Jamaican Creole

Ethnic Makeup: 90% black; 7% mixed; 3% East Indian, white, Chinese and others

Religions: 56% Protestant; 5% Roman Catholic; 39% others, including some spiritualistic groups

Health

Life Expectancy at Birth: 73 years (male); 77 years (female)

Infant Mortality Rate (Ratio): 14/1,000

Physicians Available (Ratio): 1/6,043

Education

Adult Literacy Rate: 85%

Compulsory (Ages): 6–12; free

COMMUNICATION

Telephones: 444,400 main lines

Daily Newspaper Circulation: 65 per 1,000 people

Televisions: 306 per 1,000

Internet Users: 600,000

TRANSPORTATION

Highways in Miles (Kilometers): 11,613 (18,700)

Railroads in Miles (Kilometers): 230 (370)

Usable Airfields: 36

Motor Vehicles in Use: 59,000

GOVERNMENT

Type: constitutional parliamentary democracy

Independence Date: August 6, 1962 (from the United Kingdom)

Head of State/Government: Queen Elizabeth II; Prime Minister Portia Simpson Miller

Political Parties: People's National Party; Jamaica Labour Party; National Democratic Movement

Suffrage: universal at 18

MILITARY

Current Disputes: none

ECONOMY

Currency ($U.S. Equivalent): 57.74 Jamaican dollars = $1

Per Capita Income/GDP: $3,800/$10.21 billion

GDP Growth Rate: 1.9%

Inflation Rate: 14.1%

Unemployment Rate: 16%

Labor Force: 1,130,000

Natural Resources: bauxite; gypsum; limestone

Agriculture: sugarcane; bananas; coffee; citrus fruits; potatoes; vegetables; poultry; goats; milk

Industry: tourism; bauxite; textiles; food processing; light manufacturers; rum; cement; metal

Exports: $1.7 billion (primary partners United States, European Union, Canada)

Imports: $3 billion (primary partners United States, CARICOM; European Union)

SUGGESTED WEBSITES

http://www.cia.gov/cia/ publications/factbook/index.html

Jamaica Country Report

JAMAICA: "OUT OF MANY, ONE PEOPLE"

In 1962, Jamaica and Trinidad and Tobago were the first of the English-speaking Caribbean islands to gain their independence. A central problem since that time has been the limited ability of Jamaicans to forge a sense of nation. "Out of many, one people" is a popular slogan in Jamaica, but it belies an essential division of the population along lines of both race and class. The elite, consisting of a small white population and Creoles (Afro-Europeans), still think of themselves as "English." Local loyalties notwithstanding, Englishness permeates much of Jamaican life, from language to sports. According to former prime minister Michael Manley: "The problem in Jamaica is how do you get the Jamaican to divorce his mind from the paralysis of his history, which was all bitter colonial frustration, so that he sees his society in terms of this is what crippled me?"

Manley's first government (1975–1980) was one of the few in the Caribbean to incorporate the masses of the people into a political process. He was aware that in a country such as Jamaica—where the majority of the population were poor, ill educated, and lacked essential services—the promise to provide basic needs would win him widespread support. Programs to provide Jamaicans with basic health care and education were expanded, as were services. Many products were subjected to price controls or were subsidized to make them available to the majority of the people. Cuban medical teams and teachers were brought to Jamaica to fill the manpower gaps until local people could be trained.

DEVELOPMENT

Prime Minister Patterson visited Cuba, where agreements were signed for closer cooperation between the two nations in the medical sphere and with a focus on biotechnology. Agreement was also reached on tourism issues and stressed cooperation rather than competition.

However, Jamaica's fragile economy could not support Manley's policies, and he was eventually opposed by the entrenched elite and voted out of office. But Manley was returned to office in 1989, with a new image as a moderate, willing to compromise and aware of the need for foreign-capital investment. Manley retired in 1992 and was replaced as prime minister by Percival J. Patterson, who promised to accelerate Jamaica's transition to a free-market economy. The government instituted a policy of divestment of state-owned enterprises.

FREEDOM

Despite the repeal of the controversial Suppression of Crime Act of 1974, the Parliament, in the face of persistent high levels of crime, provided for emergency police powers. Some critics charge that the Parliament in essence re-created the repealed legislation in a different guise.

The challenges remain. Crime and violence continue to be major social problems in Jamaica. The high crime rate threatens not only the lucrative tourist industry but the very foundations of Jamaican society. Prime Minister Patterson called for a moral re-awakening: "All our programs and strategies for economic progress are doomed to failure unless there is a drastic change in social attitudes…." A stagnant economy, persistent inflation, and unemployment and underemployment combine to lessen respect for authority and contribute to the crime problem. In 2001, Amnesty International noted that in proportion to population, more people are killed by police in Jamaica than anywhere else in the world. Many of the deaths are the result of clashes with gangs of drug dealers, who usually outgun the police. Jamaica counted 1,000 murders in 2002, more, proportionately, than in South Africa, and less than Colombia or El Salvador. It remains a violent society, and the nation continues to walk the narrow line between liberty and license.

HEALTH/WELFARE

Jamaica's "Operation Pride" was designed to combine a dynamic program of land divestment by the state with provisions to meet demands for housing. Squatter colonies would be replaced by "proud home owners."

As is the case in many developing-world countries where unemployment and disaffection are common, drug use is high in Jamaica. The government is reluctant to enforce drug control, however, for approximately 8,000 rural families depend on the cultivation of ganja (marijuana) to supplement their already marginal incomes.

Some of Jamaica's violence is politically motivated and tends to be associated with election campaigns. Both major parties have supporters who employ violence for political purposes. The legal system has been unable to contain the violence or bring the guilty to justice, because of a pervasive code of silence enforced at the local level.

The Patterson government moved deliberately in the direction of electoral reform in an attempt to reduce both violence and

ACHIEVEMENTS

Marcus Garvey was posthumously declared Jamaica's first National Hero in 1964 because of his leading role in the international movement against racism. He called passionately for the recognition of the equal dignity of human beings regardless of race, religion, or national origin. Garvey died in London in 1940.

fraud. Until those reforms are in place, however, the opposition Jamaica Labour Party has decided to boycott by-elections.

Reelected to fourth term in 2002, PM Patterson hoped to match Jamaica's political stability with improvements in the nation's social and economic sectors. He successfully addressed inflation through tight monetary and fiscal policies and redressed Jamaica's debt by privatizing inefficient state enterprises.

On the positive side, human rights are generally respected, and Jamaica's press is basically free. Press freedom is observed in practice within the broad limits of libel laws and the State Secrets Act. Opposition parties publish newspapers and magazines that are highly critical of government policies, and foreign publications are widely available.

Jamaica's labor-union movement is strong and well organized, and it has contributed many leaders to the political process. Unions are among the strongest and best organizations in the country and are closely tied to political parties.

Long-term Prime Minister Patterson stepped down from office in 2006 and was

Timeline: PAST

1509
The first Spanish settlement

1655
Jamaica is seized by the English

1692
An earthquake destroys Port Royal

1944
Universal suffrage is proclaimed

1962
Independence from Great Britain

1990s
Violent crime and strong-armed police responses plague the island

Percival J. Patterson is elected prime minister

PRESENT

2000s
Gun battles break out in Kingston

Patterson reelected to a fourth term in 2002

2006
Portia Simpson Miller elected Jamaica's first woman prime minister

replaced by Portia Simpson Miller, Jamaica's first woman leader. Popular with labor, she will follow essentially the same policies as Patterson.

St. Kitts–Nevis (Federation of St. Kitts and Nevis)

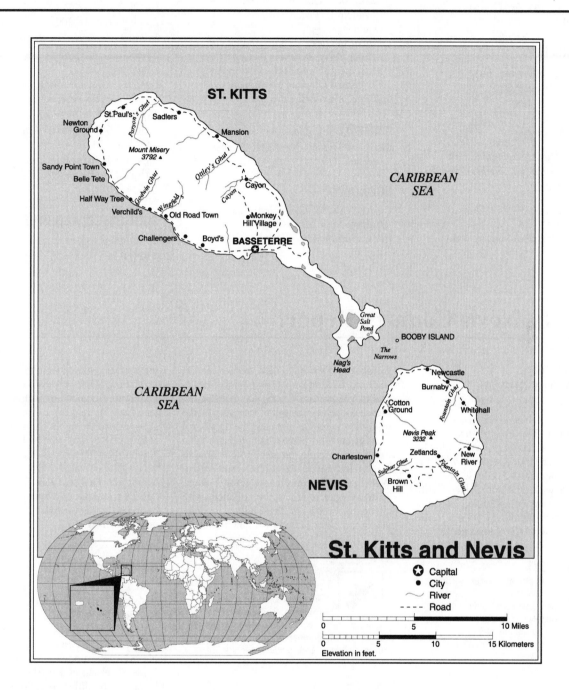

St. Kitts–Nevis Statistics

GEOGRAPHY

Area in Square Miles (Kilometers): 101 (261) (about 1½ times the size of Washington, D.C.)

Capital (Population): Basseterre (12,600)

Geographical Features: volcanic, with mountainous interiors

Climate: subtropical

PEOPLE

Population

Total: 38,836
Annual Growth Rate: 0.25%
Rural/Urban Population Ratio: 66/34
Major Language: English
Ethnic Makeup: mainly of black African descent

Religions: Anglican; other Protestant sects; Roman Catholic

Health

Life Expectancy at Birth: 68 years (male); 74 years (female)

Infant Mortality Rate (Ratio): 16.3/1,000

Physicians Available (Ratio): 1/1,057

Education

Adult Literacy Rate: 97%

Compulsory (Ages): for 12 years between ages 5 and 18

COMMUNICATION

Telephones: 23,500 main lines
Televisions: 241 per 1,000
Internet Users: 10,000

TRANSPORTATION

Highways in Miles (Kilometers): 199 (320)
Railroads in Miles (Kilometers): 36 (58)
Usable Airfields: 2

GOVERNMENT

Type: constitutional monarchy within Commonwealth

Independence Date: September 19, 1983 (from the United Kingdom)

Head of State/Government: Queen Elizabeth II; Prime Minister Denzil Douglas

Political Parties: St. Kitts and Nevis Labour Party; People's Action Movement; Nevis Reformation Party; Concerned Citizens Movement

Suffrage: universal at 18

MILITARY

Current Disputes: Nevis has threatened to secede

ECONOMY

Currency ($U.S. Equivalent): 2.67 East Caribbean dollars = $1

Per Capita Income/GDP: $8,800/$339 million

GDP Growth Rate: -1.9%

Inflation Rate: 1.7%

Unemployment Rate: 4.5%

Labor Force: 18,200

Natural Resources: negligible

Agriculture: rice; yams; vegetables; bananas; fish

Industry: tourism; cotton; salt; copra; clothing; footwear; beverages

Exports: $70 million (primary partners United States, United Kingdom, CARICOM)

Imports: $195 million (primary partners United States, CARICOM, United Kingdom)

SUGGESTED WEBSITES

http://www.cia.gov/cia/
publications/factbook/index.html

St. Kitts–Nevis Country Report

ST. KITTS–NEVIS: ESTRANGED NEIGHBORS

On September 19, 1983, the twin-island state of St. Kitts–Nevis became an independent nation. The country had been a British colony since 1623, when Captain Thomas Warner landed with his wife and eldest son, along with 13 other settlers. The colony fared well, and soon other Caribbean islands were being settled by colonists sent out from St. Kitts (also commonly known as St. Christopher).

DEVELOPMENT

In an attempt to improve an economy that is essentially stagnant, the government of St. Kitts–Nevis, under the auspices of CARICOM, supports the idea of a Caribbean free-trade area. Of particular interest is the inclusion of Cuba in the agreement.

The history of this small island nation is the story of the classic duel between the big sea powers of the period—Great Britain, France, and Spain—and the indigenous people—in this case, the Carib Indians. (Although much of the nation's history has centered around St. Kitts, the larger of the two islands, Nevis, only two miles away, has always been considered a part of St. Kitts, and its history is tied into that of the larger island.) The British were the first settlers on the island of St. Kitts but were followed that same year by the French. In a unique compromise, considering the era, the

British and French divided the territory in 1627 and lived in peace for a number of decades. A significant reason for this British–French cooperation was the constant pressure from their common enemies: the aggressive Spanish and the fierce Carib Indians. The Caribs, for a while, played a role similar to that of Indians in the French and Indian War in North America a century later. They were adept at forming alliances with either the French or the English to drive one or the other or both from the region.

FREEDOM

The election in 1984 of Constance Mitcham to Parliament signaled a new role for women. She was subsequently appointed minister of women's affairs. However, despite her conspicuous success, women still occupy a very small percentage of senior civil-service positions.

With the gradual elimination of the mutual threat, Anglo–French tensions again mounted, resulting in a sharp land battle at Frigate Bay on St. Kitts. The new round of hostilities, which reflected events in Europe, would disrupt the Caribbean for much of the next century. Events came to a climactic head in 1782, when the British garrison at Brimstone Hill, commonly known as the "Gibraltar of the West Indies," was overwhelmed by a superior French force. In honor of the bravery of the defenders, the French commander allowed

the British to march from the fortress in full formation. (The expression "peace with honor" has its roots in this historic encounter.) Later in the year, however, the British again seized the upper hand. A naval battle at Frigate Bay was won by British Admiral Hood following a series of brilliant maneuvers. The defeated French admiral, the Count de Grasse, was in turn granted "peace with honor." Thereafter, the islands remained under British rule until their independence in 1983.

AGRICULTURE

Before the British colonized the island, St. Kitts was called Liamiuga ("Fertile Isle") by the Carib Indians. The name was apt, because agriculture for most of its history played a big role in the economy of the islands. Tourism and offshore banking and business facilities definitively replaced sugar has the largest generator of foreign exchange.

HEALTH/WELFARE

The demise of the sugar industry in 2005 resulted in the loss of employment for about 4 percent of the population. Effected workers will likely seek employment in other kinds of agriculture, the tourism industry, or out-migrate. Although a minimum wage exists by law, the amount is less than what a person can reasonably be expected to live on.

Because the sugar market was so unstable and because world market prices were so low, the decision was made to phase out the sugar industry altogether. The last mill closed its doors in 2005. Agricultural production will now likely be geared toward local or regional markets.

ECONOMIC CHANGE

Unlike such islands as Barbados and Antigua, St. Kitts–Nevis for years chose not to use tourism as a buffer to offset any disastrous fluctuations in sugar prices. On St. Kitts, there was an antitourism attitude that can be traced back to the repressive administration of Prime Minister Robert Bradshaw, a black nationalist who worked to discourage tourism and threatened to nationalize all land holdings.

That changed under the moderate leadership of Kennedy Simmonds and his People's Action Movement, who remained in power from 1980 until ousted in elections in July 1995. The new administration of Denzil Douglas promised to address serious problems that had developed, including drug trafficking, money laundering, and a lack of respect for law and order. In 1997, a 50-man "army" was created to wage war against heavily armed drug traffickers operating in the region. Agriculture Minister Timothy Harris noted that the permanent defense force "was critical to the survival of the sovereignty of the nation." Simmond's promotion of tourism took root. By 2001, tourism had become a major growth industry in the islands. Major airlines refused to schedule landings in St. Kitts until there were an adequate number of hotel rooms. Accordingly, the government promoted the construction of 1,500 rooms. A positive side-effect are the jobs produced in the construction trades and service industry.

ACHIEVEMENTS

St. Kitts–Nevis was the first successful British settlement in the Caribbean. St. Kitts–Nevis was the birthplace of Alexander Hamilton, the first U.S. secretary of the Treasury Department and an American statesman.

The future of St. Kitts–Nevis will depend on its ability to broaden its economic base. PM Douglas's economic policies include the promotion of export-oriented manufactures and off-shore banking. A potential problem of some magnitude looms, however: The island of Nevis, long in the shadow of the more populous and prosperous St. Kitts, nearly voted to secede in a referendum held in August 1998. The Constitution requires a two-thirds majority for secession; 61.7 percent of the population of Nevis voted "Yes." Not surprisingly, the government is working to fashion a new federalism with "appropriate power sharing" between the islands. That has not diminished the move toward independence for Nevis' 10,000 people. Prime Minister Douglas has also said that difference between the two islands should be the subject of constitutional reform, not repeated referenda on secession.

Timeline: PAST

1493
The islands are discovered and named by Christopher Columbus

1623
The British colony is settled by Captain Thomas Warner

1689
A land battle at Frigate Bay disrupts a peaceful accord between France and England

1782
The English are expelled by French at the siege of Brimstone Hill

The French are beaten at the sea battle of Frigate Bay; the beginning of continuous British rule

1967
Self-government as an Associate State of the United Kingdom

1983
Full independence from Great Britain

1998
A referendum on Nevis secession is narrowly defeated

PRESENT

2004
Denzil Douglas reelected for a third consecutive term

St. Lucia

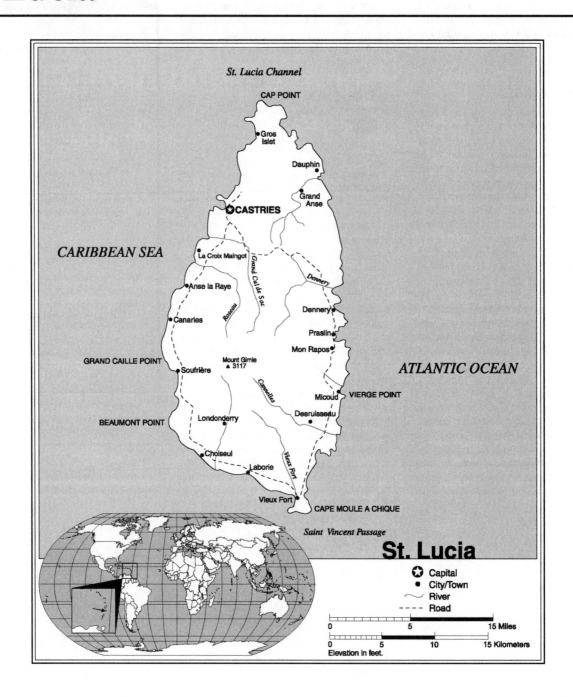

St. Lucia Channel

CAP POINT

• Gros Islet

Dauphin •

CARIBBEAN SEA

La Croix Maingot •

• Anse la Raye

• Canaries

GRAND CAILLE POINT

Soufrière •

Mount Gimie
▲ 3117

BEAUMONT POINT

Londonderry •

• Choiseul

Laborie •

Vieux Fort •

CAPE MOULE A CHIQUE

Grand Anse •

⊛CASTRIES

Grand Cul de Sac

Rozeau

Dennery

Dennery •

Praslin •

Mon Rapos •

Canelles

Micoud •

Desruisseau •

VIERGE POINT

ATLANTIC OCEAN

Vieux Fort

Saint Vincent Passage

St. Lucia

⊛ Capital
• City/Town
∿ River
- - - Road

0   5   15 Miles

0   5   10   15 Kilometers
Elevation in feet.

St. Lucia Statistics

GEOGRAPHY

Area in Square Miles (Kilometers): 238 (619) (about 3 times the size of Washington, D.C.)

Capital (Population): Castries (13,600)

Environmental Concerns: deforestation; soil erosion

Geographical Features: volcanic and mountainous; some broad, fertile valleys

Climate: tropical maritime

PEOPLE

Population

Total: 164,213

Annual Growth Rate: 1.23%

Rural/Urban Population Ratio: 63/37

Major Languages: English; French patois

Ethnic Makeup: 90% black; 6% mixed; 3% East Indian; 1% white

Religions: 90% Roman Catholic; 3% Church of England; 7% other Protestant sects

Health

Life Expectancy at Birth: 69 years (male);
  76 years (female)
Infant Mortality Rate (Ratio): 13/1,000
Physicians Available (Ratio): 1/2,235

Education

Adult Literacy Rate: 67%
Compulsory (Ages): 5–15

COMMUNICATION

Telephones: 51,100 main lines
Televisions: 172 per 1,000 people
Internet Users: 13,000

TRANSPORTATION

Highways in Miles (Kilometers): 451
  (1,210)
Railroads in Miles (Kilometers): none
Usable Airfields: 2
Motor Vehicles in Use: 19,000

GOVERNMENT

Type: constitutional monarchy within
  Commonwealth
Independence Date: February 22, 1979
  (from the United Kingdom)
Head of State/Government: Queen
  Elizabeth II; Prime Minister Kenneth D.
  Anthony
Political Parties: United Workers Party;
  St. Lucia Labour Party; National
  Freedom Party
Suffrage: universal at 18

MILITARY

Current Disputes: none

ECONOMY

Currency ($U.S. Equivalent): 2.67 East
  Caribbean dollars = $1
Per Capita Income/GDP: $5,400/$866
  million
GDP Growth Rate: 3.3%

Inflation Rate: 3%
Unemployment Rate: 16.5%
Labor Force: 43,800
Natural Resources: forests; sandy
  beaches; minerals (pumice); mineral
  springs; geothermal potential
Agriculture: bananas; coconuts;
  vegetables; citrus fruits; root crops;
  cocoa
Industry: clothing; assembly of electronic
  components; beverages; corrugated
  cardboard boxes; tourism; lime
  processing; coconut processing
Exports: $66 million (primary partners
  United Kingdom, United States,
  CARICOM)
Imports: $267 million (primary partners
  United States, CARICOM, United
  Kingdom)

SUGGESTED WEBSITES

http://www.cia.gov/cia/
  publications/factbook/index.html

St. Lucia Country Report

ST. LUCIA: ENGLISH POLITICS, FRENCH CULTURE

The history of St. Lucia gives striking testimony to the fact that the sugar economy, together with the contrasting cultures of various colonial masters, was crucial in shaping the land, social structures, and lifestyles of its people. The island changed hands between the French and the English at least seven times, and the influences of both cultures are still evident today. Ninety percent of the population speaks French patois (dialect), while the educated and the elite prefer English. Indeed, the educated perceive patois as suitable only for proverbs and curses. On St. Lucia and the other patois-speaking islands (Dominica, Grenada), some view the common language as the true reflection of their uniqueness. English, however, is the language of status and opportunity. In terms of religion, most St. Lucians are Roman Catholic.

DEVELOPMENT

The government negotiated a loan with France to construct new water pipelines. Provision of potable water is critical not only to agriculture but also to the tourist industry.

The original inhabitants of St. Lucia were Arawak Indians who had been forced off the South American mainland by the Carib In-

dians. Gradually, the Carib also moved onto the Caribbean islands and destroyed most of the Arawak culture. Evidence of that early civilization has been found in rich archaeological sites on St. Lucia.

FREEDOM

The St. Lucian parliament introduced controversial legislation in 2003 that calls for possible imprisonment for knowingly publishing false news that harms the public good. Media watchdogs have warned that this law threatens freedom of the press.

The date of the European "discovery" of the island is uncertain; it may have occurred in 1499 or 1504 by the navigator and mapmaker Juan de la Cosa, who explored the Windward Islands during the early years of the sixteenth century. The Dutch, French, and English all established small settlements or trading posts on the island in the seventeenth century but were resisted by the Caribs. The first successful settlement dates from 1651, when the French were able to maintain a foothold.

The island's political culture is English. Upon independence from Great Britain in 1979, St. Lucians adopted the British parliamentary system, which includes specific safeguards for the preservation of human rights. Despite several years of political disruption, caused by the jockeying for

power of several political parties and affiliated interests, St. Lucian politics is essentially stable.

THE ECONOMY

St. Lucia has an economy that is as diverse as any in the Caribbean. Essentially agricultural, the country has also developed a tourism industry, manufacturing, and related construction activity. A recent "mineral inventory" has located possible gold deposits, but exploitation must await the creation of appropriate mining legislation.

HEALTH/WELFARE

The minister of agriculture has linked marginal nutrition and malnutrition in St. Lucia with economic adjustment programs in the Caribbean. He noted that the success achieved earlier in raising standards of living was being eroded by "onerous debt burdens."

U.S. promises to the region made in the 1980s failed to live up to expectations. Although textiles, clothing, and nontraditional goods exported to the United States increased as a result of the Caribbean Basin Initiative, St. Lucia remained dependent on its exports of bananas. About a third of the island's workforce are involved in banana production, which accounts for 90 percent of St. Lucia's exports.

ACHIEVEMENTS

St. Lucians have won an impressive two Nobel prizes. Sir W. Arthur Lewis won the prize in 1979 for economics, and in 1993, poet Derek Walcott won the prize for literature. When asked how the island had produced two Nobel laureates, Wolcott replied: "It's the food."

St. Lucia's crucial banana industry suffered significant production losses in 1997 and 2001 in large part because of drought. Exports were half of the normal volume, and St. Lucia fell short of filling its quota for the European Union. A 1999 European Union decision to drop its import preferences for bananas from former colonial possessions in the Caribbean together with increased competition from Latin America growers have created an urgent demand to diversify St. Lucia's economy. Increased emphasis has been placed on exports of mangos and avocados. Tourism, light manufacturing, and offshore banking have also experienced growth. Despite these attempts unemployment, inflation, a high cost of living, and drug trafficking remain serious problems and have led to periodic unrest.

Timeline: PAST

638
The English take possession of St. Lucia

1794
The English regain possession of St. Lucia from France

1908
Riots

1951
Universal adult suffrage

1979
Independence from Great Britain

1990s
Banana production suffers a serious decline

PRESENT

2000s
Economic diversification becomes a critical need

Kenneth Anthony elected for a second term with an overwhelming majority.

St. Lucia, like several other islands, has also succeeded in trading on its sovereignty—a vote in the United Nations—to raise revenue. Since 1997, when banana exports reached crisis proportions, St. Lucia has supported the claims of China over the independence of Taiwan.

EDUCATION AND EMIGRATION

Education in St. Lucia has traditionally been brief and perfunctory. Few students attend secondary school, and very few (3 percent) ever attend a university. Although the government reports that 95 percent of those eligible attend elementary school, farm and related chores severely reduce attendance figures. In recent years, St. Lucia has channeled more than 20 percent of its expenditures into education and health care. Patient care in the general hospital was made free of charge in 1980.

Population growth is relatively low, but emigration off the island is a significant factor. For years, St. Lucians, together with Dominicans, traveled to French Guiana to work in the gold fields. More recently, however, they have crossed to neighboring Martinique, a French department, in search of work. St. Lucians can also be found working on many other Caribbean islands.

St. Vincent and the Grenadines

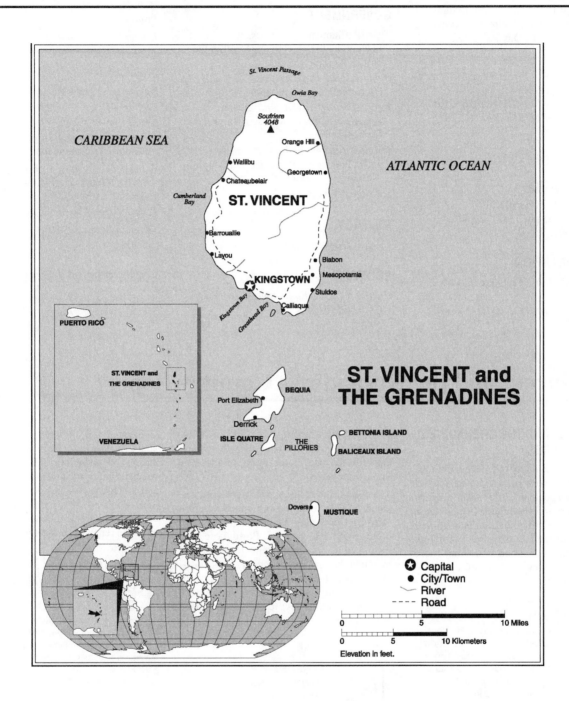

St. Vincent and the Grenadines Statistics

GEOGRAPHY

Area in Square Miles (Kilometers): 131 (340) (about twice the size of Washington, D.C.)

Capital (Population): Kingstown (16,000)

Environmental Concerns: pollution of coastal waters and shorelines by discharges from pleasure boats
Geographical Features: volcanic; mountainous
Climate: tropical

PEOPLE

Population

Total: 117,193
Annual Growth Rate: 0.31%
Rural/Urban Population Ratio: 50/50

Major Languages: English; French patois
Ethnic Makeup: mainly black African descent; remainder mixed, with some white, East Indian, and Carib Indian
Religions: Anglican; Methodist; Roman Catholic; Seventh-Day Adventist

Health

Life Expectancy at Birth: 71 years (male); 74 years (female)
Infant Mortality Rate (Ratio): 16.6/1,000
Physicians Available (Ratio): 1/2,708

Education

Adult Literacy Rate: 96%

COMMUNICATION

Telephones: 27,300 main lines
Televisions: 161 per 1,000 people
Internet Users: 7,000

TRANSPORTATION

Highways in Miles (Kilometers): 646 (1,040)
Railroads in Miles (Kilometers): none

Usable Airfields: 6
Motor Vehicles in Use: 8,200

GOVERNMENT

Type: Parliamentary democracy, independent sovereign state within the British Commonwealth
Independence Date: October 27, 1979 (from the United Kingdom)
Head of State/Government: Queen Elizabeth II; Prime Minister Ralph Gonsalves
Political Parties: Unity Labour Party; New Democratic Party; United People's Movement; National Reform Party
Suffrage: universal at 18

MILITARY

Current Disputes: none

ECONOMY

Currency ($U.S. Equivalent): 2.67 East Caribbean dollars = $1

Per Capita Income/GDP: $2,900/$339 million
GDP Growth Rate: -0.5%
Inflation Rate: -0.4%
Unemployment Rate: 22%
Labor Force: 67,000
Natural Resources: negligible
Agriculture: bananas; arrowroot; coconuts; sweet potatoes; spices; small amount of livestock; fish
Industry: food processing; cement; furniture; clothing; starch; tourism
Exports: $38 million (primary partners CARICOM, United Kingdom, United States)
Imports: $174 million (primary partners United States, CARICOM, United Kingdom)

SUGGESTED WEBSITES

http://www.cia.gov/cia/
publications/factbook/index.html

St. Vincent and the Grenadines Country Report

ST. VINCENT AND THE GRENADINES: POOR BUT FREE

Vincentians, like many other West Indians, either identify with or, as viewed from a different perspective, suffer from a deep-seated European orientation. Critics argue that it is an identification that is historical in origin, and that it is negative. For many, the European connection is nothing more than the continuing memory of a master–slave relationship.

DEVELOPMENT

A slump in banana production because of poor weather and low prices forced farmers to produce other crops, including marijuana. In a 1998 sweep, U.S. troops aided St. Vincentian soldiers in eradicating the crop, which spread animosity toward Washington.

St. Vincent is unique in that it was one of the few Caribbean islands where runaway black slaves intermarried with Carib Indians and produced a distinct racial type known as the Garifuna, or black Carib. Toward the end of the eighteenth century, the Garifuna and other native peoples mounted an assault on the island's white British planters. They were assisted by the French from Martinique but were defeated in

1796. As punishment, the Garifuna were deported to what is today Belize, where they formed one of the bases of that nation's population.

In 1834, the black slaves were emancipated, which disrupted the island's economy by decreasing the labor supply. In order to fill this vacuum, Portuguese and East Indian laborers were imported to maintain the agrarian economy. This, however, was not done until later in the nineteenth century—not quickly enough to prevent a lasting blow to the island's economic base.

FREEDOM

The government took a great step forward in terms of wage scales for women by adopting a new minimum-wage law, which provided for equal pay for equal work done by men and women. Violence against women remains a significant problem.

St. Vincent, along with Dominica, is one of the poorest islands in the West Indies. The current unemployment rate (2004) is estimated at 33 percent. With more than half the population under age 15, unemployment will continue to be a major problem in the foreseeable future.

Formerly one of the West Indian sugar islands, St. Vincent's main crops are now bananas and arrowroot. The sugar industry was a casualty of low world-market prices and a black-power movement in the 1960s that associated sugar production with memories of slavery. Limited sugar production has been renewed to meet local needs.

HEALTH/WELFARE

Minimum wages established in 1989 range from $3.85 *per day* in agriculture to $7.46 in industry. New minimums were to be presented to parliament in 2003. Clearly, the minimum is inadequate, although most workers earn significantly more than the minimum.

THE POLITICS OF POVERTY

Poverty affects everyone in St. Vincent and the Grenadines, except a very few who live in comfort. In the words of one Vincentian, for most people, "life is a study in poverty." In 1969, a report identified malnutrition and gastroenteritis as being responsible for 57 percent of the deaths of children under age five. Those problems persist.

Deep-seated poverty also has an impact on the island's political life. Living on the verge of starvation, Vincentians cannot appreciate an intellectual approach to politics. They find it difficult to wait for the effects of long-term trends or coordinated development. Bread-and-butter issues are what concern them. Accordingly, parties speak little of basic economic and social change, structural shifts in the economy, or the latest economic theories. Politics is reduced to personality contests and rabble-rousing. Prime Minister Ralph Gonsalves, elected to a second term in 2005, remarked that he was tired of "perpetual warfare of a verbal kind" and has urged national reconciliation.

Despite its severe economic problems, St. Vincent is a free society. Newspapers are uncensored. Some reports, however, have noted that the government has on occasion granted or withheld advertising on the basis of a paper's editorial position.

ACHIEVEMENTS

A regional cultural organization was launched in 1982 in St. Vincent. Called the East Caribbean Popular Theatre Organisation, its membership extends to Dominica, Grenada, and St. Lucia.

Unions enjoy the right of collective bargaining. They represent about 11 percent of the labor force. St. Vincent, which won its independence from Great Britain in 1979, is a parliamentary, constitutional democracy. Political parties have the right to organize.

POLITICS AND ECONOMICS

While the country's political life has been calm, relative to some of the other Caribbean islands, there are signs of voter unrest. Prime Minister James Mitchell was reelected in 1999 for an unprecedented fourth five-year term, but his New Democratic Party lost some ground in the Legislature. In 2001 Ralph Gonsalves and his Unity Labour Party narrowly won election; in 2005 they gained 12 seats in the 15-seat parliament. Gonsalves, as reported by *BBC News*, is known to his followers as "Comrade Ralph" and campaigned on his government's economic record. He could point to meaningful economic growth and the completion of dozens of major projects.

Bananas once accounted for two-thirds of St. Vincent's export earnings. That figure fell to 50 percent in 2004 and to 33 percent in 2005. As is the case with other Windward Islands, St. Vincent's economy has been hurt by the 1999 European Union decision to phase out preferential treatment to banana producers from former colonial possessions. Not surprisingly drug trafficking, marijuana cultivation, and money laundering have increased as a result of the general economic malaise.

In 2001, along with other islands in the Windwards, St. Vincent entered talks with European Union officials with an eye to improving both yields and quality of bananas. There was general agreement that

Timeline: PAST

1498
Christopher Columbus discovers and names St. Vincent

1763
Ceded to the British by France

1795
The Carib War

1902
St. Vincent's La Soufrière erupts and kills 2,000 people

1979
Independence from Great Britain

1990s
A new minimum-wage law takes effect

PRESENT

2000s
The country's financial problems remain severe

2001
Ralph Gonsalves assumes the post of prime minister

2005
Gonsalves wins second term

the entire Windward Islands banana industry needed restructuring if the industry is to survive.

Trinidad and Tobago (Republic of Trinidad and Tobago)

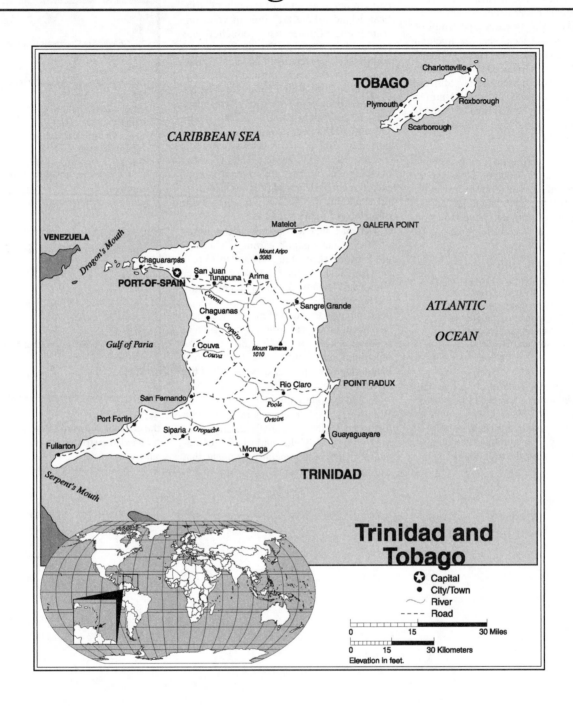

Trinidad and Tobago Statistics

GEOGRAPHY

Area in Square Miles (Kilometers): 1,980 (5,128) (about the size of Delaware)

Capital (Population): Port-of-Spain (44,000)

Environmental Concerns: water pollution; oil pollution of beaches; deforestation; soil erosion

Geographical Features: mostly plains, with some hills and low mountains

Climate: tropical

PEOPLE

Population

Total: 1,096,585

Annual Growth Rate: -0.71%

Rural/Urban Population Ratio: 28/72

162

Major Language: English

Ethnic Makeup: 43% black; 40% East Indian; 14% mixed; 1% white; 1% Chinese; 1% others

Religions: 32% Roman Catholic; 24% Hindu; 14% Anglican; 14% other Protestant; 6% Muslim; 10% others

Health

Life Expectancy at Birth: 66 years (male); 71 years (female)

Infant Mortality Rate (Ratio): 25/1,000

Physicians Available (Ratio): 1/1,191

Education

Adult Literacy Rate: 98%

Compulsory (Ages): 5–12; free

COMMUNICATION

Telephones: 325,100 main lines

Daily Newspaper Circulation: 139 per 1,000 people

Televisions: 198 per 1,000 people

Internet Users: 138,000

TRANSPORTATION

Highways in Miles (Kilometers): 5,167 (8,320)

Railroads in Miles (Kilometers): minimal agricultural service

Usable Airfields: 6

Motor Vehicles in Use: 155,000

GOVERNMENT

Type: parliamentary democracy

Independence Date: August 31, 1962 (from United Kingdom)

Head of State/Government: President George Maxwell Richards; Prime Minister Patrick Manning

Political Parties: People's National Movement; National Alliance for Reconstruction; United National Congress; Movement for Social Transformation; National Joint Action Committee; others

Suffrage: universal at 18

MILITARY

Current Disputes: none

ECONOMY

Currency ($U.S. Equivalent): 6.12 Trinidad/Tobago dollars = $1

Per Capita Income/GDP: $9,500/$10.6 billion

GDP Growth Rate: 4.5%

Inflation Rate: 3.7%

Unemployment Rate: 10.9%

Labor Force: 559,000

Natural Resources: petroleum; natural gas; asphalt

Agriculture: cocoa; sugarcane; rice; citrus fruits; coffee; vegetables; poultry

Industry: petroleum; chemicals; tourism; food processing; cement; beverages; textiles

Exports: $4.9 billion (primary partners United States, CARICOM, Latin America)

Imports: $3 billion (primary partners United States, Venezuela, European Union)

SUGGESTED WEBSITE

http://www.cia.gov/cia/
publications/factbook/index.html

Trinidad and Tobago Country Report

TRINIDAD AND TOBAGO: A MIDDLE-CLASS SOCIETY

The nation of Trinidad and Tobago, which became independent of Great Britain in 1962, differs sharply from other Caribbean countries in terms of both its wealth and its societal structure. More than one-third of its revenues derive from the production of crude oil. Much of the oil wealth has been redistributed and has created a society that is essentially middle class. Health conditions are generally good, education is widely available, and the literacy rate is a very high 98 percent.

DEVELOPMENT

The economy has experienced rapid growth thanks to vast reserves of natural gas, which has attracted investors from developed countries. The government has also promoted the use of natural gas, instituting a program to encourage consumers to switch from gasoline.

The country also enjoys an excellent human-rights record, although there is a good deal of tension between the ruling urban black majority and East Indians, who are rural. The divisions run deep and parallel the situation in Guyana. East Indians feel that they are forced to submerge their culture and conform to the majority. In the words of one East Indian, "Where do Indians fit in when the culture of 40 percent of our people is denied its rightful place and recognition; when most of our people exist on the fringes of society and are considered as possessing nothing more than nuisance value?"

The lyrics of a black calypso artist that state the following are resented by East Indians:

If you are an East Indian
And you want to be an African
Just shave your head just like me
And nobody would guess your
    nationality.

The prosperity of the nation, however, tends to mute these tensions.

Freedom of expression and freedom of the press are constitutionally guaranteed as well as respected in practice. Opposition viewpoints are freely expressed in the nation's Parliament, which is modeled along British lines. There is no political censorship. Opposition parties are usually supported by rural Hindu East Indians; while they have freely participated in elections, some East Indians feel that the government has gerrymandered electoral districts to favor the ruling party.

Violent crime and political unrest, including an attempted coup by black fundamentalist Muslim army officers in 1990, have become a way of life in the nation in recent years. Prime Minister Basdeo Panday, elected in 1996, noted that there were still agendas, "political and otherwise," that divided Trinidadian society. "How much better it will be," he stated, "if all in our society, and particularly those in a position to shape mass consciousness, will seize every opportunity to promote and mobilise the greater strength that comes out of our diversity...."

FREEDOM

Freedom of expression on the islands is guaranteed by the Constitution. The independent judiciary, pluralistic political system, and independent and privately owned print media assure that free expression exists in practice as well as in theory.

Trade-union organization is the most extensive among Caribbean nations with ties to Britain and includes about 30 percent of the workforce. In contrast to other West Indian states, unions in Trinidad and Tobago are not government-controlled, nor are they generally affiliated with a political party.

Women are well represented in Parliament, serve as ministers, and hold other high-level civil-service positions. Several groups are vocal advocates for women's rights.

HEALTH/WELFARE

Legislation passed in 1991 greatly expanded the categories of workers covered by the minimum wage. The same legislation provided for 3 months' maternity leave for household and shop assistants as well as other benefits.

In an attempt to redress imbalances in the nation's agricultural structure, which is characterized by small landholdings—half of which are less than five acres each—the government has initiated a land-redistribution program using state-owned properties and estates sold to the government. The program is designed to establish more efficient medium-size family farms, of five to 20 acres, devoted to cash crops.

The islands' economic fortunes have tended to reflect the prices it can command from its exports of oil and liquefied natural gas. In 2004, with prices high, government revenues grew significantly. In 2001, British Petroleum began development of the Kapok gas field with a completion date of 2003. The project will give the nation one of the largest offshore gas-handling facilities in the world. Importantly, the company has

indicated that the facility will conform to the most stringent environmental safeguards.

Of some concern to the government are the inroads made by Venezuela into its Caribbean market for refined petroleum. Venezuelan foreign policy has used oil to buy influence in the region and its low prices undercut Trinidad. A possible solution was discussed in 2006 whereby Venezuelan crude would be refined in Trinidad.

ACHIEVEMENTS

Eric Williams, historian, pamphleteer, and politician, left his mark on Caribbean culture with his scholarly books and his bitterly satirical *Massa Day Done*. V. S. Naipaul is an influential author born in Trinidad. Earl Lovelace is another well-known Trinidadian author. He won the 1997 Commonwealth Writers' Prize for his novel *Salt*.

TOBAGO

Residents of Tobago have come to believe that their small island is perceived as nothing more than a dependency of Trinidad. It has been variously described as a "weekend resort," a "desert island," and a "tree house"—in contrast to "thriving," "vibrant" Trinidad. Tobagans feel that they receive less than their share of the benefits generated by economic prosperity.

In 1989, the Constitution was reviewed with an eye to introducing language that would grant Tobago the right to secede. The chair of the Tobago House of Assembly argued that, "in any union, both partners should have the right to opt out if they so desire." Others warn that such a provi-

bind two peoples into one. Trinidadian opposition leaders have observed that the areas that have historically supported the ruling party have more and better roads, telephones, and schools than those backing opposition parties.

Timeline: PAST

1498
The island now called Trinidad is discovered by Columbus and later colonized by Spain

1797
Trinidad is captured by the British

1889
Tobago is added to Trinidad as a colonial unit

1962
Independence from Great Britain

1980s
Oil-export earnings slump

1996
Basdeo Panday is elected prime minister

PRESENT

2000s
Further development of the natural-gas industry

Patrick Manning elected prime minister, October 2002

2005–2006
Tension between Venezuela and Trinidad over competition for petroleum markets in the Caribbean region

Latin America's Populist Turn

"Latin America's political landscape, highly complex and variegated, defies easy categorization and raises fundamental questions—including whether it might be better to jettison the term 'left' altogether."

MICHAEL SHIFTER AND VINAY JAWAHAR

When Tabaré Vázquez won an impressive victory in Uruguay's presidential election on October 31, 2004, some newspapers could not resist proclaiming that the triumph solidified a wider, regional pattern. "Uruguay Completes the Leftward Realignment of the Southern Cone" was a typical headline. Given Vázquez's pedigree—the new president represents the Broad Front, a coalition of democratic socialists, communists, and former Tupamaro urban guerrillas—he fit right in with the region's other leaders: Ricardo Lagos, Chile's first socialist president in more than three decades; Luiz Inácio "Lula" Da Silva, Brazil's president from the leftist Workers' Party; and Néstor Kirchner, the Argentine president whose political roots can be traced back to the strand of leftism practiced by the Peronist party in the 1970s. The entire lineup now ruling the southern cone of South America exhibits strong "leftist" credentials.

Yet if this is Vázquez's—and the left's—moment, it is unclear just what that moment means. The broad category of "leftist" offers a variety of possibilities. The moderate, even orthodox economic policies that the Southern Cone's "leftist" leaders have recently undertaken contrast sharply with other variants of leftism found in Latin America. Cuban President Fidel Castro has of course largely embodied and practically defined the leftist label over almost half a century. Castro's revolutionary project centered on the radical reordering of Cuba's economy, marked by confiscation and nationalization of private property. And since coming to office in early 1999 as Venezuela's democratically elected president, Hugo Chávez has often been described as a leftist, in part based on his close relationship with Castro and also because of his highly charged rhetoric.

Other so-called leftists, still aspiring to be presidents, include Bolivian indigenous leader Evo Morales and former Salvadoran guerrilla figure Shafik Handal. Few doubt that Nicaragua's Daniel Ortega, who formerly led the Sandinista regime in the 1980s, hopes to return to his old executive office, this time via the ballot. So does Peru's rehabilitated former president, Alan García, who governed in the late 1980s and in the past gladly embraced the leftist label. Curiously, even the president whom

García hopes to succeed in 2006, Alejandro Toledo, has been depicted as a leftist, as has Ecuador's president, Lucio Gutiérrez.

In fact, Latin America's political landscape, highly complex and variegated, defies easy categorization and raises fundamental questions—including whether it might be better to jettison the term "left" altogether. Does "left" actually provide a useful handle for understanding the forces today shaping the region's politics, or for anticipating the policies that a president might pursue once in office? Does it capture what is happening in Latin America, or is it merely an artificial construct that obfuscates more than it illuminates? Are observers confusing a natural concern for acute social conditions, cast in markedly populist rhetoric, with "leftist" agendas? Or are "leftists" simply those who identify themselves as such?

The Region and Its Discontents

It is not surprising that Latin America has been undergoing political ferment in recent years. Economic and social progress has been meager, and expectations for a better life have largely not been met. Over the past 25 years the only Latin American country that has witnessed a significant increase in its real per capita income has been Chile. Regionally inflation has successfully been brought under control, and most governments have exercised fiscal discipline. But the results of economic recipes applied throughout Latin America—contained in the so-called Washington consensus and advocating greater privatization and liberalization—have been disappointing.

It is hard to discern coherent proposals and policies that could constitute a viable, alternative approach to the prevailing economic model in Latin America. The region has witnessed greater concern for the urgent social agenda and appeals to the popular sectors of society—traditionally excluded and recently mobilized—not only in Lula's Brazil, Lagos's Chile, and Chávez's Venezuela, but also in Álvaro Uribe's Colombia and Vicente Fox's Mexico. Unsettled national politics have combined with a perceptible tendency across the region to resist pressure from the world's only superpower, the United States, and an attempt to chart a more independent economic and political course. But an effort to tackle thorny social problems with practical solutions, coupled with a more autonomous foreign policy, is a far cry from leftism—at least as generally understood and practiced in Latin America.

It is now common to point out that, consistent with global trends, most Latin Americans are increasingly unhappy with politics as usual and are seeking new political options. Since 1995, Latino-barómetro, the public opinion survey carried out by a Santiago-based organization, has shed light on this public disenchantment. Dissatisfaction with government performance in a number of critical areas, especially the provision of economic and physical security, has grown considerably. Unemployment, crime, and corruption typically top the list of public concerns.

At the same time, there is little evidence that Latin Americans are systematically rejecting either the principles that underpin the democratic system or the market economy. In fact, in 2004 Latino-barómetro reported that some 56 percent of the region's respondents favor the market economy. It is true that the prescriptions associated with the Washington consensus—distinct from, or at least a subset of, the market economy—have yielded unfavorable results for most Latin Americans. Rates of poverty and inequality, long the region's Achilles heel, have remained stubbornly stagnant, or have deteriorated.

Only in 2004—ironically, the same year that the leftist label seemed to acquire greater appeal in Latin America—was overall economic performance reasonably robust. The 5.5 percent growth rate for the year was the region's highest for several decades. Experts attribute the performance mainly to favorable commodity prices, the extraordinarily high demand from China, and the fact that statistics for many of the region's key countries—Argentina and Venezuela, most notably—had risen from an extremely low base. Whether a similar growth rate can be sustained in 2005 and beyond, and whether it will effectively translate into more balanced and equitable development, remains a key question.

If Latin Americans show few signs of being eager to abandon the market economy, they do appear keen to soften the rougher edges of policies commonly associated with the Washington consensus. The substantial scaling back of an array of government functions in the 1990s is widely viewed as having gone too far, and is therefore in need of redress. Perhaps most alarmingly, the privatizations that took place in a variety of sectors, while not objectionable in principle, were accompanied by high levels of corruption and significant social strains. The protests triggered by the attempted privatization of electrical companies in Arequipa, Peru, in 2002, or the popular mobilizations in Bolivia surrounding the fight for control over water in 1999 and gas in 2003, should be construed as demands for honest government and rightful sharing of wealth. But they do not necessarily reflect a defense of state-owned and operated enterprises.

Prescriptions and Politics

Indeed, the problem is less the prescriptions for liberalizing economies than the fragile governance structures in most of Latin America that have proved ill-equipped to accommodate and sustain such reforms. To succeed, privatization of state enterprises and assets needs to be well managed politically, and in many of the countries where it has occurred, regulatory frameworks and oversight mechanisms were manifestly deficient. Political parties and their leaders have failed to modernize government structures and properly prepare them to handle these important reforms. As Human Rights Watch and other respected groups have regularly reported, adherence to the rule of law sadly remains more the exception than the norm in much of the region.

Despite the prominence of rule of law in political speeches and on policy agendas, corruption is still a profound and vexing problem. Last year public opinion regarding this issue became highly galvanized in two of Latin America's most unlikely countries: Costa Rica and Chile. Both had long enjoyed reputations as having relatively clean governments, exceptions in a region where corruption is rampant. In Costa Rica, two former presidents, Rafael Ángel Calderón and Miguel Ángel Rodríguez, were charged with having engaged in corrupt practices during their administrations. (Rodríguez was forced to resign as secretary general of the Organization of American States just two weeks after assuming the post, causing enormous embarrassment for the organization and the region.) Similar allegations of corruption were also brought against another former Costa Rican president, José María Figueres.

In perhaps the most notorious case, former Chilean President Augusto Pinochet, long accused of having presided over massive human rights violations, was recently found to have accounts holding millions of dollars at Riggs Bank in Washington, DC. The exposed impropriety further disgraced Pinochet, even among his previous supporters, opening the way for judicial prosecution of past crimes. While these cases highlighted public concern about corrupt activities and the ability of the judicial systems to respond, at least in Costa Rica and Chile, they also seriously tarnished the image of both countries.

Although political and public sector institutions in Latin America are generally held in low regard, polls consistently show that most citizens want democracy to work. A majority of respondents in the region recently agreed with the statement: "A democracy is preferable to any other form of government." A major United Nations Development Program report in 2004 revealed that many in the region could well be tempted by a more authoritarian option if it better addressed their economic and social needs. But it is far from clear whether that is the fundamental choice citizens are likely to confront. (For that matter, it is far from clear whether, faced with a similar choice, citizens of advanced Western democracies would express a significantly different opinion.) The critical, often frustrating task is to devise more effective policies to address complex economic and social problems within the democratic framework.

The Southern Cone's Pragmatism

In this regard, the experience of the Southern Cone countries is instructive. Compared with much of Latin America, the political contours of the Southern Cone countries are substantially smoother. This is particularly so in the case of Chile, increasingly in Brazil, and is even evident in Argentina. Although leaders in all three countries have been called leftists, they are pursuing policies that blend a market economy and democratic politics. At the same time they are attempting to give higher priority to the long-pending and formidable social agenda—at least rhetorically and, when possible, through concrete actions. As in the case of Uruguay's Vázquez, their ascension to the presidency can in part be attributed to the electorate's perception in the three countries that social policies would be at the top of these leaders' agendas. In addition, Lula's Workers' Party, like Vázquez's Broad Front, had ample experience at the local level and had demonstrated its capacity for effective governance.

In Latin America generally, Chile is widely regarded as the premiere success story, having forged a broad consensus and fashioned a recipe for democratic stability and relatively broad-based economic growth. Following the end of the Pinochet regime in 1989, Chile has had three successive governments of the Concertación de Partidos por la Democracia, or Coalition of Parties for Democracy, the latest headed by Ricardo Lagos. Under Lagos, the country's first socialist president since Salvador Allende in the early 1970s, Chile's economy has grown admirably and poverty levels have continued to decline. Income inequalities remain a huge problem, although Lagos, building on his Concertación predecessors, has sought to reduce the gap between rich and poor through progressive social policies, particularly education reform.

Sergio Bitar, the education minister in the Lagos administration and the only member of the current cabinet to have also served in the Allende government (he was then minister of energy and mines), perhaps best epitomizes the dramatic evolution of "leftism" in Chile, and in Latin America, over the past three decades. Bitar is directing an ambitious program known as "English Opens Doors" that seeks to make all of Chile's 15 million people fluent in English within a generation. Although the effort has aroused some questions because of its excessive identification with the United States, Bitar has emphasized its democratic character, describing it as "an instrument of equality for all children" in Chile. And as *The New York Times* reported in December 2004, "that argument seems to resonate deeply with working-class families eager to see their children prosper in an increasingly competitive and demanding job market."

Lula's Accommodations

While a comparable program would be politically unpalatable in Brazil, where anti-American sentiment is more pronounced than in Chile, Lula of the Workers' Party has pursued markedly orthodox market-friendly economic policies as well. In 2004, Brazil's economy grew by over 5 percent, and Lula's support correspondingly rose—above 65 percent as of December 2004, according to one poll. Lula's policies have been regarded by some as a betrayal of his professed radical stance, and have created fissures within his own party. But Lula has responded pragmatically to a national and global context that leaves little margin for radical policy experimentation, and has tempered his goals accordingly. Midway through his term, Lula has achieved noteworthy political success, and is in a strong position—provided current trends continue—to win reelection in 2006.

Curiously, supporters of the previous, more centrist government of Fernando Henrique Cardoso have criticized the former metal worker for failing to push Brazil's social agenda sufficiently. Lula's social programs, including health policy and agrarian reform, along with the much touted "zero hunger" initiative, have so far failed to generate much enthusiasm or yield important results. In a region anxious for answers to complex social problems, the timidity and moderation of the greatest hope for "leftist" renewal in Latin America's largest country have broad and significant political implications.

Internationally, the Lula government has also been, to the dismay of some, notably accommodating and pragmatic. Lula has devoted considerable energy to going beyond the Southern Cone trade group known as MERCOSUR and seeking to construct a South American trade bloc—to some degree as a counterpoint to the United States. But this effort has been fraught with difficulties and has gained little traction. The Lula government has, however, successfully built on the efforts of the Cardoso administration and has made important inroads in its campaign to secure a permanent seat on the United Nations Security Council. Perhaps most noteworthy has been the Lula government's fine standing with Wall Street, the IMF, and the rest of the international financial community because of its sound macroeconomic management and performance.

In trade policy, too, Washington and Brasilia have been able to work together constructively. Following the sharp disagreements and tensions—chiefly around the issue of agricultural subsidies in the United States—that accompanied the September 2003 trade talks in Cancún, Mexico, the two governments made headway in narrowing their differences in 2004. At the conclusion of the Doha round of global trade negotiations in Geneva in July 2004, US Trade Representative Robert Zoellick praised Brazil's interest in pursuing common ground with the United States. And at the Asia Pacific Economic Cooperation meeting in Santiago in November 2004, Zoellick appeared more sanguine about the prospects for reenergizing the stalled process for creating a Free Trade Area of the Americas—a shift based in part on having developed a better understanding with the Brazilians.

Recovery in Argentina

In contrast with Lagos or Lula, Argentine President Néstor Kirchner has taken a more critical stand toward the prescriptions advocated by the international financial community. In particular, Kirchner has strongly disagreed with the position taken on his country's substantial foreign debt by the IMF and has refused to be rushed into signing a debt-schedule agreement. So far, Kirchner's gamble seems to be working. Argentina's economy has recovered spectacularly from its meltdown in late 2001 (growth in both 2003 and 2004 was 8 percent), and Kirchner has benefited politically from his defiant, independent posture. His resistance to the IMF's demands has been reinforced by other gestures in protecting human rights and fighting corruption that have similarly yielded political dividends.

Nonetheless, it would be a mistake to overstate Kirchner's deviation from the policies pursued by Lagos and Lula. Despite strong disagreement on debt rescheduling, Kirchner's management of the economy has been, on the whole, fairly orthodox. He has carefully eschewed any public spending that could risk another bout of high inflation. There are budget surpluses at both the central and provincial levels. And private investment in Argentina—by the Chinese and South Koreans, other Latin Americans, and Argentines themselves—is on the rise. Judged by historical standards, and by some of the rhetoric coming from the Kirchner administration, these policies show considerable pragmatism, moderation, and acceptance of the tenets of the market economy. In neighboring Bolivia, unfortunately, the situation is slightly more unsettled.

Bolivia's Turbulent Politics

Few recent elections in Latin America have so eloquently illustrated the breakdown of ossified and discredited political institutions as did Bolivia's municipal elections in October 2004. In that vote, the country's traditional political parties imploded, and new and independent political forces emerged on the scene.

Morales, the indigenous leader who has successfully extended his support beyond his original base of coca growers, gained some ground in the vote (although his party did not win in any of Bolivia's 10 largest cities). More than any other figure, Morales, who just barely lost the presidential election in 2002, symbolizes the aspirations of the country's majority indigenous population, and underscores Bolivia's highly complicated, fluid, and precarious political landscape.

The man now in charge of the executive office, Carlos Mesa, struggles to maintain order and hold the country together until the next elections, which are scheduled for 2006. Mesa, who has no political party base, had been vice president before moving into his current post following the forced resignation of Gonzalo Sánchez de Lozada in October 2003. The mounting social protests and accompanying violence sparked by the proposed export of Bolivian natural gas—compounded by the fact the gas would be routed through Chile, a country that Bolivia has had a sensitive relationship with for more than a century because of the "War of the Pacific" that stripped Bolivia of access to the sea—highlighted the frustration among many poor Bolivians. The protests also reflected these groups' heightened ability to organize on behalf of their interests, and rendered the Sánchez de Lozada government unsustainable.

Although Mesa gained some breathing space with a national referendum on the gas question in July 2004, the respite has proved short-lived. His ambivalence and tendency to postpone key decisions have generated mounting suspicion with radical national groups and foreign investors alike, with both pressing for more favorable, friendly policies.

Underlying Bolivia's agitated politics and uncertain future is the need to find practical ways to balance a more just distribution of resources with a formula for sustained growth. In key respects, Morales, with his emphasis on social justice, comes closest to the classic definition of a leftist. But in such a transformed context, where Morales is seeking to construct a more hospitable institutional order for more equitable economic development, even he resists that label.

Some analysts believe that Bolivia could split into two separate entities: the overwhelmingly poor, indigenous altiplano; and the more modern and industrial lowland region centered in Santa Cruz. These predictions may be overstated, but some change in the prevailing, highly skewed order is inevitable and desirable, given the mostly legitimate demands of a previously excluded majority. Whether the constitutional assembly planned for 2005 will help find the right mix and satisfy key constituencies is unclear.

Venezuela's Dissenting Voice

As Bolivia struggles to find its footing and move forward, Venezuela, after six years under Chávez, has set out on a dramatically different path. Cuba aside, Venezuela is the Latin American country that has most sharply deviated from the regionwide acceptance of the market economy and the principles of liberal democracy. Evidence can be found mainly in Chávez's own rhetoric, with its harsh condemnation of capitalism's ills and free trade and what he calls the "rancid oligarchy" associated with Venezuela's previous civilian, constitutional governments. Chávez has been especially unsparing in his remarks about the nefarious role of US imperialist designs in the world and Washington's presumed determination to impose its own economic and political model on weaker governments and societies. Chávez has also resisted the expanding notion of sovereignty—that setbacks in democratic progress are matters of hemispheric concern—which has gained considerable ground in the region since the end of the cold war.

The Venezuela factor is especially significant regionally. First, the country's social and economic conditions have deteriorated more dramatically than in any other Latin American country over the past two decades. This decline can be attributed to widespread mismanagement and corruption along with excessive reliance on petroleum. As a result, Chávez's charged discourse becomes more compelling, and has wider resonance. Second, with oil prices rising toward $50 per barrel, Chávez has money to spend, and corresponding political muscle, which makes him an important player in hemispheric affairs.

Still, whatever the rhetoric, it is hard to make the case that Chávez is steering a markedly revolutionary or even "leftist" course in the traditional sense of that term. He has welcomed foreign investment in the petroleum sector. Since investors are generally making money, one hears few complaints: provided the oil is flowing, Wall Street is pleased. In this regard, Chávez has been quite shrewd, since he calculates that any political pressure in response to his more authoritarian measures will be tempered by recognition that he is courting foreign investment in a strategically important industry. More radical actions such as land reform have been carried out half-heartedly at best. State-led attempts to instill revolutionary fervor and fashion a "new man" have an anachronistic quality to them, and suggest more posturing and experimentation than a serious effort at sustained, institutional transformation.

It is questionable, moreover, whether Chávez's tightening grip on Venezuelan institutions, and the growing presence and political role of the military, can properly be seen as reflecting a "leftist" orientation. They suggest instead a conscious attempt by the Chávez government to consolidate control and amass power. The president has continued to build on the momentum of a failed April 2002 coup against him (which enabled him to solidify control over the military) and a general strike in early 2003 (which allowed him to further dominate the state petroleum enterprise). In 2004, Chávez emerged stronger than ever after he defeated an August referendum aimed at removing him from office. He has subsequently achieved greater international legitimacy.

With an opposition disoriented and in disarray, Chávez gained further ground in local elections in October 2004, and seems likely to do as well in congressional elections later this year. Also in 2004, Venezuela's Chavista-led legislature passed bills that pack the Supreme Court and authorize the government to determine whether radio and television programs meet standards of "social responsibility." Concerned about the ominous climate in Venezuela, the Inter-American Commission on Human Rights noted that such measures further undermine judicial independence and risk the onset of government censorship of the media. None of this, however, makes Chávez a leftist. (For similar transgressions, Russia's Vladimir Putin is called a rightist.)

The Chávez government's displays of concern for the poor—and occasionally virulent attacks against a popular target like the United States—no doubt resonate among certain sectors throughout the region. Chávez's control of ample resources also makes him highly attractive, and will likely enhance his power and ability to cause mischief in an already unsettled Latin America. But the essential features of the Chávez model, which is likely to continue in force at least until presidential elections in late 2006, hold little appeal for a region searching for viable alternatives and practical solutions to problems.

The Test for Washington

Whatever the actual policy orientation that prevails in Latin America, it is undeniable nevertheless that the leftist banner in recent years has been politically wise and effective. This can be attributed in part to the failure of previous governments, many of which could be regarded as "rightist," and the generalized sense of frustration and disappointment that pervades the region. At the same time, the political rhetoric—much of it with a populist flavor—that has recently been heard in Latin America is inseparable from a growing distrust of, and resistance to, the United States.

Although such a reaction to US power has historically been evident, the region's current resentful mood has been compounded by several factors. One is a sense that the United States has been disengaged from Latin American concerns—even by

historical standards. The gap between the rhetoric coming from Washington and the actual US commitment to the region is striking. So, too, is the gap between the agendas and priorities of the United States and those of Latin America. Indeed, the disconnect has seldom been greater. In this regard, the climate significantly shaped by Washington's preoccupation with the war on terror—and particularly with what is widely regarded as a disastrous military adventure in Iraq—has only aggravated the strain.

Against the backdrop of a region whose politics are especially sensitive to the words and actions that emanate from Washington, it is crucial to have a nuanced appreciation of Latin America's differentiated political landscape. Exaggerating the challenge posed by "leftist" governments would only harm the quality of inter-American relations and prove extremely counterproductive. Washington's excessive concern about Ortega's potential return to power in Nicaragua, for example, suggests a hangover from the cold war mindset.

To its credit, the United States has generally understood and supported the pragmatism displayed by leaders like Lagos and Lula. One of Lagos's chief accomplishments, after all, was the signing of a free trade agreement with the United States in December 2003. Despite differences over Iraq policy and some attendant friction, relations have been excellent between the Bush administration and Chile's socialist president, who presides over the region's most robust economy and most stable democracy. Similarly, Washington has not treated Lula as the threatening leftist some initially feared he would become. There have been differences, some of them rather sharp, over trade and other matters, but in general a sense of mutual accommodation has dominated. One would expect that a similar relationship may greet the new Uruguayan administration led by Vázquez.

Washington's relationship with Chávez's Venezuela has been far more problematic. Indeed, Chávez poses a vexing policy challenge for the United States. As in other situations throughout the world, the dilemma is how to reconcile a pragmatic relationship that takes into account a vital interest—Venezuela provides about 15 percent of US oil imports—with serious concerns about the erosion of democratic practices and safeguards within the country, and with the leader's support (at a minimum, financially) for political forces that oppose US interests. Washington so far has lacked a thoughtful, strategic approach in dealing with the Chávez government. Its overly reactive posture has resulted in major, costly blunders, such as its initial support of the April 2002 coup against Chávez. Washington needs to do a better job of thinking through how to balance conflicting policy goals and of consulting more systematically and at higher levels with other key Latin American governments. Otherwise, it risks repeating mistakes and further fueling anti-American sentiment throughout the region.

The situation presented by Bolivia's fluid and complicated politics is less clear-cut and poses another severe test for Washington. It may be tempting to regard Morales, who has fiercely opposed US drug policy and has been denied a visa as a result, as a threat to democratic stability in the region. But common sense would suggest an effort to engage such figures and understand their objections to a policy that has destroyed the livelihoods of many coca growers and their families. What is striking in the case of Bolivia is not only that Washington's criticism of Morales has boosted him so much politically but also that the Bush administration failed to support a loyal ally like Sánchez de Lozada when he requested additional aid in 2002. If Washington had been more responsive—and less shortsighted—the collapse of his government might have been averted.

Leaving "Left" Behind

Whatever governments are in place in Latin American countries—and whoever is in charge—they must deliver concrete results for broad sectors of the population that have not seen much, if any, improvement in their well-being in recent years. Absent such results, citizens will again become frustrated and will inevitably be drawn to different political banners. (Meanwhile, it is worth noting that none of the five Central American countries could even remotely be considered left.)

There are many obstacles to attaining effective performance. In Latin America, retiring buzzwords such as "left" and focusing instead on practical solutions to difficult problems would be a welcome step forward.

MICHAEL SHIFTER, a *Current History* contributing editor and adjunct professor at Georgetown University, is vice president for policy at the Inter-American Dialogue. **VINAY JAWAHAR** is a program associate at the Inter-American Dialogue.

Latin America's Populist Shift

JUAN FORERO

LIMA, Peru, April 14—The past is always on display at the imposing headquarters of the Popular Action Party. Meeting halls are adorned with black-and-white pictures of party leaders, men whose hold on Congress was once indisputable.

But in a trend mirroring the sagging fortunes of traditional political parties across Latin America, Peruvians elected only four Popular Action candidates to the 120-member Congress this month, and the party's candidate for president finished a distant fifth.

From Venezuela to Argentina, many of the traditional parties that built dynasties through patronage and hard-knuckle politics—but also offered stability, a clear ideology and experienced functionaries ready to govern—are disintegrating. Disillusioned by corruption and a failure to deliver prosperity, voters are increasingly captivated by new, mostly leftist movements promising to redistribute wealth, punishing traditional parties and turning political systems on their heads.

The upheaval has come as Latin Americans have grown frustrated with Washington-backed economic prescriptions like unfettered trade and privatization. The new leaders and movements they bring to power, though, threaten to create a political free-for-all that could weaken already unstable countries.

"There's a crisis in the political system in Latin America that goes hand in hand with the economic crisis," said Iván Hinojosa, a political analyst at Catholic University in Lima. "Some parties recuperate, but many do not, and in their place you have all these new, unpredictable movements."

In Peru, voters in the recent presidential election gave the most votes to Ollanta Humala, whose Nationalist Party was formed just last year. Mr. Humala, 43, said traditional politicians simply had not delivered, leaving voters looking "not just for a new message but a new messenger."

"These people are the same candidates from 20, 30 years ago," he said in an interview, speaking of traditional politicians and their parties. "They are grayer, a little fatter, but they are the same people, and they've destroyed the country."

The change is seen as far south as Argentina, where one of two longtime governing parties, the Radical Civic Union, has been on the margins of power since its leader, Fernando de la Rúa, resigned as president in 2001 as the economy collapsed. As far north as Costa Rica, the Social Christian Unity Party has been left in disarray by corruption scandals that enveloped two of the party's former presidents.

In Venezuela, Democratic Action and Copei, two parties that divided the spoils of an oil-producing economy for 40 years, have been so debilitated by Hugo Chávez's seven-year presidency that they backed out of parliamentary elections in December and lost all representation in the 167-seat National Assembly.

But it is in the five Andean countries where traditional parties have been most buffeted, and where the alternatives have been the most unpredictable.

In Bolivia, the election in December of Evo Morales, an Aymara Indian, as president signaled the obliteration of one traditional party and upheaval for three others that had dominated politics since the country's return to democracy in 1982. Even the once omnipresent National Revolutionary Movement, which led the country's epic 1952 revolution, won just a handful of congressional seats.

Colombia's two traditional parties have been so battered by President Álvaro Uribe's influence that one of them, the Liberals, lost 12 of their 29 Senate seats in elections in March, while the other, the Conservatives, have been co-opted into a coalition of pro-Uribe movements.

Across Latin America, the political tumult has gathered momentum with the introduction of decentralization, which since the 1990's has permitted voters in several countries to choose their own mayors and other local leaders for the first time. Increasingly aggressive and sometimes independent news media have also heaped scorn on old parties, while lending visibility to new movements.

Chris Sabatini, senior director of policy at the Americas Society-Council of the Americas, said the shifting political terrain had given voice to long-ignored regions and made issues like schools, crime and public works crucial in local elections.

"We shouldn't romanticize the old parties," Mr. Sabatini said. "They were not democratic, and they were patronage-driven. They were tied to the economic elite old order, and they were simply not up to the task of adapting."

But the new movements often lack the cohesion and direction of traditional parties and, in many cases, much of an ideology.

Some movements, like Mr. Chávez's Fifth Republic Movement in Venezuela or Mr. Uribe's U Party in Colombia, are beholden to the cult of personality built around their leaders. Many lack capable technocrats that the most successful traditional parties drew on to fill crucial government posts.

Moreover, the new movements sometimes appear and disappear so quickly that voters are never really able to determine what they are offering, aside from nebulous promises of change. In Peru there are now 36 parties, or one for every 450,000 voters, and only six of them are more than a decade old, said Rafael Roncagliolo, who studies political parties for the Lima-based Institute for Democracy and Electoral Assistance.

Even Mr. Humala's movement, which is expected to become the largest bloc in Congress once votes are tabulated from the April 9 election, is such a loose assortment of politicians that desertions are considered inevitable.

"They do not have a doctrine to support a plan of governance," said Gastón Acurio, 75, a former senator and member of Popular Action since 1956, when it was founded. "You don't know what you're going to get with these movements. If there's no ideology, then the politician does what he wants."

Lloyd Axworthy, who led the election observers here for the Organization of American States, said having so many movements could make reform difficult. "You've got to get to a point where you have 3 or 4 parties, not 21," Mr. Axworthy said. "You have to get majorities to pass law."

Nonetheless, the resentment, even fury, at the old-line parties is so great that Latinobarómetro, a Chilean public opinion group that surveys political attitudes across the continent, says political parties ranked last, with only a 19 percent confidence level, among Latin American institutions.

In Peru, the breakdown of the parties began with Alberto K. Fujimori, who won the presidency 16 years ago by railing against the party system and, within two years, dissolved Congress.

After Mr. Fujimori's government collapsed in scandal in 2000, many parties felt that the parties would regain legitimacy. But as regional parties won big victories, some of the traditional parties were left with little representation in rural Peru.

Now, after the April 9 general elections, Peru's political landscape has been further redrawn. The party of President Alejandro Toledo, Peru Possible, once the majority party in Congress, is virtually gone. In its place are Mr. Humala's movement and others like the Alliance for the Future, which is led by Keiko Fujimori, the former strongman's daughter.

Valentín Paniagua, who was Popular Action's candidate for president, said traditional parties had become easy scapegoats for populists looking to score points with voters.

The adjustment is not easy for Popular Action, the party that is famous in Peru for its founder, Fernando Belaúnde Terry, who was twice president and renowned for bringing infrastructure to the countryside. The party's politicians know they have less influence, and they have a harder time raising money to keep the party operating.

"There are leaders who, through their own jealousies and selfishness, did not let in new leaders, and you can see the results in the latest voting," said Yohny Lescano, a Popular Action congressman.

Taking Root: The Practicalities of Latin American Democracies

RUSSELL CRANDALL

These days, news reports from Latin America suggest that citizens throughout the hemisphere are fuming with anti-capitalist and anti-American rage. The recent elections of leftist presidents in Chile, Brazil and Uruguay, as well as the fulminations of Venezuela's Hugo Chávez, are cited as evidence that the region has turned against Washington's "hegemony", including its despised and failed free market policies.

Are these impressions correct? Did the economic and political reforms undertaken during the 1990s impoverish Latin Americans, and is there a rising tide of anti-Americanism that jeopardizes the U.S. relationship with Latin America?

Assessing the Washington Consensus

While the term "Washington Consensus" has been misused and co-opted to the point of meaninglessness, it is important to recall that in its initial incarnation it represented the understanding that newly democratized governments needed to pursue economic reform to secure hard-won freedoms. In Latin America, this meant, in part, the privatization of state-owned enterprises, macroeconomic reform with an eye to controlling inflation, and trade and price liberalization.

We forget that by the end of the 1980s, Latin America was dangerously close to economic implosion from hyperinflation, negative growth, high unemployment and crushing foreign debt payments. In contrast, today's Latin America is much healthier without rampant inflation, uncontrolled fiscal profligacy and the other economic ailments that plagued the region during the "lost decade" of the 1980s.

No one should have expected the Washington Consensus would act as a magic pill that Latin America could swallow to alleviate centuries of economic instability; wrenching poverty and inequality still beset the region. But the frustrating persistence of poverty does not negate the success of these reforms.

Perhaps no country in Latin America is more closely associated with the alleged failures of the Washington Consensus than Bolivia. Indeed, Bolivia has become the poster child for everything wrong with "U.S.-backed" economic reforms. The international press zooms in on colorful anti-globalization protests

and riots, ignoring the fact that before liberalization began Bolivia's average real GDP growth rate was negative. During the height of the reforms, the GDP growth rate was 4 percent, and hyperinflation was eliminated. In the past five years, Bolivia's growth has averaged about 2.5 percent—a growth rate certainly inadequate to meet the country's pressing socio-economic needs but nevertheless a vast improvement. Bolivia's "much improved, much improvement needed" situation echoes the regional reality, too.

Latin America's economic growth has not been nearly adequate to keep up with the region's pressing social agenda. Weak government institutions and weak rule of law hinder sustained economic development. Citizens often have little faith in their elected leaders. As a result, the region is stymied at times by a vicious cycle of voter apathy, poor public institutions, anemic economic activity and continued social unease.

But the most encouraging sign is that Latin Americans seem predisposed to solve social and economic problems via the ballot box. Popular dissatisfaction with the pace or outcome of reforms has not lead to revolutions or coups d'état. Increasingly, democracy has become the only game in town in Latin America. Over the past several years, there have been several instances where threats to democratic rule have been resolved (some more effectively and permanently than others) through constitutional means. Guatemala in 1993, Paraguay in 1997, and, more recently, Bolivia and Ecuador (repeatedly) are but some examples.

One major step toward the maturation of democracy is the electoral success of the democratic Left. In the immediate aftermath of the democratic opening, conservatives won presidential elections in most countries. More recently, leaders such as Argentina's Nestor Kirchner, Uruguay's Tabaré Vásquez, Chile's Ricardo Lagos and Brazil's Luis Inacio Lula da silva (or Lula, as he is known) have come to power, ending the conservative monopoly.

Yet, while these leftist leaders hold unquestionably different ideological perspectives from their more conservative predecessors, their performance in office has usually been far from radical. Many observers expected them to govern in a radical manner, but these left-leaning governments of the region have, even with their social agendas, continued on the general path of economic reform set out during the 1990s. This is the "pothole" theory, whereby utopians or revolutionaries often become more pragmatic when faced with practical governing challenges. It's telling that the current leftist presidents have dyed-in-the-wool, pro-liberalization ministers running their finance ministries. Were Lula to shave his beard, he and his economic policies would be almost indistinguishable from his more neo-liberal predecessor, Fernando Henrique Cardoso.

These new leftist governments recognize that supporters voted for them to lead their governments toward more responsible and humane policies, not down a previously traveled path to the dark past. They understand that, while imperfect, the Washington Consensus path is part of the solution to, not the cause of, Latin America's ills.

In Brazil, Lula does not blindly follow in the footsteps of his predecessor as he navigates the tightrope between his social agenda and the austere financial measures needed for macro-economic stability. His balancing act has no doubt angered former supporters who accuse him of selling out Brazil's poor for the favors of Washington and Wall street. Yet Brazil is currently enjoying a much more sustainable period of economic expansion than experienced under Cardoso, which should allow Lula more flexibility for progress on the social front in the future. While it is unbelievably difficult, Lula's efforts demonstrate that a social agenda and economic reform are not incompatible.

There is a consensus between the Right and the Left about the success of the Chilean model as a fascinating example of a surprisingly stable and lasting combination of economic reform, deepened democracy and gains in the social arena. In the 1970s and 1980s, Augusto Pinochet's military government imposed the liberal economic model that remains the foundation for Chile's current economic stability and dynamism. Yet, since the transition to democracy in the late 1980s, a series of governments have worked to "humanize" Chile's economic model in order to address what is still a glaring deficiency on the social side.

This "social liberalism" has continued under President Lagos, someone who well knows that returning to the quixotic policies of the Marxist former President Salvador Allende is neither practical nor appealing. For Lagos, old-school populism is not a painless way to utopia. Instead, social and institutional gains must be made within the framework of an economy marked by fiscal and monetary stability. Lagos's policies model how liberal economics and an aggressive social agenda can help deepen democracy's roots and give citizens a stake in their society. Chileans now talk with justifiable pride about virtually eliminating severe poverty within the next few decades; given the way that its socio-economic indicators are tracking, the country may be the first in Latin America to be considered a fully developed economy.

The Chávez Factor

Still, there are other developments in the region that are of serious concern. Hugo Chávez's "Bolivarian Revolution" is often cited as the most effective and popular counterweight to a "U.S.-imposed" order in Latin America. Chávez's rhetorical flair and focus on social issues is thus welcomed as a long overdue contrast to the orthodox policies peddled by Washington and its "surrogates" in the international financial community.

Elected in 1998 at a time when the price of oil was barely into double digits, Chávez has subsequently used his swollen oil revenues to support his "revolutionary" political agenda at home and in the region. Similar to its first cousin, "Fidelismo", "Chavismo" represents both rhetorical panache and active policies fashioned as an aggressive alternative to the alleged yankee-imposed neo-liberal model.

In April 2002 the Bush Administration severely damaged its credibility on the democracy question when it failed to immediately condemn the coup attempt against Chávez. Since this time, Washington tried a policy of "watch what he does, not what he says", but this approach has been abandoned over concerns about Chávez's increasing efforts to tighten his grip domestically and promote regional instability.

There is no question that Chávez has tapped into latent public frustration with ineffective and unresponsive governments and chronic unemployment and inequality—mostly inside Venezuela but also regionally. In April a faction of Argentine *piqueteros* (protestors) announced that it was joining as "volunteers of the civil force that in Venezuela is defending the Bolivarian Revolution."

But Chávez's bark is much stronger than his bite in terms of fomenting any sort of viable region-wide Bolivarian movement. Witness the vituperative reaction of many Bolivian citizens in June of this year to his verbal support for groups calling for the removal of their then-President Mesa. Protestors were ultimately able to pressure Mesa to resign, but if anything, some of the more radical elements in Bolivia were weakened by the suspicion that they were doing Chávez's bidding. Many Bolivian citizens are visibly frustrated with their political and economic situation, but few see Hugo Chávez or his revolution as a viable alternative to democracy, however weak or unresponsive democracy may be.

Examining Chávez's rhetoric and actions illustrates why he has garnered so little regional support. His rhetoric on his weekly television show, *Hello, Mr. President*, tends to echo Marxist guerrillas in Colombia and Fidel Castro in Cuba. While Chávez's policies are not identical to those held by Colombian guerrillas or Castro, the ideological cohesion is undeniable. Chávez increasingly governs with the Castro playbook, supporting undemocratic movements throughout the region, while clamping down on civil liberties and promoting a zero-sum populist agenda at home.

Paradoxically, some observers are so eager to embrace the Bolivarian Revolution as the real deal, an authentic and preferable response to what they perceive as savage U.S. imperialism and global capitalism, that they are willing to overlook Chávez's militarization of Venezuela and his attacks on democracy and civil rights. These are the same individuals who were first to condemn abuses in countries such as Pinochet's Chile or Fujimori's Peru. But the fact that Chávez is providing the country's many desperate citizens with more handouts and educational opportunities is not sufficient grounds for ignoring increasingly gross abuses.

Thus arises the question of Chávez's relationship with the democratic Left. Do these leaders share Chávez's revolutionary vision? Will the memory of the 1970s persecution by right-wing military dictatorships lead leftist presidents to oppose instinctively any serious effort by Chávez to promote the Bolivarian agenda at home and abroad?

Behind the scenes in private bilateral and multilateral settings, these governments often profess their profound concern with Chávez's antics and his ability and desire to challenge the democratic consensus. Yet, too often various Latin American governments indulge Chávez rhetorically in a display of "hemispheric solidarity." As has been the case for decades with Castro, there is often a strong temptation to overlook Chávez's alarming actions so that governments can bolster their "independent" or "non-aligned" *bona fides*, even if they totally reject such undemocratic practices in their own countries.

The recent case of the controversy over the election of a new secretary general of the Organization of American states (OAS) draws out this point. In their efforts to secure the election of Chilean José Miguel Insulza, the Chilean government modified its behavior toward Chávez, knowing full well that he supported Insulza's candidacy and would thus use oil largesse with numerous Caribbean countries to secure their votes for him.

What's more, Latin American governments are all too willing to allow Washington to do the heavy lifting on criticizing Chávez, a "good cop, bad cop" position that invariably leaves Washington on the receiving end of Caracas's ire for meddling in Venezuelan affairs.

The good news is that the democratic Left knows that Chávez's regional influence is antithetical to democracy and stable social reform; they are loathe to see him champion himself as leader of the region's poor. Yet, tacit acceptance of Chávez's antics and rhetoric is a weak way out, with unknown and potentially devastating consequences for democracy in the long run.

Washington Ignores Latin America?

It is common to hear that the Bush Administration is ignoring the region; distracted by its military and political efforts in Iraq and Afghanistan and its policies in China, the thinking goes, an apathetic Washington has turned a blind eye to Latin America at the very time when the region is in the throes of instability.

There is no question that many critical global issues take priority over much of the Western hemisphere agenda, but given Washington's historic relationship with its Latin American neighbors, perhaps a little bit of distance between Washington and Latin America is not such a bad thing.

Of course, what is interesting about any sort of interventionist approaches toward Latin America is that they often backfire. Take, for example, Bolivia's 2002 presidential election when the U.S. ambassador publicly commented that the United States would cut assistance if voters elected indigenous candidate Evo Morales. The comments sparked a meteoric rise in Morales's support, vaulting him to within less than two percentage points

of the presidency. Sometimes words and actions can have unintended, deleterious effects, especially given the sensitivity of the region's relationship with the United States. What is needed is a not a non-interventionist policy, but a low-key approach. While Morales now appears poised to win election in December, given the divided vote, his victory would likely not signify majority support from the population.

A number of Latin American governments—especially the leftist ones—are hesitant to be seen as too close to Washington; yet, behind the scenes they are developing increasingly deep and trustful relationships with the United States. The increasingly intimate and direct Lula–Bush dynamic comprises one of the most unexpected and overlooked odd couples in global relations right now. Journalists and other observers love to focus on the more visible rifts in the U.S.–Brazilian relationship, and trade is one area where disagreements abound. But this approach overlooks the frank and constructive ties that continue to grow away from the headlines. Indeed, the bilateral relationship is arguably the strongest in almost fifty years. To take one example, U.S.–Brazilian bilateral cooperation on terrorism and narcotics trafficking is encouraging other nations to become involved in what is undeniably a regional concern.

All of this does not mean, of course, that there are never differences of opinion between Washington and its Latin American counterparts. But even a fair amount of public friction is a sign that relations are increasingly mature and frank, devoid of the paternalism that characterized earlier eras.

Washington can point to Colombia as an example of successful U.S. engagement in the region. Starting under the Clinton Administration in 1999, Washington embarked on an aggressive and costly effort to support Colombia's fragile democracy and eradicate drugs. Known as Plan Colombia, the program first focused on the drug war, but by 2002 the Bush Administration expanded it to help the Colombian government defend its citizens against pernicious narco-insurgencies.

For many, the term "Plan Colombia" quickly became a symbol for U.S. imperialism. Human rights groups and European governments immediately concluded that Plan Colombia would further "militarize" Colombia's domestic conflict. A veritable library of academic work outlined the ills of Plan Colombia, and numerous experts predicted that the United States was blindly heading into another Vietnam.

But once Plan Colombia was being fully implemented in 2002 and 2003, the situation in Colombia improved dramatically. Kidnappings dropped by 60 percent, many key roads are free of insurgent roadblocks and a critical state presence has been established in many parts of the country that until recently were in a state of anarchy or controlled by insurgents. Thousands of judges, prosecutors and criminal investigators are working to bring justice to areas of the country where impunity reigns. Moreover, while controversial in the United States and Europe, U.S. assistance to Colombia is backed by an overwhelming majority of the Colombian people. Plan Colombia did not magically save Colombia, but it did provide vital support to Bogotá at a critical and lonely time in its war against narco-terrorists and drug traffickers.

Despite continued eradication failures, the broader Plan Colombia represents a resounding policy success for Washington, one that has enabled Colombians to gain more control of their country and has set the stage for future success. And all of this has been accomplished without sacrificing adherence to human rights principles, as happened at times during the Cold War. For one, aggressive U.S. engagement with the Colombian military has made it less abusive, not more. Colombia is still an extremely violent place where injustice is common, but prolonged support from Washington has made the situation significantly better. Compared to Colombia's even more precarious situation prior to Plan Colombia, human rights and other peace groups should be relatively encouraged about what has occurred over the past few years.

There are some areas where Washington has made critical errors, however. Perhaps the most glaring mistake has been the application of the American service Members Protection Act (2002), which bans U.S. security assistance and most military cooperation unless a country rejects the International Criminal Court (ICC) or signs a bilateral immunity agreement with the United States. Meant to protect U.S. service personnel from politically motivated prosecution at the ICC, the net result has been that Washington has been cut off from its normal engagement with its Latin American military counterparts.

Training of Latin American officers in U.S. schools has dropped precipitously. What makes this development especially worrisome is that China has moved to fill this void by offering Latin American militaries both training and hardware. And, unlike the United States, China has a "don't ask, don't tell" policy on human rights and civil-military affairs issues.

The Bush Administration's Venezuela and Cuba policies are its most controversial. And there is no question that these policies are far from perfect. In particular, Washington's hesitation in condemning the coup against Chávez severely weakened its credibility on the democracy front. Even more damaging was that the coup episode occurred at a time when Washington was making serious and significant gains on helping push the democracy agenda through hemispheric organizations such as the OAS.

As for Cuba, the Bush Administration's policy is essentially an extension of the same economic embargo and political isolation employed by Washington for the past half century. And there are certainly worse policies than ones intended to expedite the removal of a dictator. Yet the argument is often made that this hard-line policy is ineffective because it provides Castro with a convenient bogeyman with which he can justify his repression. This is likely the case—and the argument that liberalizing our policy toward Cuba might expedite the transition to democracy is a strong one. But, the efficacy of the policies aside, we must not somehow conclude that current Bush policies toward Cuba are particularly radical or represent a departure from previous approaches.

Partnership for Democracy

Alarmist headlines notwithstanding, Latin America is not on the verge of violent, anti-American revolutions nor has the United States abandoned its backyard. To be sure, leftist leaders at times will keep a healthy distance from certain U.S. policies, but we should not interpret that as a wholesale rejection of market-led economic policies, democracy or general interaction with Washington.

For its part, the United States can help Latin America consolidate its democracy and promote socio-economic development by recognizing that we don't have all the solutions nor are we able to determine outcomes in the region—for better or for worse. But the United States must play a significant supporting role as the region continues to consolidate different degrees of democratic and economic practices. Trade, technical assistance and military training are some of the critical areas where Washington should continue to act as a partner. It is in our national interest to see that democracy flourishes in Latin America under both right-wing and left-wing governments. A strong democratic foundation is necessary if equitable and lasting socio-economic development is finally to thrive.

In the long run, the Castro-Chávez "revolution" will fall under the weight of its own ineptitude and anachronistic authoritarianism. But, in a manner not dissimilar to what President Kennedy preached regarding combating communism in the early 1960s, to make this seductive ideology even less appealing in the short run, democratic governments must show that democracy provides its citizens with both material and political benefits. This will not be easy work, but Washington must continue to be a partner in this process.

RUSSELL CRANDALL is a professor at Davidson College. His upcoming book is *Gunboat Democracy? U.S. Interventions in the Dominican Republic, Grenada, and Panama* (2006). In 2004 and 2005, supported by the Council on Foreign Relations, he served as director for the Western hemisphere at the National Security Council. He would like to thank Rebecca Stewart for her assistance with this article.

Democracy's Ten-Year Rut

Latin Americans do not want to go back to dictatorship but they are still unimpressed with their democracies

IF ANYONE ever imagined that building strong democracies in Latin America would be a swift and easy task, this *year*'s Latinobarómetro poll should disabuse them. Economies have been growing strongly across the region and governments are spending more than ever on social programmes, but the poll—taken in 18 countries and published exclusively by *The Economist*—suggests that only about half of Latin Americans are convinced democrats and only one in three is satisfied with the way their democracy works in practice. Those figures have remained almost identical for three years in a row—and are down on those of a decade ago.

This year's poll points to a slightly sunnier mood: political institutions are a little less reviled and presidents are still quite popular even though many are nearing the end of their term. Respondents are slightly more optimistic about their economic prospects, and a bit less hostile towards the United States. They are even starting to warm again to privatisation.

Latinobarómetro, a Chilean organisation, has carried out similar surveys each year since the mid-1990s. So the poll has captured shifts in opinion in the region during a decade that saw initial enthusiasm for democracy and free-market reform tempered by recession (severe in places), and followed by the advent of leftish governments and then a strong economic recovery. Through this switchback, says Marta Lagos, Latinobarómetro's director, what is striking is the underlying stability of opinion.

Support for democracy is lower in a dozen countries today than in 1996. It is worryingly low in Peru, parts of Central America and Paraguay (the only country with a strong authoritarian streak). In Brazil, some of the shine brought by the election of Lula da Silva in 2002 appears to have been removed by a recent corruption scandal involving his party. On the other hand, support for democracy is very high in Venezuela, perhaps because both supporters and opponents of Hugo Chávez, the socialist president, claim it as their banner. It is high, too, in two small countries, Uruguay and Costa Rica, which many political scientists say are the region's only "consolidated" (ie, fully fledged) democracies. It is rising in Chile (which many would say now qualifies for the "consolidated" tag) and in Mexico. But only in Uruguay and Venezuela are a majority of respondents satisfied with the working of democracy.

Nevertheless, the poll suggests a growing resilience in Latin American democracy. Some 62% say that in no circumstances

would they support a military coup (though only 51% in Ecuador, 49% in Peru, and 31% in Paraguay). And 70% agree with the Churchillian notion that whatever its problems, democracy is the least bad system of government.

But much of the machinery of democracy is missing or defective. Only 26% of respondents said that citizens in their country are equal before the law—the same number as in 1998. Only a fifth express much faith in political parties and only a quarter in the Congress and the courts—though in both cases that is a slight improvement on recent years. In some countries, mistrust of political institutions has led citizens to take to the streets—in Bolivia, where protests have toppled two presidents in as many years, 11% of respondents said they had taken part in roadblocks and another 12% said they might do so.

The poll shows that a clear majority believe that a market economy is the only means by which their country can develop. Sentiment towards privatisation is improving—perhaps, Ms Lagos suggests, because more people appreciate the service improvements delivered by privatised utilities now that they have a bit more money with which to meet their bills. Latin Americans continue to see their main problems as being unemployment, crime and poverty. Just 31% (up from 27% last year) think their country is progressing. Only in Chile and Venezuela do a majority see progress. But across the region, expectations are rising: 54% think their children will live better than they do, up by 4% compared with last year.

Almost everywhere, opinions towards the United States are thawing, though they are yet to reach the warmth of the late 1990s. There are two exceptions. One is Venezuela, where Mr Chávez accuses (without proof) the United States of planning to invade his country. The other is Uruguay, where a left-wing government took power this year. The most anti-American country remains Argentina, which has long had difficult relations with the United States (except for an interlude in the 1990s). In many other countries, respondents thought that relations with the United States were becoming closer. That may be because the memory of the Iraqi war, which was very unpopular in Latin America, is fading. Central America, with which the United States this year enacted a free-trade agreement, is the most pro-*Yanqui* part of the region.

The most popular leader among Latin Americans seems to be Brazil's president, Lula da Silva, despite his party's recent woes. However, fewer than 50% of respondents expressed an opinion about Lula. Mr Chávez is more popular than his mentor, Fidel Castro, and his arch-enemy, George Bush. But the appeal of *chavismo* in the region may be more limited than is often claimed. Only in the Dominican Republic, a generally pro-American country, did more than 10% of respondents choose Venezuela as the Latin American country they most trusted; in Bolivia and Ecuador, two countries seen as vulnerable to Venezuelan influence, only 5% and 9% did respectively. And the poll suggests that most Latin Americans place themselves in the political centre.

The poll also indicates that crime remains a big problem in the region. Some 41% of respondents said they knew someone who had been a victim of crime in the past 12 months—up from 33% last year. But 30% think progress is being made in reducing corruption in their country, up from 26% last year. The poll also reveals the steady rise of Protestantism in the world's most Catholic continent. In 1995, 80% of respondents said they were Catholic and only 3% Protestant. This year, those figures were 70% and 15% respectively.

After a decade of polling, two things are clear. Latin Americans will not easily revert to authoritarianism, even in hard times. But on the other hand, building consolidated democracies amid poverty, inequality and a legacy of past undemocratic practices, is a long, slow job.

Falling Off a Cliff

Millions of garment workers worldwide stand to lose their jobs with this year's changes in global textile trade rules.

KEITH YEARMAN AND AMY GLUCKMAN

anuary 1, 2005, was just another New Years' Day for most Americans, but for millions of garment workers in developing countries around the globe, from Lesotho to Bangladesh to Jamaica, the date symbolizes cataclysm. On that day, a 30-year-old international trade arrangement known as the Multifiber Agreement (MFA) was officially ended. Under the MFA's quotas, which guaranteed them a share of the world clothing market, and with the encouragement of international financial institutions, dozens of poor countries had developed apparel industries. Now, stores in Europe and the United States are likely to be deluged with clothing made in China and India, and millions of garment workers elsewhere are likely to be unceremoniously dumped into the ranks of the unemployed. The sweatshop jobs may have paid little, and the apparel industries may have contributed little to nations' genuine economic development. Nonetheless, you can hardly blame Bangladeshi or Salvadoran workers for feeling jerked around by shifts in global trade policy over which they have virtually no say.

Okay, We'll Export Garments

Though most people have probably never heard of the MFA, to see its impact one only has to open the bedroom closet. The MFA imposed a global quota system for textile and apparel production, limiting the output of manufacturing giants such as China while allowing substantial clothing industries to develop in small countries which would not have been able to compete otherwise.

Nearly 50 nations were given market access to the United States and Europe under the MFA. For example, "Cambodia ... this year can export to the U.S. 1,721,232 cotton pillowcases, 72 silk dresses, and 37,896 playsuits—in all, $1.4 billion worth of clothing and textiles," *Business Week* reported in 2003. The agreement was not originally aimed at boosting Third World economies. In the 1960s, the Kennedy administration implemented a quota system to protect domestic cotton producers. This was expanded in the 1974 MFA to include textiles and clothing of all materials (hence a "multifiber" agreement). "The original idea of the quotas was to afford some protection to the declining textile industries of the developed countries. The re-

ality was different. With quotas effectively guaranteeing market access, manufacturing sprang up in such unlikely places as Jamaica and Sri Lanka, which before the quotas had no significant textile industry," notes *Business Week*.

The MFA guaranteed market access for these nations, and the neoliberal policies imposed on them by international institutions such as the IMF helped too. For example, the elimination of agricultural price-stabilization programs and the removal of tariffs and quotas on food imports in many countries over the past 20 years has forced countless farmers off their lands and into the urban economy, where a formal garment factory job, however low-paid and tedious, can look a lot better than eking out a living in the informal sector. Under the structural adjustment programs many nations adopted as a condition of refinancing their foreign loans, governments privatized public-sector enterprises, often resulting in mass layoffs and further softening labor markets.

Large supplies of desperate workers, cheap financing for factory construction (for example, from the U.S. Agency for International Development), and guaranteed market access led many nations to become dependent on their textile exports for jobs and revenues. In 2001 clothing and textiles accounted for nearly 80% of Bangladesh's total exports, up from 39% in 1990. Other countries that have become deeply dependent on clothing exports include Cambodia (72.5%), El Salvador (60.2%), Mauritius (56.6%), the Dominican Republic (50.9%), Sri Lanka (49.8%), and Honduras (41.3%).

Then the Rules Change

Now that they've followed the neoliberal prescription to switch from an economic development model that emphasizes production for domestic markets ("import substitution") to one that focuses on building up export industries like apparel, these countries are about to have the ground ripped out from under them. In the United States, textile and garment manufacturing has continued its long-term decline even under the MFA; it's now small enough to provide little incentive for continued quotas. So the United States has gone along with a decade-long phase-out of the MFA, which had been attacked all along by the business press, by many economists, and by clothing retailers as "nonsense" and a barrier to free trade.

Ironically, in the 1990s smaller nations *sought* removal of the quota system. After all, the MFA's original purpose had been to protect textile manufacturing in the rich countries from growing Third World exports, and many of these countries believed they would gain even more market share once the quotas were dropped. At the time the phase-out plan was signed in 1994, China was not a member of the World Trade Organization or its predecessor, the GATT, and was thus not allotted a quota. But once China joined the WTO in 2001, it stood to dominate the world textile trade. So instead of shifting opportunity in the textile industry from rich nations to poor ones as advertised, the elimination of quotas is likely only to shift production out of lots of developing countries and into just a few: India and particularly China.

It seems implausible that smaller nations would not have realized the threat China posed. Plans for bringing China into the world trading system had been afoot for years. As early as July 1994, for example, German Chancellor Helmut Kohl announced he would give China "full support" in its attempt to join the new WTO. China had already come to dominate production of many manufactured goods. And the country spent the years leading up to the MFA's expiration building textile factories. "Hundreds of new textile mills are now sprouting up in Changzhou and Guangdong provinces, alongside megafactories that will dwarf anything found in Latin America," the *Wall Street Journal* reported in 2004. China also has a massive base of cheap labor to staff these megafactories. China's textile wages are not the lowest in the world, but its relatively low wages, in combination with factors such as a strong infrastructure and the domestic technical expertise the country has built up under its proactive industrial policy, give it an insuperable edge over most other developing countries.

Forecast: Disaster

Quota removal, which smaller nations once welcomed, now poses a grave danger. The predictions for the post-quota world are quite literally of disaster: projections suggest as many as 30 million jobs will be lost worldwide.

The most dire forecasts are for Bangladesh. "At stake are 1.8 [million] jobs in the factories and as many as 15 [million] more in related industries, from button-making to insurance underwriting," notes the Financial Times. Projections are that the country will lose 40% of its total exports and face social upheaval, with a massive number of newly unemployed workers who have no social security, welfare, or unemployment benefits.

The forecast for Mongolia is dim: tens of thousands of jobs are likely to be lost there as a result of the quota expiration. Likewise a number of African and Caribbean countries: "Among the people who will be destroyed by this are the African and Caribbean people who have been building investments based on the special quotas," former U.S. trade negotiator Seth Bodnar told the Miami Herald. Latin America is projected to lose at least half of its 500,000 garment jobs by 2010. And the U.S. colony Saipan, long a major center for textile production, has already seen four plants close in 2005, with nearly 1,600 jobs lost. Saipan's garment sales are projected to drop by 50% in 2005.

There's a technical term for what these nations are facing: falling off a cliff.

Actually, the destruction began even before last January 1, as companies readied for the MFA's termination by shedding hundreds of thousands of jobs around the world. In the months and years prior to the expiration of the quota system, for example, 6,000 Salvadorans and 235,000 Brazilians lost their textile jobs. Sara Lee closed factories in the mainland United States, Puerto Rico, Honduras, and Mexico, and laid off more than 4,000 employees, in what was described in the business press as a quota move.

Chinese-made garments are now flooding markets. To point this out has been derided in the *Wall Street Journal* as "hysteria," but the facts speak for themselves:

- After quotas on baby clothes ended, China's exports to the United States rose 826%. Soft luggage exports rose fivefold. Production of these items in Mexico, Thailand and Indonesia has dropped by half.
- During the first three months of 2005, exports of Chinese-made cotton knit shirts and blouses to the U.S. rose 1,250%. In January 2004 (under quotas), China shipped 941,000 knit shirts to the United States. In January 2005, it shipped 18.2 million.
- During the first three months of 2005, exports of Chinese-made trousers to the United States increased by 1,500% and exports of underwear by 300%.
- From 2001 to 2003, during the partial phaseout of quotas, China's share of the United States sock market jumped from 2% to 40%.

The World Bank estimates that China's share of the global trade in textiles will grow from 17% to around 45% in just a few years. Over the same period, U.S. clothing importers expect they will go from buying goods in about 50 countries down to less than 10.

A Small Backlash

In the United States, 12,000 textile jobs were lost in January 2005 alone, and projections suggest more than 500,000 jobs will disappear over the next few years. A strong backlash from unions, the textile industry, and Congress has forced the Bush administration to take advantage of a clause in the MFA phase-out agreement that allows countries to reimpose some quotas. The curbs are temporary though, lasting for just a few years, and granting China a yearly quota increase of 7.5%. China may challenge the new quotas, but even if they remain, this essentially amounts to a brief stay of execution. Economist Dean Baker of the Center for Economic and Policy Research believes that there is no chance of reviving an MFA-type quota agreement in the long run. Given that, he says, "the best thing that could be argued is that the proponents of getting rid of the MFA should feel an obligation to provide special assistance to the victims of their policy. This could take the form of debt forgiveness, for example, or relaxing the new WTO rules governing intellectual property."

For investors in clothing retailers and manufacturers, the expiration of the MFA means good times ahead. Thirty million textile workers, on the other hand, have just been shoved off the cliff. The institutions that regulate global trade, the powerful nations that dominate them, and the corporations whose interests they promote are committed to reshaping global trade rules along neoliberal lines, even if the changes cause upheaval for tens of millions of workers worldwide. There's nothing inherently wrong with clothes being manufactured in China or India rather than in Mauritius or Bangladesh. But there is something wrong with a global trade regime that pushes millions of poor workers into one sector then, with little ado, kicks them out of it.

KEITH YEARMAN is assistant professor of geography at the College of DuPage. **AMY GLUCKMAN** is a coeditor of *Dollars & Sense*.

From *Dollars & Sense*, September/October 2005, pp. 8-9, 36. Copyright © 2005 by Dollars & Sense. Reprinted by permission.

Conservative Wins in Mexico in Final Tally

JAMES C. MCKINLEY JR. AND GINGER THOMPSON

MEXICO CITY, July 6—After days of uncertainty, election officials declared Thursday that Felipe Calderón, a conservative, had won the race for president by less than 1 percent of the official count. His leftist rival refused to accept the results and vowed to go to court and demand a recount.

As he pulled ahead in a tally overnight that entranced the nation, Mr. Calderón said he would fight to keep his victory, however narrow, over the populist former Mexico City mayor, Andrés Manuel López Obrador. Election officials said Mr. Calderón had won by 243,000 votes out of 41 million cast on Sunday.

By the evening, Mr. Calderón, 43, appeared before supporters at his party headquarters and gave a half-hour victory speech, declaring that the forces of peace had won over those of violence. He reached out to the supporters of the other candidates and urged Mexicans of all political parties to come together, declaring that the voters demanded it.

"I assume as my personal responsibility the hopes of the people who have voted for other candidates," he said.

The official tally opened a new phase in the bruising political battle between the men. Mr. López Obrador's refusal to concede defeat set the stage for a legal challenge that could take weeks to decide who would be the next president.

He called on his supporters to rally in the historic central square of the capital on Saturday in a show of strength that suggested he would use huge street demonstrations to put public pressure on the court to grant his request for a recount.

"We cannot accept these results," Mr. López Obrador, 52, declared. "We are going to ask for clarity. We are going to ask for a vote count, polling place by polling place."

Mr. López Obrador's determination to challenge the results means that a special Federal Electoral Tribunal, set up to handle electoral disputes, will end up deciding whether there will be a recount. Some legal scholars said that while that outcome was unlikely, it was not impossible.

Mr. López Obrador said the election had been riddled with irregularities and the official count could not be trusted. He and the leaders of his Party of the Democratic Revolution complained that, during the official tally on Wednesday and Thursday, local election officials had ignored demands that boxes of ballots be recounted from polling places that they thought had unusual results.

Aides to Mr. López Obrador said he would argue in court that a recount was needed because poll officials had tossed out large number of ballots—904,000—because they could not tell the intention of the voters. These null votes could be enough to change the results of the election, they said.

Mr. López Obrador is also likely to point out that, in the few cases where election officials did recount votes during the official tally, mistakes had been found. Many of those mistakes hurt Mr. López Obrador and benefited Mr. Calderón, they said.

But, announcing the vote, Luis Carlos Ugalde, the chairman of Federal Electoral Institute, maintained that electoral officials had "complied with the law and guaranteed that the votes of Mexicans have been counted with absolute transparency."

Mr. López Obrador's decision to hold a rally on Saturday revived concerns of continued political turbulence. The populist former mayor has a history of using marches to protest what he has considered fraudulent elections that did not go his way. He also used large demonstrations to beat back an attempt to knock him off the ballot with a legal challenge last year.

"Building a democracy has cost a lot in this country, and we are not going to give it up easily," said Federico Arreola, a campaign adviser to Mr. López Obrador. "There is no reason for López Obrador to back out or defend a system that he doesn't belong to."

The Federal Electoral Institute released the final vote count on Thursday. It will submit the count to the electoral tribunal for approval on Sunday, usually a pro forma process. Mr. López Obrador then will have until Monday to present his case for a recount, officials at the electoral institute said.

Mr. Calderón, a technocrat, campaigned on promises to make Mexico more competitive in the global economy, to attract foreign investment and to continue the free trade policies that his opponent blamed for impoverishing many Mexicans.

A native of Morelia, the capital of Michoacán State, Mr. Calderón is the son of one of the founders of the National Action Party, or PAN, the governing party.

He was groomed to be a politician from a young age, earning a law degree and a master's degree in economics in Mexico, before going to Harvard for a master's in public administration. He first ran for office at 26, winning a seat in Mexico City's legislature. Later he won and served two separate terms in Congress, but lost a race for the governorship of his home state in 1995.

In 2000, the PAN's candidate, Vicente Fox, made history by winning the presidency and ending seven decade's of one-party, authoritarian rule. Mr. Calderón rode his coattails.

Mr. Fox first appointed him the director of a Banobras, a national development bank, then made him secretary of energy in 2003. Mr. Fox asked him to step down after Mr. Calderón made known his ambition to be president.

He ran a tough, frequently negative, campaign against Mr. López Obrador, accusing him of being an irresponsible leftist who would bankrupt the country and suggesting he was a dictator in the making, with comparisons to Hugo Chávez of Venezuela.

It worked. Polls showed that Mr. Calderón started the year 10 points behind Mr. López Obrador, came up fast, ended in a dead heat with the former mayor and, according to the official tally, won by a nose.

The election was the most competitive and transparent in Mexico's history, and it polarized the nation, between haves and have-nots.

The confusing results kept the country in suspense, and to some, revived concerns over the soundness of the electoral process from a not-too-distant past when elections were marred by fraud and manipulated by the state.

Some political analysts said that unless there was a full and open recounting of the ballots, Mr. López Obrador's legal challenge could permanently taint the legitimacy of a Calderón government, or lead to unrest.

"The culture of fraud is still so strong that unless there is a recount, it is going to be impossible to generate confidence in the system," said Denise Dresser, a political scientist at the Autonomous Technological Institute of Mexico.

José Antonio Crespo, who sits with Ms. Dresser on a citizen's committee at the Federal Electoral Institute, agreed: "It is the best way to dispel any doubts about whether Felipe won."

That decision will likely fall into the hands of the Electoral Tribunal, a court of seven magistrates who are nominated by the Supreme Court and approved by the Senate for 10-year terms. Created 15 years ago to review complaints about state and federal congressional elections, its powers were expanded in 1996 to cover presidential elections, and its findings are final.

The tribunal's decisions have made sweeping changes on the political landscape. In the last 10 years, the court has annulled gubernatorial elections in the states of Tabasco and Colima, and it has imposed multimillion-dollar fines for illegal campaign financing.

But challenges to presidential elections are unprecedented in Mexico, so this, like many parts of electoral law, will be tested for the first time.

Legal scholars say there is nothing in the election law providing for a recount, but there is nothing prohibiting it either. The tribunal has the power to order any number of ballot boxes opened to make its decision.

Lorenzo Córdova, a legal scholar who specializes in election law at the National Autonomous University of Mexico, said annulling the election would be possible, but improbable, under current law.

A presidential election can be annulled only if the military had intervened or the party in power had exerted influence, he said.

Yet, he said, the tribunal would have to break new ground in deciding on a recount. Whatever the outcome, he said, it would be better than the old system, under which the government declared who had lost and candidates had no legal recourse.

"It is natural that there are complaints in an election as close as this one," he said. "What would be worrisome is if there were not legal mechanisms and all we had were the streets."

Uncovering Mexico's Dirty War

The scholar Sergio Aguayo seeks the truth about his nation's history in government files—and takes his quest for justice to the streets

MARION LLOYD

S ERGIO AGUAYO revels in exploring contradictions. He is a former gang member fighting for human rights. A left-wing academic who writes books with gringos. A scathing critic of Mexican politics who has run for office—twice.

When Mr. Aguayo labels his life as "schizophrenic," he is referring to more than his maneuvers outside the conservative halls of the elite College of Mexico, where he has held the post of research professor in international relations since 1977. He sees his life as divided into two halves by one pivotal event: a contract taken out on his life by a member of a government-backed death squad in 1971, during Mexico's so-called Dirty War of the late 1960s and 1970s.

Mr. Aguayo was a member of *los Vikingos*, a street gang in Guadalajara, a hotbed of political strife in an era when the government killed or "disappeared" hundreds of leftist opponents. Mr. Aguayo's gang, a motley group of disaffected youths and working-class students with leftist sympathies, was locked in a violent political turf war with a gang of pro-government university students. When the Dirty War heated up in the late 1960s, many members of the rival group, the Federation of Students of Guadalajara, were recruited by the Mexican Army to join its death squads. While the squad members' job was to hunt down suspected leftist activists, they often used their power to settle personal scores.

Mr. Aguayo made the mistake of defeating one of the squad's main hit men, Carlos Morales, during a brawl. Soon after, he says, he heard through friends that the hit man wanted him dead. "It was horrible. You find out you're on the death list, and it's your problem. I didn't have any way of defending myself," says Mr. Aguayo, 57, shuddering at the memory even after more than 30 years. (He says it wasn't until 1989, when Mr. Morales, then an accused drug trafficker, was killed, that he could visit his family in Guadalajara without fear.)

Mr. Aguayo fled from his childhood home to Mexico City. The journey changed his life. He won a scholarship to the College of Mexico and later earned a Ph.D. in international relations from the Johns Hopkins University's Paul H. Nitze School of Advanced International Studies, in Washington.

His academic work includes 20 books on Mexican foreign affairs, democracy, and national security, often written in collaboration with scholars in the United States. But his reach extends far beyond academe. Mr. Aguayo has co-founded half a dozen human-rights and civic organizations, and a social-policy think tank. He also writes a weekly syndicated column, and he has made two unsuccessful runs for Congress in Mexico.

His disparate activities have created a 17-page résumé—and a cloud of controversy that has resulted in frequent death threats and police protection. But what unifies Mr. Aguayo's work in academe, activism, and journalism is a single strand: a commitment to advance democracy and human rights in Mexico.

"There is a mutual distrust between activists and academics," says Mr. Aguayo, speaking from personal experience. He belongs to both camps. "The activists distrust the academics, with their lofty ideas, and the academics scorn the activists, who are sometimes very simplistic in their analyses. But they are two different kinds of knowledge that have to be fused to bring about change."

Dirty Research

Mr. Aguayo's commitment to social justice has its roots in his childhood. Abandoned by his father at birth, he watched his mother struggle to make ends meet as a seamstress in the working-class neighborhood of San Andres, on the outskirts of Guadalajara. At 16, Mr. Aguayo quit school and went to work along the border, landing a job in a seedy bar in Tijuana that offered prostitutes to American tourists. He also did a brief stint as an illegal migrant worker in Northern California, where he was caught and jailed for two months before being deported.

The Dirty War period—when Mr. Aguayo found trouble and fled it to start a new life—is a central theme in his academic research. In 1997 he requested permission from several government agencies to review archives related to one of the pivotal events of that era: the October 1968 massacre of student protesters in Tlatelolco Plaza, in downtown Mexico City.

To his surprise, all but the Secretariat of Defense agreed.

"They thought we wouldn't be able to do it because the information was so disorganized," says Angeles Magdaleno, a historian who was the lead research assistant on the project.

Ms. Magdaleno describes her own surprise when an archive employee referred to the volume of papers on the subject as one kilometer of back-to-back documents. Even more daunting, since no scholar had ever been given access to the files, there was no index to the mass of papers, which successive governments had literally dumped into boxes.

While Ms. Magdaleno concentrated on Mexico's mammoth National Archives, Mr. Aguayo shuttled among various archives in Mexico, Europe, Canada, and the United States, including the Lyndon Baines Johnson Library, in Austin, Tex., and the National Security Archive, in Washington. He also interviewed more than 160 people—including former government officials, police and army officers, security agents, diplomats, and student activists—who were witnesses to the events or had access to information.

His book, *1968: The Archives of Violence* (Editorial Grijalbo, Mexico, 1998), was timed to coincide with the 30th anniversary of the massacre. It provided the first documentary proof for what many had long suspected: Gustavo Díaz Ordaz, who was president from 1964 to 1970, and died in 1979, had as president ordered his security forces to fire on some 8,000 mostly unarmed protesters. The book also gave details on the measures taken by the government to erase traces of the massacre— whose victims are estimated at anywhere from several dozen to 300—before the start of the Olympic Games in Mexico City 10 days later. *The Archives of Violence* also dispels myths surrounding the event, including the notion that the students were merely passive victims of the violence. One chapter ("The Two Violences") opens with a description taken from the archives of two city policemen rushed to the hospital after students bathed them in acid.

"The difference between using government archives versus 30-year-old eyewitness accounts and newspaper columns to shape what we know happened under the ruling party, the PRI, is the difference between writing history and writing a fictional story," says Kate Doyle, director of the Mexico Project for the National Security Archive in Washington. "One of the things Sergio did was to prove to other analysts and historians and students that this could be done."

Getting Personal

Two years later Mr. Aguayo delved further into the Dirty War period, becoming the first scholar to gain access to the files of Mexico's now-defunct Federal Security Directorate, an intelligence agency created in 1947. Disbanded in 1985, the directorate remains synonymous with the worst abuses of that authoritarian era.

This search was a deeply personal one for Mr. Aguayo. Among the hundreds of victims of the regime were many of his childhood friends from Guadalajara. He read with indignation the government's conflicting versions of the death of his fellow gang member, Enrique Guillermo Pérez Mora. Pérez Mora, who had joined a leftist guerrilla group, was reportedly killed in a shootout with the police in 1976.

Other disturbing personal surprises awaited Mr. Aguayo in the files. Among a list of civilians acting as secret agents was the professor's father, Jesus Aguayo, a journalist who died when Mr. Aguayo was 9. Mr. Aguayo's first reaction was disbelief. But he later accepted the information as consistent with what he already knew of his father's questionable character. The older man moonlighted smuggling arms from the United States into Mexico, and spirited Mexican migrants in the other direction. (He also physically abused Mr. Aguayo's mother—which later inspired the professor's commitment to women's rights.)

In 2001 Mr. Aguayo published the results of this research as *The Badge: A History of the Intelligence Services in Mexico* (Editorial Grijalbo). The book weaves the tragedy of Mr. Aguayo's childhood neighborhood of San Andres into a scrupulously documented history of state repression, based on the government's own files.

Days after its release, he received a written death threat that he believes was sent by a former member of the security agency.

That the book won Mr. Aguayo some enemies among former officials is not surprising. But he was not prepared for the reaction from his allies on Mexico's political left. In a letter posted on the Internet in 2003, family members of the "disappeared" accused Mr. Aguayo of being a traitor to their cause, partly because he doesn't absolve the guerrillas and student activists of all blame. They also accused him of working on behalf of the CIA, an old allegation stemming from his work monitoring elections. (His organization, Civic Alliance, received money from the National Endowment for Democracy, a group paid for by the U.S. Congress.)

"In Mexico, the best way to discredit someone is to align them with the gringos," says Ms. Magdaleno, Mr. Aguayo's former researcher, who also received death threats for her role in uncovering Dirty War secrets.

Mr. Aguayo was sickened by the charges, which he says are rooted in the myopic vision of many in the Mexican Left, who view any cooperation with the United States as betrayal. "I'm not afraid of relating with people in the United States," he says. "In fact, I think it's necessary to collaborate with the left in the United States, with those who share our values."

He filed a defamation lawsuit this past July against the person responsible for spreading the rumors, Primitivo Rodríguez, a political analyst and former friend. That case is pending.

However, Mr. Aguayo today says he finally understands the reaction from some former guerrillas. "I committed the sin of robbing them of the romanticism of their movement by suggesting that they had also committed excesses," he says, adding, "but there is no comparison between the abuses committed by the Mexican state and the abuses that the guerrillas might have committed."

Politics and Prose

Mr. Aguayo points to another early experience that helped shape his life. In 1969 a fellow gang member handed him a rifle and invited him to join a newly formed urban guerrilla movement against the government. Mr. Aguayo declined.

"I didn't want to take up arms, because I didn't believe it was the solution," he says. "I thought it was suicide."

He says that decision haunted him for years, as dozens of his childhood friends ended up dead or "disappeared."

Today it is hard to imagine Mr. Aguayo ever wielding a gun. His image is too indelibly linked with the peaceful, grass-roots struggle for democratic reforms in Mexico.

"What Sergio has done is to bring the fight for democracy and human rights out of the margins and put it at the center of the national debate, with solid research to back him up," says Marieclaire Acosta, a former Mexican undersecretary of human rights and a longtime activist. "That's no small thing."

She first met Mr. Aguayo in the jungles of southern Chiapas state in the early 1980s, when both were working on behalf of the estimated one million Guatemalan refugees who had fled their country's brutal civil war. Mr. Aguayo "brought to national attention the fact that the Mexican state expelled people who came to the country in search of asylum, and sent them to their deaths," she says.

Mr. Aguayo also played a key role in bringing down the autocratic regime of the Institutional Revolutionary Party, or PRI, which ruled Mexico from 1929 to 2000. In 1994 he led an army of tens of thousands of citizen observers to monitor the first clean presidential elections in Mexican history. The success of that campaign helped pave the way for President Vicente Fox's historic victory in the elections of July 2000, which ousted the PRI.

He also campaigned for the creation of the government transparency that helped make such a victory possible. In 1996, while at the helm of Civic Alliance, he sued the government to make public the president's salary and the far larger discretionary fund authorized to him by the Mexican Congress. (From 1983 to 1997, that fund placed $1.3-billion dollars at the disposal of successive presidents.) He was also an instrumental force behind the country's first freedom-of-information law, approved by the Congress in June 2002. As with most of his causes, Mr. Aguayo made use of his weekly column to shame the government into taking action.

Mr. Aguayo has even tested his own appeal at the ballot box, making two unsuccessful bids for Congress in 2000 and 2003. In the most recent election, the Roman Catholic family man served as the bellwether candidate for the upstart Mexico Possible Party, whose radical platform included proposals to legalize gay marriages and marijuana use. The party won so few votes that it lost its federal registry. But Mr. Aguayo says he gained valuable insights into the sordid world of Mexican politics.

Some of Mr. Aguayo's colleagues at the College of Mexico were unhappy with his runs for public office. They felt it was unbecoming for a scholar of his stature to dirty his hands in politics.

"In an institution like the College of Mexico, there is a way of life that rewards those who devote themselves to conducting archival research and producing books, but not those who get involved in daily politics," says Lorenzo Meyer, a leading historian at the university and a longtime friend of Mr. Aguayo's. Politics, he adds, are "viewed as something negative." He believes that Mr. Aguayo has proved his critics wrong by playing a major role in the campaign for democracy and conducting groundbreaking research into national security and human rights.

Pesos and Problems

Though not in public office yet, Mr. Aguayo helps shape policy through Fundar, the think tank he founded in 1999. The organization monitors government spending in such key areas as women's health and indigenous rights, and also tracks how the government uses the billions of dollars it receives annually from the national oil company, Petroleos Mexicanos.

Fundar's annual budget has mushroomed from $40,000 at its start to $1.2-million this year, thanks largely to the John G. and Catherine T. MacArthur Foundation and the United Nations.

"Part of the tragedy is that Mexico devotes huge sums to protect human rights, but little reaches the people," says Mr. Aguayo during a tour of his center, on a quiet, tree-lined street in the capital. "We're working to change society, so society can start monitoring the government."

Those efforts have not always been well received.

Last year the Morelos Academy of Human Rights, a nongovernmental organization co-founded by Mr. Aguayo in the state of Morelos, requested information about how the state's family-welfare agency was using its substantial budget. The unprecedented petition, invoking the state's newly enacted freedom-of-information law, struck a nerve, since the agency's president, Maica Barbolla de Estrada Cajigal, was the governor's wife. Aides of the governor, Sergio Estrada Cajigal, fought back with a smear campaign against the female researcher in charge, Vera Sisneaga. (Tactics reportedly included creating an Internet porn site that included her name as its main attraction.) Cristina Martin, the president of the human-rights group, says the page was removed after Mr. Aguayo organized a news conference denouncing the dirty tactics.

Such attacks, and the virulent reaction from both sides of the political spectrum to his most recent book, The Badge, have made Mr. Aguayo think hard about how much to risk on behalf of the campaign for democracy. After much agonizing, he decided in August to postpone plans for a current history of the federal intelligence agency under President Fox. His thesis, that the agency remains largely under the political control of the PRI, would have been a political bombshell.

"I decided it wasn't the right moment. It would have been too dangerous," he says, particularly if, as looks increasingly possible, the party regains the presidency in 2006. Instead, he has decided to write a book on what he calls "the sickness of Mexico's democracy," which he hopes to publish before the presidential elections.

But he says he hasn't abandoned the idea of writing a sequel to The Badge.

He adds, as if preparing for the inevitable, "I came out of a tough neighborhood, and I'm not afraid of a good fight."

"There is a mutual distrust between activists and academics."

Grim News in Central America: Wave of Gang Violence Grows

KARI LYDERSEN

M urders involving mutilations and beheadings have become a chillingly common occurrence in El Salvador, Guatemala and Honduras. Governments and the public place much of the blame on gangs.

In October, the head of a young girl was found in a burlap bag in Puerto Cortes, Honduras, along with a note saying the killing was in memory of a Mara 18 gang member killed by police. In Guatemala, five people were beheaded during a recent prison riot, where gang members forced other prisoners to eat the remains. In El Salvador, four women were beheaded earlier in the year.

While gangs have long existed in Central America, the number of members and their levels of brutality have skyrocketed in the past few years. Some media reports put the number of gang members in Guatemala, Honduras and El Salvador at 25,000. The Honduran police place the number at 35,000 in Honduras alone. Nicaragua and Panama are home to large gangs as well.

In addition to known gang violence, more than 700 young women and girls have been found murdered in Guatemala since 2001, many of them ritually mutilated and raped. This number is significantly higher than the epidemic of femicide in Ciudad Juarez, Mexico, where 300 to 400 women have been killed in a decade. While the Mexico murders have received increasing international attention over the years, the situation in Guatemala is mostly ignored. Police and the public blame most of the Guatemala killings on gangs who abduct women on their way to or from work.

Roots of Gang Violence

There are several reasons for the explosion of gang activity and bloodshed. One is the delayed effect of the end of the civil wars in El Salvador, Guatemala and Nicaragua. War in these countries has been over for about a decade or less—El Salvador found tenuous peace in 1992, Guatemala in 1996, and Nicaragua in the late 80s—while the years since have been marred by ongoing violence.

As guerrilla factions and paramilitary groups have slowly disbanded, weapons have flooded the market and become easily available to youth—many still suffering from the emo-

tional and social havoc wreaked by war. Thousands of children saw their families killed or were forced to flee their homelands. Some 2 million Salvadorans became refugees during its 12 years of civil war.

"The social fabric in so many communities was completely destroyed," notes Margaret Swedish, director of the Religious Task Force on Central America and Mexico. "Millions became refugees, there was huge internal displacement, and a lot of people ended up orphans in big cities, lost in the streets."

Central American gang members are identified by the tattoos that blanket their bodies. They are boys as young as 10 who feel hopeless and are looking for a sense of belonging, according to Central American immigrants and advocates. Many of them are forced to join a gang. In Honduras, for example, gang members recently killed the mother and grandmother of a boy who refused.

U.S. immigration policy appears to be another key reason for the increase in Central America's gang violence. The draconian 1996 immigration reform laws known as IIRIRA (the Illegal Immigration Reform and Immigrant Responsibility Act) are just now being broadly implemented. Combined with pressure on immigrants since September 11, the result is more deportations of longtime undocumented or even documented residents. Under IIRIRA, the list of crimes for which legal residents can be deported was expanded to include not only felonies but also various misdemeanors.

Many of the deported immigrants are youth and young adults who grew up in U.S. cities with hugely active gang cultures. "We're seeing the deportation of all these young men whose families fled to the U.S. during the wars or economic crises of the 1980s and 90s," notes Geoff Thale, senior associate at the Washington Office on Latin America. "They grew up in immigrant neighborhoods in L.A. and Chicago, in gangs like *Salvatrucha* and *Diez y Ocho*. These are U.S.-based gangs that are *exported* to Central America, where the men show up culturally disoriented but much more sophisticated in criminal activity."

Latino immigrants in the U.S.—documented or not—often cluster in low-income, crime-ridden neighborhoods. "The families that fled through Mexico to the U.S. ... ended up in very stressful environments in big urban communities," says Swedish. "These kids who grew up very marginalized, living in the streets in the U.S., are now being sent back to countries they barely know. Their families are gone, so the gangs provide them family and protection."

Police and Vigilante Street Justice

Swedish notes that police are so poorly equipped to deal with the gang problem by legal means that many of them end up resorting to barbaric street justice, even executing suspected gang members on sight.

"The police in the region are completely overwhelmed and probably outgunned by the gangs," she says. "Some of the countries have received more criminal aliens than they have people in prison in the country—they can't possibly absorb these people. In countries like Honduras, where most of the people in prison have never even been in front of a judge, that's a big problem."

Youth killings known as "social cleansing" are on the rise in Central America, with gang members and homeless children as the primary targets. Casa Alianza, an advocacy group for street children, has documented that the police carry out at least some of these killings, while vigilantes are also reported to shoot young gang members on sight. In Honduras, the UN concluded that the rate of youth slayings by security agents was among the highest in the world. According to Casa Alianza, more than 2,050 Hondurans aged 23 or younger have been killed in the past five years, one of the highest murder rates for youths in the hemisphere.

During civil wars and dictatorial regimes, the police routinely function as a military arm of the government, freely carrying out intimidation, torture and even extra-judicial executions. Now, according to a recent study of the police departments in El Salvador, Honduras and Guatemala by University of New Mexico professor William Stanley, police corruption and human rights abuses have been significantly reduced. But a side effect of these positive reforms is that the police are far less effective in preventing and punishing crimes like murder, assault, rape and theft. In Guatemala, physical assaults and rapes hit a six-year high in 2001. There were 3,210 reported murders, the highest rate in several years.

Part of the reason for this is that the former police ranks—made up mostly of political partisans with violent histories—were disbanded and replaced by civilians with little training.

"In this context of demilitarization, political opening, and state reform, individual citizens have sometimes faced greater insecurity than during the wars," writes Stanley. "In El Salvador, the annual rate of violent death for civilians in the first few years of peace was higher than it had been during the war."

The increase in crime is likely to keep swinging the criminal justice situations in these countries back toward oppressive policies.

Government Response

The governments of the countries hardest hit by gang violence have responded with anti-gang policies known as Mano Duro (Iron Fist). A terrified public greeted the policies with widespread support, but most experts and legal advocates believe the policies have only exacerbated the situation. In effect, horrific violence has been joined by human rights and civil liberties abuses.

In Honduras, president Ricardo Maduro modeled his zero-tolerance policies after those of former New York City mayor Rudolph Giuliani. Maduro's policies include prison sentences of 3–12 years just for membership in a gang, with members as young as 12 tried as adults. Tattoos or other small pieces of evidence are enough to convict youth of gang membership. El Salvador recently passed a similar law, and Guatemala is in the process of passing one.

Youth are being arrested for activities that may not actually be criminal or gang related, leaving them in overcrowded prisons full of violent offenders. "It's not a constructive approach to solving crime," says Thale. "There's not much evidence in Central America or the U.S. that broadly arresting young men and throwing them in jail does very much to orient them away from crime or drug activity."

"You have to look at the underlying social problems," says Alexy Lanza, a Honduran immigrant and political activist living in Chicago. "The majority of the people involved in gangs live in extreme conditions of poverty. They are people that have been marginalized all their life."

Lanza believes the hard-line approach will fail. "It's never going to end, because the causes that produce this phenomenon will still be there—poverty, oppression. You need to take the problem from the roots. That means providing education, social programs, things that will give people an opportunity to change their lives."

U.S.–based advocates say that while it is clear the Iron Fist *Mano Duro* policies are the wrong approach, there is no easy solution. The roots of the problem lie in the lingering effects of civil wars, along with the devastation created by decades of economic and political exploitation in these countries. The issue of gang violence could be best addressed by improving unfair economic systems and fixing corrupt political systems dominated by foreign governments and a wealthy elite.

"It's going to be a problem until we see the international community and financial institutions putting some priority on dealing with these underlying social and economic factors," says Swedish. "Meanwhile, we've got to change our immigration policies so that we don't keep exporting our criminal problems to other countries."

KARI LYDERSEN is a Chicago-based journalist and regular contributor to AMERICAS.ORG. She writes for *In These Times* magazine, Alternet, the *Washington Post* and various publications. Contact her at karilyde@aol.com.

Touched by Oil and Hope in Belize

SIMON ROMERO

SPANISH LOOKOUT, Belize, Feb. 17—Near this small Mennonite town carved out of the thick jungle, a farmer dug a shallow water well a few years ago and found a viscous black liquid seeping into the water. Given Belize's disappointing record of oil exploration, stretching back to its years under British rule, nearly everyone shrugged at the story except a stubborn Denver geologist.

Now Belize is the newest exporter of oil to the United States, a development that is starting to upend this small country of 280,000 people. A roughneck crew, backed by investors from Ireland and Colorado, struck oil in its first drilling attempt last year.

Their wells, dotting the dairy farms of German-speaking Mennonites who moved here a half-century ago from Canada and Mexico, are producing 2,000 barrels a day of oil similar in quality to the prized low-sulfur crude from the oil fields of West Texas.

"We need some help from fuel prices in this country, but people aren't too happy living near a smelly well," Jake Letkeman, the operator of the small Mennonite-controlled electricity plant here, said. "We're waiting to see how this thing plays out." Much of Belize is on tenterhooks regarding the oil and its ramifications, but the small companies behind the discovery, Belize Natural Energy and CHX Energy of Denver, are reveling in their good fortune. Together with other independent companies that have recently struck oil and natural gas in locations once written off, including Paraguay, Syria and Uganda, these entrepreneurs are proving that wildcatting is alive and well.

As in Belize, the quantities of oil discovered in these places are relatively small, which partly explains why the largest and richest oil companies, Exxon Mobil, Chevron and Royal Dutch Shell, shun such gambles for larger so-called elephant projects with more promising returns.

But with oil fetching more than $60 a barrel on world markets, smaller companies are willing to risk just about everything these days in hopes of finding even tiny oil fields.

[Oil prices rose to $61.46 . . . in reaction to rebel attacks in Nigeria.]

"There were 50 dry wells drilled in Belize over 50 years until we came along," said Susan Morrice, a geologist from Denver. She is the wildcatter behind Belize Natural Energy, a venture she formed with the backing of her husband, the Colorado oil executive Alex Cranberg, and more than 70 small investors from her native Ireland." We simply felt we could not fail in our search for oil in such a promising, if neglected, country."

Ms. Morrice's company has been remarkably swift in turning the discovery into cash. In January, Belize Natural Energy loaded 40,000 barrels onto a barge destined for a refinery in Houston, netting the company about $2 million.

With other wells planned in Spanish Lookout, it soon expects to be producing 5,000 barrels a day, and some geologists say Belize as a whole may one day produce 50,000 barrels a day.

That is a drop in the bucket compared with neighboring Mexico, where daily output is 3.4 million barrels a day. But it is significant for a small country on the margins of the global economy that has long scrounged for enough hard currency to import all its oil.

Belize imports about 5,000 barrels of oil a day, and gasoline costs nearly $5 a gallon. So the crude in Spanish Lookout has allowed this country to dream of energy independence.

Still, Belize, known as British Honduras until it was granted autonomy from Britain in 1981, faces some serious obstacles before it becomes anything resembling the Kuwait of Central America. About the same size as nearby El Salvador, it has only 4 percent of that country's population. It also has no refineries or pipelines and, unlike many developing countries, it has no national oil company or even an oil ministry.

But Belize does have a hidden asset in a civil servant, André Cho, who spends his time in a modest bungalow with linoleum floors and a screen door, in the capital city of Belmopan.

"I've been under a lot of stress lately, man," said Mr. Cho, 29, Belize's inspector of petroleum. The phone in Mr. Cho's office, which holds stacks of dog-eared copies of Oil & Gas Journal and British-era geological maps, has been ringing repeatedly in recent weeks with inquiries about drilling licenses from small American and European oil companies.

"We don't want to repeat the mistakes of other oil countries, like Nigeria," said Mr. Cho, wearing jeans and a gold earring. He said the government had recently approved his request to hire more staff geologists, as well as a former United Nations consultant from India who specializes in organizing the petroleum industries of poor nations.

Despite such moves and the formation in December of a government petroleum advisory board, there is considerable skepticism throughout Belize that the country can develop its oil resources without the corruption and environmental damage that afflict other poor oil-producing countries.

"If oil wealth brings millions, even billions, to Belize, who is to say that the wealth will not vanish just the same?" Amandala, the country's largest-circulation newspaper, said in a recent editorial, citing a string of recent corruption scandals. In one report, government pension funds were said to have been used to pay the foreign obligations of a telecommunications start-up. "Belizeans," the editorial said, "need to keep their eyes on the oil and the money."

Much of the tension around the oil discovery is focused on the 7.5 percent royalty that Belize Natural Energy is required to pay the government, which is much less than in other oil-producing countries. (Royalties to Norway for exploration in the North Sea, for instance, are more than 70 percent.)

Prime Minister Said W. Musa has said the royalty was kept low to provide a strong incentive for companies to explore in a country where oil had never been found before.

Sheila McCaffrey, a director in Belmopan of Belize Natural Energy, said the government would end up collecting overall taxes of about 30 percent on the oil. That includes the royalty and agreements that give the government a minority stake in the company, along with control of 10 percent of production from the oil wells.

The company is also trying to avoid ill will among Belizeans by channeling 1 percent of its revenue to a fund for protecting the country's fragile environment, which is about 40 percent jungle.

In Spanish Lookout, no one is waiting to find ways of profiting from the oil. The 1,400 Mennonites in the town still want a small share of the government's royalties to be transferred to them, but many are already using some of the low-sulfur oil by mixing it directly with diesel fuel in their small electricity plant, tractors and pickup trucks.

George Remple, the owner of Farmer's Choice Gas, said he had a steady stream of customers dropping in to buy the fuel, which he acquired from Belize Natural Energy for $1.60 a gallon and sold to customers for $1.80. "As long as the engine isn't too computerized" he said, "it runs fine."

Oil here is low in impurities, or "sweet" in the parlance of the oil industry, making it relatively easy to process into fuel. So Belize Natural Energy, according to Ms. McCaffrey, plans to import a small plant that would enable it to produce diesel fuel from crude locally, which would alleviate the country's need to import some of its refined fuel.

On the drawing board as well, she said, was a project to use natural gas from the oil wells to fuel electricity plants, which might allow Belize to avoid costly and environmentally controversial hydroelectric dams. Other projects include a pipeline and an export terminal on the coast.

These ambitious plans, though, hinge on a smooth political environment in Belize. The United States is transferring its embassy from hurricane-battered Belize City to Belmopan, the centrally planned capital in the interior, laid out by the British in the 1970's, that resembles a small Brasília. The American embassy complex, under construction, would dwarf the capital's other structures, including federal buildings designed along Mayan temple motifs.

The most acute political risk for Belize's nascent oil industry may be a long-festering territorial dispute with neighboring Guatemala, the most densely populated country in Central America and home to 12 million people. Guatemala waited until 1992 to recognize Belize's independence officially.

Generations of Guatemalans have been taught in school that "Belice es nuestro," or "Belize is ours," a slogan that might acquire new resonance if abundant oil is found in Belize.

Representatives of the two countries agreed this month to begin negotiations to resolve territorial claims, but areas of Belize where oil exploration is taking place or planned remain squarely in land still claimed by Guatemala. Spanish Lookout is just a 20-minute drive from the Guatemalan border, where migrants seeking available land, many of them Maya Indians, have settled.

Irma Uck, a shopkeeper at the border crossing of Benque Viejo del Carmen, and who said her father was Guatemalan, said the oil discovery would add to tension in the area.

"Guatemala has a little oil, but they want more," Ms. Uck, 52, said. "Everyone here has heard that Belize now has oil."

Costa Rica's Elections: Not the Cleanest Game Around

MICHAEL LETTIERI

- Sunday's election will underscore the fact that smug Costa Rica, once called the "Switzerland of Latin America," is now almost indistinguishable from its disreputable Central American neighbors.
- Voters hope to punish those whose venality gave their country a bad name, but the near certain return of former President Oscar Arias hardly achieves that goal.
- Arias' ties to Mexico's telecommunications mogul, Carlos Slim, have disturbing echoes, as several of the country's recent presidents have been linked to bribery scandals involving European cell phone companies.

S tung by a string of political scandals, after revelations that the country's three most recent presidents have been on the take from European cell phone providers, Costa Ricans have reflexively recoiled from politics. Thus when the country selects its next president on February 5, many will be hoping to erase these memories, and voters may resurrect a figure from the country's glory days as "the Switzerland of Latin America." But that epoch is long gone, and the moniker was ill-deserved in the first place, as the smug little Central American nation was always more form than substance. In this sense, the election is a desperate attempt to reclaim past rectitude, as former president Oscar Arias (1986–1990), the country's most prominent statesman, will likely coast to victory after leading the race wire to wire.

But beneath the veneer of *gravitas*, Arias' candidacy floats on troubled waters, and he may fall far short of restoring the country's lost luster. Specifically, Arias' vehemently pro free-trade stance, which has included vocal support for the yet to be ratified CAFTA-DR agreement (Costa Rica is the only signatory which has not done so), raises significant questions. Linked to Arias' passionate support for CAFTA-DR is his involvement in highly controversial proposals to open the nation's telecommunications sector, leading to a new generation of allegations of ties between the candidate and Latin American cell phone mogul Carlos Slim. While the taint has not weakened Arias' chances on Sunday, once in office he could find himself sucked into a messy battle over the management of state enterprises which might threaten his reputation and shatter the country's hopes of a return to idyllic yesteryears.

A Parade of Rogues

The 2006 election campaign has taken place against a backdrop of distrust and skepticism, as Costa Ricans have been unable to staunch the spreading stain of political corruption, which has spread over the country's once vaunted democracy. The scandals began to break in 2004, when three former presidents were linked to bribe and kickback schemes. Rafael Ángel Calderón (1990–1994) was charged with receiving funds as part of his government's administration of a Finnish governmental loan to the Costa Rican Social Security Agency. Calderón's successor, José María Figueres Olsen (1994–1998) was linked to a high-profile scandal involving contracts with the French telecommunications firm Alcatel, and was charged with accepting a $900,000 bribe (Figueres has not returned to Costa Rica since and is currently residing in Switzerland). Near the end of 2004, Miguel Ángel Rodríguez (1998–2002), who followed Figueres in office, was also implicated in an Alcatel bribery case, and furthermore was connected to illicit Taiwanese campaign donations. The fact that current president Abel Pacheco has been similarly embroiled by accusations of malfeasance regarding Alcatel and Taiwan has led many Costa Ricans to fear that their country is now fully in the coils of the region's endemic rot of venality.

The common thread connecting these incidents is the relationship between Costa Rican presidents, foreign investment, and state monopolies—principally the *Instituto Costarricense de Electricidad* (Costa Rican Electric Institute, ICE). The ICE was established in 1949 as the sole provider of electric and telecommunications service in the country, and was responsible for creating an unparalleled national infrastructure. Costa Rica has the best telephone coverage rate for Central America with 95% of the population having access to services, and is second in Latin America only to Chile in terms of internet penetration.

Yet recently the ICE has stumbled in modernization efforts, particularly in the realm of cell phones, as it had to cancel a contract with Ericsson to install 600,000 new GSM lines. A component of the ICE's struggles comes from the fierce international competition for government contracts, which has helped to make the institution, and its governmental administrators, particularly susceptible to bribery. As the presidential campaign draws to a close, the future of the ICE has become the biggest hot-button issue in a largely low-key election, and current runaway poll leader, and likely president, Oscar Arias is far from bleach white on the subject.

A Low Intensity Campaign

Arias' candidacy was facilitated by the Costa Rican Constitutional Court's 2003 annulment of a 1969 law which barred presidential reelection, a controversial decision which allowed the popular former president to stand in the 2006 race as he had been out of office for the requisite period of two terms. Arias has run a successful campaign centered around his own personal standing—his greatest political asset—rather than an issue-oriented platform. He has even been able to roundly reject his opponents' calls for a televised debate, noting that, "It wouldn't interest me even if the Holy Father asked me himself," and seems quite secure, as well as content, with his current lead, which is around 10 points, according to a poll published yesterday by *La Nación* which put him at 42.6%.

The program that Arias has put forward centers around further opening the country to foreign investment, as he sees unrestrained free trade as an unstoppable and positive path forward. This encompasses not just pushing hard for the CAFTA-DR ratification, but also furthering international integration as a means for creating "quality" jobs. Arias also favors trimming the state, ending state monopolies, and allowing competition, while encouraging private investment in those sectors, seeing such liberalization as a way of increasing efficiency.

While there are 13 other presidential candidates besides Arias, the only real challenge has come from Ottón Solís, founder and two-time presidential candidate for the Citizen's Action Party (PAC), which was founded in 2000 as an alternative to the two traditional parties—Arias' National Liberation Party (PLN) and Pacheco's Christian Social Unity Party (PUSC). In the 2002 election Solís was able to parlay his outsider status into a fairly impressive 26% showing, and has managed to somewhat build on that platform, as he is currently polling at 31.5%.

Part of the reason for Solís' relatively weak showing could be that he has not catalyzed the country behind a program that is radically different than Arias'. Solís has not vociferously opposed CAFTA-DR—which Arias ardently supports—instead only favoring its renegotiation, claiming that the existing agreement is one-sided and will harm Costa Rican farmers and industry. But his rejection is far from wholesale, as he still maintains a belief in the benefits of free trade if agreements are balanced, and their premises are tweaked a bit. While this mushy stance might be part of Solís problem, there has not been widespread discontent over the agreement, suggesting that if he had run an aggressive anti-CAFTA campaign, he could still have been trumped by the political veteran.

The fallout from the campaign's lack of zest has added to the already existing national apathy about politics. A July 2005 poll gave President Pacheco a 19% approval rating, and in that survey 57% of respondents evaluated the Legislative Assembly as "useless." This disaffection, compounded by the corruption scandals, has led some to fear for the country's democratic virtue, as the abstention rate could possibly reach as high as 35%. The sad truth is that today, Costa Rica represents more the Golgotha, than the Switzerland, of Latin American politics.

CAFTA as Campaign Issue: Free Trade and Managing the ICE

Despite the CAFTA-DR agreement's highly controversial nature, it has failed to play much of a role in recent Central American elections, as both Honduran candidates backed the accord, and the stances of the two Costa Rican candidates are only slightly differentiated on the matter. Although the electorate may not have seized on CAFTA-DR itself as a wedge issue, in Costa Rica a parallel component of the measure has attracted a surprising amount of attention. During the negotiations, San José held a hard line over telecommunications, and nearly withdrew over pressure to open that sector completely. In the end, it was agreed that the country would open itself to internet competition by 2006, and then open its cell phone market by 2007. Although the stalled ratification process has held up the implementation of these measures—the original January 2006 target date has been revised to a hopeful February or March timeframe—the question of how to manage the ICE, with or without CAFTA-DR, still looms large in Costa Rica.

Most Costa Ricans staunchly oppose an out and out privatization of the ICE, and are split on whether the industry should be opened to competition. Oscar Arias, however, has been among the most vocal proponents of opening the telecommunications sector to private competition, which has raised more than a few eyebrows and rankled some Costa Ricans. Although Arias has avoided the suicidal suggestion of privatization, his plans for the future of the ICE, and the forces behind his ideas, have led to deep suspicions about the ultimate intentions of the once-revered leader.

Going Movil

The controversy, which is beginning to envelop Arias' previously unimpeachable stature, involves the possibility that his interest in opening Costa Rica's cell phone market to private competition does not spring from high-minded economic theorizing, but rather from his personal relationships with Mexico's Carlos Slim and former Spanish Prime Minister Felipe Gonzalez.

Slim, a billionaire, and Latin America's richest man, built much of his fortune upon the voracious expansion of a telecommunications empire throughout the region. After snapping up Mexico's phone service giant Telmex when it was privatized in 1990 under President Carlos Salinas, Mexico's crown prince of corruption, Slim's wealth grew exponentially. Since then, Slim has embarked on a campaign to dominate Latin America's cell phone and internet markets through a subsidiary company known as América Movil. The company, which has moved aggressively throughout Central America and currently operates in Guatemala, Honduras, Nicaragua and El Salvador, has made no attempt to hide its interest in the Costa Rican market, and recently registered its Telcel logo in the country.

Although up to this point, the ICE's constitutional monopoly has kept América Movil out of Costa Rica, Arias, and the possible ratification of the CAFTA-DR agreement, could open the country to the company's advances. Arias has specifically proposed to end the ICE's monopoly, although he denies any privatization plans. In the event this occurs, América Movil would be well positioned to hoist its flag over Costa Rica.

A Team Effort

The commercial machinations of América Movil have coincided with growing suspicions around the ties between Arias, Slim, and Gonzalez. All three are acquaintances, and Slim and Gonzalez are close friends, who have collaborated in the past. This seeming "old boys" network led to serious discomfort among Costa Rican's tiny "good government" elements, when Gonzalez visited San José on January 25, and held a private luncheon engagement with Arias.

Accusations were quick to fly, and the head of a powerful union within the ICE, Ricardo Segura, led the charge. Segura gave voice to the misgivings of many when he labeled Gonzalez as merely Slim's "place holder," and alleged that the Arias reunion was used to discuss plans to allow América Movil's entry into the country. The union leader went on to note that even if the opening did not include outright privatization, it would be tantamount to it, as Slim's commercial steamroller would quickly dominate the country.

Although both Arias and Gonzalez quickly refuted the charges, with Arias quickly denying that the meeting was "to cook up the opening of telecommunications," and commenting that, "Slim is such a close friend that he has never asked any-

thing of me that related to his business interests." Gonzalez too rejected the charges, saying that Arias' status (as he is still a candidate, not the president) by definition impeded the possibility that they would have discussed any sort of business interests.

Yet these watery demurrers have hardly silenced critics, and some may remember that while Arias' presidency preceded the corruption-fraught administrations of Figueres, Calderón and Rodríguez, he has himself not been immune from scandals regarding the telecom sector. During his first presidency, the ICE granted a free radio frequency concession to Millicom (although the value of the concession was estimated at $120 million) to develop a cellular phone network, which at the time the ICE was in no position to finance. At the time a questionable move, the issue eventually led to conflict when, in 1995, the Supreme Court ruled the initial concession to be in violation of the constitution, and forced Millicom to either abandon the market or operate under contract with the ICE.

A Tough Call

When Costa Ricans cast their ballots on Sunday, it appears unlikely that these rumors will prove lethal enough to erode Arias' commanding lead. The country's direction after February 5, however, is murky. Although it now appears as though either CAFTA-DR or Arias himself will ultimately force an opening of the Costa Rican telecommunications market, what remains to be seen is whether América Movil will be able to leverage a personal relationship with the incoming president into propitious enough conditions that would effectively allow it to swallow up the ICE. Any opening will face considerable opposition from the ICE's unions, whose protests have affected policy decisions in the past, and conceivably arouse discontent in the society at large. If it appears that Arias is playing a similar game as his predecessors did, the controversy would represent one more lash mark for a nation that is urgently trying to heal past wounds.

Just Garments

A worker-run factory tries to wring the sweat out of the apparel business.

JAY BLAIR AND DANIEL FIRESIDE

When the workers at a garment-assembly factory (known as a *maquila*) in El Salvador started a union drive, their goal was simply to improve their working conditions and earn a living wage—they never imagined that they would be running the place. But when the owners responded by trying to shutter the factory and move production to another country, the workers had no other choice if they hoped to keep their jobs. Now, as they help write a new chapter in the history of low-wage workers in the global South, they must also deal with the more pressing concern of turning a profit as the global apparel industry undergoes a wrenching transformation.

The remarkable story of the factory that is now aptly named Just Garments began in early 2002. Soon after workers joined the Textile and Industrial Union, known in Spanish as STIT, and asked the managers of the Taiwanese-run Tianan *maquila* to negotiate a contract that would provide higher wages and safer working conditions, the bosses shut the factory doors and put the organizers on an industry-wide blacklist. As has happened after every other successful union drive in Central American *maquilas*, the owners announced plans to move production to another country with a more docile labor force. Led by veteran union leader Gilberto Garcia, the two-dozen strikers knew they were in for a long struggle: striking workers at other factories in El Salvador had been subjected to beatings, arbitrary arrests, and death threats.

But the Salvadoran workers joined with student and labor activists in both the United States and Taiwan, and initiated a consumer campaign against the company's American buyers—big-name retailers like Kohl's, Target, and Gap. In the face of this pressure, Tainan relented, and in November 2002 signed an agreement to reopen the factory under worker control, overseen by a two-member board of directors, one from the company and the other from the union. As part of the deal, Tainan agreed to provide machinery and technical support as well as startup capital. The factory was legally established under the new name "Just Garments" in April 2003.

It turned out that the real battle had only begun. Government officials put up roadblocks at every turn, releasing the machinery and allowing the factory a spot in the export free trade zone only after another pressure campaign. The workers spent the better part of a year fixing up their dilapidated factory and getting ready for business. They survived by doing pick-up work when they could find it, and by getting donations from international supporters.

When Just Garments finally began filling clothing orders in April 2004, it was managed by a two-member board of directors: the union leader Garcia, and a representative from Tianan. "The company put in $160,000 in cash and $240,000 in machinery. This meant that they had a 99% stake in the factory and the workers only 1%," explains Garcia. In the past year the union has increased their stake to 55% thanks to loans and donations from unions in the United States and Canada, as well as cash, machinery, and material from clothing giants Land's End and Gap. But even with this support, Just Garments is still struggling to build up its production capacity so it can handle major orders. "Right now we can only work as subcontractors for other factories," says Garcia. "We have customers asking for huge orders of T-shirts—one rock band wants 70,000!—but we don't have the capital to buy the cloth."

In the apparel business, as in other industries that export products made in poor countries to be consumed in wealthy ones, only a tiny amount of the consumer dollar ends up in the hands of the producers. As Garcia explains it, "The big brands pay about 20 cents to make a T-shirt that they sell for $15 just by putting their label on it and maybe adding a few cents of value. With that 20 cents, the factory pays for electricity, rent, and labor. With these prices the owners are practically forced to exploit their workers if they want to make a profit."

Just Garments' plan for getting out of this trap is to start producing under their own label rather than only working as subcontractors. "We've figured out that if we can develop the means to distribute on a larger scale we could sell a T-shirt for two dollars instead of 20 cents. Of course we'd have to invest about 80 cents of that in material, but with that extra dollar or so we could keep the factory going and pay decent salaries to the workers. We'd also like to start using organic cloth. But the first step is to get a source of financing so that we can buy the materials for the big orders."

Until they are able to make apparel under their own brand, Just Garments is only paying its workers 5% over the minimum wage—not a bad deal, since many employers don't even honor the legal minimum, but well short of the 150% increase that the union considers a living wage. But the change in management has brought other tangible improvements that mark a sharp contrast to standard industry practices. Sick days and legal holidays are honored without question. Social Security payments are paid up. No one is forced to work overtime. All work stations have ergonomic chairs. And new ventilation has been installed to control the airborne fabric dust. "You can't imagine how much dust is generated to make each shirt," says Garcia. "Sadly, few factory owners are willing to spend the money to keep the dust out of the air and the workers' lungs. For us, the safety and health of the workers has been our top priority." But beyond the material benefits, the most important has been "the feeling of mutual respect and cooperation."

A new threat is on the horizon. January 1 of this year saw the end of the Multifiber Agreement, a textile trade arrangement that for decades has allowed many poor countries, including El Salvador, to export a set volume of textiles and apparel. Now many of the major brands are buying from China, where wages are low and the only unions are tightly controlled by the Communist Party. Although the Bush administration sold the Central American Free Trade Agreement (CAFTA) to the region's leaders in part by suggesting that it would help the *maquila* sector, it's far from clear that it will help factory workers.

"CAFTA's worker rights provisions, such as they are, represent a giant step back from worker rights provisions that existed prior to the passage of CAFTA," says Stephen Coats, director of the Chicago-based U.S. Labor in the Americas Project, or US/LEAP. "CAFTA standards are lower (compliance with national law rather than international standards) and the sanctions are weaker (potential fines are paid to the government instead of trade sanctions)."

While Just Garments can't compete with China on wages, Garcia thinks they'll survive by marketing to the growing niche of ethical consumers, and hope that by getting the word out that niche can turn into the mainstream. "Just think of all the T-shirts and sweatshirts that are sold in universities," beams Garcia. "Now imagine if all the uniforms of firefighters, police, hospitals, and city workers had to be sweat-free. We're just scratching the surface. Remember, it took 20 years for the fair trade coffee movement to grow to where it is now. We're just getting started."

Coats agrees. "Just Garments has chosen a future that seeks to sidestep the race to the bottom in the post-MFA world. But its future depends on the development of the sweat-free market." Stay tuned.

From *Dollars and Sense*, September/October 2005, pp. 6-7. Copyright © 2005 by Dollars & Sense. Reprinted by permission.

Honduras' President Softens Stance on Gangs

Amid allegations of police executions, Honduras' new president said he will narrow his focus toward gang leaders and stop harsh treatment of other gang members.

JOE MOZINGO

TEGUCIGALPA, HONDURAS—The country that invented the harsh *Mano Dura* crackdown on notoriously violent street gangs is softening its stance as its new president addresses allegations of police executions and arbitrary arrests of suspected criminals.

Honduras led Central America over the last few years in its tough policies against the gangs, Mara Salvatrucha and Mara 18, born among Central American immigrants in Los Angeles but now spread throughout the region. Anyone with a tattoo risked going to jail, and just associating with a gang was a crime.

But now newly elected President Manuel Zelaya says he wants to narrowly focus the attack on violent gang leaders, arguing that *Mano Dura*—Hard Hand—gave rise to death squads, imprisoned countless innocent youths and caused hysteria while doing little to lower the crime rate.

Zelaya, in an interview with *The Miami Herald*, called *Mano Dura* "a show" launched by his predecessor to generate political support through fear, and to divert attention from what he called the true source of violence—the traffic through Honduras of Colombian cocaine bound for U.S. streets.

"There was a . . . political campaign to blame the crime problem on the youth," said the left-of-center Zelaya, who took office Jan. 27. "It was governing under a specter of fear. If there is fear, the protector can appear."

Oscar Alvarez, the former security minister who oversaw the *Mano Dura* approach under former President Ricardo Maduro, declined to comment for this story. In the past, he has highlighted the brutality of the gangs and downplayed reports of police abuse as isolated incidents by rogue officers.

Homicide Rate

Police estimate there are up to 30,000 gang members in Honduras, a deeply impoverished nation of seven million with one of the highest homicide rates in the Americas.

The *maras* often beheaded or dismembered their victims and left the remains in public for all to see. And in December 2004, they opened fire on a bus near the northern city of San Pedro Sula and killed 28 people.

Maduro's zero tolerance approach was popular, particularly among owners of Honduras' duty-free assembly plants, local business owners and residents of poor neighborhoods where the rival bands often clash.

But Zelaya tapped into an increasing concern over police repression. On Election Day Nov. 27, Zelaya eked out a close victory over his opponent, Porfirio Lobo Sosa of Maduro's National Party, who wanted to continue *Mano Dura* and reinstitute the death penalty.

Zelaya said he will continue to go after gang crime and will form a new military unit to help police patrol violent areas. But he added that he also would consider a truce, easing up on youths who may be inclined to straighten out and providing them with job-training programs.

"I have gotten calls from the bosses from Mara 18 about the possibility of starting a social dialogue so that both sides could receive a pardon," said Guillermo Jiménez, executive director of the government's gang prevention program. "For what gangs have done to society and what society have done to gangs."

Zelaya said he would not offer any type of amnesty, but believes that dialogue alone could help cut down on the violence. The prisons are filled far beyond their official capacities and crime has not diminished.

Global Outcry

Instead, over the last five years, there have been increasing reports by international human rights groups and the media here of police executions of suspected criminals, even street children. Amnesty International reported in 2004 that at least 2,300 "children and youths [had] been murdered or extra-judicially executed in the country" since 1998.

Witness: Cops Killed

The former internal affairs chief of the national police, María Luisa Borjas, told *The Miami Herald* that she had found evidence that business groups were paying police to kill delinquents they thought were hurting business. And she alleged that top levels of the government sanctioned the killings.

"This was state policy," Borjas said. "The previous minister of security was in charge of carrying out a policy of social cleaning." Alvarez, the former security minister, said he would not comment on this allegation either because Maduro administration veterans have agreed not to make public comments in the first 100 days of Zelaya's government.

A 25-year-veteran of the police, Borjas said no fewer than 3,000 youths—many who were not delinquents at all—were killed in the past five years, and that she began investigating the killings in March of 2002.

She said she had a witness who had been a police informant, pointing out alleged gang members. The witness believed he was helping officers detain delinquents, but learned that the people he was identifying were being killed, she added. Their bodies were often found with hands tied behind their backs, and single bullet wounds to the back of their heads.

She said the witness gave secret testimony to prosecutors, judges and the country's human rights commission, but all the officials dismissed his information. "They determined he was mentally incompetent," she said. "But he had dates and all the chronology. He was very logical."

'They Know'

Borjas was suspended after she publicly accused Alvarez, her boss, of covering up extra-judicial killings. The official reason for her suspension: illegally revealing classified information.

Officers from the anti-gang Cobra police unit took the internal affairs files, she said. "They know who all the protected witnesses are," she added.

Amnesty has criticized the police for doing little to investigate such deaths ever since. "Despite the fact the government [has] admitted that police officers have been involved in many of the killings, only two policemen have so far been convicted," it reported in 2004.

Police Denial

The national police director, José Roberto Romero Luna, denies his officers have carried out killings.

Mano Dura, he insisted, dramatically reduced the level of gang-related crimes, particularly the extortion of bus drivers and small businesses. He did not provide statistics reflecting such a trend.

"Now things are much calmer," Romero said. "We stopped finding the dismemberments. We're not finding the heavy weaponry."

Gangs Retreating

Indeed, many Hondurans agree the *maras* have retreated. But leaving a gang is not easy, and many Hondurans don't want them back. Employers sometimes require applicants to remove their shirts and pants to inspect for tattoos.

Churches have been funding tattoo-removal clinics. But in a poor country, most do not have the money to buy modern laser equipment.

In a storefront clinic in Chamelecón, a suburb of San Pedro Sula, José Celaya was recently having his tattoos slowly cauterized by an infrared wand designed to remove hemorrhoids.

He never joined a gang, he claimed, but got tattoos when he lived in Los Angeles, mainly because he thought women would find it cool. Across his back and chest are not traditional gang markings, but Mexico's Virgin of Guadalupe, the face of a lion, a rose inside a heart, his last name.

Now with two children and in desperate need of a job, he watched the nurse turn big swaths of his body into mottled white scars.

"People will see you different without your tattoos," he said. Celaya understands people's fear. For not ratting out a friend, *Maras* once attacked him so savagely with stones that his left eye is white and dead, and a .38 bullet is lodged in his back.

Nurse Gloria María Torres, 46, said the clinic has treated more than 5,000 people over six years—sometimes 80 a day. Still, others are getting new tattoos every day.

"It's like a plague," she said. "Some are taking them off, others are putting them on."

Super-Sizing the Canal

Panama plans to add a third set of locks so waterway can handle much bigger vessels

LUCY CONGER

The plan unveiled this week to expand the Panama Canal to accommodate *super*-size ships would increase the flow of goods to Houston and other ports along the Gulf Coast and East Coast, trade experts say.

Panama's president, Martin Torrijos, introduced the $5.2 billion master plan for a third set of locks. They would be large enough to handle the giant ships increasingly used to move containers from China to the United States.

The plan calls for the third set of locks to begin operating in 2015—the year after the centennial year of the canal, which today operates at near-capacity—with locks large enough to handle "post-Panamax" ships, able to carry more than 9,000 standard-size cargo containers.

"I have no doubt this will make Panama the most important logistics and transshipment hub of the Americas and transform the way goods are moved," the canal's chief executive, Alberto Aleman Zubieta, said this week during a conference call.

And it's seen as good news for the Port of Houston.

"A new canal with new dimensions will absolutely put Houston in a position to better compete with East Coast ports" such as Savannah, Ga., Charleston, S.C., and New York, said Tom Kornegay, executive director of the Port of Houston Authority.

Reaching that goal will require meeting a series of challenges.

The spending will have to be authorized by a public referendum. At the moment, polls suggest there's strong support, but its critics say the project is too big a financial risk for this small country.

Influential foes say building a megaport to ship containers across the country for reloading on vessels on the eastern coast would cost far less and serve the same market as a set of locks that would be about 180 feet wide, more than half again as big as the current ones.

A Lot to Fret Over

As with the plans for any huge project, there's the danger that the demand projections will not pan out, or the planners have underestimated the cost or time needed to build it.

The project's cost is huge when compared with the small country's economy.

Maritime professionals expressed confidence in the professionalism of the canal staff. But finding skilled labor in Panama is a problem, and the government has begun to address the issue by creating a job-training program to prepare 7,000 Panamanians for the construction work.

Keeping costs in line is another concern.

If the lock project performs like other recent transportation projects and the price tag is "neither more nor less accurate than cost estimates for other large construction projects, then we may predict the risk of cost overrun will be 80 to 90 percent and an expected cost overrun of 30 to 40 percent in constant prices," said Brent Flyvbjerg, professor of planning and a specialist in construction costs at Aalborg University in Denmark.

Higher Tolls

To pay for the improvements, the canal authority has predicted that tolls will double over the next 20 years. Shipping experts say the money saved on a direct water route would more than justify the higher fees.

For the giant ships, the alternatives for getting cargo from Asia to the eastern United States are moving it by ship to the West Coast and then by rail across the U.S., or heading east through the Suez Canal.

"Once the Panama Canal is able to handle post-Panamax vessels, my opinion is shipping lines will see this as the uncorking of the bottleneck" and will choose that route, said Robert West, managing director of global trade and transportation at Global Insight, a Boston-based forecasting firm. "There is going to be enough cargo for everyone."

Global Insight estimates the worldwide container trade is growing 8.2 percent a year.

West Coast port managers agree.

Don Snyder, director of trade and maritime services for the Port of Long Beach, said he is sure that all Gulf Coast and East Coast ports would see higher volumes of inbound trade from the canal expansion project.

Houston shippers will have an opportunity to learn the details firsthand in May when Alemán Zubieta visits the city to explain the plan.

"We'll read through it, develop questions, and when he comes to talk about it, we'll have a good discussion," Kornegay said.

Indications of Support

Among Panamanians, support appears strong. In a survey released this week, 70 percent of those asked favored the project, up from 56 percent in a survey earlier in April.

There is opposition. Critics question the wisdom of this small country taking on the cost of the project with a price tag equal to a good percentage of Panama's GDP, which stood at $13.7 billion in 2004, according to the World Bank.

"It's a high-risk investment because no one can guarantee infrastructure projects nor the flows of transits," said Fernando Manfredo, a leading opponent and the first Panamanian administrator of the canal.

Former President Jorge Illueca and Manfredo are part of a group proposing an alternative route for containers: a major port at the Pacific entrance to the canal, where containers from ships too big for the canal would be moved across the isthmus on rail cars or smaller boats.

They also argue that the funds would be better used on better schools, health care, credit for small businesses and other services in this country where 40 percent of the population lives in poverty.

"The argument of alternative use of canal resources is very, very strong," said Guillermo Chapman, a former finance minister and president of Indesa, an economic consulting firm in Panama City.

Paying for It All

The canal authority plans to spend roughly $200 million per year from its own funds on the construction project, which will be largely funded by borrowing. During this period, Alemán Zubieta predicted, the canal will continue to provide the federal government more than $500 million annually.

Environmentalists also will track the project closely, because a fragile rain forest rich in biodiversity flanks the Panama Canal and its waterway of lakes. The project design includes water-saving basins parallel to the locks that allow reuse of 60 percent of the water used in the locks to raise and lower ships.

While tolls will rise sharply, shipping experts say the savings should justify this cost.

"The economies of scale for larger ships are such that the average toll can be spread out," Peter Drakos, president of the Connecticut Maritime Association, the world's biggest international shipping trade group.

Maritime industry traders expressed optimism about the project's feasibility.

Asked whether the project can be built successfully, Roberto Boyd, the largest shipping agent in Panama, said, "I have no doubts. This canal was built 90 years ago, and the technology is pretty much the same—water flowing by gravity into locks—so they're not sending a man to the moon."

No Left Turn

ÁLVARO VARGAS LLOSA

Washington

IN 1781, an Aymara Indian, Tupac Katari, led an uprising against Spanish rule in Bolivia and lay siege to La Paz. He was captured and killed by having his limbs tied to four horses that pulled in opposite directions. Before dying, he prophesied, "I will come back as millions." To judge by the overwhelming victory of Evo Morales, an Aymara, in Bolivia's elections on Dec. 18, he kept his promise.

Mr. Morales's election has been interpreted as confirmation that South America is moving left. Mr. Morales does not hide his admiration for Fidel Castro and Hugo Chávez, and his proposals include the nationalization of the oil industry, the redistribution of some privately owned estates and the decriminalization of coca plantations in the Chapare region. He opposes the Free Trade Area of the Americas and blasts "neoliberalism."

It would be a mistake, however, to think that Mr. Morales will become another Hugo Chávez even if that is his wish. The new Bolivian president will not have the resources that Venezuela commands and his popular base is shakier. Moreover, Brazil has an important presence in Bolivia and will be in a position to exercise a moderating influence.

Unlike Venezuela, where skyrocketing oil prices brought Mr. Chávez a windfall that allowed him to build a strong social network based on patronage, Bolivia has little revenue. The only reason its fiscal account is not showing a $1 billion deficit is foreign aid, mainly from the United States. Because Mr. Morales's followers toppled the two previous presidents and forced the authorities to impose heavy royalties on multinational companies exploiting natural gas, foreign investment has dried up: only $84 million worth of investment came into the country this year.

And the possibility of suddenly turning Bolivia's natural gas reserves (potentially a whopping 52 trillion cubic feet) into an exporting bonanza has been precluded by the cancellation of a project that sought to export natural gas to Mexico and California through Chilean ports. (Bolivia and Chile have been at odds since the late 19th century, when Bolivia lost its access to the sea to Chile in the War of the Pacific.)

Bolivia's indigenous population, which wants results quickly, may also hold Mr. Morales in check. His party, Movement Toward Socialism, is a loose amalgam of competing social groups. If Mr. Morales tries to concentrate power, he will need a sturdy, permanent base of support that is by no means guaranteed. Furthermore, the residents of many provinces, especially in the east, are agitating for local autonomy and have warned that they will resist attempts to centralize even more power in La Paz.

Bolivia has had left-wing governments before that were toppled by the same people who made them possible. President Carlos Mesa, who replaced Gonzalo Sánchez de Lozada in 2003 after violent demonstrations, had the support of the population when he reneged on natural gas contracts with foreign investors and led a virulent campaign against Chile. Yet the masses still turned against him, forcing his resignation in June.

Finally, Brazil's pragmatic president, Luiz Inácio Lula da Silva, could also constrain Mr. Morales's ambitions. Brazil is now effectively Bolivia's only foreign investor, and its role is likely to grow even more crucial, because Mr. Morales promises to nationalize the subsoil and keep the high royalties on oil and natural gas exploitation that have kept out investors from other countries. Bolivia therefore will need Petrobras, the Brazilian energy giant, to expand its investments. Mr. da Silva has not been able to rein in Mr. Chávez, but he will have leverage over the more vulnerable Mr. Morales.

Of course, whether Mr. Morales will draw closer to Mr. Chávez will in part depend on American policy toward Bolivia. And that, in turn, will depend on whether Mr. Morales decriminalizes coca growing. If he does so, the United States should not overreact, because nothing much will change. Even with the restrictions that are in place now, there are already as many plantations in Chapare as the demand for coca—and Bolivia's capacity to make cocaine from it—warrant. In any case, cocaine production and distribution will still be banned in Bolivia, Mr. Morales says. If Washington were to respond to coca decriminalization by hindering Bolivia's exports of clothing and jewelry to the United States, tens of thousands of families in El Alto, one of Mr. Morales's indigenous power bases, would lose their source of income, and anti-American sentiment would pull Mr. Morales leftward.

Thomas Shannon, assistant secretary of state for Western Hemisphere affairs, recently told me that the United States aims to eliminate its remaining protectionist measures (which hamper some South American economies by restricting United States imports of their goods). Few Latin Americans have heard about this endeavor. If the goal is to promote development and foster good relations across the hemisphere, eliminating protectionist policies will be far more effective than making coca plantations the paramount issue in Bolivia–United States relations. Fractious politics and ethnic tensions already make for a delicate situation in the Andes. Let's not make it worse.

ÁLVARO VARGAS LLOSA, the director of the Center on Global Prosperity at the Independent Institute, is the author of "Liberty for Latin America."

Lula's Leap

The Economist *talks to Brazil's president*

THE press says he's shed 14 kilos (30lb). His aides confirm more than ten. But there is no doubt about the improvement in the political fitness of Brazil's president, Luiz Inácio Lula da Silva. Last year, Brazil's worst scandal in a dozen years nearly finished him. The polls now predict his victory over likely rivals in next October's presidential elections. Lula does not admit to being a candidate: he may wait until June to declare himself, while his main rivals must leave their current jobs by next month. Yet his frenetic trips around the country inaugurating crowd-pleasing public works make his intentions plain.

Why is he now likely to win? Speaking to *The Economist* in a rare interview, Lula cited over and over what he regards as his twin triumphs: economic stability plus social progress. "How many countries have achieved what we have: fiscal responsibility and a strong social policy at the same time?" he asks. "Never in the economic history of Brazil have we had the solid fundamentals we have now." Brazil is ready for "a leap in quality", he says.

Such a leap is what Brazil—a country with a population (186m) equal to that of the whole of the rest of South America and a land area bigger than all 25 EU countries combined—has been waiting for since the early 1970s, when it was one of the world's fastest growing economies. Then its economy stumbled into debt and inflation, while other emerging economies like China and India began to take off, generating more global buzz. In his interview at the presidential ranch, Granja do Torto, Lula defended a slow and steady approach to growth and promised further reform in a possible second term. "The future", he says, "will be built on strong investment in education and training, with tax relief to encourage new investment, notably in science and technology." Since becoming president in January 2003, he has achieved much of what he set out to do, but has not yet cleared all obstacles to Brazil's great leap forward.

Popular, but No Populist

Solid fundamentals are not what the world expected from Lula. His pre-presidential career consisted mainly of leading a trade union that defied Brazil's military dictators, and a political movement, the Workers' Party (PT), that denounced the "neoliberal" policies of the dictators' democratically elected successors. The victory of a worker born dirt-poor in Brazil's poverty-stricken north-east was celebrated as a victory for poor people everywhere. Yet Lula did not turn out to be a populist like Venezuela's Hugo Chávez. Instead of spending recklessly, reigniting inflation and perhaps defaulting on debt as Argentina has done, Lula clamped down on inflation and saved extra money to pay the debt. "I will not throw away the opportunity the people gave me," he says.

Lula sees himself as a negotiator, not an ideologue. He has befriended both Mr Chávez and the Venezuelan leader's American antagonist, George Bush. On a state visit to Britain next week, he will try to prod the Doha round of global trade negotiations into life.

For a leader adept at reconciling opposites, Lula has proved a surprisingly polarising figure. Disappointed with his orthodox economics, the left wing of the PT has harried the government with "friendly fire", deterring Lula from reforming as boldly as he might have done. Yet, for his foes, Lula remains the party's creature. He allowed the PT to replace experts from the government bureaucracy with loyalists and to abort programmes that had proved their worth. Then came the *mensalão*, revelations that the PT had been funnelling money illegally to both its own congressmen and those from allied parties. Millions had voted for the party because it proclaimed itself above the grubby norm of Brazilian politics. That image is now in tatters. Lula is popular among the poor, say the polls, but has lost ground among Brazilians from the middle class up.

That the mass of Brazilians seems prepared to overlook these misdeeds suggests that Lula got two big things right: the economy and poverty alleviation. Comparing Brazil's vital indicators when Lula took over with the same ones now "is like looking at two different economies", says Vinod Thomas, former head of the World Bank in Brazil. In the autumn of 2002, Brazil's currency, the *real*, plunged, largely because the markets feared Lula's arrival. Inflation, already in double digits, threatened to spike higher and the yield on Brazil's dollar bonds was 25 percentage points above that of American Treasuries. The new government swerved away from disaster. The finance minister, Antonio Palocci, raised the target for the public sector's primary surplus (before interest payments) by half a percentage point to 4.25% of GDP, persuading the markets that Lula could be trusted to pay Brazil's public debt. The central bank steadied the *real* and raised interest rates to choke inflation.

An economy that swooned every time confidence in emerging markets wobbled now looks steadier. Spurred by a devaluation in 1999 and buoyant demand for commodities, exports have boomed, turning a current-account deficit into surplus. Mr Palocci has used the inflow of dollars to pay off foreign creditors, including the IMF. Soon, Brazil will no longer have to worry about a falling *real* driving up its debt burden. The risk premium has fallen to a record low of two percentage points.

Much of the grumbling is about the price Brazil has paid for stability. Under Lula, economic growth has averaged just 2.6% a year, barely better than the dismal average of the last 15 years. There are at least three culprits. At around 11%, Brazilian real interest rates are among the highest in the world. Government grabs an estimated 38% of GDP in the form of taxes and contributions, well above the tax take of most other Latin American economies. Even with all that revenue, central government investment has shrunk to a derisory 0.5% of GDP.

Barely a day has passed since Lula came to office without shrill denunciations of the central bank, often from his own vice-president, José Alencar. Tight monetary policy has stifled investment and pushed the *real* to levels that threaten exports and scare local producers. But Lula insists that "you can't make the central bank the villain", not least because the government sets the inflation target. The government is doing its part, for example by reducing import tariffs "on products that we know are increasing in price more than they should", such as steel, he says.

Steady as She Goes

Turning to Brazil's crushing tax burden, Lula points out that the government has not raised a single tax rate yet. Revenue is up because profits are higher and tax collection is better. As this improves, "we'll be able to reduce the tax burden by cutting rates and expanding the base of contributors". For Lula, sure growth is worth more than fast growth. "I don't want to grow 10% or 15% a year. I want a lasting cycle of growth averaging 4% or 5%." There will be "no magic in the economy", he says. This year growth should be around 3.5%.

But stability has its own subtle magic. It protects the value of salaries and encourages business to plan long term. "The capital market is now an option" for financing infrastructure, says Paulo Godoy, president of the ABDIB, a group representing infrastructure firms. Despite high interest rates, consumer credit surged after the government let banks lend to consumers against their paycheques. This contributed to what will no doubt be the PT's favourite campaign statistic: 3.5m jobs created in the formal sector between 2003 and 2005.

This points to a second achievement: a reduction in poverty and inequality—the blight that Lula was elected to combat. A poverty index tracked by the Fundação Getulio Vargas (FGV), a business school, fell from 27.3% of the population in 2003 to 25.1% in 2004. Strong economic growth in 2004 helped. More important, says Marcelo Neri of FGV, was a sharp drop in inequality, which is "now at its lowest level in the past 30 years, and still falling."

The reasons for this are complicated and only partly down to Lula. His predecessor, Fernando Henrique Cardoso, universalised primary education, which accounts for much of the reduction in inequality. He also tweaked Brazil's job-killing labour law, encouraging formal employment. Declining informality and inequality are "new elements on the Brazilian scene which analysts don't fully understand," says Mr Neri.

After a stumble, Lula has helped. Upon taking office, he unveiled an anti-poverty programme called *Fome Zero* (zero hunger), which was clearly unworkable. Lula retreated, replacing it with *Bolsa Família* (family fund). This consolidated five pre-Lula programmes that transferred cash to poor families, raised the benefit and expanded the number of beneficiaries so far to 8.7m families, roughly a fifth of Brazil's population. This makes it "the most important income transfer programme in the world", says Lula. In the poor north-east, with the largest concentration of beneficiaries, the programme can mean the difference between hunger and sufficiency and sustain small-town economies.

Bolsa Família draws sneers, too, notably that it provides subsistence, but no exit from poverty. Lula retorts that the conditions attached to the transfer—beneficiaries must keep their children in school and vaccinate their babies—make it more than a handout. "It's an emergency programme," he says. "My dream is that one day we won't need *Bolsa Família* any more because it will have generated employment and aided income distribution."

More lasting is Lula's other gift to the poor, a real 25% rise in the official minimum wage, which also affects publicly financed pensions. Lula claims this is necessary to ensure "that the poorest part of the population has the right to eat". But it does so inefficiently, with a bias toward the elderly. Just 3% of poor families include a pensioner, while 85% have children.

This points to the Lula government's blind spot. The rise in the minimum wage is symptomatic of an overall increase in government spending, one of the main reasons debt, taxes and interest rates are so high. Non-financial spending by the federal government rose from 17.7% of GDP in 2002 to an estimated 18.8% last year, says Raul Velloso, a budget expert. That is part of a deeper failure: to come to grips with a state that is overgrown but is neither efficient nor fair. That omission may well be one of the roots of the *mensalão*, which has blotted the second half of Lula's mandate. Reinventing the state is no simple task, but it is probably the most urgent one facing the winner of October's elections.

Mr Palocci recently proposed a "social accord" to reduce spending and improve its quality. Although he did not spell it out, this would probably involve capping spending as a proportion of GDP, breaking the link between the minimum wage and pensions, and reforming the pension system, Brazil's version of welfare for the rich. Lula's chief of staff, Dilma Rousseff, scorned one version of this idea as "rudimentary", a hint of the resistance it will face from within the government.

Lula says that Mr Palocci and Ms Rousseff differ only over timing. "In an election year it's hard to achieve a social accord," but "in a quieter period everyone will agree that we need a commitment not to spend more money than we can." Lula says that he started the job by reforming civil-service pensions (taxing them, for example) and that a campaign to strike fraudsters from the benefit rolls is paying off. But he may not swallow Mr Palocci's ideas whole. Delinking the minimum wage from pensions, for example, "is easy to say and very difficult to do". As for raising the retirement age, "as longevity increases, the pension system will have to adapt".

The *mensalão* revealed defects of a different sort. It remains a sea of supposition dotted with islands of fact. What is known is that the PT channelled millions of *reais* to friendly congressmen, mainly through an intermediary who doubled as a campaign consultant. Off-the-books campaign financing is illegal, but common. Still unproved are more sensational claims that congressmen accepted the *mensalão* (monthly stipend) in exchange for backing the government and that the money came from state enterprises or their pension funds. A report by a congressional committee later this month may back these claims. Fact and suspicion forced a purge of the PT's top officers along with the resignation and subsequent expulsion from Congress of Lula's chief aide, José Dirceu.

Lula blames two groups of people: those who perpetrated a "massacre" of the PT with unfounded accusations, and a few bad apples in the PT itself. "You can't judge a party because a half-dozen people made mistakes." Yet he admits that the massacre was "justifiable". The PT "will have a lot to explain to society", he says, avoiding explanation himself.

The *mensalão* crystallised a belief that the PT's historic rise to power was a setback for Brazil's institutional development. Its rise seemed to confuse party with government, injected ideology where expertise was needed and pushed government into areas where it had no business. Lula says encouraging things about withdrawing the state from the economy and professionalising the civil service, but has not done much of either. More disappointingly, "Brazil has done less than expected on education and health," says Mr Thomas. Lula has tended the orchard but planted no new trees, critics say.

There are examples enough to justify these criticisms, from the needless scrapping of the *provão*, an exam used to evaluate universities, to a hare-brained proposal to install government-appointed auditors in independent regulatory agencies. But this demands qualifications. One is that the Lula government sometimes learns from its mistakes. It spent years tinkering with a concession law, during which time no new federal roads were handed over to private management. But under the new law, disputes will be submitted to arbitration, which investors like. The orchard analogy misses some trees. A bankruptcy law, for example, has lowered leasing costs for airlines. A judicial reform should speed cases through the notoriously slow courts.

What other trees might Lula plant? The next president should disentangle state sales taxes, restructure trade unions and "update" labour law to make it "less burdensome for an employer to hire a worker", Lula says. Political reform would discourage future scandals. If "you create a public fund for elections, prohibit private money and you have better control by the electoral authority, you can reduce the errors that a political party can commit." Could it be Lula's destiny to preside over a transition to cleaner politics?

Language Born of Colonialism Thrives Again in Amazon

Larry Rohter

S ÃO GABRIEL DA CACHOEIRA, Brazil, Aug. 23— When the Portuguese arrived in Brazil five centuries ago, they encountered a fundamental problem: the indigenous peoples they conquered spoke more than 700 languages. Rising to the challenge, the Jesuit priests accompanying them concocted a mixture of Indian, Portuguese and African words they called "língua geral," or the "general language," and imposed it on their colonial subjects.

Elsewhere in Brazil, língua geral as a living, spoken tongue died off long ago. But in this remote and neglected corner of the Amazon where Brazil, Colombia and Venezuela meet, the language has not only managed to survive, it has made a remarkable comeback in recent years.

"Linguists talk of moribund languages that are going to die, but this is one that is being revitalized by new blood," said José Ribamar Bessa Freire, author of "River of Babel: A Linguistic History of the Amazon" and a native of the region. "Though it was originally brought to the Amazon to make the colonial process viable, tribes that have lost their own mother tongue are now taking refuge in língua geral and making it an element of their identity," he said.

Two years ago, in fact, Nheengatú, as the 30,000 or so speakers of língua geral call their language, reached a milestone. By vote of the local council, São Gabriel da Cachoeira became the only municipality in Brazil to recognize a language other than Portuguese as official, conferring that status on língua geral and two local Indian tongues.

As a result, Nheengatú, which is pronounced neen-gah-TOO and means "good talk," is now a language that is permitted to be taught in local schools, spoken in courts and used in government documents. People who can speak língua geral have seen their value on the job market rise and are now being hired as interpreters, teachers and public health aides.

In its colonial heyday, língua geral was spoken not just throughout the Amazon but as far south as the Paraná River basin, more than 2,000 miles from here. The priests played by Jeremy Irons and Robert de Niro in the movie "The Mission," for example, would have communicated with their Indian parishioners in a version of the language.

But in the mid-18th century, the Portuguese government ordered the Jesuits out of Brazil, and the language began its long decline. It lingered in the Amazon after Brazil achieved independence in 1822, but was weakened by decades of migration of peasants from northeast Brazil to work on rubber and jute plantations and other commercial enterprises.

The survival of Nheengatú here has been aided by the profusion of tongues in the region, which complicates communication among tribes; it is a long-held custom of some tribes to require members to marry outside their own language group. By the count of linguists, 23 languages, belonging to six families, are spoken here in the Upper Rio Negro.

"This is the most plurilingual region in all of the Americas," said Gilvan Muller de Oliveira, director of the Institute for the Investigation and Development of Linguistic Policy, a private, nonprofit group that has an office here. "Not even Oaxaca in Mexico can offer such diversity."

But the persistence and evolution of Nheengatú is marked by contradictions. For one thing, none of the indigenous groups that account for more than 90 percent of the local population belong to the Tupi group that supplied língua geral with most of its original vocabulary and grammar.

"Nheengatú came to us as the language of the conqueror," explained Renato da Silva Matos, a leader of the Federation of Indigenous Organizations of the Rio Negro. "It made the original languages die out" because priests and government officials punished those who spoke any language other than Portuguese or Nheengatú.

But in modern times, the language acquired a very different significance. As the dominion of Portuguese advanced and those who originally imposed the language instead sought its extinction, Nheengatú became "a mechanism of ethnic, cultural and linguistic resistance," said Persida Miki, a professor of education at the Federal University of Amazonas.

Even young speakers of língua geral can recall efforts in their childhood to wipe out the language. Until the late 1980s, Indian parents who wanted an education for their children often sent them away to boarding schools run by the Salesian order of priests and nuns, who were particularly harsh with pupils who showed signs of clinging to their native tongue.

"Our parents were allowed to visit us once a month, and if we didn't speak to them in Portuguese, we'd be punished by being denied lunch or sent to sit in a corner," said Edilson Kadawawari Martins, 36, a Baniwa Indian leader who spent eight years as a boarder. "In the classroom it was the same thing: if you spoke Nheengatú, they would hit your palms with a brazilwood paddle or order you to get on your knees and face the class for 15 minutes."

Celina Menezes da Cruz, a 48-year-old Baré Indian, has similar memories. But for the past two years, she has been teaching Nheengatú to pupils from half a dozen tribes at the Dom Miguel Alagna elementary school here.

"I feel good doing this, especially when I think of what I had to go through when I was the age of my students," she said. "It is important not to let the language of our fathers die."

To help relieve a shortage of qualified língua geral teachers, a training course for 54 instructors began last month. Unicef is providing money to discuss other ways to carry out the law making the language official, and advocates hope to open an Indigenous University here soon, with courses in Nheengatú.

And though língua geral was created by Roman Catholic priests, modern evangelical Protestant denominations have been quick to embrace it as a means to propagate their faith. At a service at an Assembly of God church here on a steamy Sunday night this month, indigenous people from half a dozen tribes sang and prayed and preached in língua geral as their pastor, who spoke only Portuguese, looked on approvingly and called out "Hallelujah!"

But a few here have not been pleased to see the resurgence of língua geral. After a local radio station began broadcasting programs in the language, some officers in the local military garrison, responsible for policing hundreds of miles of permeable frontier, objected on the ground that Brazilian law forbade transmissions in "foreign" languages.

"The military, with their outdated notion of national security, have tended to see língua geral as a threat to national security," Mr. Muller de Oliveira said. "Língua geral may be a language in retreat, but the idea that it somehow menaces the dominance of Portuguese and thus the unity of the nation still persists and has respectability among some segments of the armed forces."

The Harnessing of Nature's Bounty

The inexorable rise of Brazil as an agricultural superpower forms an important backdrop to world trade negotiations

IF GOD is Brazilian, as national folklore would have it, His hometown must be Petrolina. That, at least, is the belief of Arnaldo Eijsink, head of agri-business in Brazil for Carrefour, a French supermarket chain with lots of Brazilian stores. Nature made this district in Brazil's poor north-east an open-air greenhouse, with persistent sun, fertile soil and low humidity, a natural barrier to disease. With the arrival of irrigation, drawn from the São Francisco river, in the early 1980s Petrolina became a horticultural prodigy. Grapes mature in 120 days, compared with 180 in the rest of the world, allowing two harvests a year, says Mr Eijsink. Asparagus can be cut twice as often as in temperate climes.

Other Brazilians might disagree with Mr Eijsink, but only to assert their region's claim to being agriculture's paradise. The state of São Paulo, in the south-east, produces the world's cheapest sugar and orange juice. The endless savannahs of the centre-west are ideal for growing soya, by far Brazil's biggest agricultural commodity. Brazil is the world's largest exporter of beef, coffee, orange juice and sugar, and it is closing fast on the leaders in soya, poultry and pork. Unlike its competitors, Brazil is not running out of land. Agriculture occupies 60m hectares now; it could stretch out to another 90m hectares without touching the Amazon rainforest, says Silvio Crestana, director of Embrapa, the main agricultural research institute.

If rich countries suddenly demolished trade barriers and zeroed out subsidies, Brazilian farming would really shift into overdrive. Full liberalisation would boost the real value of agricultural and food output by 34% and real net farm income by 46%, according to calculations by the World Bank. Under a more realistic scenario, Brazil's income would rise by $3.6 billion a year. That is why the Doha round of multilateral trade talks, which Brazil hopes will dramatically lower barriers to agricultural trade, are so important. Brazilians fret that the round may merely cut "water", that is, deliver impressive-sounding reductions in maximum tariffs without lowering much the ones actually applied. "A 50% cut can mean nothing," says Marcos Jank of ICONE, a pro-liberalisation think-tank. This will be a major topic of conversation when George Bush visits his Brazilian counterpart, Luiz Inácio Lula da Silva, on November 5th–6th.

At the moment, Brazil's farmers are feeling more cursed than blessed. The early 2000s were miraculous years, with buoyant international prices for several of the main export commodities and a competitive exchange rate, which gave exports an extra push. But prices have retreated and, more damagingly, Brazil's *real* has surged against the dollar. Drought struck farmers in the south during the latest growing season. The value of agricultural output (not including ranching) is expected to drop in local currency terms by 16% to 80 billion *reais* ($35 billion) in 2005. Exports of beef, one of the most promising sectors, have been hit by an outbreak of foot-and-mouth disease in the south. Brazil's real interest rates are the world's highest; its system for transporting commodities befits a third-world backwater, not an agricultural superpower.

In the short run, output is likely to grow slowly, if at all. Agroconsult, a consultancy, forecasts a "strong reduction" in the amount of land to be planted with cotton, rice and, for the first time in six years, soya. In June 20,000 farmers and 3,000 tractors descended on Brasília, the national capital, to demand financial relief from the government, the third such demand in little more than a decade. If the government does not comply, "Brazil will lose important markets," warns Homero Alves Pereira, head of FAMATO, which represents growers in the centre-western state of Mato Grosso.

Brazil's vocation for agriculture will outlast this crisis. It has enhanced its natural endowments with decades of investment in research and development, creating the world's "first competitive tropical agriculture", in the words of José Roberto Mendonça de Barros, head of MB Associados, an economic consultancy. China's growing appetite for Brazil's produce, sharpened by urbanisation, seems as inevitable as its rise to superpower status.

Yet the pace of Brazil's development is uncertain. It will be determined partly by foreign exchange, interest rates and economic growth. The willingness of producers and the government to grapple with deficits in transport and management will play a big role. Some types of small farm will be left behind. Other obstacles lie in the rich world, whose subsidies and trade barriers undermine Brazil's exports. Within Brazil a debate over what to concede in return for liberalisation of farm trade has revived an old suspicion that the export of commodities is a second-class activity for an ambitious country. Free farm trade by all means, say the doubters, but not at the expense of industry. Through farm trade Brazilians are arguing about what sort of country Brazil should be.

Nature the Provider

Agriculture is the Cinderella of Brazil's economy. Brazil's dictators thought industrial development the mark of an advanced country and until the late 1980s exploited agriculture to provide resources for industry and cheap food for the urban masses. Exports and prices were controlled. Cotton farmers, for example, faced quotas on exports, obliging them to supply their product cheaply to the textile industry. The government compensated partially for such restrictions by guaranteeing minimum prices to producers. In the 1990s subsidies shrank and restrictions were abolished. At the same time, Brazil cut tariffs for imported inputs, improving terms of trade for agriculture.

Foreign investors, some of which had been biding their time in Brazil, seized the opportunity. Trading houses like Cargill, Bunge and Archer Daniels Midland brought relatively cheap finance, infrastructure and international connections to the soya beans and grains. Multinationals like Danone of France and Nestlé of Switzerland snapped up distribution of milk and other dairy products. In 1997 the government eliminated export taxes on commodities, cutting costs by 10–20%, "maybe the biggest stimulus to agriculture in Brazil," says Sergio Barroso, head of Cargill's local operation. A sharp devaluation of the *real* in 1999 gave another push.

This coincided with an epic migration that began in the late 1970s from the south, the traditional breadbasket, to the savannahs of the centre-west. The movement is still in progress. Land is cheap, so ranchers and farmers can trade in small southern properties for large spreads in the *cerrado*, and the climate is more reliable. The establishment is joining the pioneers. Brascan, a Brazilian-Canadian company, is shifting its beef production from expensive São Paulo to Mato Grosso. The biggest producer of poultry, Sadia, is concentrating new production in the same region. The attraction, says Luiz Murat, the company's financial director, is "the lowest grain cost in the world". It makes much more sense to ship high-value chickens via Brazil's inefficient transport network than low-value chicken feed. The frontier is spreading to the western fringes of Brazil's impoverished north-east, creating boom towns in Bahia, Piauí and Maranhão.

This has been an undeniable boon for Brazil's economy. At 8.8% of GDP agriculture's share is no higher than in comparable economies, notes a new report by the OECD. Unusually, though, that share has not declined as development advanced. More important, trade in agriculture and related industries accounts for 40% of Brazil's exports and in 2004 for 100% of the $34 billion trade surplus, a vital prop for an indebted economy still vulnerable to crises of confidence. Rural success is not merely a stopgap, shoring up the economy until industrial development kicks in. "Knowledge applied to nature" can be a foundation of Brazil's development, as it was for Nordic countries, argues Mr Mendonça de Barros. Nokia, Finland's mobile-phone star, was once big in wood pulp.

Brazil has yet to produce a Nokia, but farming provides the outstanding examples of Brazilians inventing technologies rather than importing them. Since the late 19th century agricultural research has "received special attention from the state," observes Guilherme Leite da Silva Dias, an economist at the University of São Paulo. While planners carved out "market reserves" to defend local industry from competition during the 1970s, Embrapa underwrote the education of its scientists at American and European universities. The conquest of the *cerrado* is the fruit of breakthroughs like the invention of soya varieties that thrive in tropical conditions.

In sugar, a 1970s programme to fuel cars with sugar-based alcohol rather than gasoline combined with Brazilian brainpower to create a high-tech cluster based in the state of São Paulo. In addition to producing the world's lowest-cost sugar and alcohol the state is developing spin-offs that lower the cost further and extend the product line. Bagasse, the crushed dregs of sugar cane, is being burnt for energy and mixed with urea to feed cattle. Eventually it could yield more alcohol and provide the raw material for biodegradable plastic. The top of the sugar chain is flex-fuel cars, which burn alcohol and gasoline in any combination and account for nearly two-thirds of the new cars sold in Brazil.

Worst Foot Forwards

Nordic sophistication sits alongside decrepit infrastructure, spotty adherence to the law and lax sanitary practices that are more reminiscent of the third world. Brazilians were rudely reminded of this in October when foot-and-mouth disease broke out in the southern state of Mato Grosso do Sul, prompting the main importers of Brazilian beef, including Russia, Egypt and the European Union, to impose partial bans, marring what had been shaping up as a record year for exports. Ranchers were quick to blame neighbouring Paraguay, which may have been the origin of the infected cows, and the government, which has cut funding for monitoring animal health. But part of the fault apparently lies with ranchers themselves, some of whom ignored some of the regulations requiring the vaccination of their herds.

Ranchers are traditionally a headstrong breed with little patience for the niceties of the law. Some, especially in the north, do not hold clear title to their land, which makes them reluctant to invest; they often hire labour from shady contractors called *gatos*, who sometimes abuse their workers, exposing ranchers to charges of using slave labour. "What we have are good rural producers; what we lack are rural entrepreneurs," says Frederico Diamantino, a director of the Associação Brasileira dos Criadores de Zebu, the world's largest group of ranchers.

Ranching is a notorious case but not an isolated one. Brazil's world-beating soya farmers have flouted contracts to sell beans to trading companies when they could fetch better prices elsewhere. Southern farmers routinely sow genetically modified soya seeds smuggled in from neighbouring Argentina. Seed piracy has undermined the local industry and lowered the quality of crops. Weak institutions and feeble contracts constitute "the most important challenge to the agricultural sector," argues Decio Zylbersztajn, another economist at the University of São Paulo.

If so, a close second is Brazil's shaky infrastructure, which blunts much of its edge in the cost of land and labour. Just 10%

of the country's roads are paved, compared with 29% in neighbouring Argentina, according to the OECD report. Brazil has neglected its railways, a more sensible way than road to transport grain. Its navigable rivers do not traverse the heart of the country like America's Mississippi but veer off into the Amazon rainforest. Agriculture's march to the *cerrado* has been a march away from consumers. Despite the larger scale of farms in the centre-west, their break-even point is 12% higher than that of southern farms, calculates Fernando Pimentel of AgroSecurity, a consultancy, due largely to higher transport costs. This is also where ranching and agriculture impinge on the Amazon rainforest, the gravest threat to Brazil's image abroad.

The Customer Is Always Right

Brazil is addressing these failings, though fitfully rather than systematically. Consumers, both foreign and domestic, are taming agrarian unruliness. Foreigners make their expectations known through chains of enterprises joining retailers in importing countries to farmers in Brazil. With soya, the vital links are the big foreign trading houses along with a few Brazilian firms, such as Incopa. In poultry and pork Brazilian multinationals such as Sadia and Perdigão supply feed and veterinary services among other things to thousands of small farmers, then kill, package and ship the mature animals, often under their own brand. At Sadia's abattoirs in the south-eastern state of Paraná some 50m chickens a year face Mecca for slaughter.

In sectors where the processors are small, weak or sloppily run they are becoming less so. The intertwined requirements to export, invest in technology and food safety and raise external finance are encouraging the emergence of big companies that are transparent enough to withstand public scrutiny and strong enough to take over competitors.

Beef abattoirs are coming round. A decade ago Sadia withdrew from the business because it could not compete with tax-dodging firms. After a doubling of beef exports in the past five years, slaughterhouses are seeking respectability and scale, a trend that will accelerate after the shock of the foot-and-mouth outbreak. More than 20 large and medium-sized slaughterhouses have been sold or rented in the past year, says Marcus Vinícius Pratini de Moraes, head of Brazil's association of beef exporters. Among the acquirers is Friboi, which recently bought the Argentinian operations of Swift Armour. Sadia has re-entered the market.

Foreign investors will join in. Nordzücker, which will close two of its 15 sugar mills in Germany after a tribunal ruled against export subsidies, is scouting for mills in Brazil. Louis Dreyfus, a French company, has bought three sugar mills since 2000. Cargill recently acquired Seara, a poultry and pork company. According to the UN Conference on Trade and Development, $3 billion of foreign and domestic investment is poised to enter the alcohol sector. Beef processing will be another target.

The ideal is "farm-to-fork" food security, which would govern producers as well as processors, but is still some way off. Poultry processors already bring discipline to the "integrated producers" which supply them. Fruit is making progress. Mexican inspectors, familiar with the ins and outs of the United States' customs requirements, help pre-clear Brazilian mangoes for export. Some 500 growers of apples, grapes and mangoes participate in Brazil's "Integrated Fruit Production" programme, which is accepted in the EU. Many ranchers had imagined that their grass-fed beef, thus protected from mad-cow disease, needed no other credential. But the foot-and-mouth outbreak has imparted new urgency to Brazil's project of tagging and tracing each animal from birth to slaughter. About a third of Brazil's 200m-head herd meets this requirement. Friendliness to the environment is another demand with growing weight.

Transport is inching forward. The funnel for grain from the centre-west widened a bit earlier this year when Brasil Ferrovias, an ailing railway company, had its finances reconditioned, clearing the way for the expansion of Ferronorte, a line running from Mato Grosso to the port of Santos in São Paulo state. At its full capacity of 15m tonnes it will cut by 20–25% the cost of shipping out soya compared with the traditional route, through the port of Paranaguá, says Paulo Fleury of COPPEAD, a business school in Rio de Janeiro. Santos itself is more efficient. Three years ago lorries queued up for 60 hours; the outsourcing of traffic management to a private consortium has cut the wait to 18 hours, says Mr Fleury. Santos has now eclipsed Paranaguá as the main outlet for Brazilian soya. Much more needs doing. A new law allows private-public partnerships for infrastructure projects, but investors are still awaiting its implementation.

Farms v Factories

Will the Doha round bring down barriers sufficiently to create new trade? America's recent proposal, which is aggressive on tariffs and export subsidies but timid on domestic subsidies, would create more trade than the EU's position, which leans toward slashing domestic support but would limit additional market access. This should somewhat lighten the atmosphere at this week's Bush-Lula talks.

But Brazil has its own inhibitions about the haggling ahead. Farmers fume that by pandering to competition-shy industries the government is spoiling prospects for a free-trade agreement between Mercosur, a trade grouping of four South American countries of which Brazil is by far the biggest member, and the EU. A proposed Free Trade Area of the Americas, to encompass all 34 western-hemisphere democracies, is in cold storage. Farmers fear that protectionist countries will exploit Brazilian defensiveness to stymie the Doha round.

Trade talks have also set industrial interests based in São Paulo and Manaus, seat of the electronics industry, against the agrarian centre, which is "gaining political weight," says Marcelo de Paiva Abreu, an economist at the Pontifical Catholic University in Rio de Janeiro. Free trade would hurt some industries. But thanks to sun, soil, science and water, Brazilian agriculture should be a sure winner.

A Leader Making Peace with Chile's Past

LARRY ROHTER

S ANTIAGO, Chile, Jan. 15—Michelle Bachelet, who was elected Sunday as president of this male-dominated, prosperous and deeply religious nation of 16 million, is a woman and an agnostic, a guitar-strumming child of the 60s, a former exile who spent part of her childhood in the United States, and a physician who has never before held elective office.

Running as a Socialist on a platform that promised "change with continuity" and showcased her warmth and affinity with ordinary people, Ms. Bachelet, a fair-haired, vibrant 54-year-old, won more than 53 percent of the vote, according to the official tally. She made few promises beyond "social inclusion"—vowing to better meet the needs of women and the poor—and preserving Chile's economy, the most dynamic in Latin America, and the country's close ties with the United States.

But Ms. Bachelet has other qualities that explain how, in barely a decade, she has gone from being a pediatrician at a humble, underfinanced clinic here to the first woman to be her country's chief of state, and one of only a handful of women elected to lead any country in the Americas.

Some of those qualities are personal, while others stem from her real and symbolic connections to Chile's recent history. She is a toughened survivor of the Pinochet dictatorship, which was responsible for her father's death and her imprisonment, torture and exile, and she embodies for many Chile's painful reconciliation with those dark years.

"Violence ravaged my life," Ms. Bachelet said Sunday night, in an impassioned victory speech to a jubilant crowd gathered on the main downtown avenue here. "I was a victim of hatred, and I have dedicated my life to reversing that hatred."

Verónica Michelle Bachelet Jeria was born in Santiago on Sept. 29, 1951, the second child of an air force officer who rose to a general's rank and a housewife who became an archaeologist. Her early years were spent in the restrictive but sheltering environment of the Chilean Armed Forces, moving from one military base to another around the country.

In 1962, her father, Alberto Bachelet Martínez, was assigned to the military mission at the Chilean Embassy in Washington. For almost two years, the family lived in Bethesda, a Maryland suburb, where Ms. Bachelet attended middle school, learned to speak English fluently and developed a lifelong love of pop and folk music.

"It was hard for her in the beginning," Ms. Bachelet's mother, Ángela Jeria, recalled in an interview here last week. "For the first three months, she cried when she came home from school, because she didn't understand any of what was being said. But after six months she was fully integrated, and so we were able to travel around and get to know the United States and Canada and visit places like Niagara Falls and Rehoboth Beach."

Friends and relatives recall that the pre-adolescent Ms. Bachelet was shocked by the racial segregation she saw in America and by the assassination of John F. Kennedy. She returned to Chile with her family at the end of 1963, and encountered many other influences that would mark the 60's generation, from the Beatles to the debate over the war in Vietnam and the May 1968 uprising of students in France.

"We were teenagers immersed in the political and social movements that were transforming Chile and the world," said a cousin, Alicia Galdames, with whom Ms. Bachelet formed a folk duo whose repertoire included songs of Joan Baez and Bob Dylan. "The seeds of her ideals were planted in this period."

Ms. Bachelet's enrollment in college coincided with the start here of the left-wing Popular Unity government of Salvador Allende. She studied medicine at her father's urging and joined the youth wing of the Socialist Party. Colleagues remember her as holding views that were moderate for an era that became the most polarized in Chilean history.

"She was really studious, very disciplined and responsible and sure of herself, but with a tremendous capacity for empathy," said Gladys Cuevas, a fellow student and close friend. "It was a time of black and white, but she managed to get along with everybody, no matter what their political persuasion. She wasn't one to look for fights; on the contrary, she was the one who was tolerant, always looking for consensus."

With food shortages growing in Chile and a black market developing, her father was lent by the air force to the Allende government and put in charge of food rationing and distribution, where he worked closely with the Socialists and other leftists. When Gen. Augusto Pinochet led the coup that overthrew the

Allende government on Sept. 11, 1973, the military viewed General Bachelet with suspicion. Spurning a chance to go into exile, he was jailed, and in March 1974, after months of torture, died in prison of a heart attack.

Months later, both Ms. Bachelet and her mother were detained and sent to Villa Grimaldi, one of the most notorious of the Pinochet dictatorship's secret prisons. While there, Ms. Bachelet was also subjected to physical and psychological torture—being hit during interrogations, blindfolded and tied to a chair for long periods, and told that her mother would be executed. She minimized those experiences in an interview in 2002, saying, "There were others, even in my own cell, who had it much worse than I did."

"I haven't forgotten," she said. "It left pain. But I have tried to channel that pain into a constructive realm. I insist on the idea that what we experienced here in Chile was so painful, so terrible, that I wouldn't wish for anyone to live through our situation again."

Ms. Bachelet and her mother were freed within months, thanks to the lobbying of an Air Force general who was a relative. They went into exile in 1975, first in Australia, where her older brother Alberto had moved, and then, after a few months, to East Germany, at the request of the Socialist Party directorate, which wanted them to take part in Chile solidarity campaigns in Europe.

Initially, Ms. Bachelet worked as a hospital orderly and lived with her mother in Potsdam. But she resumed her medical studies at Humboldt University in East Berlin, after she became proficient in German.

While in exile, Ms. Bachelet married Jorge Dávalos, an architect and fellow exile, and gave birth to the first of her three children, Jorge Sebastián Alberto, now 27. The marriage ended in the mid–1980's, after a second child, Francisca, 21, was born here. Ms. Bachelet has not married again, though she has a third child, Sofía, 13, from a now-lapsed relationship with a doctor.

Upon her return to Chile in 1979, as the expulsion order against her mother was being lifted, Ms. Bachelet finished medical school, specializing in pediatrics and public health. Though she graduated near the top of her class, her family name and political affiliations made it difficult for her to find employment. She ended up working at a clinic financed by Sweden that treated children from families that had been victims of torture and political repression.

She remained there through the rest of the Pinochet dictatorship, which ended in 1990 after elections put in power the center-left coalition that still governs Chile. In 1994, after having worked in AIDS and epidemiological programs, she became an adviser to the Ministry of Health. But she retained her familial fascination with military affairs, and in 1996 enrolled in a program in strategic studies at the national war college.

Ms. Bachelet excelled there, and was invited to study at the Inter-American Defense College in Washington. She did so in 1997, and after her return, she went to work in the Defense Ministry and was also elected to the political commission of the Socialist Party, specializing in defense and military issues.

Six years ago this month, Chile elected a Socialist president, Ricardo Lagos, for the first time since the fall of Mr. Allende. Mr. Lagos appointed Ms. Bachelet minister of health. In that capacity, she became identified with a partly successful campaign to reduce waiting time for patients and emerged as a familiar figure at hospitals and clinics all over Chile.

After two years, Ms. Bachelet was shifted to lead the Defense Ministry, becoming the first woman to hold that post, and she became nationally known, photographed in an armored vehicle, inspecting troops and wearing army camouflage or an aviator's leather jacket on her official rounds.

The symbolism of her leadership of the institution that had killed her father appealed greatly to Chileans trying to reconcile with their bitter past.

Ecuador without Forests in Twenty Years

Ecuador will lose all its forests within 20 years if deforestation is not halted a top official in the Environment Affairs ministry warned Wednesday in Quito.

Alfredo Carrasco said the ministry has determined that the country is losing between 168,000 and 198,000 hectares (420,000 and 495,000 acres) of forests each year and only 48% of the Colorado-sized country's land area currently retains its natural tree canopy.

He told foreign correspondents that the deforestation process has caused the disappearance of almost all the wooded areas in the country's Andean highlands.

Carrasco said that the provinces that have experienced the greatest deforestation are Esmeraldas, on the coast, and Napo, Pastaza, Morona and Zamora, all four of which are in the Amazon region.

He added that the loss of forests was due to the expansion of farming, the building of highways and the indiscriminate cutting of trees, claiming that the latter accounts for between 10 and 15% of deforestation.

"If the country doesn't take a serious and long-term position on forestation and reforestation, in 15 or 20 years we will have serious problems with wood supply" and Ecuador will be forced to import it, Carrasco said.

Carrasco revealed that the Environment Affairs ministry had developed a plan including projects to plant and control forests, as well as declaring a state of emergency. The plan became effective March 7 and includes the reforestation of some 50,000 hectares (125,000 acres) per year and a total reforestation of one million hectares (2.5 million acres) over the next 20 years.

The process includes the incorporation of reforestation into farming practices, as well as the planting of trees to hold soil in zones considered to be "sensitive," such as river basins. The plan anticipates a strong participation of the private sector in the exploitation of wood for commercial purposes.

Andean Indian, Mixed-Race Culture Blossoms

In Peru, 'Serrano' people gain as political, economic and consumer force

Rick Vecchio

LIMA, Peru AP—When Dina Paucar takes to the stage, swathed in 40 pounds of petticoats and singing of love, hopes and her Andean hometown, she represents much more than just a pop craze.

The singer's popularity is emblematic of deep social change in race-conscious Peru, where the Indian and mixed-race majority are increasingly being recognized as a political, economic and consumer force.

The trend, which has been building for some 20 years, passed a landmark in 2001 when Alejandro Toledo became Peru's first freely elected president of Indian descent. Now it is being felt everywhere from college campuses to supermarket shelves to popular music.

At 36, Paucar, aka "the Beautiful Goddess of Love," is one of the nation's biggest stars. The one-time housemaid's fan base is the new generation of "serranos," from the word sierra, or highlands—Andean Indian and mixed-race mestizos raised in the shantytowns and slums that surround Lima and other cities.

Today, two-thirds of Lima's 8 million people live in those sprawling neighborhoods, where a burgeoning underground economy has produced an entrepreneurial class of its own.

"The people from these zones, who are basically Andean, are starting to have money to spend, and there is nothing more equalizing," said Rolando Arellano, president of the Arellano Marketing Investigation firm.

For them, "being called serrano is no longer an insult," Arellano said. "That's a very important social change and the case of Dina Paucar is clear. It is a vindication of the sierra tradition.

"Racism is starting to diminish."

That would seem inevitable, after four years under a president of mixed but mainly Indian extraction. But it is also being felt elsewhere in the Andean zone—in Ecuador, where Indians have repeatedly flexed their political muscle, and in Bolivia, which has just elected leftist Evo Morales, a full-blooded Indian, as president.

In Peru, the 80 percent Indian and mestizo majority has always occupied the lower rungs of society under a European-descended upper crust. But change is subtly felt on many fronts.

The Wong supermarket chain, which offers fancy pastas, cheeses and imported wines to the lighter-skinned elite, recently began selling guinea pig, cleaned and individually wrapped, at the fresh meat counter. To the upper class it's tailless rat, but in the Andes it's a delicacy.

For years, human rights attorney Wilfredo Ardito, who is mestizo, pressured TV network Frecuencia Latina to cancel "Paisana Jacinta," a slapstick comedy series featuring an overtly racist caricature of a stupid, toothless Andean migrant woman. Last year the network finally halted production of "Paisana Jacinta" and is cleansing the reruns of material that might be judged racist. It also ran a weeklong miniseries based on Dina Paucar's life and music, garnering record ratings and rave reviews.

Indian newcomers to the cities, many of them Quechua-speakers with poor Spanish, still face intense discrimination, Ardito, cautions. But he acknowledges that "there have been advances."

"For example, there are more people with Andean features in the private universities. Increasingly, there are Quechua last names in those places. Before, all doctors were white, but not anymore."

From Spanish colonial times, there was passive acceptance in Peru that prestige, wealth and power lay with the European-descended elite, later augmented by Asian-descended Peruvians such as the Wong family, originally Chinese, who founded and operate Peru's largest supermarket chain, and former President Alberto Fujimori, who is of Japanese ancestry.

Indians and mestizos might be descended from the mighty Inca empire, but in modern Peru they were ridiculed for their Quechua language and customs and relegated to work as maids, laborers or street merchants.

The outside world long ago fell in love with Andean music, popularized by the breathy flutes in Paul Simon's interpretation of Peruvian composer Daniel Alomias' tune "El Condor Pasa." But in Peru, the imperative for many Andean migrants was to assimilate into the mainstream, where salsa and Spanish rock predominated.

Paucar, who left home in the Andes when she was 11 to work as a street vendor and live-in maid in the capital, sings of her roots in "I Will Return," one of her biggest hits. "Now, I am far away, missing the village where I was born," she sings. "Oh, my children, I know I will return. Do not judge me. I did not abandon you. I just wish to build the things of which I always dreamed. I will return."

Her style of music is called huayno (pronounced WHY-no), a fusion of Andean and European instruments and rhythms, and she sees it as her mission to raise it "to a higher level so that no one is ashamed to dance to it."

"Dina is one of us," says Jorge Luis Gutierrez, a 28-year-old clothing salesman who left the Andes when he was 13.

"She is an example for all people who come from the provinces," he said at a recent Paucar concert.

"Most everyone loves her."

From *Associated Press*, January 9, 2006, pp. A2. Copyright © 2006 by Reprint Management Services. Reprinted by permission.

The Chávez Challenge

Venezuela's Leader Is a Regional Nuisance

MARK FALCOFF

IT'S Sunday in Venezuela, which means it's time for President Hugo Chávez to go on radio and television to "dialogue" with his people. Dialogue is actually not the right word; except for this week's special guests (Cuban dictator Fidel Castro by telephone from Havana, and later, Cuba's health minister), Chávez does all the talking—endlessly, tediously, often jumping from topic to topic in no apparent order. This time it's a full eight hours. The subjects include the evils of capitalism and "neo-liberalism," the unspecified contribution Cuba can make to solving *Venezuela*'s energy problems, the nefarious George W. Bush, the dangers of a free-trade agreement with the United States ("a grinding stone to crush peoples"), the vast wave of support that Venezuela and its president now supposedly enjoy throughout the hemisphere and even the world . . .

Welcome to South America's newest revolution, if that indeed is what is going on here. To the casual visitor who knew Venezuela before Chávez's first election in 1998 it's difficult at first to see what's so new and different. Despite the increasingly incendiary rhetoric issuing from government sources, almost everything seems remarkably unchanged. The Venezuelan capital is still the same, sprawling, overdeveloped city it always was—part Los Angeles, part Third World slum—plagued by too many cars trying to squeeze into excessively narrow streets. The hotel lounges are full of foreign businessmen in deep conclave with their Venezuelan counterparts. The restaurants are heavily booked. The malls are stocked with foreign imports. The newspapers carry ads for vacations in Miami and Europe, as well as for luxury cars. The only important news—today, as always—is the price of oil. Good news, too, since it's inching up to $60 a barrel, with reasonable hope of rising yet further. It's only when one looks beneath the surface that one can perceive that something very sinister is afoot.

To say that Venezuela is all about oil is an understatement. For nearly a century the black gold has underpinned every regime here, military and civilian, good and bad. Venezuelans know this: Surveys show, in fact, that an overwhelming number think their country is the richest in the *world*. This claim seems remarkably inconsistent with widespread poverty, malnutrition, and substandard housing on one hand, and all the luxury high-rises and elegant villas on the other, but that is precisely the point. As one mulatto woman, the hostess of my hotel dining room, explained to me on the eve of Chávez's first election, "We have *everything*. The only reason we are poor is that the politicians have robbed us." She had it half right; the politicians *did* stuff their pockets during the boom years. But the real problem was oil prices. After spiking in 1972 and 1979, they collapsed in 1982. During the good years there was plenty of jam to go around; then, for nearly two decades, depressed prices deprived successive governments of much of the resources—subsidized bus fares, cheap gasoline prices, and other amenities—with which to buy painless social peace. The economic slump, juxtaposed against a rising population and growing unemployment, was bound to take its toll. The great beneficiary turned out to be a once-unknown lieutenant colonel who convinced the underprivileged masses that the simple act of electing him would turn oil prices around and bring back the good times.

Not surprisingly, this didn't happen—at least not immediately. In fact, during Chávez's first three years in office oil prices averaged slightly more than $20 a barrel. Failure to deliver the goods overnight caused support for the leader to slip precipitously; by some reckonings, by early 2001 as much as 60 percent of the population had turned against the president. A militant opposition took to the streets and public disenchantment peaked in April 2002 when Chávez barely survived a bungled military coup involving elements of the business community and the labor movement. In December, a general strike produced widespread economic chaos but failed to force Chávez's resignation. Since 9/11, however, oil prices have turned sharply northward, pushing Chávez well into the clear. The latest surveys now show him with as much as a 70 percent approval rating.

This year alone Venezuela will receive $36 billion from its oil exports. Government accounting since Chávez took power has become something of a murky science, but it is known that of this amount the president has helped himself to $5 billion for his "discretionary budget." He has further, unlawful plans to raid the Central Bank treasury for another $5 billion, apparently for his social projects. Another $3 billion is earmarked for a new chain of government supermarkets selling foodstuffs to the public at greatly reduced prices. In addition, Chávez announced a 50 to 60 percent increase in the pay of military personnel, which might well peg the salary of a noncommissioned officer higher than that of a university-trained professional. Another $2 billion is being appropriated to buy military hardware from Russia, ostensibly to secure Venezuela's troubled frontier with Colombia, and also to equip a huge "reserve" force.

A Familiar Setup

In some ways the Chávez regime represents nothing new at all in Venezuela or indeed for the region as a whole—it is merely an exaggerated version of the classical Latin American populist regime, one that rewards loyal followers and buys off potential opponents through the promiscuous use of government funds. But unlike its predecessors elsewhere, this regime survives not by borrowing heavily from abroad, or expropriating foreign investors' assets, or printing money (or all three), but by earning hard dollars from the export of oil by the state oil company, PDVSA. Nor is Chávez himself a unique phenomenon in Latin America—he merely represents the latest incarnation of the phenomenon pioneered by the late Argentine strongman Juan Perón in the 1940s: the authoritarian by popular consent. Chávez, we should recall, has been elected twice, was reaffirmed in a referendum last year, and is a sure bet for reelection next year. While in theory Venezuela is a constitutional democracy, in practice Chávez has packed the courts, converted the armed forces into a private constabulary, and disobeyed his *own* new constitution which, on paper at least, established a limited system of checks and balances. Where the rules cannot be bent, the government often reverts to low-grade thuggery and intimidation.

Chávez resembles Perón in another important respect: He regards his country as too small a stage for the role he is called upon to play. His plan is to become the leader of Latin America, perhaps even of the entire Third World. Thus Venezuelans are not to be the only beneficiaries of his largesse. A new regional alliance, Petrocaribe, has been established to buy influence among Venezuela's Caribbean and Central American neighbors by selling them oil at a deep discount (delivery free of charge). There are plans for something still bigger: a South American energy company, Petrosur, servicing Argentina, Brazil, Ecuador, and Peru. He is promising to build a $1 billion oil refinery for Uruguay and a fleet of 40 oil tankers for Brazil (price tag: $2 billion). Chávez also has plans for his own network (Telesur) to take his "Bolivarian" message to the far corners of the earth.

No doubt some of Chávez's plans are delusionary, but the regime has introduced a new element into the equation, namely, the presence of Castro's Cuba in places high and low. In exchange for 80,000 to 90,000 barrels of oil a day—much of which the Cuban dictator resells on the world market for desperately needed hard currency—Havana has dispatched thousands of doctors, dentists, teachers, and sports trainers, as well as police, security personnel, and intelligence experts.

Meanwhile, Cuban medical personnel are assigned to Chávez's "missions," which fan out across the country to provide services—most of them mediocre and second-rate, to be sure, but in many cases brought to people whom no previous government thought it worth bothering with. These benefits offer little hope of real improvement over the longer term. As one Catholic priest from Spain, who has worked in Caracas's slums, recently told the British press, they are no substitute for a thoroughgoing reform of the health-delivery system. "What we have now in the end is a waste of time and resources . . . I expect a collapse in less than six years." The statistical result is already in: The poverty level in Venezuela since Chávez took office has increased from 44 to 54 percent.

Venezuela as Chávez imagines it to be can be glimpsed on state television. There viewers are treated to a parade of images familiar to anyone who has ever attended a radical film festival in the United States—toothless hags and decrepit pensioners uttering effusive thanks to Señor Presidente, interviews with schoolteachers, excerpts from concerts by well-scrubbed children's choirs. When the president takes to the air he lectures his people endlessly on the virtues of the Castro regime and also the supposed value of its contribution to his country's development—so vehemently, in fact, as to suggest that there might be considerable private grumbling about his billion-dollar oil giveaway to Cuba.

The Opposition

Historically, Venezuela has been controlled by two large centrist-populist parties, one of social-democratic orientation (Accion Democratica, or AD), and one styling itself "social Christian" (COPEI). Both today languish in deep discredit, partly deservedly, for over time they built a wasteful and inefficient economic and social system shot through with corruption and jobbery. Even so, if oil prices had remained where they were in 1979, it's safe to say nobody would ever have heard of Hugo Chávez. As it is, he can credibly claim that the only alternative to his regime are the bad old days, an era that at this point is still quite vivid in the memory of most Venezuelans.

"The old parties are dying," one Venezuelan friend of many years' standing assured me. Another disagreed: "They aren't dying; they're dead already." While Chávez is promising Venezuelans effortless prosperity and an unearned international importance, the opposition has no vision of its own to offer—merely a return to the day before the strongman's first election. Worse, all the opposition forces—not just AD and COPEI, but the smaller groups that have evolved to replace them—are hopelessly divided and confused.

The only really serious opposition in the country these days is the privately owned media. Not surprisingly, to counteract their influence Chávez has been toying with a new media law. Instead of imposing outright censorship—which might call down the wrath of the international media establishment—the new legislation has the quiet potential to make these enterprises financially unrewarding. At present, given Chávez's popularity, such extreme measures seem unnecessary. In any case, the media cannot overthrow Chávez or—so long as oil prices remain high—even dent his popularity.

Evidently the real source of Chávez's power is not the weakness of his opposition—striking as that may be—but his virtually unlimited access to the accounts of the state oil company. But these may not always be the windfall they are at present. Aside from the distinct possibility that oil prices will decline at some point, the government's management of its basic resource leaves much to be desired. Since the general strike there has been a massive purge of the company's upper management, as well as the dismissal of some 18,000 engineers, exploration personnel, and financial specialists. The effects are already being felt. In 2004 PDVSA produced roughly 2.65 million barrels per day, which was well below the 3.3 million anticipated by the government. Just to keep the operation going requires a minimum investment each year of $3 billion; over the last three years the figure has reached barely $2 billion. As one foreign oil-company executive told *Le Figaro* (July 12), "Chávez believes it's enough to put a soldier behind each oil well to assure production, but with oil it's not like that." This is particularly true for Venezuelan crude, which is exceptionally heavy and imposes intensive maintenance routines on the machinery. Meanwhile, PDVSA's share of production is declining vis-à-vis that of the multinationals that set up shop in the 1990s. Chávez's solution is to change the royalty arrangements agreed to a decade ago, a move to which the companies have no choice but to submit—for the moment. Over the middle and longer term the government may succeed in discouraging new investment and thus drastically reduce the size of the golden egg.

What to Do

Is Venezuela on its way to becoming another Cuba? In spite of superficial similarities and even Chávez's stated intentions, the answer is: probably not. The country is simply too informal, too disorganized, too corrupt—and too vulnerable to foreign, particularly U.S., cultural influences—to be easily pushed into a totalitarian template. Chávez has not even bothered building a political party of his own; the ranks of his regime are drawn from an undifferentiated mass of pocket-lining military officers, opportunists, and leftist ideologues. Nor is there a clear blueprint for where the president intends to take the country. Priorities change without warning, for instance, so that no cabinet minister dares miss the president's Sunday broadcasts: He may not find out what next week's agenda will be.

To be sure, none of this is cause for celebration. Chávez has plenty of money to throw around, and its effects have already been felt in nearby countries like Bolivia, where Venezuelan-funded NGOs and "indigenous" organizations recently brought down a constitutional government. "Anti-imperialist" books and magazines of a type formerly financed by Soviet embassies are suddenly reappearing in other Latin American countries. And security experts around the hemisphere are worrying aloud that some of the weaponry Chávez is buying will end up in the hands of Colombia's FARC guerrillas or Chiapas in Mexico. Such concerns provoked secretary of state Condoleezza Rice's South American trip this past April, intended to isolate Chávez diplomatically from his neighbors.

Because the Venezuelan president uses the ballot box so successfully there is a movement afoot, presumably sponsored by our own State Department, to compel the Organization of American States to define more precisely what might represent a departure from democratic practices above and beyond the actual act of electing officials.

But it is difficult to see how such efforts can succeed. A country that supplies oil to half the hemisphere, including the United States (which relies on Chávez's country for as much as 15 percent of its imports), cannot be, by definition, isolated. By providing cheap oil to his hard-pressed Caribbean neighbors, Chávez is now assured of support from the largest bloc of votes at the OAS. Even if this were not so, our long experience with Castro should have taught us by now that the Latins can be expected to hide under tables any time a difficult political decision shows up on the agenda. We can draw some consolation, however, from the fact that Chávez, unlike his Cuban mentor in his great days, enjoys virtually no popular support in the region, even among the Left—many of whose leaders privately refer to the Venezuelan president as a clown. If the clown feels like mindlessly lobbing cash in their direction, the Latins seem to be saying, they'd be crazy not to take it. And who can blame them? But judging by our more than half a century's experience in these matters, you can't buy friends. A policy that holds out more hope for us over the longer term is the effort by our National Endowment for Democracy to help nurture the Venezuelan civic organizations attempting to rebuild the country's shattered democratic political culture. But this cannot be accomplished overnight and certainly not wholly from the outside.

Is the United States vulnerable to a shutoff of Venezuelan oil? Chávez has lately threatened such a measure, particularly if he is the subject of an assassination plot, an invasion, or another coup attempt. In fact, he would find it extremely difficult to carry out such a threat. For one thing, Venezuelan industry is heavily oriented toward the United States and it would take at least two years to redirect it. During that time Chávez would run out of the ready cash on which he is so heavily dependent for power and popularity. Even China, which lately has become a major customer, could not absorb such a large quantity of oil immediately, and in any case, at this point Beijing lacks the ability to refine Venezuelan crude. An oil boycott of the U.S. by Chávez would simply induce other suppliers to step in and replace him in our huge and profitable market.

The United States would therefore be well advised to take a low profile on Chávez and treat his regime as an unpleasant fever that will eventually pass, which it surely will when either oil prices decline or the Venezuelan oil industry begins to fully register the effects of politicization. Most likely, both will happen. To be sure, this may take some years, perhaps even decades. The country will have wasted perhaps the equivalent of five or ten Marshall Plans and have nothing whatever to show for it at the end of the day. Venezuela will not become a better educated, more productive, more socially integrated society no matter how many billions Chávez throws at it. Moreover—again, borrowing a page from Perón's Argentina—when the great man finally does go he will leave behind him a deeply divided society and the prospect of semipermanent political instability.

To be sure, this is a huge misfortune for Venezuela but merely a moderate inconvenience for the United States. In any case, we cannot save the country from its unwisdom and it would cost us more than it would be worth even to try. Indeed, by seeing Chávez in his proper dimension and treating him as a purely folkloric phenomenon we will go a long way toward denying him the prestige and influence he so desperately seeks. We can afford to wait until the curtain falls—inevitably and ingloriously—on Latin America's latest *opéra bouffe*.

What Are They So Scared Of? Are They Scared of Being Discovered to Be Liars?

OSCAR HECK

VHeadline.com commentarist Oscar Heck writes: I think we all need to keep some things in mind ... especially the people who are against Chavez and his government. Based mostly on information from Vheadline.com and Wikipedia:

1. Chavez was elected by the people *(56% support)* in 1998.
2. The Chavez government put to national referendum a new Constitution which was approved with 71% support in 1999 *(88% of voters gave the go-ahead to re-write the constitution).*
3. Chavez was re-elected in 2000, under the new constitution with 59.76% support.
4. A new *(first)* **elected** National Assembly was created under the new Constitution.
5. Based on the new Constitution, any elected official, including the president, can be challenged through a national referendum half way through his or her period of office ... the only Constitution in the world that I know of which allows for this exercise in true participative democracy.
6. After the National Assembly opened the doors for reformatory laws in late 2001, the heat began to rise. The reform laws included possible reforms in many areas of Venezuelan society, including land laws. This is what mostly infuriated the opposition *(opposition to Chavez).* The trouble began and by April 2002, the opposition, financed by the US government mostly through the NED, led a bloody coup against Chavez. Within three days, Chavez was back in power after the general population who elected Chavez came down from the shantytowns and forced the coupsters to leave the presidential palace and return Chavez to power.
7. In late 2002 and early 2003, the opposition led a mass economic sabotage of the country, again, financed by the US government ... in hopes that Chavez would be forced from power through, sedition, chaos and violence. The sabotage did not work.
8. In February 2003, the opposition led an illegitimate signature campaign to try to call for an early referendum against Chavez. That failed. The National Electoral College (CNE) directorship was fired by the National Assembly for openly *(on TV)* siding with the opposition. They are supposed to be neutral. A new CNE board was created through the National Assembly and with the help of worldwide experts and the Venezuelan courts. After months of haggling, the opposition finally accepted and approved the appointments to the new CNE in the fall *(or late summer)* of 2003.
9. By August 2004, the opposition had their referendum against Chavez. Chavez won with a clear 59% majority. The opposition blamed their loss on the CNE and on CNE fraud *(they had agreed with the choice of CNE directors in the first place!).*
10. In December 2005, National Assembly elections were held. All opposition parties dropped out of the elections at the last minute. The result was that 100% of the seats at the National Assembly are now pro-Chavez. Ironically, they subsequently yelled that democracy does not exist in Venezuela.

Today, a new CNE board is being appointed through the National Assembly. The opposition will scream and yell till all hell breaks loose ... why? Because until ***all*** board members at the CNE are anti-Chavez, they will never be happy with the CNE board. The problem is that the National Assembly, elected by the Venezuelan people, is entirely pro-Chavez ... and the main cause is the fact that all opposition candidates dropped out of those elections.

There is no logic in the opposition's stance, words or actions. They have to get it through their heads that the Venezuelan people elected Chavez, voted for the new Constitution, elected the National Assembly ... and as a consequence, the National Assembly is entrusted with choosing the board of the CNE *(with consultation and nominations from many sectors of Venezuelan society, including opposition sectors!).*

All the opposition has to do is to get some measurable amount of support from the Venezuelan people so that they can get elected to the National Assembly ... and perhaps try to win the presidency as well. That can't be too difficult, especially considering the fact that the opposition claims that Chavez is ruining the country!

If Chavez is so bad for the country, why then does he continue to win the support of the majority of Venezuelans?

Why is the National Assembly 100% pro-Chavez?

(Even if the opposition parties had not dropped out of National Assembly elections, it is highly probable that at least 80% of the seats would have been pro-Chavez anyway.)

Why is it that Chavez appears to have close to 80% support now?

What is he doing wrong?

If he is doing something wrong, then the opposition should have some kind of proposal which the majority of Venezuelans would support ... but where is the plan?

The answer is simple, there is **no** plan ... and the opposition must be lying through their teeth. If they are so convinced that Chavez is doing such a bad job, why do they have such little support from the voters *(less than 20%, I believe)*? They must be lying, for if it were true that Chavez is no good for the country, Chavez would have much less support than he does. **That is logical.**

What are they so scared of? Are they sacred of being discovered to be liars?

Again, if what they claim about Chavez is true, then they have nothing to fear ... and they will easily win every election against Chavez or against any Chavez-supporting politician.

Simple as That

(How come they weren't able to win the August 2004 referendum against Chavez? Venezuela was in even worse shape then than it is now since it was still coming out of the economic sabotage led by the opposition itself?)

We are only 7–8 months away from presidential elections *(December 2006)* and these self-proclaimed *"educated, demo-cratic and civilized"* opposition leaders *(and followers)* have done squat to get their act together ... and I doubt they will. If they do enter into the presidential elections, they will be shamed in public due to very low support ... and Venezuelans hate to lose face in public!

If they decide to sabotage the presidential elections, they will further lose their reputations and the trust of the Venezuelan people *(which is very low at the moment)* ... Venezuelans don't like cowards.

The opposition is cornered ... and they know it.

I think the Venezuelan opposition would have a better chance of winning elections in Florida ... or on Mars...

Oscar Heck
oscar@vheadline.com
http://www.vheadline.com/heck

OSCAR HECK has been a VHeadline.com commentarist for over 3 years and has contributed close to 500 articles. Born in Canada, Oscar has spent most of his life working as an executive recruiter and corporate investigator. He has traveled to 34 countries and lived/worked in 12, including Kuwait during the Gulf War (1991). Oscar's love affair with Venezuela began 28 years ago when he first went to work as a missionary in the shantytowns (barrios) of Caracas and in the Barlovento area, east of Caracas. Over the years, Oscar has traveled and worked throughout much of Venezuela, living mostly in the barrios. Oscar's strong anti-US-government stance stems mostly from his experience in the Gulf War and from his vast exposure to the inside workings of large corporations. His strong pro-Venezuela stance stems from his love for the Venezuelan Pueblo and from his unwavering belief that Hugo Chavez, Venezuela's current President, is taking positive steps toward enhancing the lives of the traditionally exploited, abused and excluded 80% majority. Oscar is fluent in English, Spanish and French. You may contact Oscar at oscar@vheadline.com

They Can't Believe They're Still in Cuba

ANDRÉS MARTINEZ

IT DOESN'T TAKE LONG to figure Cuba out. The whole island is a stage putting on a rather austere production of Samuel Beckett's "Waiting for Godot." What's hard to figure out, as in the play, is exactly what Cubans are waiting for—even they don't know.

But that sense of waiting, of a suspended reality, is as palpable in Havana as is the sticky humidity that corrodes the vintage American cars and the colonial Spanish buildings. Cubans have been waiting, and waiting, for years—whether it was for the revolution to fulfill its promise or to run its course as a result of the Soviet collapse. Neither has happened, so Cubans are left to await, with a mixture of resignation and grudging respect, the death of Fidel Castro, who has been in power 47 years and turns 80 in August.

But even that begs the "what are we waiting for?" question, because no one quite knows what will happen the day after.

Certainly the day after cannot just be about Raul Castro, my host in Havana. The dictator's younger brother runs the Cuban military, which in turn runs the tourism industry, making Raul concierge in chief to the hordes of German, British, Spanish and Canadian tourists who flock to Cuba in part to spite Uncle Sam.

In a recent interview with a French journalist, Fidel seemed to dismiss his brother's future relevance when he pointed out that Raul is only four years younger than he is and that another generation would have to take over at some point. There are a number of other players vying to succeed Fidel—Vice President Carlos Lage Davila; Foreign Minister Felipe Perez Roque and Raul Alarcon, president of the National Assembly—but assessing their relative chances and merits feels like a trivial pursuit best left to those who can name the last leader of East Germany.

The real question in Cuba is whether the system, in all its kitschy, anachronistic glory, can survive the only leader it has known, the *comandante* who rode into Havana from the Sierra Maestra 47 to serve as impish nemesis to 10 U.S. presidents (and counting). That's highly unlikely, and Fidel seems to know it.

His harsh crackdown of recent years—rounding up dissidents and reversing timid steps toward a market economy—is driven by his desire to ensure that Cuba's socialism outlasts him. But the man who famously declared that "history will absolve me" when tried by his predecessor half a century ago must know that history will catch up with this island.

"We are more *fidelistas* than socialists," says Lizardo Gomez, a veterinary student at San Jose University, located on the outskirts of Havana. Gomez is an earnest believer in the principles of the revolution, but he concedes that Cuba is unlikely to be a socialist nation in five to 10 years. He thinks Fidel's successors will be able to muddle through for a year or two, but after that, who knows?

He says all this in the back seat of my rental car on the way to the city of Cienfuegos—the throngs of hitchhikers such as Gomez and the obligation to pick them up are among the charms of revolutionary solidarity.

CASTRO LIKES to bask in his "Bolivarian" partnership with Venezuelan President Hugo Chavez, and he points to the rise of Bolivia's Evo Morales and Brazil's Luiz Inacio Lula da Silva to suggest hemispheric trends are going his way. But it's self-delusional for him to ignore the fact that these and other Latin American leftists were elected, and that their cities remain teeming bastions of private consumerism, while in Cuba you'd better not lose your rationing card if you want that bar of soap you are entitled to every three months.

Cuba's nightly newscast loves to show fellow Latin Americans rallying against free-trade agreements with the U.S. The goal, once again, is to reinforce the notion that events are going Cuba's way, but the message is mixed.

"If only we could protest spontaneously like that here," says Eliezer, a bookseller in Havana, echoing a common refrain among Russians exposed quarter of a century ago to scenes of anti-nuclear protests in Western Europe. "The trouble with this country," he goes on to say, presumably ignoring the thousands of compatriots who brave the Straits of Florida each year, "is that no one is willing to die for freedom."

Eliezer sells some risque material in his bookshop, but he says the way to stay out of trouble is to not get air-conditioning (a bourgeois comfort that might raise suspicions), stay off the Internet and never learn English. That's quite a survival guide.

Over in Havana's Miramar district, Natalia Bolivar, a prominent intellectual, says: "This is a mystery island where we all manage to get by fine, thank you, despite such absurdly insufficient rations like a monthly pound of chicken. We all are scamming something, paying a high price to live in the land we love." Her survival guide: surround yourself with art, music and other forms of escapism.

A collective incredulity that dulls the imagination is afflicting the island nation's 11 million inhabitants, akin to the "I-can't-believe-

I'm-still-here" exasperation Bill Murray's character felt in the movie "Groundhog Day." Cuba's news radio station is called Radio Reloj, featuring a clock's jarring second hand ticking between its propagandistic vignettes, as if to convince the audience that time is actually passing.

Most people seem to know that they are living in a Stalinist theme park—albeit a somewhat whimsical Caribbean version in which the customs agents who grill you wear fishnet stockings and irrepressible salsa tunes still waft. But Cubans no longer dare speculate how they will transition back into the real world.

Church officials worry that much violence, of the spontaneous score-settling variety, is in store. Diplomats speculate about possible "precipitating events," beyond the obvious one of Fidel's passing. A botched hurricane response, a la Katrina? Too many blackouts during this "year of the energy revolution"? You never know. What became the tragedy of China's Tiananmen Square was triggered by the death of an ousted reformer, and protests tied to a visit by Mikhail Gorbachev in the fall of 1989 helped bury East Germany.

The U.S. embargo against Cuba has long provided Castro a convenient, all-purpose scapegoat. Yet compared to a previous visit 14 years ago, I am struck by the extent to which the drama unfolding here, or yet to unfold, is no longer about us.

Yes, most Cubans I met are bitter that Washington wants to make their lives more difficult, but on the whole they don't hold the United States responsible for their hardship.

Even Castro is downplaying the siege theme these days. He must be torn between wanting to gloat that he has stared down the empire and not giving up his scapegoat entirely. In one of his trademark marathon speeches last November, commemorating the 60th anniversary of his admission to the University of Havana—hey, any excuse will do—Castro said Cuba would never become a colony again: "This country can self-destruct; this revolution can destroy itself, but they can never destroy us; we can destroy ourselves, and it would be our fault."

THE REGIME is busy rooting out corruption and what it calls "ideological vulnerability," meaning it doesn't want to be seduced by the types of economic reforms that China's communist leaders have wholeheartedly endorsed. Castro's Chinese comrades are wagering that large doses of economic freedom will keep people so content that the Communist Party will be able to retain its monopoly on political power. Castro worries that once you cede too much autonomy to the private marketplace, your political monopoly is doomed.

Private businesses, and there were never many in Cuba, are being shut down, and Castro no longer allows U.S. dollars to circulate. Angel, a former fisherman who works as a government inspector of neighborhood *bodegas* that distribute the subsidized rations, acknowledges his country is a mess. "How are people supposed to live on a half-pound of beef a month?" he asks, pointing to his rationing card. He thinks it's unconscionable that the regime won't allow people to open up their own stores if they want.

As we sit in his cramped apartment, he shows off his pirated CD collection and offers me a Beck's beer that he obtained because in his position people like doing him *favorcitos*.

The regime's propaganda has become more muted in recent years, at least judging by the public billboards around Havana. Posters that once boasted that "we owe everything" to the revolution are now deemed perilously double-edged. So most billboards now bash the U.S. for jailing Cubans accused of spying, and for supposedly giving safe haven to Luis Posada Carriles, an anti-Castro militant who stands accused of a 1976 bombing of a Cuban airliner and who is being held on immigration charges in Texas, pending a resolution of his deportation proceedings.

Cuba's more uplifting propaganda is about Castro's foreign policy, which is all about turning the country into another Doctors Without Borders. Some 25,000 Cuban doctors are on missions overseas, and not a day seems to go by without more needy, grateful patients being flown in for treatment.

That may win some hearts and minds elsewhere, but Castro's impulse to dispatch doctors around the globe is creating a backlash at home. "It's all very admirable," says Angel, "but we are a poor nation that cannot afford this at a time when medicines are scarce here."

THE UNITED STATES, for its part, must come up with a new strategy to win over hearts and minds in Cuba as it prepares to engage Castro's successors. Even if the administration refuses to lift the ill-advised embargo, it should find a way to convince ordinary Cubans that their fellow baseball-playing nation—an older sibling, by virtue of culture and history—does not mean them harm. Creating a widely trumpeted, multibillion-dollar transition investment fund to aid Cuba once it has a democratic government would be a good start.

In the meantime, Cubans continue to wait. No experience is more emblematic of life in Havana these days than standing in line to enter the iconic Coppelia ice cream parlor in the Vedado district, a flying-saucer-like structure in the middle of a park. Uniformed guards manage the lines that converge on it from six directions. My first attempt to enter was thwarted by a cop plucking me out of the line and insisting that I go to an adjacent hard-currency ice cream stand, where there was no wait. But the next night the confusion of a tropical storm helped me gain entrance into the high temple of Cuban ice cream.

As luck would have it, I shared a table with two soldiers, Mario and Ramon, on leave and clearly mortified to be sharing a table with a foreigner. A waitress hurriedly dispensed bowls of an orangy-vanilla ice cream—no choice here—covered in chocolate sauce.

My tablemates each downed three of the bowls, and chided me for having only one after waiting in line for so long. "It's OK, it was worth it," I say truthfully, not because the ice cream was any good, but because I hadn't known what awaited me inside.

I hope most Cubans find their wait worthwhile too.

ANDRÉS MARTINEZ is editorial page editor of *The Times*.

Students Learn Nursing Lessons in Dominican Republic

Noah Bierman

MIAMI—A group of Miami Dade College students returned in April from a field trip into "modern-day slavery."

Traveling to a "batey"—a sugarcane plantation in the Dominican Republic populated by Haitian immigrants—is not on the typical community-college syllabus. But 10 nursing students who went saw conditions and diseases not present in most U.S. clinics.

They saw a 13-year-old mother playing with toys, her child sleeping in a shack while she was on break from working the cane fields. One student held a baby that nearly died as the clinic lost power.

They saw a father concerned that his 9-year-old son might be blind, a double threat because the disability would deprive him of a home if he could not work in the fields.

"I think the frustration is that you're there and you're just basically putting a Band-Aid on a bigger problem," said Lori Kelley, 36, a licensed practical nurse training online to become a registered nurse.

The visit was led by the Haitian-American Professionals Coalition and included eight doctors along with a handful of other professionals. The trip happened at the same time K.K. Bentil began pushing for a more global outlook in Miami Dade College's nurse training since becoming president of the school's medical campus in November.

On the mission's first day, 500 people began lining up outside the clinic at 5 a.m., more than four hours before the first patients were seen. Some had walked 10 miles without shoes, the students said.

"You walk off the bus and they come over and hug you and thank you," said Jay Carrion, 35, a part-time nursing student from Coral Gables, Fla., who holds a full-time finance job.

The doctors and nurses treated more than 1,000 people with a range of conditions including skin lesions, hypertension and machete wounds. The bateyes are sugarcane plantations populated by an estimated 20,000 Haitian immigrants who live in some of the Western Hemisphere's poorest conditions.

Kelley, like others who visit the bateyes, came away believing it was "modern day slavery."

The cane cutters earn small salaries and, as illegal immigrants, have little protection against threats. Most live in shacks and the students said malnutrition is rampant.

The Miami group stayed an hour away from La Higuera Batey, in a popular resort village in La Romana. Their all-inclusive hotel offered the amenities that have made the Dominican Republic a popular tourist destination in recent years—a bar by the swimming pool, a choice of four restaurants, salsa lessons and merengue lessons.

The students would donate their boxed lunches to the children of the batey and walk through the hotel's marbled lobby wearing hospital scrubs every day.

"We could eat all we want, but I could not eat," said Rita Williams, a 41-year-old letter carrier from Miramar, Fla., who is studying part-time to become a registered nurse. "To see these people not eating ... I felt like I was taking food from them."

Williams said she was not prepared for what she would see, "a child that's 4 years old and weighs 18 pounds. I wasn't looking for that."

Marie Etienne, a nursing professor at MDC, had been on a prior mission to the bateyes in October, also with the Haitian-American Professionals Coalition.

"That's when I felt, 'Oh my God, this is so good. I need to expose students to this,' " she said.

Etienne coordinates community health nursing courses, in which students are required to spend at least 23 hours serving the community. She opened the Dominican trip to anyone who could pay his or her own way—about $1,200 for the week. She's planning future trips and Kelley said she plans to donate her own money to help future students attend because the college does not cover any costs.

Beyond learning cultural sensitivity and a service mentality, the students saw diseases they would not normally encounter at home.

"You've heard of malaria, but not everybody's seen malaria. You hear of impetigo, but not everybody sees impetigo," Etienne said, referring to a blistering skin infection that afflicts many in the developing world.

Kelley got her church involved through the food bank that she directs, collecting 900 pounds of medicine, toys and clothing. The doctors on the trip donated 800 pounds of medical supplies. One church member, an American Airlines employee named Reuben Vega, escorted about half the supplies to the Dominican Republic.

Carrion said he initially signed up because he believed it would be a harmless way to fulfill a requirement, "what I call nonsense community hours," while staying at a luxury hotel.

One day, he held a 7-month-old boy in his arms who was showing severe signs of distress.

"Normally, you take this child here and the first thing that's available to you is all this technology," he said, comparing it with the situation in Miami.

The clinic had a machine and Carrion tried to hook it up. Then the power went off. He and the child's mother ran two doors away to a generator owned by a Catholic mission.

"We were able to do the whole treatment for 20 minutes, and within 15 minutes the child was jumping and alive and pushing me away, which is what you want to see," Carrion said. "I don't know what these people would have done."

Glossary of Terms and Abbreviations

Agrarian Relating to the land; the cultivation and ownership of land.

Amerindian A general term for any Indian from America.

Andean Pact (Cartagena Agreement) Established on October 16, 1969, to end trade barriers among member nations and to create a common market. Members: Bolivia, Colombia, Ecuador, Peru, and Venezuela.

Antilles A geographical region in the Caribbean made up of the Greater Antilles: Cuba, Hispaniola (Haiti and the Dominican Republic), Jamaica, the Cayman Islands, Puerto Rico, and the Virgin Islands; and the Lesser Antilles: Antigua and Barbuda, Dominica, St. Lucia, St. Vincent and the Grenadines, St. Kitts–Nevis, as well as various French departments and Dutch territories.

Araucanians An Indian people of south-central Chile and adjacent areas of Argentina.

Arawak An Indian people originally found on certain Caribbean islands, who now live chiefly along the coast of Guyana. Also, their language.

Aymara An Indian people and language of Bolivia and Peru.

Bicameral A government made up of two legislative branches.

CACM (Central American Common Market) Established on June 3, 1961, to form a common market in Central America. Members: Costa Rica, El Salvador, Guatemala, and Nicaragua.

Campesino A Spanish word meaning "peasant."

Caudillo Literally, "man on horseback." A term that has come to mean "leader."

Carib An Indian people and their language native to several islands in the Caribbean and some countries in Central America and South America.

CARICOM (Caribbean Community and Common Market) Established on August 1, 1973, to coordinate economic and foreign policies.

CDB (Caribbean Development Bank) Established on October 18, 1969, to promote economic growth and development of member countries in the Caribbean.

The Commonwealth (Originally the British Commonwealth of Nations) An association of nations and dependencies loosely joined by the common tie of having been part of the British Empire.

Compadrazgo The Mexican word meaning "cogodparenthood" or "sponsorship."

Compadres Literally, "friends"; but in Mexico, the term includes neighbors, relatives, fellow migrants, coworkers, and employers.

Contadora Process A Latin American intiative developed by Venezuela, Colombia, Panama, and Mexico to search for a negotiated solution that would secure borders and reduce the foreign military presence in Central America.

Contras A guerrilla army opposed to the Sandinista government of Nicaragua. They were armed and supplied by the United States.

Costeños Coastal dwellers in Central America.

Creole The term has several meanings: a native-born person of European descent or a person of mixed French and black or Spanish and black descent speaking a dialect of French or Spanish.

ECCA (Eastern Caribbean Currency Authority) A regional organization that monitors the integrity of the monetary unit for the area and sets policies for revaluation and devaluation.

ECLA (Economic Commission for Latin America) Established on February 28, 1948, to develop and strengthen economic relations among Latin American countries.

FAO (Food and Agricultural Organization of the United Nations) Established on October 16, 1945, to oversee good nutrition and agricultural development.

FSLN (Frente Sandinista de Liberación Nacionál) Organized in the early 1960s with the object of ousting the Somoza family from its control of Nicaragua. After 1979 it assumed control of the government. The election of Violeta Chamorro in 1990 marked the end of the FSLN.

FTAA (Free Trade Area of the Americas) An effort to integrate the economies of the Western Hemisphere into a single free trade arrangement.

GATT (General Agreement on Tariffs and Trade) Established on January 1, 1948, to provide international trade and tariff standards.

GDP (Gross Domestic Product) The value of production attributable to the factors of production in a given country, regardless of their ownership. GDP equals GNP minus the product of a country's residents originating in the rest of the world.

GNP (Gross National Product) The sum of the values of all goods and services produced by a country's residents in any given year.

Group of 77 Established in 1964 by 77 developing countries. It functions as a caucus on economic matters for the developing countries.

Guerrilla Any member of a small force of "irregular" soldiers. Generally, guerrilla forces are made up of volunteers who make surprise raids against the incumbent military or political force.

IADB (Inter-American Defense Board) Established in 1942 at Rio de Janeiro to coordinate the efforts of all American countries in World War II. It is now an advisory defense committee on problems of military cooperation for the OAS.

IADB (Inter-American Development Bank) Established in 1959 to help accelerate economic and social development in Latin America.

IBA (International Bauxite Association) Established in 1974 to promote orderly and rational development of the bauxite industry. Membership is worldwide, with a number of Latin American members.

IBRD (International Bank for Reconstruction and Development) Established on December 27, 1945, to make loans to governments at conventional rates of interest for high-priority productive projects. There are many Latin American members.

ICAO (International Civil Aviation Organization) Established on December 7, 1944, to develop techniques of international air navigation and to ensure safe and orderly growth of international civil aviation. Membership is worldwide, with many Latin American members.

Glossary of Terms and Abbreviations

ICO (International Coffee Organization) Established in August 1963 to maintain cooperation between coffee producers and to control the world market prices. Membership is worldwide, with a number of Latin American members.

IDA (International Development Association) Established on September 24, 1960, to promote better and more flexible financing arrangements; it supplements the World Bank's activities.

ILO (International Labor Organization) Established on April 11, 1919, to improve labor conditions and living standards through international action.

IMCO (Inter-Governmental Maritime Consultative Organization) Established in 1948 to provide cooperation among governments on technical matters of international merchant shipping as well as to set safety standards. Membership is worldwide, with more than a dozen Latin American members.

IMF (International Monetary Fund) Established on December 27, 1945 to promote international monetary cooperation.

IPU (Inter-Parliamentary Union) Established on June 30, 1889, as a forum for personal contacts between members of the world parliamentary governments. Membership is worldwide, with the following Latin American members: Argentina, Brazil, Colombia, Costa Rica, Haiti, Mexico, Nicaragua, Paraguay, and Venezuela.

ISO (International Sugar Organization) Established on January 1, 1969, to administer the international sugar agreement and to compile data on the industry. Membership is worldwide, with the following Latin American members: Argentina, Brazil, Colombia, Cuba, Ecuador, Mexico, Uruguay, and Venezuela.

ITU (International Telecommunications Union) Established on May 17, 1895, to develop international regulations for telegraph, telephone, and radio services.

Junta A Spanish word meaning "assembly" or "council"; the legislative body of a country.

Ladino A Westernized Spanish-speaking Latin American, often of mixed Spanish and Indian blood.

LAFTA (Latin American Free Trade Association) Established on June 2, 1961, with headquarters in Montevideo, Uruguay.

Machismo Manliness. The male sense of honor; connotes the showy power of a "knight in shining armor."

Marianismo The feminine counterpart of machismo; the sense of strength that comes from controlling the family and the male.

Mennonite A strict Protestant denomination that derived from a sixteenth-century religious movement.

Mercosur Comprised of Argentina, Brazil, Paraguay, and Uraguay, this southern common market is the world's fourth largest integrated market. It was established in 1991.

Mestizo The offspring of a Spaniard or Portuguese and an American Indian.

Mulatto A person of mixed Caucasian and black ancestry.

Nahuatl The language of an Amerindian people of southern Mexico and Central America who are descended from the Aztec.

NAFTA (North American Free Trade Agreement) Established in 1993 between Mexico, Canada, and the United States, NAFTA went into effect January 1, 1994.

NAM (Non-Aligned Movement) A group of nations that chose not to be politically or militarily associated with either the West or the former Communist Bloc.

OAS (Organization of American States) (Formerly the Pan American Union) Established on December 31, 1951, with headquarters in Washington, DC.

ODECA (Central American Defense Organization) Established on October 14, 1951, to strengthen bonds among the Central American countries and to promote their economic, social, and cultural development through cooperation. Members: Costa Rica, El Salvador, Guatemala, Honduras, and Nicaragua.

OECS (Organization of Eastern Caribbean States) A Caribbean organization established on June 18, 1981, and headquartered in Castries, St. Lucia.

PAHO (Pan American Health Organization) Established in 1902 to promote and coordinate Western Hemisphere efforts to combat disease. All Latin American countries are members.

Patois A dialect other than the standard or literary dialect, such as some of the languages used in the Caribbean that are offshoots of French.

Peon Historically, a person forced to work off a debt or to perform penal servitude. It has come to mean a member of the working class.

PRI (Institutional Revolutionary Party) The dominant political party in Mexico.

Quechua The language of the Inca. It is still widely spoken in Peru.

Rastafarian A religious sect in the West Indies whose members believe in the deity of Haile Selassie, the deposed emperor of Ethiopia who died in 1975.

Rio Pact (Inter-American Treaty of Reciprocal Assistance) Established in 1947 at the Rio Conference to set up a policy of joint defense of Western Hemisphere countries. In case of aggression against any American state, all member countries will come to its aid.

Sandinistas The popular name for the government of Nicaragua from 1979 to 1990, following the ouster of President Anastasio Somoza. The name derives from César Augusto Sandino, a Nicaraguan guerrilla fighter of the 1920s.

SELA (Latin American Economic System) Established on October 18, 1975, as an economic forum for all Latin American countries.

Suffrage The right to vote in political matters.

UN (United Nations) Established on June 26, 1945, through official approval of the charter by delegates of 50 nations at an international conference in San Francisco. The charter went into effect on October 24, 1945.

UNESCO (United Nations Educational, Scientific, and Cultural Organization) Established on November 4, 1946, to promote international collaboration in education, science, and culture.

Unicameral A political structure with a single legislative branch.

UPU (Universal Postal Union) Established on July 1, 1875, to promote cooperation in international postal services.

World Bank A closely integrated group of international institutions providing financial and technical assistance to developing countries.

Bibliography

GENERAL WORKS

Mark A. Burkholder and Lyman L. Johnson, *Colonial Latin America,* 5th ed. (New York: Oxford University Press, 2004).

E. Bradford Burns, *Latin America: A Concise Interpretive History,* 6th ed. (New Brunswick, NJ: Prentice-Hall, 1994).

David Bushnell and Neill Macaulay, *The Emergence of Latin America in the Nineteenth Century,* 2nd ed. (New York: Oxford University Press, 1994).

Franklin W. Knight, *Race, Ethnicity and Class: Forging the Plural Society in Latin America and the Caribbean* (Waco, TX: Baylor University Press, 1998).

Thomas E. Skidmore and Peter Smith, *Modern Latin America,* 6th ed. (New York: Oxford University Press, 2004).

Barbara A. Tenenbaum, ed., *Encyclopedia of Latin American History,* 5 vols. (New York: Charles Scribner's Sons, 1996).

Claudio Veliz, *The Centralist Tradition of Latin America* (Princeton, NJ: Princeton University Press, 1980).

NATIONAL HISTORIES

The following studies provide keen insights into the particular characteristics of individual Latin American nations.

Argentina

Leslie Bethell, *Argentina Since Independence* (New York: Cambridge University Press, 1994).

Nicholas Shumway, *The Invention of Argentina* (Berkeley, CA: University of California Press, 1991).

Bolivia

Herbert S. Klein, *A Concise History of Bolivia* (New York: Cambridge University Press, 2003).

Brazil

Thomas Skidmore, *Brazil: Five Centuries of Change,* (New York: Oxford University Press, 1999).

Caribbean Nations

Franklin W. Knight and Teresita Martínez-Vergue, *Contemporary Caribbean Cultures in a Global Context,* (Chapel Hill: University of North Carolina Press, 2005).

Louis A. Perez Jr., *Cuba: Between Reform and Revolution,* 2nd ed. (New York: Oxford University Press, 1995).

Central America

Ralph Lee Woodward Jr., *Central America: A Nation Divided,* 3rd ed. (New York: Oxford University Press, 1999).

Chile

Brian Loveman, *Chile: The Legacy of Hispanic Capitalism,* 3rd ed. (New York: Oxford University Press, 2001).

Colombia Frank Safford, Macro Palacios, *Colombia: Fragmented Land, Divided Society,* (New York: Oxford University Press, 2001).

Mexico

Michael C. Meyer and William L. Sherman, *The Course of Mexican History,* 7th ed. (New York: Oxford University Press, 2003).

Eric Wolf, *Sons of the Shaking Earth: The Peoples of Mexico and Guatemala; Their Land, History, and Culture* (Chicago: University of Chicago Press, 1970).

Ricardo Pozas Arciniega, *Juan Chamula: An Ethnolographical Recreation of the Life of a Mexican Indian* (Berkeley, CA: University of California Press, 1962).

Peru

Peter Klaren, *Peru: Society and Nationhood in the Andes,* (New York: Oxford University Press, 1999).

David P. Werlich, *Peru: A Short History* (Carbondale, IL: Southern Illinois University Press, 1978).

Venezuela

John V. Lombardi, *Venezuela: The Search for Order, The Dream of Progress* (New York: Oxford University Press, 1982).

NOVELS IN TRANSLATION

The Latin American novel is perhaps one of the best windows on the cultures of the region. The following are just a few of many highly recommended novels.

Jorge Amado, *Clove and Cinnamon* (Avon, 1991).

Manlio Argueta, *One Day of Life* (Vintage, 1991).

Miguel Ángel Asturias, *The President* (Prospect Heights, Il: Waveland Press, 1997).

Mariano Azuela, *The Underdogs* (New World Library, 2004).

Alejo Carpentier, *Reasons of State* (Writers & Readers, 1981).

Carlos Fuentes, *The Death of Artemio Cruz* (FS&G, 1991).

Jorge Icaza, *Huasipungo: The Villagers* (Arcturus Books, 1973).

Gabriel García Márquez, *One Hundred Years of Solitude* (Harper, 1998).

Mario Vargas Llosa, *The Green House* (FS&G, 1985).

Victor Montejo, *Testimony: Death of a Guatemalan Village* (Curbstone Press, 1987).

Rachel de Queiroz, *The Three Marias* (University of Texas Press, 1991).

Graham Greene's novels about Latin America, such as *The Comedians* (NY: Penguin, 1966), and *The Power and the Glory* (NY: Penguin, 2003), and V. S. Naipaul's study of Trinidad, *The Loss of El Dorado: A History* (NY: Vintage, 1993), offer profound insights into the region.

Index

Index